MEET
THE REAL YOU

A Recipe to Find Meaning and Purpose of Life; Master Emotions and Focus; Raise Prana Energy; Awaken Conscious; Enhance Love, Joy, Success, Growth and Happiness in Life

CHETAN BANSAL

MEET THE REAL YOU

Publisher & Author: Chetan Bansal
bansalchetan911@gmail.com
www.meettherealyou.org

ISBN: 979-85-8729-168-3

LIFE IS A GAME

Driving car is difficult and hard for those who do not want to understand, learn and practice driving. Driving car becomes like child's play for those who have understood, learnt and practiced driving.

Same is with your life; once you understand, learn and practice rules, laws, principles, techniques and formulas on which life, mind & universe thrive; you can become master skilful driver of your life. Otherwise we will keep on encountering undue struggles & miseries in life.

But for that you need a TEACHER or GURU and your best of best super intelligent GURU is sitting inside you and the best way to meet him is MEET THE REAL YOU; A REAL GAME CHANGER for effortless, easy, purposeful, prosperous, successful and joyous journey.

Your Life Transformation Journey begins...

PREFACE

MEET THE REAL YOU is about realising and strengthening the connection with your eternal reality, to master your mind, body and energies for finding success, happiness, growth, love and joy in all areas of your life. And for understanding and mastering your mind, body and energies, you must understand the connection with the source of life; universal space, time and energies.

All the success & failures in all areas of your life viz. health, wealth, relationship, career/job/profession (HWRC) is dependent upon your actions, reactions, decisions, attitude, behaviour, beliefs, habits, perception etc. **which is dependent upon the strength/weakness or degree of consciousness of your mind & body.** And the strength/weakness or degree of consciousness of your mind & body is determined by the degree of connection with source; Universal space, time and energies.

The book is about strengthening the connection with your roots; the source of your life which not only creates, maintains your life but also gives you all the natural intelligence to live a successful life. The only cause of problems in your and everybody's life is one i.e. decrease in natural intelligence & life skills due to lower consciousness which is due to low percentage/degree of connection with your source; universal time, space and energies.

The focus of the book is on ONE SOURCE of life, ONE CAUSE of problems and ONE SOLUTION....*MEET THE REAL YOU* to set your life on an automatic/natural path of life where everything that is needed by you, comes towards you in an effortless way rather than you chasing.

The book has been divided in to three parts for step by step learning, understanding and mastering your life by having in-depth insights on human psychology, physiology and spirituality for complete 360 degree solution to all your problems by working on your roots; your omnipotent eternal reality.

PART-A contemplates the understanding about your life, mind, universal and personal space...understand the connection between them to find out the root cause of your problems. **PART B and C strengthens the connection** with your omnipotent eternal reality by working on your mind & body using various tools, formulas and techniques, explained with various metamorphic diagrams, flow charts and examples.

This book will help you understand life, self, mind, body and universe from a deeper perspective opening the real truth about life breaking all limiting beliefs. The book **will help remove all accumulated garbage from all levels of your existence; physical, mental and spiritual** leading to increase in energy & consciousness and synchronising your mind, body and soul with truth. All humans are born with **preinstalled/default codes** for happy, successful, purposeful, loving & passionate life and synchronising with truth/source/eternal reality activates & balances all these codes.

The activation of these codes gives you immense focus, emotional & spiritual strength which in turn activates your super natural intelligence or life skills (intuitive powers, intellect, memory, logical abilities, creative powers, communication skills, removal of disempowering beliefs, and activation of truthful righteous perceptions, decisions & actions). The source bring in to your conscious presence your hidden talents, life purposes and attracts right opportunities to fulfil those purposes, dreams, desires and goals making your life a happy and joyous journey.

The activation of above life skills makes you master of your mind, body & senses and thus life, a strong/valuable person who is capable of creating his/her intended reality, fully focused on his goals and solutions without being perturbed by any/all situations who keep on taking righteous actions helping self & others live a purposeful, passionate and successful journey.

This book has real practical techniques, concepts and formulas developed/discovered by using WOW focus technique, which when followed will make you a skilful master of life, as follows :-

1. WOW technique- To develop laser sharp focus, immense emotional & spiritual strength, for connecting with source and activation of all life skills narrated above and thus all success in life.

2. Horizontal to vertical alignment- Concept to understand the connection of your past, present, future, mind, real you, and Universal powers.

3. I.P. thought process- A unique way to understand the working of your thoughts and to choose right thoughts in life.

4. F-TIPP technique to deal with any or all people &situations in your life.

5. Five decision making techniques for taking perfect decisions in any/all situations of life.

6. 3G to 4G model technique- To change your stubborn disempowering habits/behaviour.

7. Breathing techniques like **Deep breather (SSF to DLS breathing), Internal & external Meditation** for instant energy and connection with source.

8. PPN Scan model- Human psychology based analysing and deciding tools to understand and fulfil all your **physical, emotional and spiritual needs.**

9. A 9-point spiritual attitude to convert your disturbed/unconscious state of mind (depressive, aggressive...) to a balanced/conscious state of mind.

The result of above skills shall reflect and manifest in your physical reality i.e. health, wealth, relations, career/job/profession (HWRC) making your life a happy, successful and joyous journey. **So here in this book we shall understand our roots, work on them and make you powerful enough to get connected to your roots.**

WHO HAS CHOSEN THIS BOOK FOR YOU? It is not mere coincidence but the choice of your *SOURCE/REAL YOU* who wanted you to *MEET THE REAL YOU.* The real you trust everything that comes on its way and it immediately accepts whatever is offered to it by universe, without any doubt or resistance. This book has been waiting to meet you and you have been waiting to **MEET THE REAL YOU** and this book will definitely bring it to your consciousness, **THE REAL YOU...**source of all success, growth, happiness, love, purpose, passion and joy in life.

WHAT IS SOURCE OF THIS BOOK? This book has been written without any doubt, without any resistance, from my real me. The source of deep insights written in this book is purely from my heart and my conscious presence on life experiences of you & me; it is about the truth which is not different for me and you but one as me and you are one. Only logical mind has been used for better presentation of the book.

SOME IMPORTANT POINTS ABOUT THE BOOK... At many places in this book, words like real you, source energy, God, being, super conscious, nature, universal space & time has been used which are very difficult to separate but are used to denote the one super power which has created this universe, running this universe and has the power to destroy this universe. All these words are formless and part of the same power; the power of real you and me, the feeling of oneness with the whole universe is being only you.

      In this book, I have tried my best to give you an understanding about the concepts about life. Some topics may give the same message again and again, the reason being that they are inseparable; it is very difficult to separate the concepts of life with different names, in fact they are all one having the same source but needed to be dealt with separately to give you a deeper connection, knowledge and understanding of life.

      Most questions about life are answered in this book; in fact you can find answers to all questions related to life if not directly but indirectly for sure. You just have to be a good reader and observer of this book. All in all, all life issues have been taken care of in this book. This book is a complete manual on life and I have tried to cover every aspect of life in a logical, sequential way.

      During my journey of writing this book, many people suggested to reduce the number of pages. My simple answer was that my focus is quality which comes from complete knowledge without shortcuts.

HOW TO GAIN MAXIMUM OUT OF THE BOOK? Just read and understand this book with an open mind, forget your material identity; read it from your heart, feel it, live it and rest would be automatic. Every required change that you are looking in yourself/ life will come to you naturally. **Read this book with full acceptance and zero resistance to grasp its benefits**. So keep your heart, mind, body and soul not as separate but as one to connect, read and understand.

Read this book, chapter by chapter. Make your own key notes on every topic & chapter. Take some time to give a conscious, focused thought on every topic. Try to correlate this with your real life experiences/situations. I am sure you will enjoy this; it will broaden the horizons of your mind and expand your awareness. And when awareness expands, life expands to its full potential.

Read it again and again, at least 3 times. The more you read, the more you gain. On every repetition you will find deeper meanings and understandings which will further enhance your consciousness. **All the concepts, techniques and formulas in book are very simple** to understand and implement. **The challenge is not in understanding but practicing regularly in real life situations for real experience & gain in real time. No knowledge is complete without experience for which you need to do repetitive practice.** If you do not practice, you won't be able to experience and verify the truthfulness of any knowledge, any law or principles and unless something comes to your experience, how would you believe, preach and practice? You won't become perfect in one day it is a never ending process, it is journey n not the destination. The key to master anything in your life is practice and only repetitive practice. **With every passing day, your degree of mastery over life will keep on increasing and will set your life on a path of continual growth.**

WHO CAN READ THIS BOOK? Anyone who is breathing irrespective of age, sex, profession, religion, region, caste etc. and is looking to understand life, find meaning, purpose, love & joy in life, want success & growth in each & every area of life i.e. HWRC. This book is a complete one stop solution to all problems in life by strengthening the connection with your roots.

BLESSINGS...I have written this book with the blessings of my parents, God, my family, loved ones, my friends, your blessings and with blessings of entire Universe as all is one; one life, one universe, and one energy. Do you know the meaning of Universe? **'Uni' means One, 'Verse' means song; is equal to one song, one vibration and energy. Each & every living and non-living things are vibrating energies nothing else having different frequency vibrations. I am a vibrating energy and you are a vibrating energy.** The source of you & me is also energy; creator of the universe. We humans are all connected to each other, to supreme power through one universal mind which is capable of generating energies of different frequencies through thoughts, feelings, emotions and actions.

This book is all yours now. Come *MEET THE REAL YOU, LIVE THE REAL YOU and TAKE CONTROL OF THE STEERING OF YOUR LIFE.* BELIEVE IT, READ IT, APPLY IT, TRANSFORM YOURSELF AND WITNESS THE POSITIVE CHANGE IN

YOUR LIFE. *Best of luck My Dear Real You, Meet The Real You is waiting for your conscious presence* and remember no matter what, god is always with you...

-SD-
Chetan Bansal
A Keen observer, thinker & learner of life...
bansalchetan911@gmail.com
www.meettherealyou.org

Table of Contents

1.0 INTRODUCTION 1

PART-A: UNIVERSE AND YOU 17

  2.0 UNIVERSAL SPACE 18

    2.1 MOTHER NATURE 19

    2.2 COSMIC ENERGY AND LAWS OF UNIVERSE..................... 22

    2.3 UNIVERSAL SPACE & TIME 29

    2.4 YOUR REAL IDENTITY 32

    2.5 PURPOSE OF LIFE 37

  3.0 YOUR PERSONAL SPACE 41

    3.1 SUBTLE, PHYSICAL BODIES AND LIFE ISSUES 41

    3.2 CONSCIOUS & SUBCONCIOUS MIND 50

    3.3 THOUGHTS 56

    3.4 EMOTIONS 58

    3.5 BELIEFS AND PERCEPTIONS............................. 61

    3.6 EFFECT OF THOUGHTS, EMOTIONS AND BELIEFS ON YOUR PERSONAL SPACE AND LIFE. 73

    3.7 HOW MIND & LIFE BECAME NEGATIVE................. 76

    3.8 I DON'T BELIEVE 82

  4.0 YOUR PHYSICAL LIFE 86

    4.1 LIFE 86

    4.2 NEEDS & WANTS... 89

    4.3 RELATIONS 95

    4.4 HOW RELATIONS & LIFE BECAME PROBLEMATIC......... 106

    4.5 THE SUMMARY OF PHYSICAL LIFE 115

  5.0 A RECIPE TO MEET THE REAL YOU 118

PART B: UNCONSCIOUS TO SUPERCONSCIOUS MIND...................128

  6.0 SPIRITUAL PATH, ATTITUDE AND WOW FOCUS 129

  6.1 ACCEPTANCE 138

  6.2 VERTICAL ALIGNMENT, I.P. THOUGHTs AND WOW....... 147

  6.3 FAITH & BELIEF... 178

  6.4 GRATITUDE & COMMUNICATION.......................... 189

  6.5 HAPPINESS & ANGER..................................... 196

  6.6 KINDNESS... 207

  6.7 BHAKTI YOG 212

  6.8 FORGIVENESS AND FTIPP................................. 218

  6.9 POWER OF CELEBRATION................................. 227

  7.0 LAW OF DESTINY/LUCK 234

  7.1 ENHANCING PERCEPTION & NATURAL INTELLIGENCE THROUGH WOW 247

7.2 DECISIONS & PPN SCAN *259*

7.3 ACTIONS & 3G TO 4G MODEL *274*

7.4 RESULTS *285*

PARTC: RAISING ENERGY & CONSCIOUSNESS THROUGH PHYSIOLOGY **289**

8.0 FUELLING YOUR PHYSICAL VEHICLE 290

8.1 FOOD & WATER *292*

8.2 PHYSICAL EXERCISE *307*

8.3 REST & RELAXATION *309*

8.4 DLS BREATHING PATTERN *312*

8.5 SLEEP *315*

8.6 MEDITATION TECHNIQUES *318*

8.7 DISEASE: CAUSE & CURE *330*

8.8 PPLV *340*

8.9 GIVE TREAT TO YOUR SENSES *343*

8.10 CLEANING INTERNAL & EXTERNAL SPACE *344*

9.0 A NEW BEGINNING **350**

1.0 INTRODUCTION

YOU, ME, AND EVERYBODY: SAME LIFE SAME STORY

Let's start your **step by step journey to *MEET THE REAL YOU*** with a thought provoking story about me, you and everybody.

Without wasting any time, let's move on to what matters. Now why are you reading this book? The simple answer is that you want to live a happy and prosperous life. And for that, you should be able to fulfil your needs & wants, nothing else.

But the problem is that you are not able to fulfil all of your needs & wants. This creates anger and frustration in life. **Many questions are bombarding our mind at each and every moment of life,** for some we are able to find answers and for some we are not able to. For some, we find the answers immediately and for some, later in future. **Finding answers and solutions at the right time gives happiness and much desired success in life.**

We taste success in varying degree/percentage. Some people are able to solve majority of their problems, some say solve only 50% and some say 30% or even lesser for others. But there is not even a single person in the world that has ever solved 100% of his/her problems. If you find someone or already know someone, please let me know. I am sure you won't find them. Why is that so?

Whatever may be the degree of success....our aim is always to increase the percentage of success in all areas of life. Like in school, we want to improve our score in each & every subject; we all want growth. In school, we have subject teachers and books to help and guide us but for life we don't have any formal education and we learn from life experiences.

Most of us even don't get any opportunity/chance to know about the subject of life in a scientific and logical way. Some get the opportunity but still don't use and some seize the opportunity and become masters of life. The last ones are the lucky ones and you are one of them whose door has been knocked on by luck, to make you lucky and to find that **much desired happiness...**

But where is the happiness...? Are you happy? Have you found the secret to happiness? Do you understand the real meaning of happiness? Is there anyone who is always happy...? Yes or no? Whatever your answer is, the real truth about yourself is waiting to be unfolded and become a part of your consciousness, for you to be able to understand & live happily forever...

Even I wanted to find the secret to happiness or is there anything in life beyond happiness which does not vary with changes of time, mind or in other words, which is not dependent on anything/something and is complete in itself and for me, it's been amazing journey whose experience

1

has been recorded in this book for my reference, your reference, and everybody's reference...

THE DREAM CHANGE EVERYBODY IS LOOKING FOR....

In this quest for happiness, people are always looking to change their life or improve their life because either they have problems in life or they want to grow in life...and they want to achieve something more in life. Some problems are big, requiring a huge amount of time and effort or some problems are small and can be solved in small time or with less effort or both; the whole life of every individual revolves around this. **Most of people do not know what to change or how to change to get the desired result.** That is why they are in dilemma and in quest for more knowledge and understanding the hidden secrets of universe, to solve their problems, they are looking for *CHANGE* to change their destiny, thus life.

The change everybody is looking for, dreaming it each and every second of their life but is never happening their way or happens very slow or they do not know what they can change or what they cannot. This creates frustration in people and at the same time, challenges them to learn from life. To master life and to get what you want in life, you must know what you are doing, if it is right or wrong and what change to bring in your life in order to control your life. **Controlling your life gives immense happiness.** This very freedom of choosing and living life your way is the source of immense happiness in life. But, we do not know what to do and life of most people is controlled by others and/or their situations...Life is just happening without having any control over it, causing sadness in life; **the reason being that we are not aligned with our reality....the source of all intelligence, courage and power...**

Everybody has dreams, desires, wishes, and create many goals but how many of us take action? Most of us keep on procrastinating, giving so many excuses; wasting our time thinking negatively or just think of doing many things but never do or even try, either due to lack of confidence or skill but the real problem is just one and that is, disconnection with your roots.

Everybody in this Universe wants to live a happy and prosperous life and for that, everybody wants to be successful in all areas of life viz. health, wealth, relations, and career/job/profession. A failure in even one of the vital areas creates disharmony and misery in life. To maintain balance in all areas of life is real success and the source of everlasting happiness in life. We all have been trying this but have not been able to achieve the desired level. Why is it so?

Whatever may be your life situations today, the ultimate purpose of every human is to live a happy life and for that, real understanding of happiness is very important; Is happiness in accumulating wealth, material things or doing something for personal growth or growth of others/society or growth of all? We will understand more about happiness in detail in **PART-B of this book.**

To bring about the desired positive change in life for much desired happiness, to solve problems and to fulfil dreams, desires, wishes and goals we need to understand the source of life, get aligned to it to for the automatic installation of super intelligence, courage, skill, will, determination to make possible which once looked impossible.

LET ME NARRATE YOU MY STORY, A JOURNEY MIXED WITH HIGHS AND LOWS....

HOW THIS BOOK BECAME A REALITY......I have faced many challenges in my life from childhood till date and have tasted both success & failures and have gotten up after every fall, against all odds with only one belief that God is with me. With strong desires I have overcome/surpassed, and raised above all the challenges in my life.

During my childhood, I have faced many chronic physical diseases-- skin problems, allergy problems, physical injuries, accidents and more; used to be on medicines most of the times. All in all, there weren't any life threatening issues but at the same time I was physically unfit, making it difficult to live like other normal children. But somehow I overcame all those health challenges.

In school I was an average student, a so-called back bencher and once failed in 7th standard. It was just that I didn't have any interest in studies and I never liked memory based education. I always felt that going to school was boring. Most of the time, I just used to study for just 15 days before my final exams and always cleared my exams with a percentage between 60 to 70% and much to the surprise of my teachers as they never expected me to even pass the exams. I always believed in understanding the concept against memory of the content of topic because in real life, it is the understanding and the perception which matters and not the memory.

Education has nothing to do with intelligence. See, most of the owners of top business houses, top politicians have very less formal education, and some are even illiterate. Have you ever wondered how come average students or so-called backbenchers can be on such top positions in life because these people are just masters of their mind, thoughts & emotions either they know this science naturally or somebody taught them. But no school teaches this science; the source of life, the laws of human mind & nature and the laws which creates, maintains and destroys life. Imagine people learning & mastering this science will lead to the end of inequality and thus, misery in life; leading to a life full of life, love, happiness and prosperity.

It is not that scoring good marks in academics is bad, in-fact it's very good but what about their mastery over mind, body and thus life? See our education system shall be based on the overall development of an individual- Physical, Mental & spiritual growth leading to development of Moral & ethical values for which the subject of life-who we are, how we are, what is life, what is universe, nature, purpose of life, practical training for mind along with physical education, breathing exercises should be a part of Education system. Only then we shall be able to produce a truly natural human being, "The real human" who knows how to be happy even in the toughest of times, who knows how to convert tough situations into opportunities, and who can bring about real positive changes in their own life and others, transforming the society as a whole.

Today, our education system teaches us how to make money, gain materialism and see what the result is? Corruption, violence, tax evasion, depression, suicidal tendencies, domestic violence has become a norm of society. People are earning loads & tons of money but are they happy? Do they help others? Are they living in one home and are they having good or severe relations with parents, spouses, children, etc. **Where is humanity?** We are losing it for the race of money, which is ultimately making life miserable. **Money and materialistic things are needed but not to an extent that we forget our nature of love, compassion, care and help for others.**

COMING BACK TO MY STORY, YOU WILL NEVER FAIL TILL YOU GIVE UP IN LIFE...I failed my entrance exams for medical profession. And you know why, because it was not meant for me; attitude of my life. Then, I finally did what destiny choose for me; Master's Diploma in Software Engineering, studied arts, commerce, Business management and finally started my own manufacturing business with my Papa (Dad). I did quite well in my business but still I wanted to do more. I always had a feeling of something lacking in my life.

Everything was going well in my life but suddenly, I started observing some down trends in all areas of my life; physical health, relations, finance and business. All this seriously affected my mind. I never knew what to do or how to do; fear, anger and frustration took over my mind and also spent so many sleepless nights. During this period, I also met with a serious road accident when the car that I was driving got crashed into a truck. The whole car got damaged except my driving seat, I don't know how but only one thing **"God has been so kind to me always."**

I was constantly thinking, thinking and thinking about my bad life situations; why did this happen to me, why are there so many problems, is there a way out or not? More thinking leads to more stress and I have completely lost my peace of mind. All in all, my mind was in darkness and light looked like a very difficult and distant possibility. At that time, **I realized that I need to focus on finding solutions and for that, I need to maintain a cool & calm mind.** But maintaining cool & calm mind was a good thought but in reality, it is very difficult to practice. Whenever I encountered some adverse situation, my emotions of anger and frustration have always won over my thoughts of maintaining cool & calmness. Amazing! I was trying so hard but all in vain, what is the secret to control my emotions?

Many questions started bombarding my mind about my life and the life of others.........THIS WAS ALWAYS A BIG QUESTION I HAD FOR MYSELF.

WHY OTHERS WERE CONTROLLING MY LIFE.....?

I used to get angry easily, easily frustrated with my day to day life situations, my feelings and emotions were outside of my control. People used to say something and I would get upset. If something adverse happens which is beyond my control, I used to get upset. I wasn't able to control my thoughts, emotions and thus, my mind. I used to think why I am not happy, what is lacking in my life, why have my life situations turned from good to bad?

WHY THERE IS SO MUCH UNHAPPINESS AROUND?

I always used to think why people are not happy? Some have money but there health is bad. Some have good health but they don't have money. Some have money but their relations are bad and somehow everybody has a reason to be unhappy. People are not happy, irrespective of their success in profession, health, money matters or relations. Everybody is lacking one thing or the other and **human's untrained mind always focus on what is lacking** and somehow always find reasons to be unhappy.

WHY PEOPLE ARE SAME OR DIFFERENT OR INDIFFERENT?

Why people are different or why, once best friends end up being enemies? Why, once lovers become haters or are indifferent towards each other? Are people really different or their priorities changes with time, or having different perspective is good or bad? Or why people from different regions, different religions or different countries have some commonality or have some differences? Why people fight with each other for money, power or something else or why people love each other? Why there are so many successful marriages, divorces? Why is there harmony or disharmony in relations? Why one person is so rich and other one is very poor or why one person is so healthy and other one isn't? Why? Why? Why?

WHY IS THERE SO MUCH INDECISION IN LIFE?

Why are we not able to decide about what is good or bad? Should we forgive others or not; should we be always guilty of our mistakes or not? Why some good and some bad people, some good and some bad situations come in life? Should we let go or hold on to grudges? Should we live in the present, past or future? Why, when or how to decide in every life situation?

QUESTIONS ABOUT SELF, LIFE AND UNIVERSE

Who created this universe, what is the role of everything that is present in the universe and how they are related to us and each other? What are the guiding principles on which universe and life thrives? Why do we worry & fear so much, why do we have lack of faith, what is sleep, what happens in sleep, why we have emotions, what is luck, what is destiny or what determines our past, present and future...?

I just wanted to know if there are different causes for different problems or there is one cause for every problem or what is the source of our life? What are the roots of our life? What are the causes of problems or how to overcome the problems/challenges and remove those obstacles from life?

WHY? WHY? WHY? TO HOW? HOW? HOW?
THEN I CHANGED THIS "WHY" TO "HOW COME IT IS POSSIBLE"........TO FIND ANSWERS TO MY QUESTIONS.

Having questions, asking questions to yourself with strong curiosity and to find answers shall always lead you to answers. This is the best way to gain knowledge and learn in life.
                        -Chetan Bansal

Then, with this strong desire to understand life and find solutions to all the problems in life, I entered this world of immense knowledge about life/universe which transformed me immensely and made me who I am today. I attended 2 seminars on mind power and read 3 books. This gave me a much needed impetus to my quest of understanding life. Rest of the knowledge came from deep thoughts and focusing of my mind. I used to give deep thoughts on my real life situations, which always use to bombard newer and newer insights in my mind about each & every situation of my life.

Then, a thought came to my mind that there are so many people struggling in life. They want solutions to their problems and they want answer to their questions. So, why not write a book on life? We all have so many questions in life and the best teacher who can answer your question is only you, so my job is to just make you MEET THE REAL YOU, your true identity, your true nature and the real intelligence which has answer to your every question and solution to your every problem.

AFTER ANALYSING/OBSERVING MY LIFE AND THE LIFE OF OTHERS, I REALISED MANY TRUTHS ABOUT LIFE....

THE MOST IMPORTANT REALISATION IS PROBLEMS AND CHALLENGES ARE A PART OF LIFE...Life is a mix of good and bad times. I have seen many people complaining and not happy with their life. I have understood that everybody's life is a mix of good and bad, irrespective of their health, money and relationship status. Life is never a straight line. You must have seen poor laughing and rich crying, so money has nothing to do you being happy or unhappy, it's a part of life and is bound to happen with everybody. Being happy is your conscious choice. There is no way to happiness but only, happiness is way to happiness. You will understand about happiness in detail, in PART-B of this book.

Life itself means problems and challenges. If you have nothing to solve or nothing to work upon, life will lose its essence & charm and boredom will set in leading to sadness & depression in life. So, action is a must and action becomes exciting when you have challenges & problems. The purpose of life is to learn from challenges and grow in life.

We encounter many situations in life, some desirable and some undesirable but **the success depends upon your ability to respond in a way that is suitable to the situation and not in a way that is suitable or comfortable to us.** The right ability to respond is **called responsibility** which can only be mastered by training your mind to be at its best in all situations of life and that can only be possible by living a life from higher consciousness. **Response + ability = Responsibility.**

We get only what we choose in life. All the actions and decisions that we choose are based on our mindset and determine our destiny. But sometimes we do not get the desired results or situation becomes out of control, still we can control the situation to some extent or even fully, only with right response. Yes, we can convert the uncontrollable situation to a controllable one through our response. We may not be able to control what is coming to us but surely we can control what is going from us. **Life is all about your responses and only responses.**

The unknown zone of the future will always pose challenges and problems. Thus, problems are a part of life and accepting them is the only intelligent choice. Should we accept the problem as permanent and do nothing about it? No! Not at all, you need to act. Acceptance means understanding the problem, realizing what went wrong and how to correct it now so as to bring about the righteous change by taking righteous decisions and actions now. Worrying about the present situation is useless and waste of your precious time and energy.

You can never escape hardships in your life. Better to face it now rather than waiting for things to get worse and then act....
A) If your life situations are good today but you never know when it may become bad tomorrow. The key is to analyse and find hidden problems that are not visible today but present in any or all areas of your life which will become visible if not today but tomorrow and haunt you. Just detect the hidden problems and without wasting any time, start working on the solutions before it becomes bigger and uncontrollable.
B) If your life situations are bad today, it might become worse tomorrow if left unattended. So instead of getting perturbed by the situation, start focusing and acting on the solution.
C) If situations in your life are worse or out of your control---do whatever best that you can do, even keep on doing if not getting any results, surrender to almighty, release all resistance, and accept everything that is offered to you by the universe.
Most of the time people are unaware of the life laws & principles and eventually, become depressed and lose faith in life. They give up. Giving up

is not the solution, it is bound to attract more problems and miseries in life. Nobody is perfect and everybody has problems. Whatever may be the situation, to clear all hurdles, to solve problems, we should learn one thing i.e. **"NEVER GIVE UP...KEEP ON FIGHTING....NO MATTER WHAT"** and the rest is all automatic.

"In life, you will fall but falling is not failure, failure is not to stand up after fall. These are testing times which are countered and overcame by tools of courage, faith, belief and patience in life. Having faith & patience not only teaches you the dynamics and statics of life but also gives you the courage to sail through difficult tides..."
                                        -Chetan Bansal

Do not fear problems or big changes in your life. It has come to prepare you for your future challenges and will help you grow in life. Like a famous saying that there is always a day after every night and there is always a good time after bad time. So just have faith, things will change automatically. Good times are on their way, bad times just come to teach you some lessons, to make you stronger, to realize your mistakes, to correct your mistakes and to make you grow your intelligence, and life skills.

 There is nothing like good or bad in life. The things in balance are the source of happiness and thus, called Good. And the things which are in excess or in short become the source of problem and thus labelled Bad. Sugar is needed but only in the right balance, excess of it makes a person diabetic and deficiency causes hypoglycaemia, a source to the host of diseases. Drugs are medicines when given in right quantities cure diseases but excess of it causes addiction and becomes a source of disease. The drug is same but their different quantities cause different results. Excess or deficit of physical exercise is bad, excess or deficit of professional work is bad, excess or deficit of love is bad. Everything has to be in the right balance to become a source of happiness and we should know what the right balance is.

 I have used my bad times to learn about life and to improve my life skills. It has helped me in my personal growth and I used this opportunity to help others by creating this book. This book became a reality only because of my bad times. In a way, it's a **blessing in disguise, a nature's way of giving you something by making you uncomfortable** which you would have never achieved in your comfortable/happier times. So, if your current life situation is difficult, you should be happy. Search and seize some hidden opportunity that a difficult situation has been thrown towards you.

 Why god miraculously saved me in a deadly road accident? It's because he wanted me to understand life, its purpose and fulfil the very purpose of my life. If I hadn't met with that road accident, maybe I wouldn't have written this book today or many which are in pipeline. Maybe that accident activated my Real Me, **the inner me which gave the intelligence,**

courage, time, skill, focus, and determination to write this book which I have never ever thought of in my life.

I listened to my inner voice and acted upon it. I never knew how this book will become a reality, I just believed my instincts and started working on it and all the help & guidance came from my REAL ME. My job was just to give my time, focus and energy, rest MY REAL ME took care of.

God has been so kind to me, who has given me the immense power to write this book. The very purpose of my life is to write books or do anything in any other way for the benefit of the society which came to my consciousness at the age of 42 years. I have written this book from my intuition using WOW technique. I don't know from where the idea, or from where the matter came in my mind, I had just one intention to write a book and that is to help people transform their lives, so that they can solve their problems, end miseries and live a happy and prosperous life.

Writing this book gave me immense joy, a feeling beyond happiness difficult to explain. Any work that gives you peace, joy and happiness is your purpose of life; means you are automatically aligned and passionately mad about that work. I had never written a book earlier or even a small article. I kept on writing, analysing, reviewing and improving the matter of the book till I achieved satisfaction. Not even a single thought came to my mind that I won't be able to complete the book. I think that all these focused work connected me to my roots, which all the way guided me to write this book. I am just the medium. I dedicate this book to my roots/my source energy/my subconscious mind/my real me/the real you/the whole universe and above all my parents, the source of my physical life.

COMING BACK TO THE LIFE; PROBLEMS, FAILURE, MISERIES AND SOLUTIONS, SUCCESS AND HAPPINESS, WHAT MATTERS TO ME, YOU AND EVERYBODY?

First, you need to understand that the problems are a part of everybody's life. Being 100% free from problems is not possible in life and anybody looking for that is living in a fool's paradise. To be 100% free from problems is wishing for death and who wants that. It is only the presence of problems in life that makes you alive.

Life is never absolute or perfect; perfection is in the nature of divine. We have problems, needs & wants because of imperfection in life. We think of solutions and growth only due to imperfection in life. Problems and imperfection are interrelated and a part of life, so we need to develop not a perfection mindset but a growth mindset in life. Having imperfections, problems and challenges is nothing but an opportunity to understand and grow in life.

The problem is not having problems in life; the real problem is being stuck in a problem for a longer period of time and not being able to find a solution at all or more appropriately, not trying for solution. So these are the real problems that we should be concerned about and work upon that, like carrying an unhealthy body or overtly aggressive or overtly depressive state of mind or having unhealthy relations or being poor or all, over a long period of time.

Understand just one thing that 95% of your life is the outcome of 3 core karmas--PDA (perception/decision/action), your mindset and rest 5% of your life is the outcome of the collective action/karma/consciousness of the society/world you belong to. Most of us focus on 5% and forget 95%. **Ignoring self and expecting personal growth, success, happiness and prosperity, isn't it contradictory?**

So shift the focus of your mind onto yourself; work on your own mind, body, energy, thoughts (PDA), emotions, raise your energy vibrations & consciousness to connect with the source of life and to enhance life skills so as to set life on automatic path where everything that is needed to you come towards you in an effortless manner rather than you chasing.

Mind & body are the tools to experience life. Problems in mind & body have caused undue problems in life. The wellbeing of mind & body shall determine the happiness and joy in life. To maintain a healthy mind & body, we need to sharpen them on daily, weekly, monthly basis. The more sharp and healthy you are able to maintain them, the more successful your life becomes. **When an AXE losses its sharpness, it takes more time to cut trees,** it loses its precision and need to be re-sharpened to become effective again, same is with your mind & body, with any man made machine; car, airplane, production machines or anything/everything. All needed is preventive and curative maintenance for peak performance. The more you practice preventive maintenance, the lesser is the chance of attracting big or uncontrollable problems.

Only we humans have been given a brain size bigger than any other life on this planet earth. With this, we have the advantage to fully tap the consciousness (super intelligence of nature) and create so many things to improve the quality and standard of life. But with this advantage also comes the power of choice where some knowingly or unknowingly make their mind destructive and become source of misery for self and others. So choosing construction and creativity is the only choice for a happy and prosperous life. Life is all about choice and only choice. The difference between two or more people is the difference of choice. But do we know how?

A life will never choose to kill another life, never choose to run away from problems, never choose unhealthy food habits, never choose depression, never choose suicide, never choose hatred over love, never choose drug addiction, never give up on life, **unless and until it is operating from a unconscious or lower conscious or disturbed state of mind,** unless and until it has diverted from its nature, from its reality, the source of everlasting joy, happiness, success and growth. So, if your life or the life of anybody has become problematic, they need to raise their consciousness to raise their life. Let's start living life from higher consciousness by raising your vibrations **to MEET YOUR STATIC OMNIPOTENT ETERNAL REALITY.**

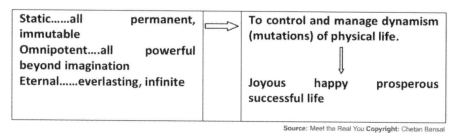

Static......all permanent, immutable Omnipotent.....all powerful beyond imagination Eternal......everlasting, infinite	To control and manage dynamism (mutations) of physical life. ⬇ Joyous happy prosperous successful life

But what are energy vibrations? How to raise them and how it will benefit us? We have been trying to find solutions to all problems in life but we are not getting results, why?

TRYING FOR A SOLUTION BUT NOT HAPPENING, WHY? WEAK EMOTIONS & FOCUS...

Most of the times we work very hard to bring about positive change in life; chase dreams, give our best and still fail and it is all more frustrating when we witness others achieve success with little or no hard work. They seem to be lucky. What is the difference? **The difference is emotional strength.** See, we **know what to do** but still we are not able to transform our decisions into actions and desired results due to weak emotions or disturbed emotions. Check this:

A) We all know that for good physical health, we need to intake healthy food, do physical exercise but still we are not able to practice as our greedy senses & weak emotional strength mostly falls for taste, excessive rest etc.

B) For good relations, we all know that we need to respect, understand, love and care the other person but again, we are not able to practice it; reason our emotions of anger, urge to control and change others is more dominant.

C) Same way, we may know how to **earn huge money** but again we are not able to practice in reality because of our emotions of fear and greed.

D) We resolve many times to change our bad habits. Say for example, you resolve not to get angry next time but again when an undesirable situation comes, you lose your temper.

See, you are failing because your decisions & actions are not being backed by your emotions. Emotions are **energy in motion and fuel for life.** And when any thought, action, decision, behaviour, perception of yours does not have the energy (fuel), how come they be manifested in life. This is like expecting the vehicle to run without fuel. Problems of mind and disturbed emotions/low energy are not letting fulfil your needs, dreams and desires. What to do? Well the problems of mind and disturbed emotions can only be solved by increasing your energy/consciousness/awareness only by connecting with your roots, source of life, universal space and supreme father divine.

Why source? Because it is the only power which has created your physical body, mind and thus, life. It also maintains your life, control the very functioning of vital organs and lack of this power means death of your physical life. It also knows about all problems and solutions in your life. The

11

problems of mind can never be solved by a mind but the guidance of higher space over mind; the creator of mind. Like when local mechanics, repair shops are not able to correct/mend complex problems of computer hardware/software, you go to the source company; the original manufacturer to get it repaired in a right, fast and efficient manner.

Your source is within you; the master was present, is present and shall always be present. It was just hidden due to the formation of clouds of disturbed emotions. To break these clouds, you have the power of choice; FOCUS on positive natural emotions. **The two most important life skills are mastery over your focus & emotions for strengthening connection with your source to raise your energy vibrations and consciousness/awareness/intelligence of your mind & body.**

My Dear, you have been trapped, *NOW YOU DON'T HAVE ANY OPTION BUT TO WORK ON YOURSELF; YOUR MIND, THOUGHTS, EMOTIONS, FOCUS, ENERGY, get connected to your roots to become highly conscious to write your own success story.* Remember one thing, the **degree/percentage of success and failures in your life are directly related to the degree of your connection with your source**, nothing else.

This book has been written for you with only one purpose, to realize and reconnect with *your roots, the source.* The whole book has one purpose and that is to enhance knowledge/awareness about the subject of life; to become master of life, to live a happy, purposeful and joyous life. God has given us immense powers and to find, realise and master those powers you need a manual of life to avoid unnecessary waste of time & energy on hit & trail (Hard work). So let's do a smart work, *MEET THE REAL YOU,* **a manual of your life; about mind, body and source.**

THE RECIPE TO MEET THE REAL YOU

To know the recipe, you just have to observe yourself and around, nothing else. For that, first you must understand life; self (personal space comprising of mind, body and energies), super intelligent nature creator of life (Universal space, time & energies) and connection between all of them, how they affect each other, what is the cause of real problem in life and lastly how to re-establish strong connection with your source to find real solutions in an effortless way. **Let's begin.....Your mind & body is made up of cells.** And all cells are made up of 5 elements of life viz. earth, fire, water, air and space, all different forms of source energy. Cells of body need continuous supply of energy/fuel to work like machines need petrol/gas/diesel/electricity etc.

You get that energy from (F) food & water that you eat, (A) attitude & focus of your mind, (B) breathing pattern, (P) physical body posture/language/voice. These are the 4 major inputs that are powerful changing agents **(FABP)** which are in your control and will determine the quality of energy in the cells of the body. The quality of energy will determine the degree or percentage of **1) consciousness/natural intelligence/mindset;**

2) Quality of physical body & health. It means the health of your mind & body and thus consciousness is in your hands.

The quality of consciousness & physical body determines your PDA and results in life. The high degree/percentage of energy means Righteous PDA and thus, righteous results in life and low degree ensures wrong PDA and undesired results in life.

When we were born, we had a strong connection with source and thus each & every cell of our body was at its natural best, vibrating with energy. As a child, you were loving & passionate about life; happy, curious, joyful, creative, playful, fearless, forgiving but as the life progresses, you somehow lost your nature of love for life, **how? You adopted wrong FABP...**

Wrong Input of FABP	Wrong Output
Wrong **F**ood & Water Wrong **A**ttitude/focus of life Wrong **B**reathing Pattern Wrong **P**hysical body posture, language & voice	Lower consciousness and Wrong PDA(Mind set) ↓ Problems in Health, wealth, relations, Career/job/profession(HWRC) ↓ Sad & disturbed Journey

Source: Meet the Real You Copyright: Chetan Bansal

Wrong/unnatural choice of FABP creates imbalance in 5 elements or emotional disturbances or low energy field/aura, leading to the disconnection with source, to lower consciousness, to loss of natural intelligence, to wrong PDA, to wrong results and problems in life.

This is what happened at a cellular level. Due to wrong FABP, the original nature/constituents of each & every cell/DNA/subconscious of body have been changed negatively; the blue print of your life pattern. The natural intelligence and path of your life has been **hijacked by your emotions,** leading to disconnection with the source of your life. Your mind & body meant for a happy life has now become weak, devoid of life energy and thus, become a source of problems and miseries in life.

THE ULTIMATE SOLUTION...ESTABLISHING STRONG CONNECTION WITH SOURCE; MEET THE REAL YOU

Due to disturbance in emotions, your mind & body has become devoid of life energy and thus become unconscious and loses its natural intelligence (life skills) to live a happy life. To get back your consciousness and natural intelligence/life skills, you just need to strengthen your connection with your roots; the source of life. Once you do that, you will get back your consciousness and thus natural intelligence which is your birth right. With this your mind & body becomes strong and valuable which is capable of dealing with any problem, be it any. The connection with your roots, your source of life is a must for you to enjoy the fruits of your life, for you to get wings to expand your experience of life. Can you imagine a tree bearing quality fruits without strong roots and if not, how come you imagine colourful life without strong connection with your roots?

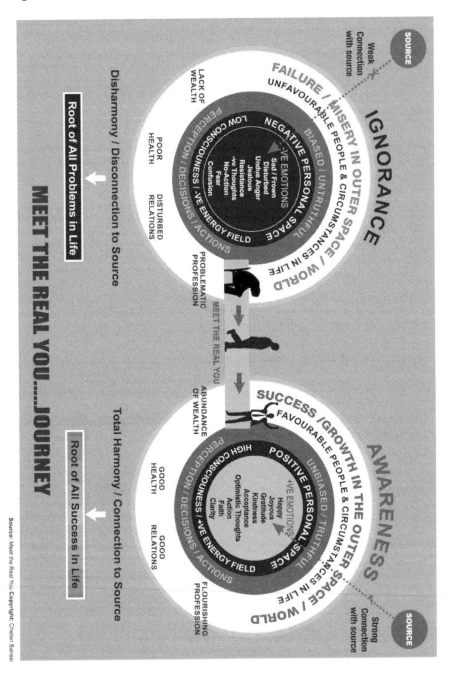

Just change the input

CHANGE THE INPUT	TO GET THE	CHANGED OUTPUT.

It's as simple as that. It works on the principle of **GIGO (Garbage in Garbage Out).**

Due to unawareness, your input was wrong but now my DEAR REAL YOU, you know what to choose

Right Input of FABP	Right Output in HWRC
Right **F**ood & Water Right **A**ttitude/focus of life Right **B**reathing Pattern Right **P**hysical body posture, language & voice	Higher consciousness & Righteous PDA(Mind set) ↓ Perfect results Health, wealth, relations, Career/job/profession(HWRC) ↓ Happy & joyous journey

OR

ALWAYS REMEMBER : CHANGE FABP TO CHANGE YOUR LIFE

ELEMENTS OF LIFE	SOURCE OF ELEMENTS	
Air	*Breathing pattern, Attitude & focus*	*THIS IS THE MOST BASIC SCIENTIFIC AND ONLY WAY TO CONTROL/CHANGE YOUR LIFE POSITIVELY*
Water	*Water, Attitude & focus*	
Fire	*Food, Attitude & focus*	
Earth	*Food, Attitude & focus*	
Space	*Energies, Emotions, Thoughts dependent upon your attitude & focus*	*MUST BE FOREMOST KARMA OF YOUR LIFE.*

FABP is the biggest power in your hand and will definitely change your life positively, you just need to understand & practice the right FABP and this must be your foremost karma, purpose of your life, to change your life from being miserable to flourishing, from being on Wrong journey to Righteous Path of Self-realization...*THE REAL YOU......ULTIMATE PATH----DESIRE AND QUEST OF EVERY HUMAN.*
Simply put together, you need to balance the 5 elements of your life by changing your FABP to enhance the quality/degree of your energy vibrations and thus your life.

You can see yourself in the above table that the common source of all the elements of life is attitude & focus which determines your energy field/aura/consciousness and PDA (mindset). Practically your mind-set is nothing but a set of your beliefs, values, perception, habits, decisions, actions and behaviour which determine the quality of results in your life.

Your food and water also gets converted to energies through the process called digestion. These energies take up the etheric space in your body and manifests in the form of thoughts & emotions which determines your mindset and also become a part of your physical cells/tissues/organs and the body as a whole. If the input of these elements is unnatural, it is going to negatively impact your physical & mental life and thus, external life situations also. **PART B & C OF THIS BOOK ONLY DEALS WITH THIS SYSTEM OF ENHANCING YOUR ENERGIES THROUGH YOUR FIVE ELEMENTS...MOST EXCITING, AMAZING, REAL KNOWLEDGE THAT A MAN CAN HAVE ABOUT HIS LIFE.**

The solutions are always simple, basic and easy. You just need to realise through your observance and when this simple system has come in to your conscious presence, then the destiny has knocked on your door to make you lucky. Now you just have to read this whole book to bring about a positive change in your FABP and only then, expect positive changes in your mind & body and thus life. Otherwise forget about the good life you aspire for.

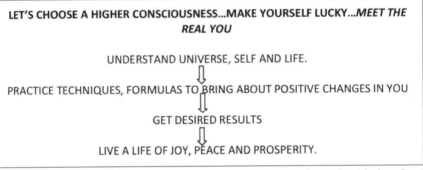

LET'S CHOOSE A HIGHER CONSCIOUSNESS...MAKE YOURSELF LUCKY...*MEET THE REAL YOU*

UNDERSTAND UNIVERSE, SELF AND LIFE.
⇩
PRACTICE TECHNIQUES, FORMULAS TO BRING ABOUT POSITIVE CHANGES IN YOU
⇩
GET DESIRED RESULTS
⇩
LIVE A LIFE OF JOY, PEACE AND PROSPERITY.

Source: Meet the Real You Copyright: Chetan Bansal

MEET THE REAL YOU

A Recipe to Find Meaning and Purpose of Life; Master Emotions and Focus; Raise Prana Energy; Awaken Conscious; Enhance Love, Joy, Success, Growth and Happiness in Life

PART-A: UNIVERSE AND YOU

Understanding the fundamentals of life

THREE CHAPTERS

2.0 Universal Space
3.0 Your Personal Space
4.0 Your Physical Life

In-depth understanding of life is the key to right perspective, right actions and right results in life

2.0 UNIVERSAL SPACE

2.1 MOTHER NATURE

2.2 COSMIC ENERGY AND LAWS OF UNIVERSE

2.3 UNIVERSAL SPACE & TIME

2.4 YOUR REAL IDENTITY

2.5 PURPOSE OF LIFE

Have you noticed, have you observed, do you observe? See the whole cosmos contains so many things, things which are mysterious, the sun, moon, stars, clouds, rainbow in sky, plants, animals, water bodies, plains, mountains, rain, storms, earthquakes, floods on Earth; always raise curiosity in my mind. Who has created all this, where is he/she is sitting. Who is controlling all this? What is the purpose of this creation? **And what about you, don't you think you to be the biggest mystery above all mysteries of life. Think over it again!**

It has been very mysterious and mankind has always been searching the mysteries of Universe. At the same time, we can't deny the beauty and perfection of this universe, the perfection of nature. When it's too hot, rain comes. There are all types of weather-winter goes summer comes, summer goes rain comes, rain goes winter comes, death and birth are happening all the time. Humans have evolved overtime, both in body & mind. New species of plants and animals keep on entering the universe and many species have already become extinct.

There is no limit to the sky, it looks endless. There is no limit to stars, we cannot count them. This is all we can see with our naked eye. Surely there shall be so much we cannot see with our naked eye or things which are present in this universe are beyond the imagination of our mind or beyond the reach of our senses i.e., eye, ear, touch etc.

Who we are, why have we come here, why are we born at the first place when we have to eventually die?

Seeing so many mysteries in nature and **science has come of ages, made so many discoveries, created so many high-tech products** like airplanes, computers, robots, and has even discovered other planets, made trips to them but can science ever discover the mysteries about universe and life? Can science ever control nature? There is no doubt that science has understood many laws of nature and is using those laws of nature for the development and progress of mankind but can they change the laws of nature?

The problem is that most of us believe in only what we can see, touch and feel and do not want to listen beyond that or do not want to believe beyond that. And going beyond the unseen is where all the answers to the mysterious of universe lies and waiting to be explored by you.

To understand life, to understand universe, we must understand energy, frequency and vibrations...
-Nikola Tesla

Understanding the energies is to know the unseen world, which is the source of creation of this seen world. **Let's start, take a deep breath and this is going to be amazing!**

2.1 MOTHER NATURE

The natural space is infinite and ever expanding. There are millions and billions of stars, galaxies, solar system, planets which are beyond the imagination and realization of human mind. Universe is ever expanding, Universe is infinite. There is no limit to sky; it is eternal.

There is abundance in Nature. Everything in this universe and planet earth is in abundance. Normally, people believe that everything on this planet is scarce but the reality is the opposite. There are enough resources on this planet earth to make every life a prosperous one. Want to see a proof of abundance? There is abundance of stars, galaxies, land, water, air, flora, fauna, energy, wealth, natural resources and abundance of products/brands.

Think of abundance, you shall surely find abundance everywhere. So everything in this world is in abundance. But why abundance is not equally distributed among people and how to get my share of it? The only difference between people is their difference in degree of connection with the source and you need to strengthen the connection to draw more abundance in your life.

Universe works on the principle of giving. See sun is constantly giving us energy, air is giving us oxygen, plants and animals give us food, and Earth gives us space to live; everything in nature gives. The act of giving is nature, nature means to give and to give is to love, so nature's nature is to love. **So I, you and everybody, in fact the nature of whole universe is to love and give unconditionally.** To live a truly happy life, we must tune into the frequency of giving of unconditional love but is this true? We will come to know as the book progresses.

THREE FORMS OF LIFE ON PLANET EARTH

All forms of life are created from same source-cosmic energy but their forms vary having different purpose and functions in life. Everybody in this universe has a role to play and all different creations are playing their part in the functioning of universe.

Primary form-Plants–Flora- This form of life is stationary, can't move and does not have the mind to think and evolve. It survives on water, air and sun rays. There are numerous species and varieties of plants beyond the imagination of human mind, all having different purposes to sustain life on planet earth. Gives oxygen and food to humans & animals and gets carbon dioxide in return means they help each other in their existence.

Secondary form-Animals-Fauna- This form of life has voluntary moving body and a small brain with a small mind. They eat other plants and animals. Their basic needs are eating, sleeping and breeding. There are also numerous numbers of species and varieties of animals from microorganisms like bacteria to big animals like whale. They become both prey and predator to other animals and complete the food chain. They also help each other live and coexist, can't exist in isolation. Due to their small brain, animals cannot utilize the powers of their mind. It's like having a small hardware (brain) for utilizing all the features of big software (mind).

Third form-Human- Humans are animals with only a difference of having a highly evolved mind as compared to animals. This form of life has control over its body movements. Their brain & mind is highly evolved and has created many materialistic things to live a luxurious & comfortable life. They eat other plants and animals. Their basic needs are eating, sleeping, mating and with evolution of mind, they have become civilized and formed society (social groups). That is why man is called a social animal. We humans are lucky enough to have big size vertical spine & brain (hardware) which can fully utilize the powers of mind (software). That is why humans have been able to create such wonderful products and are continually improving and living a very high standard of life, which by no means can be compared with any other life form. Above all man has the power to understand and live the ultimate truth of life by raising their consciousness. **All humans are same in the sense that they have same body but having different degree/percentage of consciousness of the same mind.** Due to different degree of consciousness, humans have varying degree of thoughts, beliefs and thus different degree of success, failure, achievements and life styles. **A highly conscious mind is the most successful, happy and a blissful mind.** Anybody can change his/her life from negative to positive, i.e., to become successful just by raising their consciousness. When consciousness of mind is raised, it becomes one with a universally spiritual mind, a super conscious state of mind and a mind of super intelligence where all negativity of mind is transformed to positivity.

See all forms of life are connected to each other, constantly giving and taking from each other to live. They all coexist and even if one gets eliminated, this creates an imbalance in nature. And nature knows how to balance itself; it balances through natural calamities and new creations. See in today's world, where we are playing with nature, cutting trees on mass scales, destroying the fauna are constantly polluting the air, water and soil. And when natural calamities come, we see upwards and call it destiny. It is not destiny. It is something we have created through our irresponsible actions. What you think, can we live without plants or without animals or can we play with nature? The choice is yours, the nature will and shall balance itself and we won't be able to control it ever, no matter how powerful we become.

All living and non-living forms of life are connected in some way, give and take keeps on taking place, it's all natural. Same way we humans are connected to each other and have different roles and purposes. We cannot live in isolation. Human relations also depend on give & take; this is all natural and automatic. **See when we give, we get what we want or when we do not give what we have we do not get what we want, simple law of nature.**

The basic purpose of human life is to enhance their knowledge, awareness about self, life and universe and to learn & develop life skills to lead a happy and natural life. The purpose of your life is to contribute to the well-being of self, others, society and the whole universe to improve the overall quality of life, to make this earth a paradise to live and enjoy life. The purpose of your life is to take care of mother-nature; to protect and maintain the balance of mother-nature.

But when Human Mind & Body thinks about itself as the supreme ego sets in that try to control and play with the nature. Then nature being supreme takes back the control. **The power of nature is infinite but the powers of your mind & physical body are limited.** Because nature is the creator and mind & body are creation of nature. Nature is unbiased, loves everybody, unconditionally. For nature, everything is one and same without any discrimination. Whereas, mind has duality, it can sometimes be negative, biased, may discriminate and sometimes it is positive, unbiased and believes in oneness. Creator knows its creation very well and can control, manage, destroy, recreate it in the way it has to be. It is difficult to understand the super intelligence of nature with logical mind but we can experience by tuning in to its frequency of unconditional love, gratitude, happiness and kindness, to realize and live our true nature; a life in tune to our real nature/self.

Body & mind when disconnected from nature, illusions themselves as supreme beings; ego sets in which wants to control others, suppress others, disrespects others and believes in domination and this is the cause of all disputes, wars and bloodshed in society. Many in the past became egoistic, self-centric, and some even cruel after achieving big success and thought of themselves as GOD but sooner or later, they found a place in the graveyard. They lost connection with their nature (Supreme father), there was nobody to guide them and they resorted to cruelty. **An egoistic mind is like a car without driver which is destructive not only to self but others also.** That is why a guide/ driver of your life must be nature which loves unconditionally and not your mind which can sometimes become egoistic. **That is why powers of mind and body are limited by nature and that is why powers of nature are infinite.** Nature is ultimate truth and ultimate super intelligent power beyond the imagination of human logical mind. The sooner we realize the nature, the faster we will realize the truth of universe which will lead to a happy and joyous life.

"Graveyard is full of those people who thought that world will end without them."
        --Chetan Bansal

2.2 COSMIC ENERGY AND LAWS OF UNIVERSE

There are three planes of existence; Spiritual, Mental and Physical. Spiritual world or one universal consciousness is the source of mental and physical world. Spiritual means oneness, spiritual means nothing and nothingness gives rise to everything. Duality operates in mental and physical world only. Mind is also an extension of one universal consciousness but it may vary in degree/percentage. One universal consciousness is nothing but energy called cosmic energy.

Everything in this universe is made of just energy called cosmic energy. Source of all creation in this Universe is cosmic energy. So what is the source of cosmic energy? Is it **Space? Yes, space**. A space is nothing but everything is contained in it. Nothingness creates and gives rise to everything. Space is infinite and ever expanding, space is eternal and space contains all energy and matter.

1)THE LAW OF MIND, ONE UNIVERSAL MIND (IMMUTABLE LAW OF NATURE) : The whole universe is a creation of one universal mind; everything in physical world that we see and experience has its origin in mental realm being only a creation of mind nothing else, a single universal consciousness an unseen world and an invisible reality. Everything manifests from this mental reality. This is an immutable law that can't be changed. Your mind is a part of universal mind, having same nature but with one difference of varying degrees of same nature. We humans have the power to raise consciousness and reach a level of super intelligence, Nature; one Universal consciousness. We have the ability to raise consciousness of mind, to reach and experience a state of one universal consciousness; a spiritual mind which is the creator of this universe.

Energy, Energy, Everything is energy: Everything in this universe, whether living or non-living is energy. Nothing rests and everything vibrates although at different frequencies. Everything in the universe is pure energy, one vibration including you but vibrating at different frequencies. For example solid, liquid and gas are all energy having vibrations of different frequencies. Solid is matter having low frequency, while gas is energy having highest frequency among the three and liquid is also energy having frequency in between the solid and gas. **The highest frequent energy of nature is spiritual energy/cosmic energy and is the source of all creation in the universe.** This is a universal immutable law. **The frequency of unconditional love, empathy, gratitude, happiness and kindness is the real frequency of cosmic energy.**

It is the energy by which all living or non-living things are made off, it is the energy which is present everywhere and in everything, including us. Name anything; stone, water, fire, animals, plants, earth, air, space, metals, plastics, any natural or manmade things, cosmic energy is present in and everywhere. Cosmic energy is a life force which is present in the cosmos, in between galaxies, molecules and space. You may think of any place and space, it is present everywhere. It is the one and only source of life which animates all forms of life and maintains the balance of whole cosmos. **In Hinduism, it is called "Shakti" which refers to eternal spiritual energy,** *prana* **or life energy. Scientist calls it cosmic energy.**

Energies correspond with each other: It means that physical, mental and spiritual realities of universe are connected to each other through energy vibrations and they correspond, cooperate, coordinate & harmonize or disharmonize with each other. This law is also immutable and can never be changed or transcended. **We can use our thoughts to attract desired people and situations in our physical life by using this law of correspondence.**

Want to see the example of energy vibrations around you, let's check. To connect with some person on phone, you dial his/her respective phone number, and this way the frequency vibrations of your phone matches with the frequency vibrations of the other person phone creating a telephonic connection where both persons can talk with each other. A phone transmits the sound vibrations to the other person phone and vice-versa through frequency waves present in the atmosphere.

A cricket match is being played in Australia and you are watching its live telecast on your TV screen in India, England or any other country. How can it be possible? See the match's live pictures are being converted into vibrations and those vibrations has a particular frequency which is being connected through artificial satellites revolving around Planet earth. Your TV intercepts that frequency and you are able to see the live pictures of the same match. **You are watching the physical reality in real time transported by invisible energy vibrations.**

Same way **radio works** on the concept of frequencies. You tune in to the frequency of radio channel of your choice. A broadcaster send frequencies of all channels in the atmosphere and you have a choice to listen to a particular channel by tuning your radio set to a particular frequency.

Internet, intranet, WIFI etc., all work on the law of vibrations where a huge amount of data gets transported to a place thousands of miles away in real time and without time lag.

X-ray, MRI and various machines to diagnose your physical body uses your energy field. This is again an example of every human having its own energy field, invisible to the naked eye.

Think of it. If you want to talk to somebody face to face or want to give physical papers by hand or want to go to the actual place where the match is being played, you need to move your body to get to that place and for that you need to travel by foot or by some vehicle like car, train or airplane which consumes time but manifestations through energy vibrations is instant.

ENERGY VIBRATIONS AROUND YOU

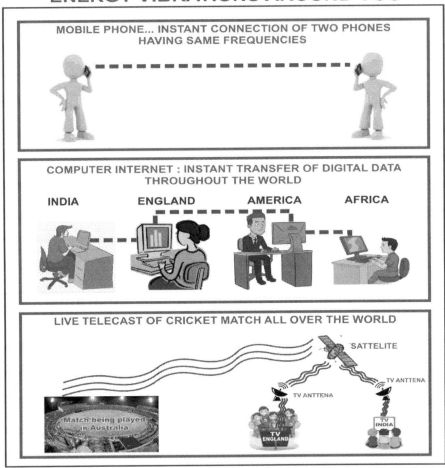

MOBILE PHONE... INSTANT CONNECTION OF TWO PHONES HAVING SAME FREQUENCIES

COMPUTER INTERNET : INSTANT TRANSFER OF DIGITAL DATA THROUGHOUT THE WORLD

INDIA   ENGLAND   AMERICA   AFRICA

LIVE TELECAST OF CRICKET MATCH ALL OVER THE WORLD

SATTELITE

TV ANTTENA

TV ANTTENA

Match being played in Australia

TV ENGLAND

TV INDIA

Source: Meet the Real You Copyright: Chetan Bansal

Have you ever noticed the glass of your window vibrating whenever an airplane passes above in sky? Do you know what happens whenever there is a frequency match between two energies; their energy enhances and causes increase in the intensity of vibrations which may even break the matter. In this case, glass is that matter resonates with the vibrations of plane, which causes glass to vibrate more and the intensity of vibrations sometimes increases so much that it causes glass to break. **See that is why soldiers are not allowed to march in the same rhythm on a bridge,** as their rhythmic march can resonate with that of bridge and can break the bridge.

What about electric current in wires? Can you see it? You can only feel it and please do not try to feel it. How much time it takes for a current to travel from a power house 10 km away to your home??? **Same way your thought is energy and can travel the distance within no time.**

Energy can neither be created nor destroyed but it can be transformed from one form to another. Think of hydro-energy being converted in to electrical energy and electrical energy being converted to mechanical energy (air fan) and electrical energy in to light energy (light bulb). We humans just use and convert energy from one form to other but we can never create energy, it is already present, we just capture it and use it. **Think of Television, phones, radios, Internet which uses the energy vibration for communication of voice, pictures, videos or any form of data.**

It cannot be seen, touched, smelled, or tasted but can be felt and heard like we can feel the air or the electric current. It is a sort of electric current and is the one & only power in the universe which has created each and everything in this universe. Like we cannot see the electrical energy, particular instruments are required to transform, transmit and use electrical energy, same way we cannot see the cosmic energy but it is present and we can feel it in our mind & body. **Have you ever felt the tingling sensation in any of your body parts like arm or leg or any other part, something tingling and vibrating trying to find its way?**

Sound of cosmic energy is AUM. Want proof of this. After a meal, sometimes we expel gases of stomach from mouth by an act called Burp. Have you ever noticed the sound of Burp? It's AUM. Next time you take a burp, notice it. Try this one now. Try to utter alphabets without moving your tongue, the only sound that comes is of AAAAA...UUUUU......MMMM, you can't utter any other alphabet without moving your tongue.

The sound of silence is AUM. Try to listen to the sound of silence by sitting in some silent place, you can try at night when everybody is asleep, when vehicles are off road, switch of all sound producing machines in your home even fans and AC's, you can sit on chair or lie down straight on bed comfortably, relax and still your body, close your eyes, take your full focus (*dhyana*) on to your ears. Try to hear the sound of silence and do it for at least 10 minutes. The more frequently and the longer you do, the faster is your experience.

Have you ever heard the sound of high tension wires of electricity supply? Next time, listen to it carefully and to your amaze, you will hear that sound of AAAUUUUUMMMMM.

Cosmic energy not only creates life but also maintains and sustains life. All living beings draw the same from Mother Nature. This action is automatic, involuntary and most of us remain unaware of this. **The presence**

of cosmic energy in all forms of life is very important for survival of life. All the simple and complex functions of our body are carried out by this energy like walking, talking, watching, thinking, functioning of all vital organs like heart, kidney, stomach etc. If this energy leaves body, life leaves our body and a body without life energy is lifeless body; a dead body.

We have seen here that everything is a creation of one universal mind or one universal consciousness or cosmic energy and everything is energy and all planes of existence, Spiritual, Mental and Physical corresponds with each other through vibrations. This is the basic laws of universe which is controlling and managing this universe, is immutable and can never be changed or transcended.

The other four laws of universe are mutable laws and can be changed or transcended; 2) Law of duality, 3) Law of Rhythm, 4) Law of Cause & Effect and 5) Law of Gender/Polarity. The understanding of these basic 5 laws of universe shall help you immensely in understanding the universe and your own life, understanding the causes of your problems and to your amaze, the solutions are also in these laws.

2) DUALITY: Everything is dual; everything has its pair of opposites. Opposites have identical nature, having difference in degree or percentage. Everything has two sides like a coin. Things that appear opposite are two extremes of the same nature.
Heat-cold; absence of heat is cold.
Peace-war; absence of peace is war.
Positive-negative; absence of positive is negative.
Good-evil; absence of good is evil.
Light-darkness; absence of light is darkness.
Energy-matter; low frequency has high density becomes matter and high frequency has less density and becomes energy.

You can change your thoughts from revenge to forgiveness, from hate to love, from fear to courage by consciously raising your vibrations. Duality operates only in mental & physical world and not in spiritual realm where all is one. You are a spirit which is omnipotent, eternal and super intelligent which is behind every thought and action of yours. And you can rise above the duality in bad situations of your life by raising your vibrations.

3) RHYTHM: The pendulum swing can be seen in everything. Everything flows out & in, up & down, all things rise and fall.
E.g. day and night, waves of ocean, rise and fall of empires, business cycles, change of thoughts from −ve to +ve or from +ve to −ve, personal success and Failure. To transcend the swing of pendulum, you must become aware of the subtle start of backward movement in all areas of your life like health, wealth relationships, career etc. When you are falling down, do not become fearful or disheartened instead keep your thoughts & actions positive, never give up no matter what, have faith in yourself/almighty that you are one with the one

universal omnipotent reality for which nothing is impossible. The upward movement is bound to happen and will surely start again, consequent of your consistent persistent focused patient faithful thoughts and actions. Soon your downfall becomes slow or less negative and positive upward movement will become inevitable. **Example:** See what happened with **Japan in World War – II**, two atom bombs were dropped in cities of Hiroshima and Nagasaki causing massive destruction to property and life. But nature (omnipotent eternal), supreme nature which always balances itself, wanted to rise again after the fall, inspired and motivated the Japanese people for reconstruction and they not only reconstructed but reached very high levels of growth in a very fast and efficient way.

4) LAW OF KARMA: Law of karma is the law of cause and effect. Every effect has some cause and every cause create some effect. Every effect in your physical world has a cause, having its origin in your inner or mental world. **This is the essence of thought power.** Every one of your thoughts, words and actions sets a specific effect in motion which will come to materialize in over a period of time. To become the master of your destiny, you must become the master of your mind (thoughts, emotions) for everything in your reality which is a creation of your mind. The luck or destiny or by chance are the words used by unaware people who do not understand law of destiny. **The law of karma is the law of destiny which you will understand in detail in PART-B of this book.** This law applies on all three planes of existence –spiritual, mental and physical. Spiritual existence's cause and effect are instant; they are inseparable as there is no duality in the spiritual world.

Your intensions are instantly manifested in spiritual world but for them to become reality in your physical world requires some time due to the concept of time and space. Concept of time and space creates a time lag between the input and the eventual output. When you decide about your physical life goals in your mind with pure intentions, it gets instantly manifested in the spiritual realms and with consistent, persistent, continual focused thoughts and actions it will become reality in the physical world over a period of time. Actions or movement is the very essence of physical reality and any thought to become reality shall only remain dream without action on your part.

5) GENDER: Gender is in everything. Everything has its masculine and feminine principles. Opposite sexes are found in humans, animals, plants, minerals, electrons and even in magnetic poles.
Dominant qualities of female: Love & care, patience, intuition and gentleness
Dominant qualities of male: Energy, confidence, logic and intellect.
All the above qualities are found both in men and women but some are more prominent in men and some are more prominent in women. The prominent qualities of women are also found in men but in a lesser degree/percentage, same way the prominent qualities of men are also found

in women but in a lesser degree/percentage. So they have duality and are not complete in themselves. **So both men and women want to experience each other's qualities which they have but in less degree** and is the only natural reason for attraction and completion of opposites genders. This is the basis of relationship between Men and Women. In fact, every relationship thrives on this principle of duality/gender/polarity, be it any; **customer-vendor, teacher-student, parent-children. We will learn more about nitty-gritty of relationships later in chapter 4 of the book.**

These are the basic laws by which the whole universe is governed, managed and controlled. **The law of universal mind having energy vibrations that correspond with each other is eternal, immutable law** and other four are transitory and mutable laws. The universe exists by virtue of these laws which forms the frame work of universe and holds the universe together. Knowing these universal laws helps you to understand your life; source, problems, needs & wants in a better way and also using these laws you can consciously choose right actions to raise your vibes and thus life.

The crux is that your life situations are dependent upon your actions which are dependent upon your thoughts and your thoughts are nothing but energy having frequencies and vibrations. How you feel inside determines your life outside. Knowingly or unknowingly, you are creating your own reality through your thoughts & emotions. So as to control your physical life, you must control your thoughts & emotions. Whatever you focus on expands in your life. The choice is yours, do you want to focus on solutions or problems, and do you want to focus on what you want or focus on what you lack. If you are happy inside, you will attract happy situations outside. If you are sad inside, you attract sad situations outside. **We have the power to choose, if vibrations of mind, body and soul are negative, we attract negative people and situations in life. And if it is positive, we attract positivity in life. Just check the MEET THE REAL YOU's JOURNEY diagram in chapter-1.** This is how it works nothing else determines your destiny but your own thoughts (understanding, perception, and decisions), behaviour and actions. **This is the essence of your thought power.**

In next chapter 3, we will understand about the basics of your mind; thoughts, emotions, beliefs etc. and in PART B & C of the book we will understand many techniques, formulas and ways to master your thoughts & emotions to transform your mind from negative to positive. All types of negative & positive energies are present in the universe.

As you have now understood the Basic laws of Universe which also governs your life, they will help you understand about the problems, solutions and the very basis of your life. The problems/failure in life is due to unintended, unaware misuse of these universal laws and the solution/success in life also lies in the right usage of these laws.

2.3 UNIVERSAL SPACE & TIME

Till now, we have understood that source of all physical life and matter is non-physical cosmic energy but another question that struck my mind is there any source of cosmic energy? The big answer is YES! It is a universal space. Space is amazing and mysterious at the same time.

Space is amazing. Everything exists in space, space is nothing yet it contains everything. For everything to exist needs space. Nothingness gave rise to everything. All planets, stars, sun, moon, air, water, earth, plants, animal, solar system, galaxies; be it anything all exists in space. The cosmic energy is also present everywhere and that everywhere is only one thing "SPACE". Where you build a house or any building? Well, you will say on land. But my dear real you land is just a support to building, it needs space; invisible space to be constructed vertically & horizontally. By making many floors or sections on same floor, you create more space to be utilized which is already present but without construction, it is of no use to you.

A space is permanent, eternal and non-physical can never change, what changes is the physical matter present in the space. Space is the witness of every creation, every change, all destruction; you cannot hide anything from space. All the past events of universe related to any or all activities of planets, plants, animals, galaxies manifests in a particular form based on specific laws of nature. Every specific action leads to a specific change, creation or destruction. All actions, reactions, manifestations only happen in a space not elsewhere.

Space is mysterious. It is infinite, limitless; it seems limited to human mind only to an extent a human mind knows and has explored it. It has no boundaries and is beyond human imagination. The more the human mind explores the universe, the bigger and limitless it seems. It has no form, no shape and it can't be touched or seen.

We may live in different houses, different cities, different countries but we all are in the same space; one universal space. The space of different places contains different energies and thus different physical forms. The presence of different forms/varieties of animals, plants, weather conditions, different soil forms, different water bodies etc. depends upon the different environment of different places. And the environment is determined by different energy vibrations. *SO ONE SPACE* having *DIFFERENT FORM OF ENERGY VIBRATIONS* results in *DIFFERENT PLACES* with *DIFFERENT ENVIRONMENTS* which manifests in *DIFFERENT PHYSICAL FORMS.* **That is why the height, skin colour, hair colour, eye colour and body structure of people living in different environment is different.**

And why the different places on planet earth have different energy vibrations? The simple answer is that the energy vibrations vary at different places because different places on planet earth have different angles in relation to other planets, moon and sun. The source of energy on planet earth is sun and the degree of sunrays is different at different places which results in different temperatures and climatic conditions. Also, various rotations and revolutions of planet earth changes the weather conditions from time to time only due to change in degree of sunrays at the same place. That is why weather conditions are always dynamic which manifests as summer, winter and rainy seasons. So, different places get different energy from sun based on degree/angle which also keeps changing with changing seasons. **This very energy is the life energy on which our mind and body thrives.** Thoughts in our mind are also energy and they keep on changing according to the external change in energy vibrations. **That is why people suffer mood swings at different places and at same place in different seasons/different times.**

Time is a creation of logical human mind based on planetary moments to record incidences of past, to plan future, to schedule actions etc. For plants, animals, soil, air, water, planets, for any life/action there is no concept of time, they are present now and performing their action now; the present space and the present time. Every thought, action and every change in the universe is present in the form of vibrations in present time and space. For space there is no such thing as past or future, for it everything/anything exists in present in the form of vibrations. From your life perspective also, life exists in present space; your action zone. There is no such thing as past or future for space. Space is present and shall always be present. The past and future are the psychological times stored in your mind in the form of vibrations. **Think, can you go back to your past and change the past action or can you go to future and take action there? No! The only action place is present space and time.** *CAN A MAN GO BACK INTO HIS PAST OR FUTURE? YOU SHALL FIND ANSWER TO THIS IN* **PART B** *OF THIS BOOK IN PRESENT MOMENT LIVING SECTION.*

Space is a witness of each & every action of the Universe. Even all your thoughts/actions are witnessed by space, are always present and stored in the form of energy vibrations. Nobody has the power to delete or remove the records of all actions present in space as it is stored in the form of non-physical eternal vibrations. **By building physical boundaries, we can only stop the entry of any physical entity within that boundary but not the energy vibrations.** You may think that you have done something in secret and nobody knows it but space witnesses all, records all in the form of energy vibrations and sooner or later shall manifest in some life situation, giving you the result of your karma. **That is why nobody can escape karma, when you have created a cause it is bound to give effect.** If the karma/actions of your past were good, they shall result in good present/future and if bad, shall result in bad present or bad future. **YOU SHALL UNDERSTAND IN DETAIL ABOUT KARMA IN PART B OF THIS BOOK.**

The **ideology of a person or group or masses living in a particular space** like the space of **country**, **society**, your **family**, **individual** etc. determines the **psychological energy vibrations (psychological atmosphere/energy field)** present in respective spaces. The ideology reflects in social, cultural, political, economic environments of these spaces. Why different families or societies or countries have different levels of growth, happiness, prosperity? It is because they have different psychological environments/energy fields. One country is democratic and gives free & fair environment to its citizens which results in growth, happiness, prosperity of individual and country as a whole but other country has a dictatorship government where humans do not get the free & fair environment which results in sadness and misery for people. *ONE UNIVERSAL SPACE having different ENERGY VIBRATIONS (THOUGHTS/IDEAS) in different PLACES (SPACES) leads to A DIFFERENT QUALITY OF LIFE.*

If the family atmosphere/society atmosphere/any group atmosphere/any country atmosphere is not good i.e., dominated by negative people with negative thoughts/ideas having vested interests and people with good human values, ethics, and morals are present in less numbers or silent, this results in bad environment leading to wrong actions and miserable life for all. To rebuild and remake a good positive environment for prosperity & growth of all requires rising and domination of good humans. Once that happen either bad elements/people transform to good ones or are vanished forever. But this can only be possible by the conscious will/choice of good people.

Same way, when the personal space of a particular person is not good and dominated with negative energies i.e. is devoid of life energy, it will manifest miseries in his/her physical body, mind and thus, physical life. **Every living organism has got their own personal space, energy field or aura which determines the quality of physical health, wealth, relations, job/career, life, death etc.** Your personal space contains your **ether body (mind, energies) and your physical body.** It also contains the record of every thought, action of self and actions of others witnessed. The amount of energy in your present space shall determine the quality of your life. The more is the presence of cosmic energy in your personal space the better is the quality of actions and thus life.

Disturbance in your personal space means disturbance in the energy field and once energy field gets disturbed, the same is reflected in your physical life (problems in all areas of your life physical health, wealth, relations, career/job/profession etc.). So if your life is disturbed you need to correct your energy field, enhance your energy levels to bring about positive changes in your life.

The viruses entered and became dominant in your personal space disturbing your positive/natural/divine energy field. This book is an antivirus which shall activate your conscious presence by raising your vibrations. The divine light where there is no space for any darkness, any negativity, and any virus (anger, violence, cruelty, hatred, jealousy, depression) but only love, happiness, prosperity. So, you can change your life from negative to positive or from miserable to joyous *BY INCREASING THE LIFE ENERGY IN YOUR PERSONAL SPACE*. And this book shall show you how to enhance your energy field/aura which is very simple, easy and in your own hands in **PART B & C OF THIS BOOK**.

2.4 YOUR REAL IDENTITY
YOUR ETERNAL NON-PHYSICAL IDENTITY

As you have already understood the concept of cosmic energy, it will now be easy for you to understand who you are. Since birth we have gone to school, college and many educational institutions but have we been ever told about the reality of life? Look the problem here is that most people are unaware about their reality; they do not understand the subject of life. We are only taught about the outer world which is visible to naked eye like our physical body, plants, animals, geography, science, professional courses on medicine, engineering, accounts, computer science, sports etc. But nobody or most of us do not want to understand that it is the invisible world that creates the visible physical world. **See for any physical visible action or creativity, an idea/thought comes in mind which is invisible thus conforming that unseen leads to seen/physical world.** Most of us, when asked who you are we normally identify our self with name, caste, religion, educational qualification, profession etc.; we just identify with our physical reality.

You are very lucky that you will now know **who you are and why you are. Most of the people die without knowing who they are, about their source, purpose of their life and how to live life???** When I understood about this mysterious subject of life, it completely changed my perspective towards life; at least I have now learned to be at peace and content in each & every moment of my life. I was surprised with the results that I started experiencing in my life after using some simple logical techniques for controlling mind & body and getting connected to nature/universe through mind & body.

WHO ARE YOU: Who are you? I am body, yes. I am body, wait, let me think, I always say my hand, my face, my eyes, my body, so if I am body I should say "I am body". This means I and my body are different.

Oh! Yes, finally I got it "I am not body but I am Mind." Yes, final answer. Wait, wait, wait, if I am mind and I think.

Yes, you think; I agree. But when you think, are you aware of your thoughts as well or someone else observes your thoughts? So who will become aware of all your thoughts? Is there something two inside you, the one who thinks and the other one who witnesses your thoughts? I don't know, I am getting confused but I am also excited. I think I am going to discover something very mysterious about myself today. Please help me find out.

Please before coming to any conclusion, think of something/anything. Think! Think! Think! Do you feel there are two different entities in you, the one who thinks and the other one who observes or there is no difference between the two?

Yes, yes, I can feel two different entities in me. Sometimes one question and other one answer, one speaks and other listens. Amazing, I never gave any thought on that.

Yes sir/madam, you are right, your mind thinks and you observe. You are an observer, you are a witness and it is your mind which thinks and most of the times it is thinking without you having any control over it. It keeps on thinking, jumping from one issue to another without your permission. Sometimes, it thinks about your pleasant memories, sometimes thinks about your bad memories, sometimes makes you fearful about your future, sometimes gives you thoughts of a bright future and makes you confident. It keeps on swaying from one thought to another. **And you cannot be what keep on changing, you are something which is permanent, you are something which is above mind & body** and also creator of your mind & body and thus life.

So am I consciousness and my mind & body are manifestation of my consciousness? No, you are not consciousness either; you are a creation of universal cosmic energy. Your consciousness is also manifestation of you; again it means that you are not consciousness but something else. **My Dear Real You! You are pure energy extension of one universal energy nothing else.** Your consciousness depends upon the quantity and flow of your presence in your mind & body, your personal space.

You are a soul/spiritual energy/cosmic energy living in physical body. The source of your creation is Universal cosmic energy, a supreme creative intelligence which has created this universe. It is this energy which religious people call God. So God is inside you, inside all of us. We all are a child of God. This energy cannot be described; it is formless, timeless and eternal. The more you become fully aware of your thoughts and circumstances, the more you are fully present; the more you can feel it, the more you can experience it.

That this energy is present in the whole universe, it is in everything, it is above you, it is below you, it is on your right, on your left, it is everywhere beyond your imagination. We all are made of same energy it means we all are alike and a part of bigger energy cosmic energy. It means we all are connected with one universal cosmic energy/God and we all are also connected with each other through cosmic energy.

The more is the presence of energy the more powerful becomes your soul the more conscious becomes your mind or more dominant becomes your nature which leads to better understanding, clear perception, right decisions, right actions and right results in life. **The less presence of energy** leads to unconscious mind and weak soul which ultimately leads to less understanding, opaque perception, wrong decisions, wrong actions and wrong results in life.

Energy never dies so you will never die. It is the death of physical body, not your death. Once your body is dead, you energy will create new body, newer circumstances in new life. **More on it is detailed in PART-B of this book (The Law of karma/luck)**. I am always within my body, the moment I leave my body, my body is dead. **I am creation of the creator** of this universe and a **part of that creative power is within me.** This means I am a creator also. **Yes, I create my whole life with my conscious thought power**. Also my sexual energy is an extension of source energy through which I have the power to produce more humans like me.

But if everybody is made of same source and that source is within everybody, so why are there differences in life of all people? Or in other words different people are doing different things, have different physical appearances, their likes and dislikes are different, their needs & wants are different, some are rich, some are poor, some are healthy, some unhealthy. **People are same in the sense that they have same source of creation, same mind but varying degree/percentage of quality/consciousness of same mind.** Some are negative, some are less negative, some are positive, some are more positive in their mind and hence **same minds having different degree/percentage of consciousness manifests different realities in physical life**. Their physical reality varies in degree in terms of health, wealth, relations, career etc.

Varying degree of presence of energy: Your presence
⇩
Varying degree of consciousness of mind will lead to
⇩
VARYING IDENTITY
Lowest consciousness: Physical identity
Next degree of consciousness: Emotional & worldly pleasure identity
Next degree of consciousness: Mind Identity
Highest degree of consciousness: Spiritual Identity
⇩
Varying beliefs, perceptions and values leading to
⇩
Varying actions, habits and behaviour leading to
⇩
Varying results in real life in terms of health, wealth, relations, career/job...

Source: Meet the Real You Copyright: Chetan Bansal

"It is not what you get but what you make out of what you get determines your destiny."
- Chetan Bansal

So, God has given you same mind and body but due to your varying degree/percentage of consciousness you have varying results in your life. Like parents give everything in equality to their children in terms of love, care, food, clothing, education, medical facilities etc. but still their children have different results in life. So, who is to be blamed, the parents or the children? **It is not what you get but what you make out of what you get determines your destiny**. If you want to change your destiny you must understand yourself; your reality, natural laws to bring about a change in your consciousness to uplift your life and destiny. **And when you raise your consciousness, you respond to a situation from higher consciousness which activates righteous perceptions, righteous decisions, righteous actions and thus righteous results**. All in all, you make yourself lucky. You were working hard but your direction was wrong, hence you got wrong results in life making you unlucky. So, two people with same resources and same situations respond differently as per their level of consciousness and thus get different results.

But can we change and raise the degree of consciousness? Yes, we have the power to raise our vibrations consciously by increasing our presence to connect with source energy/cosmic energy, to become one with the omnipotent source energy and **can thus, enhance the quality of life. We must aim at highest degree of consciousness (spiritual identity) to activate supernatural intelligence, intuitive & creative powers, and pure perception for right decisions, actions and ultimately right results in life.**

Role of source energy-The source energy knows about your past, present and future. It knows the very purpose of your life, it knows about a special quality or natural talent within you, it knows about your likes and dislikes, it has all solutions to your problems. It controls all the vital functions of your body like breathing, digestion, blood circulation, healing of wounds etc.; all functions which are beyond the control of your conscious mind. This source energy takes care of your body even when you are asleep or in unconscious state of mind. It has the power to attract desired people and situations in your life. It has the power to make your dreams/desires come true. **So connecting with your source, with your real you is the key to a happy and prosperous life**.

Establishing a conscious connection with your source is a key to a happy, prosperous and purposeful life. But we have lost connection with it that is why we are unable to understand its messages which is the cause of all misery in life.

Lost connection, getting or not getting, sounds complex.

Don't worry I will make it simpler for you......**VERY IMPORTANT FOR YOU TO UNDERSTAND THIS**.

Let me explain it. Let's say for making you understand that we are **2 parts; 1) Source energy and 2) Conscious Mind. You need to connect your conscious mind with source energy to experience the power of source energy i.e., Real You and for that you need to raise your vibrations to match the vibrations of source energy.**

Source energy ⟵⟹ **Conscious Mind**

Your source energy, being energy having highest frequency of Gratitude, Happiness, Kindness and Unconditional love is your true nature which is always positive and it is permanent.

And if your conscious thought energy is persistently consistent also of Gratitude, Happiness, Kindness, unconditional love etc., then there is a frequency match with your source energy. Now your synchronized/harmonized energy of conscious mind and source energy travels out of your mind & body and find similar energies (in the form of people & situations) of same wavelength in the outer physical world. Means your source shall bring in your real life experience, people and circumstances which are in tune with your conscious thought energy. Your source shall find each and everything that makes you happy and make it reality on your screen of life. This way it shall also bring forth the real purpose of your life. To bring the source and mediums for fulfilling your life with happiness are the responsibility of your source, your conscious responsibility is just to choose peace, joy, gratitude, happiness, kindness and unconditional love.

You can even ask your source what makes you happy, what is the purpose of your life, the answer will definitely come in some way or other but for that you need to get connected with your inner being which can only be possible **by practicing attitude of present moment living, acceptance, zero resistance, forgiveness, gratitude, happiness, kindness, love, right breathing pattern, right intake of food and water etc**. This all connects your mind with a source energy/cosmic energy. Mind when connected with source energy increases the emotional, spiritual, mental and physical power leading to the increase in the consciousness of your mind. Then your mind is transformed from negative to positive and duality of mind ends. **It becomes one with the source, one universal consciousness.**

Unconscious/Untrained mind constantly takes your focus to past problems and future worries. This generates a noise pollution of negative thoughts and negative emotions in your mind leading to depletion of energy and disconnection with the source. Thus your conscious mind becomes negative. Let's understand it with an example, when you make a phone call and if there is disturbance in phone line, you are not able to connect and communicate. Same way, when there are disturbances of emotions, you are not able to connect and communicate with the source.

Suppose you are talking to a person who only understands French and you start speaking English with him, will you be able to connect and communicate with him? No! Same way when nature of source is of Gratitude, Happiness, Kindness, Unconditional love(all high frequencies) and **your conscious thought energy is of worry, anxiety, fear, anger, jealousy(all low frequencies)** – then there is a frequency mismatch with your source energy i.e. clear indication that you have diverted from your source, your true nature. Now this disharmonized energy when travels out of your body shall attract and bring unwanted people and circumstances (negative energies) in your life, which shall make your life miserable. **As you have lost connection with your** source, leading to disconnection with the *REAL YOU* and thus you shall not be able to find peace, purpose of your life which will always give you a feeling of some lack in your life.

That is why many people complain that **"I don't know why am I feeling low or lacking something."** It's a clear indication that they are not on the right path of their journey (they haven't realized their true self, the real purpose of their life). **So they just need to raise their frequency and live life with an attitude of acceptance, presence, faith, gratitude, happiness, kindness, love, forgiveness, and celebration; a 9 point spiritual attitude to raise your vibrations, to raise your consciousness and thus, life.**

TO UNDERSTAND THE IMPACT ON YOUR LIFE OF CONNECTION AND DISCONNECTION WITH SOURCE, KINDLY RECHECK DIAGRAM (MEET THE REAL YOU...JOURNEY) IN CHAPTER-1. *NOW I KNOW YOU GOT IT RIGHT! BEFORE MOVING AHEAD TAKE A PAUSE AND READ IT AGAIN.*

Sir, I am really excited to understand and practice 9 point spiritual attitude but I don't know how? Don't lie. You already know it, you are REAL YOU who knows everything but you have forgotten it, I will remind you in PART-B of this book but for that you must read PART-A first.

2.5 PURPOSE OF LIFE

Everybody loves to play and we got this nature from the supreme intelligence which created this universe. So we can assume that he/she created this universe as a playground as playing is the nature of divine. Living life like playing a game will give you much desired enthusiasm/energy and what more you need for success in life. Different people, plants & animals have different purposes; all are helping each other by fulfilling each other basic needs of food, air, water and thus, sustaining each other's life. Knowingly or unknowingly, all are serving the higher purpose of divine who has created this whole universe. **This universe is a playground where each & every living and non-living organisms is here for a purpose, having a specific role to play. For this, the physical form of all is unique and different from each other which is beyond imagination and in control of any living organism.** Only the creator knows its creation; its purpose, its birth and death. **All is beyond the understanding and control of human mind.**

In your control is the living time for which he has given mind & body to experience life. **And Yes Ladies, he is a guy**! Just joking! Hindus believe in both God and Goddess, both are different forms of same power and complete each other. Me using here "he" is just what comes with the flow and by no means denotes any "he" being supreme. The supreme is beyond duality, is beyond masculine and feminine, in fact the supreme has both the qualities merged into one.

Life is a game to be played. The creator is supreme, he is playing bigger game and we are just working on his direction. **He is the director, creator** and has already defined roles, skills, talents by preinstalling some software in our mind. Like a film producer and director predefines every role of the actor and rest of all activities like story writing, editing, director, cameraman, other actors, other team members of production house, finances etc. are all taken care of by the producer director. **As an actor, if I am doing my role with full dedication and focus then nobody can stop me writing my success story** but if I am not doing my role properly then nobody can find me an escape route from failure. So, life is all about accepting what is being offered by the supreme nature and giving your best of actions/response to each & every situation. Non acceptance of situations and no action or action without focus and dedication is cause of all miseries in life.

And for writing that success story, not only I need to work with full focus and dedication but also need to maintain good relations with others, coordinate and cooperate with others, help others. Like an actor need to coordinate with his director, cameraman and other actors to make a scene a perfect one. And this can only be possible if we understand, love, respect and care for others. And for understanding others, I need to first understand my mind, body and needs which are universal in nature. So, understanding human mind, developing good communication skills is must for all for a successful life for it does not matter in which profession you are or which country you live in or which religion you believe in.

The good players learn, practice and improve on their skills and take help of experts. You have your own likes and dislikes, own strengths and weaknesses; you have to move according to them and not by what others think of you. Other people's consciousness is different, so different mindset having different strengths and weakness and thus different role. Do not try to copy them or compare with them, be fully focused in your role without worrying about others, without any influence of others; just be yourself otherwise you are bound to fail.

Sometimes outside situations will not be under your control as you cannot control the action of other people. In that case, you just need to accept the situation as it is without any bias and put your best foot forward without creating any internal resistance. The response/action from your side is under your control and you must focus on that only and leave the rest to the almighty/creator, **like a player in any game does not know what will be the action/response of the other team,** he just tries to understand their move counters them with full focus and dedication.

So, what is the purpose of life? The ultimate purpose of your life is to live it happily. And to live a happy life, your mind & body must be highly conscious & intelligent which can only be possible by connecting them with source. **Non acceptance and creating resistance inside disconnects you with**

source, leading to wrong actions and wrong results in life. Maintaining a cool & calm mind and keep on doing your karma with focus & dedication strengthens your connection with your inner being, your guru/guide; which guides your every action towards a happy & successful life.

So the ultimate purpose of life is to understand life, its source and getting connected to it to find meaning, purpose, joy, happiness, success & growth in life. And for that, we as humans are lucky being bestowed with large size brain and vertebrae which can tap into higher frequencies of consciousness; to understand self, life, mind and universe and to ultimately find your natural/soul path of life. For connection with source, we must practice a spiritual attitude of acceptance, surrender, conscious presence, love, faith, gratitude, kindness, celebration and forgiveness **as only this can raise your consciousness and raising the consciousness is the only purpose of human life,** in order to experience the peak of life, to experience the peak of happiness. Once you raise your vibrations you shall also find your hidden talents, hidden purposes, unique purpose for which you are born to live a happy life. Once you start living your natural inborn purposes, your actions are automatically focused, perfect and responsible. And once your actions are perfect, the results in life are also perfect. **More on it is detailed in PART-B of this book.**

Same way the purpose of humans in context to the other creatures and universe as a whole is very interesting. We the humans have been given supreme brain & vertebrae which can tap the maximum amount of consciousness as compared to other living beings and thus can live a superior life and we are already doing that. **So big brain means big power and big power means big responsibility.** With greater power comes the greater responsibility. So by giving a big brain, God has given big responsibility to us to make this world a paradise for all forms of life. **But have we misused our powers and caused more destruction than creation?** Have destructed the peace and prosperity of self and others, polluted and destructed the nature? This is the question we must ask ourselves. What do you think, the nature is going to sit back and do nothing? **No! You are mistaken, my dear. It shall bounce back in the form of natural calamities and shall definitely balance itself and in the process, only we humans shall be at huge loss. Are we ready for that?**

So the purpose of your life is to live a happy life and help others which can only be possible by connecting with your inner being and for that you need to raise your consciousness and it should be the prime focus & purpose of your life.

TO CONNECT WITH YOUR ETERNAL REALITY YOU MUST FIRST UNDERSTAND THE SOURCE OF YOUR PHYSICAL LIFE (YOUR PERSONAL SPACE) AND PHYSICAL LIFE ITSELF (YOUR NEEDS & WANTS, RELATIONS). WHAT CONSTITUTES YOUR PERSONAL SPACE, EFFECT OF YOUR PERSONAL SPACE

ON YOUR LIFE, HOW IT HAS BECOME NEGATIVE, HOW THIS NEGATIVITY IS MANIFESTING FAILURE AND MISERY IN YOUR LIFE. ALL THIS WE WILL UNDERSTAND IN CHAPTER 3 AND CHAPTER 4; YOUR PERSONAL SPACE AND PHYSICAL REALITY. ONLY THEN WE WILL MOVE TO PART B AND C OF THE BOOK TO MEET THE REAL YOU...TO STRENGTHEN THE CONNECTION WITH YOUR ETERNAL REALITY BY BALANCING 5 ELEMENTS OF YOUR LIFE BY CHANGING "FABP".

3.0 YOUR PERSONAL SPACE

3.1 SUBTLE, PHYSICAL BODIES AND LIFE ISSUES.
3.2 CONSCIOUS & SUBCONSCIOUS MIND
3.3 THOUGHTS
3.4 EMOTIONS
3.5 BELIEFS AND PERCEPTIONS
3.6 EFFECT OF THOUGHTS, EMOTIONS AND BELIEFS ON PERSONAL SPACE AND LIFE.
3.7 HOW MIND BECAME NEGATIVE
3.8 I DON'T BELIEVE

3.1 SUBTLE, PHYSICAL BODIES AND LIFE ISSUES

To get a clear understanding of yourself, you must understand your existence at the level of physical body, mind, emotions and energies (YOUR PERSONAL SPACE) in order to give you the idea of how these all are interrelated and how they affect each other and thus your life. The very basic understanding of your personal space will help you in enhancing the quality of your life by connecting with your eternal reality. Broadly speaking, your personal space can be divided in to two different layers.

YOUR PERSONAL SPACE comprises of 2 layers	
Outer body	Physical body (hardware of our body)
Inner body	Subtle body or soul (software of our body) which consists of Etheric body (energy body), Mind and Emotions

Source: Meet the Real You **Copyright:** Chetan Bansal

The focus of this chapter is on your inner bodies which creates and maintains your physical life. First a little bit about the basics of your physical body.

3.1.1 Physical body- Your body is made up of 5 elements, fire, earth, water, air and space, and also 70% of your body is water. These five elements are nothing but different forms of Universal cosmic energy/Universal consciousness. The physical body can be seen, touched, has weight and **it is through the physical body that you experience life.** So it is very important to have a healthy physical body. You need to nourish and maintain it through quality intake of food, water, right natural breathing pattern, physical exercise, sleep, relaxation, focused life with spiritual attitude etc. This enhances the health of your mind & body, steadies your emotions, keeps you connected with your eternal reality and will ultimately keep you on automatic/natural/spiritual path of life where peace, joy, success, growth and happiness is inevitable.

The full details and the importance, when, why, how and what, all your questions related to food, physical exercise, sleep, relaxation, meditation/focus, breathing pattern etc. will be shared in **PART-B AND C of this book.**

3.1.2 Subtle body is a vapour like image of your physical body and it consists of mind, emotions and etheric body. It is a formless energy field of your body. The increase in the energy field of your subtle body increases the **aura** of your body. The more is the aura or energy field, the more magnetic you become a person that attracts all positive energies in this world.

3.1.2.1 Etheric body/Energy Body consists of Energy Chakras and Nadis (energy channels/energy pipes) inside the body and through which there is flow and circulation of energy/emotions in your body. Energy Chakras and Nadis circulate energy in your body as a fan helps in circulating the air in a room. Chakras are like fans which help in proper circulation of energy in your body. All the parts of your body are connected with Chakras through these energy pipes.

The chakra is a Sanskrit word meaning "wheel" or "vortex". Each chakra is like a solid ball of energy interpenetrating through the physical body, thus making an energy field originating from chakras, penetrating and spreading outside the physical body. **The energy field of the chakras is called the Aura**. The energy field of a person is like the magnetic field of a magnet. The stronger the magnetic power, the wider is the magnetic field. In the same way, the stronger the energy of the chakras, the wider is the field of Aura. The chakras are denser than auras but not as dense as a physical body.

It is said there are about 114 chakras in your body out of which 7 are major chakras. **All 7 chakras are aligned vertically** starting from the base of spine, runs through spine till top head centre of your body.

The cosmic energy enters the mother's womb during pregnancy and creates the whole body of foetus inside the womb. After birth that cosmic energy rests at the base of the spine of the child, remain seated there for their whole life till death. The external cosmic energy enters from the top centre of your head and runs through all the chakras and ultimately meets the cosmic energy at the base of your spine. **This forms energy circuit** where a continuous flow of cosmic energy takes place. This balances, aligns, recharges all the chakras and opens up all energy blocks of Nadis leading to recharging of each and every cell of your body. This can be compared to Electric Distribution Panel (energy chakras) at your home getting power from a bigger power station (cosmic energy) outside your home and spreading electric energy throughout the home through wires & cables (nerves inside Nadis).

Cosmic energy not only creates life but also maintains and sustains life. All living beings draw the same from mother-nature. This action is automatic, involuntary and most of us remain unaware of this. **The presence of cosmic energy in all forms of life is very important for the survival of life.**

All the physical and mental ailments are due to lack of energy/inadequate energy in your etheric body. Inadequate energy in your etheric body may block one or more energy chakras, creating disturbance in the energy field of your body. Lack of energy in particular area/part/organ of body develops a patch which is an area devoid of vital energy that manifests as physical pain or some physical ailment in that particular area. Emotional disturbance reduces your vital energy and thus energy field leading to creation of energy blocks and thus physical ailments. **Every physical health problem has its root in energy body and a problem begins in subtle part of the organ first which becomes physical over a period of time.** To get the right healing, both subtle part and physical part of the body should be treated. To correct that pain or physical ailment, you need to get rid of energy blocks by channelizing the flow of energy in your whole etheric body for which you need to follow spiritual way of life; acceptance, non-resistance, conscious presence, faith, gratitude and kindness to keep you always high on energy and life.

Same happens with all electrical gadgets. Whenever at any point or any part of electric circuit of any gadget, say for example television becomes weak due to low supply of power, that point/part of television becomes weak and needs repair or replacement to become functional again.

Without it all the vital functions of body cannot be performed. All the simple and complex functions of our body are carried out by this energy like walking, talking, watching, thinking and other functions of vital organs like heart, kidney, stomach etc. **If this energy leaves your body, life leaves your body and a body without life energy is a dead body. For example if your mobile phone battery** is removed, mobile phone does not get the energy or the power to start and function. All electric gadgets without power or energy or electricity can't start or function, they are all dead without power.

Etheric/Energy body cannot be seen with the naked eye, it cannot be touched, but the flow of energy can be felt inside the body. **Have you ever felt a tingling sensation in any of your body parts like arm or leg or any other part, like something vibrating and trying to find its way?** Have you ever experienced the feeling of goose bumps in the extremes of joy or fear or both like on watching a horror movie or on achieving something extraordinary etc.? During goose bumps energy vibrations move from stomach to different parts of body, have you ever felt the feeling of presence of you within you? Next time please notice it.

Do you know what depression is? Depression simply means less energy or lowering of energy in the etheric body which creates disturbance in mind. In severe depression conditions doctors use electric shocks just to activate the energy circuits in the body which have been broken due to emotional disturbances, some physical injury or some wrong medications causing severe depression in the patient.

There are seven colours of seven chakras which correspond to seven colours of rainbow, VIBGYOR which are the colours of planets in our solar system. Is there any cosmic connection with your energy body? Well, it is said that there are complete cosmos within us having connection with solar system.

Chakras are nothing but different manifestations of one universal mind/consciousness; 7 minds, 7 default/preinstalled applications/software present in every human, installed by nature. These chakras are manifested in different forms & colour, controlling & managing different functions, emotions of your body, giving rise to different kinds of needs, wants and desires and at the same time give the energy, focus, courage & determination to fulfil all these needs.

The deactivation/over-activation of these chakras leads to all the problems, failures & miseries in life. The differences in the life of people are due to differences in thoughts and actions which are due to difference in the activation/deactivation of these 7 minds/chakras, nothing else.

The balancing/activation of these chakras will lead to fulfilment of all your needs & wants so as to enjoy all the 7 colours of life leading to a perfect life; desire of every human. The understanding and balancing of these chakras should be the purpose of human life. We will be balancing these chakras/7 human minds through spiritual attitude in PART B and through physiology in PART C of this book.

The chakras interact with our physical body through two major systems, the endocrine system and nervous system. Each chakra is associated with one of the seven endocrine glands and a particular group of nerves. And each gland is responsible for the functioning of specific organs in the body by feeding them with life chemicals called hormones. Thus, indirectly chakras control the function of all the organs of your body through glands and nerves.

The endocrine system is one of the main body control system and affects your health and well-being. It compromises a number of ductless glands that produce hormones, which are secreted in to the blood stimulating or inhibiting particular physical processes. Excess or low production and secretion of glands poorly affects physical health. So, the hormones need to be adjusted at optimum levels.

The position of seven chakras corresponds with the position of seven endocrine glands in your body. Isn't it amazing! The chakras affect the functioning of the glands. The link between the chakra and the glands emphasised the holistic nature of health and we need to maintain a balance in emotional and mental activities along with the natural diet and physical activities as all are interrelated.

Some of the functions of chakras/7 minds along with their relation to emotions, physical organs are the following which shall help us in understanding the importance of balancing/energizing of chakras with cosmic energy as balanced chakras determine the inner health that ultimately determine success and happiness in physical world.

FACT SHEET OF 7 MINDS/CHAKRAS

NAME OF CHAKRA WITH COLOR & PLANETS	POSITION IN BODY	ELEMENT ASSOCIATED WITH CHAKRA	RELATED BODY ORGANS AND ENDOCRINE GLANDS	ISSUES RELATED WITH CHAKRA, DEFAULT/PREINSTAL LED PSYCOLOGICAL NEEDS (PPN)
SAHASRARA-CROWN CHAKRA(VOILET-JUPITER)	ABOVE TOP centre of HEAD	ETHER/SPACE	TOP OF SPINAL CORD,BRAIN STEM,NERVES ,PAIN CENTRE(PINEAL GLAND-MELATONIN-AFFECTS ALL OTHER GLANDS IN ENDOCRINE SYSTEM)	CONTRIBUTION TO OTHERS-SPIRITUAL WISDOM
AJNA-THIRD EYE CHAKRA(INDIGO-SATURN)	IN BETWEEN EYE BROWS	ETHER/SPACE	PINEAL GLAND,EYES,BRAIN,NERVOUS SYSTEM,SENSES(PITUITARY GLAND-MELOTONIN-BODY CHEMISTRY)	SELF GROWTH-CLAIRVOYANCE
VISHUDDHA-THROAT CHAKRA(BLUE-SATURN)	THROAT	AIR	THROAT,TONGUE,TEETH,MOUTH(THYROID-THYROXINE-METABOLISM)	SELF GROWTH-COMMUNICATION
ANAHATA-HEART CHAKRA(GREENME RCURY)	HEART	AIR & WATER	HEART,LUNGS(THYMUS-LYMPHOCYTES-IMMUNE SYSTEM)	LOVE & CONNECTION
MANIPURA-NAVAL CHAKRA(YELLOW-SUN)	NAVAL	FIRE	STOMACH,UPPER SPINE,UPPER INTESTINE(PANCREAS-INSULIN-METABOLISM)	IMPORTANCE-POWER & CONTROL
SWADISTHAN-SACRAL CHAKRA(ORANGE-VENUS)	BELOW NAVAL	WATER	SEXUAL ORGANS,BLADDER,LOWER INTESTINE,BOWEL(OVARIES-OESTROGEN, TESTICLES-TESTOSTERONE)	VARIETY-PHYSICAL AND MATERIAL DESIRES
MULADHAR-BASE CHAKRA(RED-MARS)	BASE OF SPINE	EARTH	BACK,HIPS,LEGS,SPINE(ADRENAL-ADRENALINE-SURVIVAL)	SECURITY & SURVIVAL

Source: Meet the Real You **Copyright** Chetan Bansal

1). BASE /ROOT CHAKRA- Your life issues of security and survival are controlled by this chakra. The root chakra is about faith & belief in self/almighty. If this chakra is working properly you feel grounded, stable, secure and unperturbed by any/all situations. You don't unnecessarily distrust people. You feel present and connected to your physical body. **If your chakra is under-active**, you tend to be fearful, nervous and lacking self-confidence. **If this chakra is over-active,** you may be very materialistic and greedy. You are probably obsessed with being secure and resist change. **Physical problems** associated with this chakra are obesity, osteoarthritis, etc. **The root chakra is associated with Adrenal gland** which produces several hormones including adrenaline (emergency hormone) that stimulates fight or flight response. It is a centre of physical energy that governs the spine, back, legs, feet and hips.

2).Sacral chakra- Your life issues of physical and material desires are governed by this chakra. The chakra is about feeling and physical desires. When it is open, you express your feeling with natural flow without any resistance. You are lively, passionate and tend to enjoy your life freely. **If this chakra is underactive,** you tend to be unemotional, blank-faced and not very open to people. **If this chakra is overactive** you feel emotionally attached to people and obsessed with physical & material desires. The sacral chakra is associated with **ovaries/testicles** which produces oestrogen, progesterone and governs sexual organs, lower intestine, gall bladder, bowel etc.

3).Solar plexus- Your life issues of power and control are governed by this chakra. This chakra is about you being confident and controlling in the group. **When this chakra is underactive,** you tend to be passive, confused and indecisive. **If this chakra is overactive** you are dominating and may even be aggressive. **This chakra is associated with pancreas** which secretes insulin, governs digestion, the stomach, upper intestine and upper spine.

4).Heart chakra- Life issues of love and connection are governed by this chakra. The heart chakra is about love, kindness and affection. When it is active, you are compassionate, friendly and make harmonious relations. **When this chakra is underactive,** you are cold and distant. **If this is overactive**, you tend to suffocate people with love and you might have vested interests for your love for other. **The heart chakra is associated with thymus gland**, circulatory system and governs the heart, lungs and blood circulation.

5).Throat chakra- Life issues are communication, it being the centre of sound, communication, speech, writing and thought expression. This chakra is about self-expression. When it is active, you express yourself freely and even in a creative way. **When this chakra is underactive**, you speak less, shy and introvert. Not speaking the truth may block this chakra. **If this chakra is overactive**, you are a bad listener, you tend to speak a lot, use aggressive language, try to dominate people and people try to avoid you. **The throat chakra is associated with the thyroid gland** and governs the throat, mouth, teeth, tongue and jaw.

6).Third eye chakra- Life issues are clairvoyance. It is the centre of psychic powers, spirit energies, higher intuition and light. This chakra is about insight and visualization. When it is active, you have a good intuition and you easily find solution to your problems. **If it is underactive,** you are very poor at thinking and rely on others for your decisions. You may be rigid in your thinking relying on your beliefs, biased and invariably take wrong decisions. **If this chakra is overactive,** you may live in a world of fantasy, dreams and illusions. **The third eye chakra governs pituitary gland** and the autonomous nervous system. Physical health problems associated with this chakra are glaucoma, headache, neurological problems, cerebellum, nose, central nervous system and the left eye.

7).Crown chakra- Life issues are spiritual intelligence. It is the centre for enlightenment, dynamic thought, truth and oneness. This chakra is about wisdom and being one with the world. When this chakra is open, you are unprejudiced and quite aware of the world and yourself. You accept everything and you have zero resistance to any of the situations. **If this is underactive, y**ou are not aware spiritually and rigid. **If this chakra is overactive**, you are intellectualizing things too much. You may be addicted to spirituality and probably ignoring your bodily needs.

When all of your chakras are in harmony and balanced, each & every cell of your body becomes its natural self; vibrating with life full of energy, health free from all diseases & negativity. It sets your life on auto mode; a path to peace, joy, success, growth and happiness in all areas of your life like health, wealth, relations, career/job/profession by activating your super natural intelligence, intuition, luck, truthful perception, right decisions and courageous actions. A magical positive transformation not only amazes you, but also the people around you. At this stage, life becomes effortless where everything that is needed for you to come towards you rather than you chasing them. **And the best way to balance all the chakras is by balancing the 5 elements of life; to find balance and enjoy all the colours of life is by choosing right "FABP" which we will understand PART B AND C of the book.**

YOU) WHAT DISTURBS MY ENERGY BODY?

ME) a disturbance in one causes disturbance in the other. It means that your chakras/mind, emotions and physical body are interconnected to each other. If there is a **problem in the physical body,** there appears a problem in corresponding emotion and the chakra. Or a **problem in one or more chakras** means problem in the corresponding organs and corresponding emotions. **This means chakras/mind, body and emotions are interrelated to each other**. So we need to work at all levels of our existence for a healthy, happy and prosperous life. If you work on your energies, your energies will increase but will neglect your physical bodies or neglect your emotional health you will soon lose your energies, your energy levels shall be back to square one and you won't get the desired results. Same way, if you work on your physical body, that will surely increase your energy levels but when you are not able to handle your life situations, you become emotionally weak, you will soon lose that energy and shall be back to square one. Or if you are working on your emotions & mind but neglecting your physical body, it can disturb the energy chakra which will ultimately create disturbance in emotions. So we need to strike a balance and shall work on each and every aspect of our existence: **1) Physical body 2) Mind & emotions 3) Spiritual Energy.**

YOU) WHAT ARE THE CONNECTORS FOR ENERGY TRANSFER/ABSORPTION IN MY BODY?

ME) Like mobile phone have receptors which connects and absorbs power from external power source, **same way in your body top centre of head is a receptor of cosmic energy. Many Hindus grew choti (braid)** on the top centre of the head to enhance the reception, connection and speed of process to absorb cosmic energy.

High energy points (connectors) of your body are the top centre of the head, lips, genitals, palms, underarms or sole of a foot. These energy points are normally hotter than other parts of body. **Whenever energy connectors of two people come in contact with each other, there is transfer of energy** and enhancement of energy which gives a feeling of high, feeling of joy and happiness. **When you touch somebody's feet,** energy circuit is formed and energy gets transferred from their feet to your body through your hands. **When somebody keeps his or her hand on your head,** there is formation of circuit and thus transferring of energy. **Hindus have a tradition of feet touching** for ages, where young people touch the feet of their elders and elders give their blessings by placing their palm on the head of young ones. See this is a very strong circuit of energy and when a spiritually powerful person gives blessing to someone/anyone, they have the power to heal that person, both physically and emotionally.

When we shake hands or hug or kiss somebody/anybody, there is a formation of circuit and energy transfer. See we greet people like this only to enhance the energy; the feelings of love, happiness and friendship.

YOU) IS THERE ANY CONNECTION BETWEEN SLEEP AND COSMIC ENERGY?

ME) Yes, sleep is a natural process of recharging the cosmic energy in your body. See, a **restful mind** draws the optimum cosmic energy. And a man is **restful in his sleep. Sleep is a natural process of recharging the physical body with cosmic energy**. It is an involuntary, automatic process and we are unaware of it. After a whole day of work, you lose your vital energy and naturally, you are inclined towards sleep. When you wake up in the morning after sleep, you feel fresh and energetic but only if you had a sound sleep.

A disturbed mind or a disturbed sleep hinders the absorption of cosmic energy in your body. **That is why people with disturbed sleep or disturbed state of mind** becomes irritable, restless and are unhappy because they are lacking life energy. Nobody can be at ease without life energy. If life energy in person increases, happiness increases. Think of someone after an angry emotional outburst or after excessive physical work loses his/her vital energy, a person devoid of sleep falls asleep automatically and is not able to control his/her sleep as he/she wants to get back the lost life energy/vital energy/cosmic energy. This process is subtle, natural and automatic.

Low levels of energy makes your body lethargic and mind unconscious & negative, where you experience negative emotions like anger, fear, hatred, jealousy or anxiety. **But when you have optimum energy levels, your body & mind becomes healthy & conscious, where you** experience positive emotions like calmness, confidence, love, kindness, happiness, feelings of gratitude, etc. You can easily understand the effects of disturbed sleep on your mind & body. Some people suffer from insomnia and some feel drowsy & lethargic even after a long sleep. The simple reason for that is emotional disturbance where their mind is not at rest and it keeps on thinking negatively, hindering the inflow of cosmic energy in your body which makes you restless, tired and unhappy. *CHECK 3.6 HOW THOUGHTS, EMOTIONS AND BELIEFS AFFECT YOUR PERSONAL SPACE AND THUS LIFE.*

"The person with disturbed sleep or who is not able to sleep at all is the poorest person on this planet." Later on, in PART C of this book you will get to know techniques in order to have a healthy, sound sleep and to overcome **Insomnia** that will reduce the time/quantity of your sleep and increase the quality of your sleep.

YOU) WHY THERE IS SO MUCH HUE & CRY ABOUT CELL PHONE RADIATIONS IN TODAY'S WORLD?

ME) *MOBILE PHONE RADIATION* is another cause of concern in today's world. The radiation from laptops, cell phones etc. are **harmful radiations that disturb your etheric body** thus causing health issues. As you cannot avoid cell phones in today's world but some certain precautions shall help you tremendously avoid ill effects of cell phones:-

A). during sleep keep your cell phones at least 8 feet away from your body.

B). in office keep your cell phones at least 3 feet away from yourself.

C). Buy cell phones whose radiation levels are low.

D). Don't over use it; use it for phone calls and important work only. Playing excessive games and using other time wasting apps are just killing your precious time and also interfering with your energy field/subtle body, reducing your health of mind & body to below normal and away from happy life.

YOU) IS THERE ANY OTHER WAY TO RECHARGE MY ETHERIC BODY WITH LIFE ENERGY, OTHER THAN SLEEP?

Or can I recharge my body with cosmic energy without sleep anytime, anywhere or can I reduce my sleep?

ME) the big answer is yes. **Think of it as recharging your mobile phones**. You recharge it, as a phone devoid of energy cannot work. Recharging of mobile phones is a voluntary activity where you know about the best chargers, connectors and you have the choice to recharge your mobile anytime. But do you know how to recharge your body in a conscious way; can you control the recharging of your body? **Yes, the answer is by controlling your emotions**, by changing your thoughts from negative to positive, by achieving peace of mind; **a restful state of mind**. And peace of mind can be achieved by an attitude of "acceptance of life as it comes to you" or a spiritual way of life or focus of mind in the present moment, some simple breathing techniques, by having natural food and all. THIS IS ALL DISCUSSED IN DETAIL IN PART B AND C OF THE BOOK.

SO BEFORE DIRECTLY JUMPING TO THE SPIRITUAL ATTITUDE, TO GET THE REAL CONNECTION WITH THE "REAL YOU", FIRST UNDERSTAND YOUR SUBTLE SPACE; YOUR MIND, THOUGHTS, EMOTIONS AND BELIEFS; TO UNDERSTAND HOW IT AFFECTS YOUR LIFE, WHERE IS THE PROBLEM, HOW IT HAS BECOME NEGATIVE. SO THE FIRST STEP IN LIFE IS TO UNDERSTAND SELF, MIND, LIFE OR UNIVERSE FOR CREATING HARMONY WITHIN, WITH OTHER PEOPLE AND THE WHOLE UNIVERSE TO GET CONNECTED WITH ALL THE POSITIVE ENERGIES IN THE WORLD, FOR A HAPPY PROSPEROUS AND SUCCESSFUL LIFE.

3.2 CONSCIOUS & SUBCONCIOUS MIND

The chakras in your head and brain constitute your **CONSCIOUS MIND** and chakras in your body from base of spine till throat constitute your **SUBCONSCIOUS MIND**. Conscious mind gives direction, message and information to the subconscious mind through thoughts & emotions. And the subconscious has no choice but to honour the command of its master; conscious mind. Emotions get stored in the subconscious in the form of beliefs which affect the working of the subconscious. If the beliefs are empowering the subconscious works perfectly naturally bringing about right actions, behaviour and thus, right results in life and if the beliefs are disempowering/biased, it leads to failure & misery in life. Ultimately it is your conscious choice of thoughts & emotions which determines the action of subconscious and results in life. **So, to control your life you must control your conscious mind, thoughts & emotions, nothing else.**

If we compare our physical body with computer, our body is the hardware and our mind is the software. Now every living organism has both physical body and mind energy. But why are the humans far more superior to other living beings, why are they civilized, how they have created so much infrastructure, technology, which other living beings were not able to? The answer lies in the size & design of hardware. **Yes, the vertical vertebrae and biggest brain of humans among all living creatures of this planet earth allows them to fully tap and utilise the super consciousness of one universal mind.** Let's analyse this statement, the fact.

You see today that if you have an old computer (hardware), it cannot support the new latest application software, means that software cannot run on that old hardware or for that old hardware, that particular software is useless. In the same way, animals have both brain and mind but their hardware (brain) is too small & horizontal, not allowing them to fully utilize the power of software (mind). Mobile manufacturers keep on upgrading their hardware for better functioning of new application software. Humans having the biggest brain & vertical vertebrae are far ahead in their ability to consciously think and understand. **Mind is a very strong entity; it is the source of all creations in this world.** It is the tool/antenna which has the power to tap the vibrations/suggestions of supreme cosmic energy or life energy. The immense powers of mind are beyond imagination. So as human race, we are lucky to be bestowed with a brain and mind far more superior to other living beings, a tool to tap immense super intelligent natural powers.

It is said that we as humans on an average use approx. 3% of our mind power. Even Einstein used just 4.5% of his mind power, Swami Vivekananda 6.5%. So imagine if these great humans got tremendous results after using only 4-6% of mind power, what about using 100%. To fully utilize mind power we just need to steady our emotions by consciously choosing right thoughts, using focus of mind, right breathing pattern and other mind power exercises. It is only through mind that we can control body and life circumstances. Mind is characterized by thoughts and we knowingly or unknowingly create our own life through our thoughts. **It is a common saying that thoughts lead to things. So it is very important to understand the mind, practice the techniques to control it and use it to our advantage in order to create a life the way we want.**

Now let's understand it further. Mind can be divided into two parts: **conscious** and **subconscious mind. Conscious mind** has the ability **to think, do logical reasoning, acts as a small memory to process thoughts (like a RAM in computer), has intuitive powers which catches the ideas from super intelligent nature**. Functions like thinking, talking, walking, watching, touch, listening, eating etc. are done by our conscious mind.

Subconscious mind- The subconscious mind, in its natural state is very high on energy and thus connected with the *REAL YOU,* who is always connected to one universal consciousness i.e. the super intelligent nature that has created this life. It knows life very well and thus effectively controls all vital body functions like breathing, digestion, pumping of heart, etc. The very purpose of one's life, likes & dislikes, natural talents are hidden in the subconscious mind. The people and situations coming in your life are also determined by your subconscious mind. The intelligence of your conscious mind; right perception, decisions, actions, behaviour, habits in each & every situation of your life are also guided by your subconscious mind.

Subconscious mind/Deep memory/DNA is a store house of all the impressions/information of life; past incidences of this life and past life. All our memories are in the subconscious mind and not in brain. All life experiences are passed onto the subconscious mind from conscious mind through emotions. Either life situation makes us happy or unhappy based on the fulfilment or non-fulfilment of needs & wants in life. The more is the pain or pleasure associated with life experiences, the faster, deeper and permanent is the presence of these experiences in the subconscious mind.

All the information/thoughts pass from conscious mind to subconscious mind through emotions. Subconscious mind does not have thinking power; it only accepts the feelings & emotions of the conscious mind and brings about the positive or negative changes in the energy field/aura. So, if our energy field is positive or negative or in between, it is the thinking of the conscious mind, **it is the understanding & perception of life situations by the conscious mind which is responsible** and not the subconscious mind. This is how we create our own life through thoughts (understanding & perceptions).

But the problem is that thinking is not in our control, we do not know the right way to think. Our thinking is not by choice and thus our life situations are not by choice. **To be able to choose our life situations, we must learn the art of thinking consciously.** We should know what to think, how to think in a right way to make our life a joyous journey. Any wrong/unnatural thinking corrupts the subconscious mind and makes life difficult.

What corrupts the subconscious mind? The subconscious mind is the natural software which carries all the information/codes for making your life a happy and prosperous one. It works on its own, based on preinstalled codes which are always for health, wealth, peace, prosperity and happiness. **But the problem is that our subconscious becomes corrupted or defective by negative actions/responses/thoughts/emotions chosen by our conscious mind.** More appropriately a conscious mind operating from lower consciousness becomes negative and passes on the negative information to the subconscious, making your personal space devoid of energy and low energy field means disconnection from the source and that means only miseries in life. **When the subconscious loses its life energy or is low on energy, it starts to work in an unexpected, unnatural way leading to problems in physical & mental health and thus external life situations also.** The only key to happy life is to somehow maintain the positive energy field of your personal space for your subconscious to work perfectly in a natural manner.

TYPICAL FEATURES AND COMPARISON OF CONSCIOUS AND SUB CONSCIOUS MIND

	Conscious mind	Subconscious mind
01	Is just 10% powerful	Is 90% powerful, super intelligent(It is immutable software)
02	It can think on its own but this thinking is not uniform, it keeps on swaying, it keeps on changing which is cause of variety in perception, understanding, decision, action and thus different results.	It cannot think on its own, it just works on immutable preinstalled codes/software (PPN). But can be corrupted by wrong directions of conscious mind. Once corrupted it leads to health issues and issues of biased perception and wrong results in life
03	It understands both positive and negatives thoughts with all the logic.	It does not recognize or understand right or wrong; it just makes your energy field negative or positive based upon the feelings/emotions/mental state of your conscious mind.
04	It is active only when you are awake	It is active 24 hours a day/365 days/our whole lifetime/during our sleep/unconscious state. It is the only one power which takes care of all our body organ functions during our sleep and unconscious state.
05	**It is the watchman at the gate of subconscious mind. Whatever you think consciously percolates down to your subconscious which determines your energy field/aura and ultimately determines your emotions, behaviour and actions.**	It is the only power which governs your physical life but is controlled by the conscious or unconscious thinking of the conscious mind.
We reap only what we sow....in our mind. By conscious watching and managing of thoughts & emotions you have the power to change life the way you want.		

ILLUSTRATION OF HOW THOUGHT PROCESS OR MORE APPROPRIATELY THE FEELINGS/EMOTIONS OF CONSCIOUS MIND WORKS

Thought /prayer of	Thought/ prayer/fear /belief	What subconscious listen and rewards	Result	Correct prayer/constant belief
Student	don't fail me	fail me	you fail	God I want 70% marks in my exams. I have achieved. Thanks
Lover	Constant fear that I won't be able to marry a person of my choice	Subconscious listens that you fear the person of your own choice.	In realty you fail to marry that person	With strong feelings and emotions always pray, believe and accept that you have married that person and is happily living with that person.
Business man	Constant fear to avoid loss, somehow just want to meet expenses	You are transmitting vibes of loss, fear	You get loss, or are just hand to mouth	I know my business shall do wonders and shall reach new heights day by day giving me good name, fame and profits. Thanks my subconscious for making my business a huge success, Wonderful job by you
We just get what we consistently think, believe, act upon with strong desire and emotions				

Source: Meet the Real You Copyright Chetan Bansal

Now read and understand this carefully. When we say *'don't fail me'* or fear some loss, then our focus is on loss/failure. This leads to negative emotions & feelings, reducing the energy/consciousness which leads to disharmony with the source energy. This brings about negative changes in behaviour, actions and attitude of ours which in-turn leads to problematic relations with other people inviting wrong responses/reaction from them and thus leading to undesired situations and wrong results in life.

Always remember that negative vibes are directly proportional to low energy. Negative emotions of anger, hatred and fear drain out vital energy from our body, means it drains out the "Real Me" from my body and when my Real Me that is, when the source of my life is not with me, how can I expect peace, joy, love, happiness in my life.

But the great news is that I/we/me always have the power to bring back my "REAL ME" in my life at any time, irrespective of any life situation that might be haunting us today just by raising our vibrations which is in control of the conscious mind.

SO IN A NUTSHELL WE CAN SAY THAT IT IS THE CONSCIOUS MIND WHICH CONTROLS THE SUBCONSCIOUS MIND THAT AFFECTS THE ENERGY FIELD/AURA OF YOUR PERSONAL SPACE AND HENCE, AFFECTS YOUR PHYSICAL & MENTAL HEALTH, WHICH DETERMINES YOUR PERCEPTION, DECISIONS AND ACTIONS AND THUS RESULTS IN LIFE. SO THE REAL TASK IS

TO CONTROL & MASTER CONSCIOUS MIND AND THE BEST WAY TO DO THAT IS BY STRENGTHENING THE CONNECTION WITH THE SOURCE.

As it is the conscious thoughts which determines the actions of your subconscious mind, your focus should be to understand your conscious mind further so as to understand what is wrong with the conscious thinking and how to change it to make life a happy, prosperous and successful one.

CONSCIOUS MIND IS DUAL IN NATURE AND KEEPS ON CHANGING WITH CHANGING TIMES. HOW?

The moment a person is born, the energy field/chakra energy/ mind energy of that person is determined by the cosmic energy field prevalent at that point of time and place of birth, depending upon the positioning of the planets in terms of degree in relation with sun and moon at the place & time of birth. This energy becomes the basic energy of that person which determines his basic **Mindset**. Well, I am not an astrologer and I don't know how to make a birth chart based on planet positions but I surely know the science and Hindu astrologers use this science to make a birth chart of a person. **So every person born on a particular date, time and place has a specific unique energy field/aura making his/her mindset unique, leading to unique ways of thinking, deciding and acting in life leading to successes & failures in life.**

This is the very basis of determining common characters of various zodiac signs. So people have different thought process due to different energy field. Also with changing times, the energy field of every person undergoes a change and hence their thought process/mindset also changes. That is why we witness change in the mindset of everybody, including self. So swaying of thoughts is a natural phenomenon common to all humans. Next time, you don't have to be surprised if someone changes his/her thoughts/ideas/commitment. You have to be very careful while dealing with people. That is why a written agreement is must, specifically in all business/contractual deals.

It simply means that a duality exists in your conscious thinking process which also causes duality in your physical life situations, where sometimes you fail and sometimes you pass with changing times, even in the same field/profession. **It is this duality which is the cause of differences of opinion, belief and perception in different people and is due to varying degree of energy field/consciousness.** That is why life is never a straight line and is full of ups and downs.

Does it mean that my life is not in my control as planetary moments, my birth time is not in my control and I have to ACCEPT my life as it is; a very good and the most important question in life? Acceptance only means understanding the truth as it is, aligning with the truth and giving your 100% in your actions. No means it implies or says not to do anything about bringing a change in an undesired situation. Acceptance only means to ignore and pray for what is not in your control and give your best to change what you can change.

See my birth time and planetary moments is not under my control and they **are just affecting my energy field/aura by impacting my mind, either positively or negatively.** So this is causing changes in my mind, when positive, it helps me grow and when negative, it causes my downfall. So you can't do anything, nothing is in your control and you have to be slave of planets and thus, your mind. There is no escape from miseries. **Just joking! Now listen carefully, you have to somehow increase your energy field or maintain your high energy irrespective the negative impacts of any time/planetary moments.** By understanding these various laws of mind and practicing various techniques, you can convert an unconscious mind into a super conscious mind. **And that can only be possible by connecting with the REAL YOU where you become timeless (having no negative effect of changing times or planetary movements on your energy field/aura).** The spiritual way of life i.e. acceptance, present moment living, meditative (focus) techniques, faith in self/god, happiness, gratitude, kindness, love, forgiveness, celebration will keep you high on energy irrespective of time and that is when the luck comes in your hand; you learn, understand, practice and align with your source of life.

So in your control are your thought and your emotions which shall determine your aura/energy field and thus, your destiny. Connecting with your omnipotent reality is where the duality of mind and physical life ends or become bare minimum. **Choosing to remain positive, balanced and centred even in most difficult times** keeps your subconscious at its natural best and when subconscious is at its natural best, there is nothing which can disturb you or defeat you. **This is the only secret to happy life and the foremost purpose of life. And I choose to work on it. What is your choice?**

3.3 THOUGHTS

A thought is just energy and nothing else. Whatever you see in the physical world is just a manifestation of thoughts. The whole universe is a manifestation of one universal mind and your whole life is just a manifestation of your thoughts. Your every action is caused by a thought. Everything is first created in your mind that is to be manifested on the screen of your life over a period of time. You can co-relate this to your own life; your every action is guided by your thought. Your whole life is a result of your thought, nothing else. If you are not happy with your life, then my dear "**REAL YOU**", **you** must understand the science of thoughts as the real problem in your thought process; how to change/correct thoughts, how to direct your thoughts towards your goals and how to master your thoughts?

Everything is a thought. An emotion is a thought in action/motion, beliefs are thoughts stored in mind and perception, decision and actions are all thoughts, nothing else. A feeling is a thought, being sad and happy is a thought; anything coming from your mind is a thought. I am a thought, you are a thought and every creation is a thought of one universal mind.

A mind has its existence due to thoughts. Thought becoming zero means no mind. Life is about either wrong thinking or right thinking and not about zero thinking. For thinking to end means end of mind and end of mind means end of life. So, we need to balance our thoughts. Excess of thoughts or no thoughts, both are harmful and create miseries in our life. Although, we do some meditative techniques to shut that overthinking mind but that is only temporary, having a purpose to achieve peace of mind i.e. a restful state of mind. **It is like clearing the over-jammed RAM caused by simultaneous working of many applications (many thoughts). Meditation/focus is about bringing the focus of mind from many to one.** Like when your computer hangs, you close all applications just to clear the RAM and to bring back the normal functioning of the computer. This enhances the speed and accuracy of the processor of your computer. Same way, meditation/focus enhances the speed/accuracy of your mind. **We will understand some very simple, easy and amazingly effective techniques of meditation/focus in PART B & C of this book.**

What are thoughts? The process of thinking or an idea or opinion produced by the act of thinking is a thought. Whatever you think about, a thought or an idea about that thing comes to your mind or in other words, whatever you focus upon draws more thoughts, ideas and insights about that thing. **A thought is just energy/information having a particular frequency and wavelength.** Thoughts travel a distance within no time and at the speed of light. A cool, calm and focused mind can always tap any information/thought that is present in space, in the form of vibrations.

How thoughts are attracted to your mind? Thoughts and ideas are not created in your mind rather they are attracted to your mind. **Mind is a tool/instrument which has the power to tap all the information present in the universe in the form vibrations, like your TV antenna is a tool/instrument which catches all the frequency vibrations present in the atmosphere**. A thought can be related to your past experiences or future imaginations, or to the present circumstances or some new idea or creativity about anything that you focus upon. It is the universal law/fact that every mind gets approx. 60,000 thoughts on a daily basis and on variety of issues related to life.

Mind is a store-house of all information; past, present and future. It is like a hard disk but the only difference is that the memory of a hard disk is limited, whereas, mind memory is unlimited. You can retrieve all the information stored in your mind just by focusing on the issue or information that you want to retrieve. Like you search on a Google and it immediately shows you all the information about that thing. The same way when you focus on something, your mind shows all the information about that thing in the form of dreams, hunches, intuition, ideas etc. Sharper and longer is the focus of mind, faster and clearer is the information that you retrieve.

All the inventions, creations and discoveries in this world have been done by people with good intuitive powers which come only from a sharp focus of mind. So, the things you focus upon are brought into the conscious presence of your mind. The power of focus is enhanced by a happy state of mind, whereas, an emotional disturbance reduces the focus of mind, leading to a biased PDA and wrong results in life.

A thought needs emotion to travel and manifest. The best way to sharpen your focus is by giving your emotions. That is why a prayer of a loving, passionate person is heard by the universe instantly. That is why the pain of a truthful person becomes a curse for those who hurt them intentionally. That is why a loving, caring and a helpful person always attract blessings.

Thoughts can be a voluntary or an involuntary activity. **During voluntary thoughts,** you control your mind which means you are able to control the focus of your mind. So whatever you focus upon draws more thoughts about that thing. This way you get deep insights/understanding about that thing and once that happen you are able to see the truth as it is leading to right decisions, actions and desired results in life.

Involuntary thoughts, however, means that your mind is not under your control or focus of mind is not under your control, it keeps on jumping from one issue to another, from one topic to another, from past to future, from future to past and to present without your permission. It is like a money mind, an untrained mind which does not follow your commands. **As your focus keeps on shifting from one issue to another, you are not able to get sharp focus and thus there is no deep insight into any of the topics and you end up with only superficial knowledge.** You depend on others for guidance and you might get biased guidance from others as they might have vested interests or their knowledge and understanding is also superficial. That is why you are not able to see the truth as it is, biasness guides your PDA and most probably, you end up having undesired results. **So, the key to right results is learning & mastering the art of focus of your mind which you will understand in detail in PART-B & C OF THIS BOOK.**

3.4 EMOTIONS

Emotions are energy in motion activated by your liking/disliking of some thoughts/information. Many thoughts/information come to your mind but all information is not able to generate interest in you. The information that you find to your liking/disliking is immediately moved to deeper memory/subconscious mind. The movement of information/thought from conscious mind to subconscious mind is what we call information/thought in motion. **So thought being energy and when in motion, it is called energy in motion; Emotion.**

Emotions lead to the movement of energy in body like emotions of anger, hatred, envy, happiness, love, gratitude or faith, depending upon your state of mind triggered by information/thoughts/ideas that you get through your senses (eyes, nose, ears, touch, feelings). Emotion reflects your state of mind. Negative emotions reflect disturbed state of mind. Positive emotions reflect a happier state of mind.

Mind is a seat house of all emotions which are triggered as reaction to your thoughts. **Mind interacts with body through emotions**. **For example**, an emotion of anger is triggered when somebody scolds, betrays or misbehaves with you. Suddenly, the state of your mind and whole body becomes aggressive and your voice becomes harsh & rude. **An emotion of happiness is triggered when someone praises** or shows respect to you. This makes your mind & body cool, calm and joyous; your voice becomes soft and loving. **An emotion of sadness** is triggered when you think about your bad past experiences. **An emotion of anxiety** is triggered by your fearful thoughts of future.

Emotions bring about biochemical changes in your body. **Positive emotions** increase the energy in your body which activates and balances the energy chakras, which in turn activates endocrine glands, that further releases the required amount of biochemical (hormones) in blood stream making each and every cell, tissue and organ of your body healthy.

On the other hand, negative emotions decrease the vital energy/life energy in your etheric body that deactivates/blocks energy chakras leading to the malfunctioning of endocrine glands. Thus, your blood does not get the required amount of biochemical (hormones) leading to unhealthy cells, tissues and organs. This causes diseases and medicines are prescribed to fulfil the deficiency of biochemical in your blood stream. So the choice is yours, either chose and maintains positive emotions to remain happy and healthy, or choose negative emotions to become unhappy & unhealthy and thus, take medicines.

Also, **negative emotions having low-energy frequency vibrations lead to disharmony with source energy/life energy**. This way your mind loses connection with super intelligence of nature, leading to biased understanding, biased perception, wrong decisions, wrong actions and wrong results in life. Thus it becomes very important for you to control and manage your emotions.

Negative emotions lead to depletion of cosmic energy and positive emotions lead to enhancement of cosmic energy. That is why a person in depression has low energy and a normal person or a person in happy state of mind has optimum levels of energy. So we can easily correlate a negative state of mind leading to serious depletion of cosmic energy/life energy in the body. And to recover that cosmic energy people need more sleep, as sleep is a natural process to regain the lost cosmic energy. **That is why you must have heard that people, who are sad & depressed, sleep more.**

If your mind is happy/it is feeling good, it will generate positive energy of love, peace, joy, gratitude and kindness. So it is very important to manage and steady your emotions in order to be connected with your source, *THE REAL YOU*. As mind is a seat house of all emotions, **it is very important to control and master your mind**. There are many ways to control mind and one of them is through physiology. The particular emotional state has set patterns of body physiology as mind and body are interconnected, a change in one brings about a change in other.

Let's check the reality of this statement "Mind and body are interconnected".

When somebody scolds or misbehaves with you or does something which annoys you or when you encounter some unpleasant situation like failure in exams/sports/business or loss of some loved one etc., it directly impacts your mind which activates emotion of sadness, fear, anger, hatred, etc. Now when you experience these emotions, they are easily reflected in your physiology (body). Like in sad emotion (shoulders are down, very slow body movement, head is down, voice is low, that is, total body language is down, low in energy) and in a happy state, emotions of joy, thrill (shoulders are up, head up, strong voice, fast moving body, very joyful, full of energy etc.) are perceived.

So mind has an impact on body, means your body language (physiology) changes with change in the state of mind. **But the question here is that if change in mind can bring about a change in body, can change in body bring about a change in mind?** Yes, you are right. With change in **physiology (physical body posture, language and voice),** you can change the state of **mind**. Yes, mind also changes with change in body postures. As physiology changes, it brings about changes in thoughts & feelings, which in turn changes the state of mind. Yes it's the universal truth. It's science. Wow! I can control my mind by changing the physiology of my body. **WHAT AN AMAZING REALISATION!** *YOU WILL LEARN ABOUT THE RIGHT USE OF YOUR PHYSIOLOGY IN PART-C OF THIS BOOK.*

It means that by changing your physiology to a particular pattern, you can positively change your **emotions/energy vibrations/feelings, control your mind, and thus establish a strong connection with your source** leading to **fulfilling, joyous and a successful life. Isn't it amazing!**

MIND & BODY INTERCONNECTED THROUGH EMOTIONS

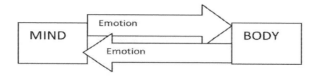

ALL TECHNIQUES, TOOLS AND FORMULAS REQUIRED TO MASTER YOUR MIND, TO RAISE YOUR VIBRATIONS, TO ACTIVATE YOUR SOUL PATH, TO MAINTAIN A COOL & CALM MIND, TO MASTER YOUR THOUGHTS, TO MASTER YOUR EMOTIONS AND TO MASTER YOUR ENERGIES ARE EXPLAINED IN DEPTH IN PART B & C OF THIS BOOK.

3.5 BELIEFS AND PERCEPTIONS

3.5.1 WHAT ARE BELIEFS?

A THOUGHT IS ENERGY; AN ENERGY/THOUGHT IN MOTION IS EMOTION; AN ENERGY/THOUGHT STORED IN MEMORY IS A BELIEF. So, a belief is a thought stored in deep memory/subconscious. It is the emotion which carries the thought from conscious mind to the subconscious mind.

Beliefs are thoughts (ideas) dependent on some reference for its support like a floor needs support of pillars and walls to stand. Belief is a thought to interpret a situation or event based on references drawn from the past experiences. We may develop belief about almost all things for which our mind starts searching for references to support it. The references are drawn from our personal experience, our own imagination, or the information that we get from other people, mass media like books, videos, audios, advertisements etc. **The strength of belief depends upon the repetition of references, emotional intensity** about the belief and **number of references.**

For example, there is a guy A and guy B. Both are your friends but they do not know each other. Now you being a common friend helped them enter a business deal with each other. After sometime, **A** came to you and told you that **B** has cheated him. Upon your mediation, **B** was rigid, adamant and instead of listening to you in a cool & calm manner, **B** out rightly rejected your proposal of mediation. Now you feel very humiliated and angry over B. A proper communication did not happen between you and B and a belief was developed in you that B is a cheater. After some days, another person came to you complaining that B has cheated him. **Now boss, what will you think? Obviously your belief is now permanent that B is a big cheater.** Now this is a **typical example of repetition of reference (twice), emotional intensity** of yours as B did not behaved well with you, and **2 references** from different people. Now the next time if **someone, say C questions** you about the creditability of B, obviously you are going to say **"do not work with him, he is a cheater"**. This is how you analyse, interpret and perceive your present moment based upon your past experiences. But what you think is this the right approach to deal with any situation. In this case, your answer to **C** can be right or wrong. See when there was a dispute in between **A and B,** there was no proper communication between you and B, so there might be some hidden truth about B and also if B was a cheater in past, it does not mean he is a cheater for life. All in all you need to understand the truth of the present situation as it is, without any bias and without any dependency on any belief. Let the truth pop up from your conscious presence through proper communication with **B** and not from the memories of your mind.

Beliefs are generalizations about past based on interpretation of your pleasurable and painful experiences. These generalizations become a reference to interpretation of a situation in future. We can also call them as filters through which we analyse, interpret and perceive situations in life. But perceiving life situations through filters of belief can always be dangerous and most likely create problems in life. **For example, if you had a good relationship** with somebody, **a belief is developed that relationship is good and will always be good.** But if now you have been experiencing some problems in that relation and still believe that the relationship is good or soon going to be good again then you are still living the belief which is away from the truth of the present situation. **Mere believing that the relationship is good or soon become good again won't work and soon it is going to be worse if not acted upon wisely.** You have to understand the truth. How problems have come into your relationships, what wrong actions you and others have taken and how to correct now to bring the relationship back to normal?

Beliefs are generalizations developed from the identification of similar pattern. For example, to open a door you will move the door lock handle downward, even if you are dealing with this door handle for the first time because you have the reference from your previous experiences with door lock handles that in order to open them you need to move them down. So a similar pattern for door lock handles developed in to a belief that all door lock handles should be moved downwards to open them. But this new handle is designed differently and it opens on upward movement and not on downward movement. So, your belief is based upon past experiences which may not hold truth in the present situation. **Thus a belief may or may not be true today.**

So, **it will be foolish on our part to perceive the present situation based upon past experiences as it may give biased perception away from the truth** leading to wrong decisions/actions and thus wrong results in our life. **The belief is a child of mind. Mind having duality is the cause of varying beliefs for same situation.** Even the beliefs of the same person keep on changing with changing time. All **beliefs are not universal truths,** it may sometimes, be true or false. It is dual in nature and we cannot trust something which keeps on changing with changing time. **The only thing that we can trust is our FOCUSED CONSCIOUS PRESENCE which is permanent, timeless and universal for perceiving the truthfulness of any situation as it is without any bias.**

Some beliefs are **real, based on truth** (like touching fire will burn us) and some beliefs are **contrasting beliefs;** people having opposite beliefs for a similar situation, depending upon their life experiences. Like for some, they believe that **"money is easy to earn"** and for some **"money is difficult to earn".**

Examples of some more beliefs

1). A child when sees a cup of hot tea for the first time, he/she will try to touch or hold it out of curiosity, as he is unaware about the risk of getting burned but the second time, he will not touch that hot tea cup as he is already aware of the information in his/her subconscious mind through past experience of touching a hot cup **(reference to belief). This is a belief they will develop automatically and permanently in their mind because this is a universal fact/truth.**

2). If we have been told from childhood that money is hard to earn, it takes years to earn money, people use unfair means to earn money and we have seen our parents, relatives, or may be even our neighbours who struggle for money **(no. of references are high)**, so a **strong belief** is formed in our mind that **"money is hard to earn"** and now at present someone is suggesting us some business model where we can earn huge money in a short span and that too in an easy manner by totally fair means, but our belief system won't believe the business model and we will miss the opportunity to earn big. **This is not universal fact, meaning for some it is true and for some it is not true. For some, belief is "Money is very easy to earn by fair means in a short span of time".**

3). If someone has seen his/her parents in a violent relationship, a belief is formed in their mind that marriages are bad, which in-turn negatively impact their future relations. So the **reference here is "bad relationship of parents"** and belief is that **"in married relations, violence/disharmony is inevitable".** Again this belief is not same for everybody. For some having experienced good loving relations between their parents, the belief is **"in married relations, there is love, care and harmony."**

3.5.2) BELIEFS ARE THE CAUSE OF CONFLICTS AND DISPUTES BETWEEN DIFFERENT PEOPLE, DIFFERENT RELIGIONS AND DIFFERENT GROUPS.

A person who lives in coastal area eats fish and sea food since his/her childhood. **For him/her, eating non-vegetarian food is normal & healthy.** Other person who lives in plains, away from sea where he is being given vegetarian food from childhood and at the same time, he is taught that eating non-vegetarian food is unhealthy. When these two people meet from different regions, there might be a conflict between them on which food is healthy, either vegetarian food or non-vegetarian. They have contrasting beliefs but why should they create a conflict on this unless and until they are not forcing each other to believe and practice each other's belief.

People having same sex, caste, religion, cultures, regions, social status and economic status have one thing in common, and that is their belief system. People having common interests, beliefs and values can be categorized in to a Group. It simply means that people with different religions, caste, regions and social status have different beliefs only because their life experiences are different and they have different life styles, nothing else.

These different beliefs lead to different rituals and practices in one's religions. Although, the purpose of every religion is same, to find peace of mind, to help weak people, to find God but their ways/practice of worship is different which causes a dispute. Everyone wants to prove oneself right and other wrong. These disputes in religions, between two people or between two countries is just a dispute of different beliefs and nothing else.

If someone's belief is not harming me in any way or hindering my freedom of life, then what is the harm in letting him/her live their beliefs? The best would be to understand, respect and accept each other beliefs. This can only be possible once we understand that we all are same but different manifestations of one universal consciousness. The very differences in opinions, beliefs and perceptions are an advantage. It opens up new possibilities, creative ideas away from monotony and should be promoted and appreciated for healthy discussions and arriving at right decisions which are beneficial to all. It is only through love that we can respect and accept the differences, be it any of the caste, religion, race, belief, opinion etc. **For real understanding of LOVE, read PART-B of this book.**

3.5.3 WHEN WE TALK OF BELIEFS, THERE ARE TWO MAJOR TYPES OF BELIEFS:
1) BELIEFS BASED ON EXPERIENCE/MIND/TIME. **2)** BELIEFS COMING FROM INNER VOICE/REAL YOU/TIMELESS.
1)   BELIEFS BASED ON EXPERIENCE OR UNDER THE INFLUENCE OF OTHERS.
Mind is nothing but a memory and memory is nothing but a set of beliefs absorbed subconsciously from the people & environment that you have experienced till now. Beliefs are based on what we see, listen, and feel from others which can be illusionary and away from the truth. We always believe what looks apparent and do not go into the detail which leads to wrong/biased beliefs. **Beliefs which are not aligned to the truth or away from the truth are called disempowering beliefs.** Disempowering beliefs make

your perception biased, leading to wrong decisions/actions and thus wrong results and miseries in life.

A wrong belief is like a slow poison which can ruin the whole life of a person if not corrected in time. A person who believes himself unlucky; becomes emotionally disturbed, loses faith/belief in self/god and once that happen, it leads to disharmony in his mind, body, emotions and soul, leading to non-action or wrong actions creating further miseries in his life. Thus, he himself proves his belief right that he is unlucky.

2) BELIEFS COMING FROM INNER VOICE/REAL YOU/CONSCIOUS PRESENCE.

Right beliefs are the empowering beliefs which are aligned to truth, come from your conscious focused presence. Empowering beliefs activate your natural power to see the truth as it is without any bias. Truthful perception leads to right decisions/action and thus, right results in life. Empowering beliefs align your mind, body, soul, and energies with reality empowering you to create anything based on laws of nature/universe.

It is your belief system which controls your whole life, the interpretation and outcome of all situations in your life is controlled by your beliefs. So, it is very important for you to master the art of perceiving the situation guided by truth and not blind belief.

3.5.4 HOW BELIEFS ARE FORMED AND AFFECT US.

Most of our beliefs are created subconsciously based on misinterpretation of our past life experiences. All the misinterpretations have been due to excessive mind activity of emotional disturbance and interpretations taken in haste. These beliefs have not been developed consciously. All information/suggestions that we get from our parents, friends, teachers, neighbours, books, media or any source of information since our birth enters our subconscious mind through five sensory organs, Eye, Ear, Nose, Skin, Feelings and becomes belief depending upon the interpretation of information/situation/experience. These beliefs become filters in conscious mind through which we analyse, interpret, understand, perceive and take decisions in life.

At birth, our mind was fresh & energetic, free from any baggage of bitter life experiences and having no bitter life experiences means zero fear for future. We are born curious, joyous, happy and playful. We have no doubts, fears and we always think big as a child; to be a big businessman, pilots, scientists, big politicians or a movie star; thinking big was our nature.

But with the passage of time as we get older, something goes wrong. As we start to grow old, we are being told please don't do this, please don't do that, you can't do it, it is very difficult for you, this is dangerous, you are incapable, life is difficult, money is hard to earn, world is full of bad people etc. We absorb all this subconsciously and start suppressing our dreams/desires/wishes/goals. This creates resistance and negativity in our mind and once that happen, sadness/unhappiness becomes state of our mind. We, as a child are unaware of the facts/laws about nature/our own existence/our own mind/body. We don't know about the truth and just believe in what is being told to us.

A child's mind is an empty mind which does not have any memories/beliefs. He just believes in what is being brought to his conscious presence. **It is up to the parents or the teachers to teach him/her the truth of life, to impart human values but what about the belief system/awareness of the parents or teachers?** Are they aware about the truth, are they living the truth or are they biased and living a life of misery? If that is so then you can only expect them to unconsciously impart wrong/biased beliefs in their children. This makes their children live life on the beliefs of their parents/teachers and at the same time experience, same life patterns as of their parents. **Hindus call these as childhood impressions/karmas which determine the future of a child.**

Terrorists are being created like this only by imparting wrong beliefs/impressions from early childhood. At very young age, these unlucky children are being trained for cruel, violent actions against humanity. These poor children are not aware about the truth. Once the wrong beliefs have been imparted from an early childhood, it is very difficult to change those negative beliefs. So these poor terrorists either die at the hands of various law abiding agencies or given life imprisonment. Only the right awareness from childhood, right knowledge and right education is the way out of destructive/disempowering beliefs.

It is your utmost prime responsibility to enhance your awareness by practicing focused conscious presence and at the same time impart right awareness among your children. You don't have to teach your children anything, they subconsciously absorb what they see, listen and feel. So your actions are being absorbed by your children subconsciously. If your attitude is of love, happiness, kindness, gratefulness, faith, care, empathy, respect or forgiveness, then your children are also going to learn the same. If you practice too much anger, fear, hate, jealously, sadness or violence, then your children are also going to become like that. Now the choice is yours, what you want to be and what you want your children to be. **And for the sake of God, don't blame luck or destiny. Luck or destiny is in your hands. Your knowledge, your awareness and your conscious presence determines the result in your life, nothing else.**

Belief is the only reason for successes or failures in life. One person succeeds and the other fails in the same business having equal resources and the only reason is both having a different belief system. Why people think and behave differently? The answer is the belief system. Have you ever wondered that some people who are mediocre in their studies are the ones who are great political leaders, CEO's /owners of big companies etc? On the other hand, some people who are bright in studies are not able to achieve big in their life. The only difference is their belief system. Successful ones believe in themselves, are aligned to the truth, know what to do and how to do, work hard & smart are passionate about their dreams and achieve them. **Self-belief aligns mind, body and soul with the truth**. Once the truth is brought to your conscious presence, all perceptions, decisions and actions are guided by **REALITY**, leading to right results in life.

'A knowledgeable man without a strong belief/self-confidence may or may not achieve his goal but a man with strong belief/faith in self shall definitely achieve his goal'.
    -Chetan Bansal

Now the big question is, if it is the beliefs which determine the outcome in our lives, can we change our beliefs? Yes, the answer is yes. My dear friends, we have the power to change beliefs we can convert /change our disempowering beliefs to empowering beliefs, such is the power of human mind. Belief is a very powerful directing force in our life. Belief can turn on or shut off the flow of ideas. So, truthful beliefs empower to achieve success in life and everybody wants to be successful. Right! **So to change life, we need to identify disempowering beliefs that are hampering growth or causing failure and changing those to empowering beliefs.**

Before changing the disempowering beliefs, let us first understand how these beliefs develop under the influence of others.

3.5.5 HOW MIND, THOUGHTS AND EMOTIONS ARE INFLUENCED, LEADING TO DEVELOPMENT OF NEGATIVE BELIEFS

Let us first understand how the memory is formed in mind. **THIS IS HOW EVENTS FIND A PLACE IN MEMORY OF YOUR MIND. Your mind is influenced by what you see, hear and feel.** You experience life or gather information through five senses (five pathways through which information enters personal space: **1) See-Eyes, 2) Hear-Ears, 3) Feel-Nose (smell), 4) Feel-Skin (touch) and 5) Feel-Tongue (taste).** All the incidents/experiences in your life that invoke strong emotions (pleasant or unpleasant) create a strong memory of that event in you. **That is why you tend to remember and reconcile immediately like your birthdays, wedding dates, traveling experiences, deaths of near and dear ones, natural calamities, wars etc.** And the experiences of day to day normal activities are very difficult to remember because emotions are not attached to them. That is why if somebody asks what you ate or wore, even 10 days back, say for example on 20th June 2019, you won't be able to tell as you do not remember. **But you still remember your wedding dress colour, design and even if you have been married for 50 years.** The only reason is having strong emotion/feeling attached to your marriage.

Information with strong emotion travels very fast and gets stored in each & every cell of your body. This way information becomes a part of memory/subconscious/DNA. Many use this science of human mind to become popular. **A person who does something either very positive or very negative becomes the attraction of mass media and people in general.** We *LOVE (STRONG EMOTION)* the good qualities/skills of someone which we lack and thus get naturally attracted towards them. That is why famous politicians, film stars, sports persons or writers become the centre of attraction and immensely popular among masses. **Same way, we *FEAR (STRONG EMOTION)* the bad actions/qualities of someone which is not to our liking and thus natural repulsion towards them.** That is why we hate hard core criminals, terrorists, cruel politicians, rapists, murderers or other bad elements but again they are the centre of attraction because we fear them.

Either of the cases, whether we love someone or hate someone, both occupy the space/memory in our mind but normal people with normal profile don't because they are not extra ordinary and thus not able to move us emotionally. That is why we do not remember normal people but always remember people with extra ordinary positive or extra ordinary negative qualities/actions/profile because either we strongly like or dislike them, nothing else.

The more are the senses involved in absorption of information, the more is the influence and stronger memory. A movie having a mixture of good audio, video, dialogues and good looking actors are able to generate positive emotions in people. **Out of two what would influence people more, TV or Radio and** for sure the answer is TV because it influences people through all five senses as compared to radio which primarily uses only audio.

Reading books has the maximum impact on mind. While reading, we read and speak in mind. We are reading through eyes, try to understand in mind and if not understood, we read it again and again. **In reading, all our five senses are being used to gather information and then process it in mind.** So reading books is the best way to enhance the development of all five senses and it also helps in the development of mind, increases knowledge and understanding and helps in the expansion of consciousness. Reading, a voluntary activity enhances the focus which tremendously speeds up the understanding and intelligence level of mind. As compared to listening or viewing or both, reading is the best way of gathering and understanding instructions. **If we can read, listen and discuss with somebody, watching videos on particular topics then that topic/concept shall become a lifelong memory in mind.** That is why reading books is the best way to increase knowledge and develop mental faculties.

HOW A MIND COMES UNDER THE INFLUENCE OF OTHERS.

As it is through five senses, all the information enters the mind it is only through five senses that a mind is influenced by outside people & situations. This is how our senses work:-

-**Smart/physically attractive** people influence mind through **eyes.**

-**Good speakers/writers** influence mind through **ears and/or feelings**.

-**Music and songs** influence mind through **ears and/or feelings**. Music has no language. A good music of even some foreign language can influence mind positively. Noise from vehicles and machines negatively impact the mind.

-**Fragrance** of good food, plants or environment influences mind positively through **nose** and negatively in case of bad smell.

-**Good taste of food** influences mind by evoking positive emotions through **tongue** and tasteless food invokes bad feelings.

Human mind, unaware about the truth of his mind, body, thoughts, emotions or beliefs are influenced in several ways by others leading to the development of biased beliefs. The ways are as follows:-

1). HUMAN MIND HAS A TENDENCY TO ATTRACT NEGATIVITY MORE THAN POSITIVITY. That is why even a single negative action after 999 good actions/deeds on our part can tarnish our image permanently, even if that act was unintentional because a human's unaware mind tends to remember & prioritize negative feelings/emotions over positive ones. **That is also the reason we see, read and listen to negative news in detail** and leave the positive news only after listening, seeing or reading the headline. Sadly, this mind tendency of people has been used by news and media people to raise their popularity. They show and write more about negative news and also give in-depth information and analysis of negative news to attract more people on their TV channels, radio channels and newspaper. This negatively impacts the human mind. We all know that negative news are only few and media highlighting it impacts the mind of people negatively making them believe that this world is full of bad people and negativity.

2). HUMAN MIND IS INFLUENCED BY FAMOUS PERSONALITIES. Famous singers, musicians, dances, actors, sports persons, politicians etc. had a responsibility to show people the truth but many of these famous personalities are being used by big companies or political parties to refer & promote poor quality products & services through speeches, advertisements, seminars etc. in order to gain money and power. **People do not bother to go into the depth of information given by these famous personalities as their natural intelligence is hijacked by looks, words or personality etc. of these famous people and just believe in what they preach.** This creates a biased belief in people about the quality of the products & services leading to wrong decisions/actions by people helping a few corrupt people with vested interests.

3). A PERSON TOUCHES A PAIN POINT TO GAIN TRUST AND MOST LIKELY MISGUIDE YOU. There are always some people looking to make you medium to fulfil their unethical wishes and dreams. He/she will first find a place in your heart via **emotional connection by touching your pain point.** Then after gaining your trust they will misguide you and motivate you to take wrong, unethical or inhuman actions against those whom have given you pain. And by the time you realize your mistake, your life has already been ruined.

Let's understand it with an example. A child witnessed the killing of his parents/family by armed Govt. forces. A poor child is unaware of anything and he/she develops a traumatic memory of this incidence. For him/her the armed forces or the Govt. is never right. They are inhuman/ cruel and the child is right in believing that and why not, his/her whole life has been ruined. Nobody can understand the pain/trauma of witnessing the killing of his parents/family in front of his own eyes. Nobody can imagine this pain except those who witnessed it.

But the poor child does not know that his family was living with a tribe of terrorists who were killing innocent people every now and then. The armed forces gave many chances to these terrorists to surrender but all in vain and ultimately they were forced to kill the terrorist. And now the innocent family of this child also got killed as they were living among these terrorists and it was very difficult for the forces to differentiate and isolate good people among terrorists.

So, the child lost his family/parents. **He became a victim of social stigma** being tagged terrorist by others, feels isolated, rejected, dejected and has nobody to take care of his needs. **His mind and emotions are in total disarray suffering from immense emotional disturbances and psychological pain.** At this point of time, there comes the entry of some person in his life, an opportunist person with vested interest, having no feelings for the traumatic life condition of the child. He just uses the child as a tool; touches his pain point and tags the armed forces, Govt. and general public bad, cruel and against him or his community as a whole. **He cites various similar examples including himself who suffered same type of misery.** He takes him to a place where he finds people with similar stories. **The reference of other people confirms and affirms in his mind that he is being subjected to suppression, aggression and violence by the other community intentionally.** But there is nobody to tell him the truth. A negative, painful and disempowering belief is created in his mind which is enough to make him a future terrorist, not by conscious choice but based on painful belief. This is how a painful point of a person has been exploited by a person with vested interest. **So, can we blame?** Everybody is right in their own perspective and acting under the influence of their biased beliefs. Their whole life of humanity has been a fight of beliefs. Everybody wants to prove their beliefs right and others wrong.

See, this is an extreme example of infusing biased beliefs by others. But if you dig deep in your life, you will find yourself being misused/negatively influenced by others in some way or the other at some point of life but by the time you realize your mistake, it's already very late. But in life, there is nothing late or early. **Whenever you realize your mistake, the best would be to correct it immediately, learn from it and never to repeat in future.** This is all you can do and your focus should always be on what you can do.

So you need to rise above the emotions to understand the truth to align your decisions and actions with truth for right results. Your belief, perception, decision and action become biased under the influence of other people who play with your emotions leading to wrong results in life.

And once a biased belief is formed, it leads to biased PDA and misery in life. Miseries or wrong results cause more emotional disturbances, leading to more loss of energy, consciousness and thus natural intelligence which further leads to wrong actions and more miseries. **So, everybody using any form of mass communication, whether it is TV, radio, social media, films, books** or any kind of mass media must understand this and become more responsible towards what they publish, to show people the full truth, not to highlight the negative news, to highlight the positive news so as to develop a feel-good factor and good empowering beliefs in people for a better world and not for a bitter world. **Even if you need to highlight some negative news, it must be supported by the truth and not based on biased opinions.** But the problem is that media people, instead of focusing on news/information try to influence people with their own opinions and beliefs, either unknowingly or knowingly for some vested interests. It is not that all are giving wrong information and creating biased beliefs, but very few.

But why to depend upon others, it will be foolish on your part to expect others to be responsible and show you the right path, they are not under your control. The best would be to work on your own mind—thoughts, emotions, beliefs and perceptions rather than trying to change or control things/issues outside you. It is your responsibility to help, not only self but others also in order to come out of darkness by showing them the truth. But the big question is how?

3.5.6 CHANGING BLIND/BIASED/DISEMPOWERING BELIEFS TO TRUTHFUL/EMPOWERING BELIEFS

When we start gathering and assembling references of pain, failures, defeats, adversities into a belief that "I am a Failure", "Nothing is possible now", and "everything is destroyed", a feeling of hopelessness, helplessness or worthless becomes our state of mind. Negative beliefs and emotions make our state of mind negative that reduces our personal power and drains vital energy – a state of mental depression. With this our mind becomes self-destructive which has already destroyed our self-confidence and fear, anxiety, doubt and unexplained psychological pains in some parts of our body have become a norm.

We need help!

You are lucky that help has come in the form of knowledge- knowledge about self, life and universe to transform life by breaking all negative beliefs. **See it is not what you see, listen and feel but what you understand & perceive that matters and determines your destiny.** See the outside information is not in your control, you cannot control the beliefs of other people but you can work on your own perception by increasing awareness & expanding consciousness by rising above your emotions so that you do not come under the influence of any situation, event or people and should be able to see the truth as it is and choose your thoughts & emotions wisely which can serve you based on truth and not the thoughts & emotions which can disturb you based on biased/untruthful information.

For example, a child with an experience of disturbed relations of parents may develop a belief that **"men and women can't live in peace"**. If he carries this belief in his mind, his behaviour towards opposite sexes is most likely to suffer from prejudice leading to disconnection, misunderstandings and problematic relations with his/her spouse in future. This is what is happening in this world, children of parents with problematic relations also suffer problems in their marriages unless and until he/she uses his consciousness/awareness to understand the differences in the mindset of male & female and then try to accept & accommodate with them instead of trying to change them. The belief in this case that the child carried in his subconscious was **"Men and women can't live in peace"**. He/she can convert this to empowering/truthful belief **"Men and women are different. They complete each other and can live in harmony with each other once they understand, respect and accept the differences of each other"**.

SAME WAY, WE CAN CHANGE OTHER DISEMPOWERING BELIEFS LIKE:
From "Believe that the problem is permanent" **To** "Believe this too shall pass, the problem is temporary".
From "My whole life is ruined" **To** "Just a challenge in my particular aspect of life, I will definitely found a way out ".
From "I am the only failure" **or** "why it happens to me only" **To** "Failures are stepping stone to success" **or** "It can happen to anybody".

The simple way to find out whether your belief is biased or truthful is to correlate all your beliefs with 5 universal laws discussed in chapter 2 of this book. Anything that is dependent upon time, changes with time, can't be permanent, so why should we give permanent space to that thing in our mind and believe it to be permanent. The best would be to remove all beliefs from mind which are governed by memory of the past and which are most likely lead to biased perception in present moment. Also life is all dynamic and what may have been useful yesterday might not be useful today. Instead we should fill our mind with all the universal laws which govern our mind and physical life.

The simple reason/truth for problematic life situation is your biased/untruthful PDA taken in the past. And now to change your life positively you need to develop truthful/righteous PDA which can only be possible by practicing a 9 point spiritual attitude discussed in **detail in PART-B of this book.**

SO THIS IS ABOUT YOUR PERSONAL SPACE MADE UP OF MIND, BODY AND ENERGIES. NOW WE WILL UNDERSTAND THE EFFECT OF NEGATIVE AND POSITIVE THOUGHTS, EMOTIONS & BELIEFS ON YOUR PERSONAL SPACE AND ULTIMATELY LIFE.

3.6 EFFECT OF THOUGHTS, EMOTIONS AND BELIEFS ON YOUR PERSONAL SPACE AND LIFE.

WE HAVE BEEN TALKING SO MUCH ABOUT NEGATIVE AND POSITIVE IN BOOK. ALWAYS REMEMBER NEGATIVE MEANS LESS OR REDUCTION IN LIFE ENERGY AND POSITIVE MEANS HIGH OR INCREASE IN LIFE ENERGY.

FIG. 1) UNDERSTANDING THE SCIENCE ON EFFECT OF LESS COSMIC ENERGY IN YOUR PERSONAL SPACE DUE TO NEGATIVE THOUGHTS, EMOTIONS AND BELIEFS.

A thought is energy and thought/energy in motion is emotion and emotion stored in memory is belief. Negative belief makes your attitude of life unnatural where negative emotions of hate, anger, fear, anxiety, envy and internal resistance become your way of life. This leads to disturbances in mind with too much focus on past and future. The negative emotion depletes the vital energy and reduces your energy field. **The low energy frequency vibrations of negative thoughts & emotions does not match with the high frequency cosmic energy vibrations present in the space and thus repulses the cosmic energy.**

A high frequency cosmic energy is the source of life and is always present but we lost it due to our unnatural way of negative thinking, acquired/learned subconsciously from other people in life. The loss of this energy is the real cause of miseries in life. **How can I expect my body, mind and life to work perfectly without energy, it is like expecting a mobile phone to work without battery.**

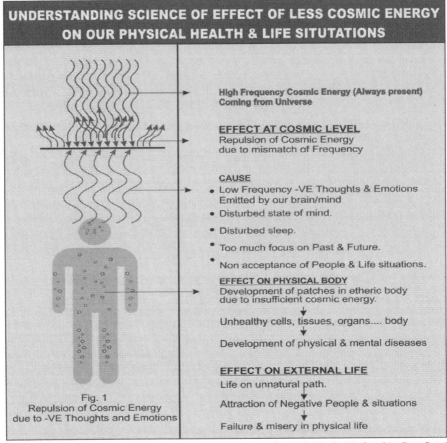

UNDERSTANDING SCIENCE OF EFFECT OF LESS COSMIC ENERGY ON OUR PHYSICAL HEALTH & LIFE SITUTATIONS

High Frequency Cosmic Energy (Always present) Coming from Universe

EFFECT AT COSMIC LEVEL
Repulsion of Cosmic Energy due to mismatch of Frequency

CAUSE
• Low Frequency -VE Thoughts & Emotions Emitted by our brain/mind
• Disturbed state of mind.
• Disturbed sleep.
• Too much focus on Past & Future.
• Non acceptance of People & Life situations.

EFFECT ON PHYSICAL BODY
Development of patches in etheric body due to insufficient cosmic energy.
↓
Unhealthy cells, tissues, organs.... body
↓
Development of physical & mental diseases

EFFECT ON EXTERNAL LIFE
Life on unnatural path.
↓
Attraction of Negative People & situations
↓
Failure & misery in physical life

Fig. 1
Repulsion of Cosmic Energy
due to -VE Thoughts and Emotions

Source: Meet the Real You Copyright: Chetan Bansal

Difficulty in solving problems and inability to fulfil needs induced compulsive negative thinking in mind or disturbs the focus of mind. Unable to find solutions, our mind starts analysing and blaming life as it is unaware of the truth that the problems in life are due to its own wrong attitude and response. It is easy for mind to find excuses and blame others but very difficult to find and correct its own mistakes. It has lost focus and thus energy & consciousness; super intelligence of life. It has forgotten its nature of love, acceptance, happiness, focus, faith, gratitude, kindness etc.; choice of high frequency vibrations is where the solution lies.

The effect of excessive, irrational thinking has doubled negative impact on my energy field.

1) There is no absorption of cosmic energy in the present space.
2) The negative emotions deplete the already present energy from my personal space.

This results in:

1) **Effect on physical body & mind:** Development of patches (areas low in energy or no energy) in our etheric body. The cells, tissues and organs of our body don't get the required amount of its natural food

74

(cosmic energy) and thus becomes faulty and defective leading to development of physical and mental diseases.

2) **Effect on external life:** The low energy field of personal space means the lost connection with natural intelligence or clouding of natural intelligence with disturbed emotions leads to biased PDA and thus, attraction of wrong people & situation and finally manifestations of wrong results in our life.

FIG. 1A) UNDERSTANDING THE SCIENCE OF EFFECT OF HIGH COSMIC ENERGY IN YOUR PERSONAL SPACE DUE TO POSITIVE THOUGHTS, EMOTIONS & BELIEFS.

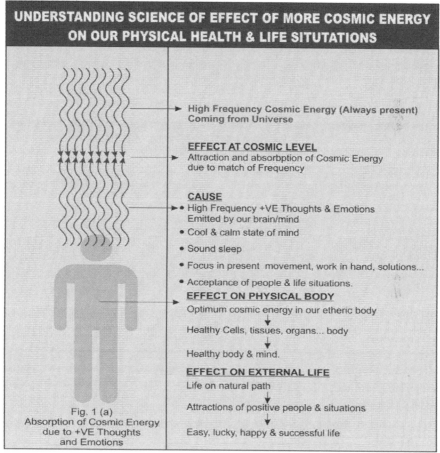

Source: Meet the Real You Copyright: Chetan Bansal

Fig. 1A) is exactly opposite of fig. 1 where the solution lies which is dealt in detail in PART-B of the book. Just understand that a **cool & calm mind, focus of mind on one thought/issue at a time rather than many, having a sound sleep, conscious presence, acceptance of people & situations steadies your emotions, making your conscious vibrations highly positive and leads to attraction & absorption of high frequency cosmic energy**; source of life and when that happens, your mind and body becomes extremely conscious &

healthy leading to truthful PDA, attraction of desired people & situations and thus right results in your life. This is a simple science of your personal space and life which you must understand to bring about a positive change in your life.

Knowing about the harmful effects of negative thoughts & emotions on your physical health and life is a first step to give up negative thinking and choose your nature of love, care, happiness, acceptance, celebration, faith etc. Still, to change your compulsive conditioned state of mind a further clarity with many formulas and techniques for real working on your mind & body is required which we are going to deal in PART-B & C of this book.

DIFFERENCE BETWEEN NATURAL MIND AND DISTURBED MIND

NATURAL MIND	DISTURBED MIND
Higher consciousness	Lower consciousness
Positive emotions increase energy field/aura	Negative emotions decrease energy field/aura
Acceptance, present moment living, faith, gratitude, happiness, kindness, forgiveness, love, celebration etc.	Non acceptance, doubt, blame, complain, sadness, hate, revenge etc.
When we talk of nature/space above mind, we are talking about the higher consciousness above lower consciousness of the mind, only we are talking about raising the consciousness of disturbed mind by choosing a spiritual/natural/super-conscious attitude of life.	

Source: Meet the Real You Copyright: Chetan Bansal

3.7 HOW MIND & LIFE BECAME NEGATIVE

OR LOSES ITS BALANCE OR BECOMES AGGRESSIVE OR DEPRESSIVE OR EGOISTIC OR DISTURBED OR IDENTIFYING SELF WITH LOWER CONSCIOUSNESS?

NON-FULFILLMENT OF NEED CAUSES EMOTIONAL DISTURBANCES. Once a psychological pain of non-fulfilment engulfs mind, it loses its vital energy, leads to physical ailments and emotions of anger, hatred, depression or aggression becomes a part of life. Emotional disturbance clouds our natural intelligence leading to biased PDA which leads to more failures and miseries in life.

Once emotional disturbance becomes habit, our mind will keep on reacting negatively leading to further loss of vital energy. These people will always be low on energy & consciousness. Having low energy all the time will only cause mental and physical disease. The mindset of a person becomes negative leading to negative actions, reactions and behaviour, which will only attract negative responses from others leading to unpleasant situations, more negative emotions, and the person finds himself entangled in the vicious cycle of negative actions and reactions. **The psychological pain has become part of their mind and thus life.**

That person has lost the ability to think & act wisely and now has become a source of misery, not only to self but to others also. A person's mind is not working the way it has been designed but has become faulty and corrupted making anger, hatred, bias and confusion his dominant state of mind.

These layers of negative emotions keep getting thicker and thicker, clouding the connection and thus blocking the divine light from the REAL YOU. The person now starts accumulating bad experiences of his life in to a belief that everything is lost and his life has been ruined forever. All the hope is lost and there is nobody to guide him.

At the subtle level, there is a severe loss of energy causing reduction in energy field/aura by constant state of negative emotions. He just becomes the attraction of all negativity and he wonders why he is the only one attracting more and more negativity in his life. This makes him think a lot, he is not able to find the reason. He is in deep analysis of his bad life experiences and based on those experiences keep on fearing the repetition of those experiences in future. The fear & anxiety has gripped his mind leading to loss of peace of mind and sleep. God gave mind to humans in order to be able to solve all problems, to grow in life so that they can live a happy, successful and prosperous life but instead, it has become a source of misery and torture.

The person is in deep pain by non-fulfilment of desire, in deep negative thoughts, not able to bear rejection; rejection in love, failure in profession. He is in total disharmony with himself, with other humans, with nature. Somehow he wants to come out of negative thoughts but don't know how. He has lost control over his thoughts & emotions and he is in a state of compulsive negative thinking. His mind keeps wandering from one thought to another, from past to future to present, from one issue to another without having any control over it. He has lost his power to focus his mind.

At this stage, negative beliefs become dominant making his mind rigid and life fragile. He doesn't want to understand, listen about anything/everything. He rejects any/all guidance coming from others as he has lost trust in life. He perceives everything based on his memory of negative beliefs, lost the flexibility of mind and finally lost the ability to see the truth as it is.

Our true nature of joy, peace, happiness, love is being covered by the clouds of anger, frustration, fear, threat, comparison, competition etc. Our mind is playing games and we have become victims of our mind. We are under control of our mind, instead I/my real being/my true nature should control my mind and emotions. A mind devoid of energy is like a machine without power which can never work in a way it has been designed.

When mind is operating from lower consciousness, it thinks that the source of happiness is material things and gets attached to them. Too much of attachment to your needs, wants and desires make you either overtly AGGRESSIVE OR DEPRESSIVE or both are EGOISTIC OR DISTURBED state of mind.

When we get **too much attached to our desires**, there are two outcomes:-

1) FULFILMENT OF DESIRES MAY MAKE A PERSON EGOISTIC WHICH DETACHES HIM FROM HIS TRUE NATURE OF LOVE. He starts identifying himself with material achievements that I am this, I am that, I have achieved that and his mind gives him a feeling of superiority over others. Slowly he becomes indifferent to others; wants to control/change/manipulate/betray others. He/she wants to control everything exactly the way he/she wants. And when things don't happen their way, they become angry, rude, harsh or violent and may even choose unfair means to achieve his goals/desires. This way he may achieve success but that would only be temporary as the negative vibes/curses of person/s he betrayed, oppressed shall come back to him making him lose his balance of mind and ultimately making him negative, unhappy and unsuccessful. The pain that he get back from others either makes him aggressive or depressive, if he doesn't want to change himself positively. This way egoist state of mind keep on becoming more and more severe day by day.

2) THE NON-FULFILMENT GIVES US A STRONG FEELING OF REJECTION WHICH IN TURN GIVES PAIN TO MIND. The pain is either converted to aggression or depression if the person is not conscious. In depression, a person becomes mentally and physically weak, loses hope/faith in life and stops living life. He stops all his life activities and confines himself in his deep negative thoughts. Or he may become aggressive to fulfil his needs and desires by using unfair/unethical means. In either of the cases psychological pain is inevitable and returns back to him.

So, **attachment to desires is like an obsession for desires** which invariably makes a person use unfair means to fulfil his desires. **The identification of mind with material things make the person egoistic** where he focuses only on his own gains even by inflicting pain or loss to others. The result is disagreements, fights, quarrels and ultimately bad relations with others leading to disturbance in the emotions of self and others. Mind loses connection with omnipotent reality and thus ultimately become negative.

Whenever a person becomes aggressive or depressive, both states of mind separate them from other people. **The feeling of separation from others is called EGO.** When someone thinks of himself/herself superior or inferior to others in terms of caste, religion, sex, job/profession, financial status, skin colour etc., his/her mind creates a self-illusionary identity of being superior or inferior to others thus creating a wall between himself/herself and others. This illusion of mind separates him from his nature and from the nature of others. The **constant feeling of only I, ME, MINE is EGO.** EGO gives importance to self only and neglects the others, thinking them as different. **Ego forgets that there is only one nature; nature of me/others/the whole universe is same.** So ego loses connection with nature of self thus losing connection with everybody else.

The cause of Ego is some deep, unresolved pain, developed on some disempowering beliefs or hurt caused due to some misunderstandings or real misdeeds of others like disrespect, breach of trust by others, violence, untimely or unnatural death of some near and dear ones, which makes them lose faith in self, God and thus humanity. That pain and hurt makes them negative and they may resort to illegal activities, or anger, hatred, revenge, sadness becomes their permanent state of mind which separates them from their own nature and nature of others. These people are the source of problem for anybody or everybody, everywhere in their house, office and society. They find pleasure in creating problems for others. They just become indifferent to self, life and to other people.

An egoist mind constantly thinks about past and worries about future, forgets to live in the present moment, feels angry and sad about past and feels anxious about future. Ego gets involved/entangled in the life of others; loves to control, blame, compare, curse, judge, suppress, manipulate, disrespects, hate, betray and envy others. Ego identifies himself with material gains, gives more importance to materialism over humanity, lose connection with the higher self (REAL YOU). Egoist mind connects with other egoist people and creates more negative situations for itself to make life worse, day by day, moment my moment. An egoist state of mind is very dangerous and needs to be mended urgently to prevent spread of hate, anger, pain, aggression, depression etc.

The lower consciousness/low energy field is the EGO and higher consciousness/high energy field is the REAL YOU. Ego makes the person either aggressive or depressive or the same person goes through cycles of both aggression and depression, having lost peace of mind. This makes their personal space devoid of energy or unbalances their energies. The low energy field in his personal space becomes a chronic state which might lead to a mental disorder called Depression. Being unaware about the science of self, life, mind and universe, people are not able to handle difficult life situations, loses faith in life and many resort to drugs or suicide. With depression or aggression, the energy chakras become defective and with defective chakras, the endocrine system of the body becomes defective. The defective glands leads to either under or over production of bio-chemicals called hormones. Here comes the role of drugs, medicines, sleeping pills, alcohol or nicotine which is alternate to biochemical but having many side effects in the long run. The person when not getting that biochemical produced in his body becomes overtly addictive on these drugs; as drugs give a temporary feeling of much desired high pleasure which they are lacking in their personal life. These drugs give relief from the psychological pain by relaxing the overthinking mind.

Weaker/unconscious or mind having lower energy will always focus on psychological time of past or future and forgets to focus on present. Focusing on past problems and future fears always gives pain. That is why to avoid pain we need to be mindless; bringing the focus to present space & time. Drugs/tranquilizers make you mindless relieving all pains temporarily and as soon as we come out of the effect of drugs, the consciousness comes back to our mind activity along with its pain. Drugs if taken on regular basis immensely reduces energy field/consciousness of mind and damages body organs in the long run and are serious threat to our health and may even cause untimely death. **That is why drugs are given only in case of emergency and that too for a short period.**

So drugs is not the solution, then what is the solution? **Either we continue to take drugs and make our life miserable** or choose to rise above our mind, to go beyond mind to cure our mind by understanding our mind, body, soul and the techniques to conquer it **through our mind & body** by only going beyond it to meet and realize our true power, true nature.

By too much attachment to my desires and trying to control the life of others, I have lost the health of my mind & body and made my life miserable. So what should I do? Should I forget about my needs & wants? Can I survive without fulfilment of my needs & wants? What is the way out?

I am not saying to forget about your needs & wants. I am just saying to detach from your desires, from the life of others and start focusing on to you. Detachment does not mean forgetting your needs & wants and not doing something about them, but just going about in a right manner where you create win-win situations for all, so that you achieve everything with less hard work and that too in a short span of time.

Detachment from your personal desires and detaching from the life of others activate your highest level of consciousness (Real You) which flowers the qualities of acceptance, patience, love, care, respect, empathy, gratitude, happiness, kindness and forgiveness. The person is unperturbed by any/all of the negative/undesired people or situation and maintain his cool & calm, focus and keep working towards his goals with a never give-up attitude.

Let's try to understand this. For **Example 1,** if you are in love with somebody and that person rejects your proposal, that rejection gives you pain but instead of choosing pain or trying to enforcing your wishes on others, you should respect the feelings of the other person and start searching a new and better option where you both shall be in love with each other. You should be happy that the previous person rejected as you were not a match with each other and due to that rejection, you have found your true love.

Example 2: It is good to have desire for material things, everybody wants to be rich. It is good to be rich and financially free. Money is very important even if you want to help somebody/society you cannot, if you are not rich but what if your material desires are not met, should you resort to drugs, should you become negative/pessimistic, should you use unfair means (betray trust of others, hurt others, use illegal means) to fulfil your needs? **No! Instead, you should tell your mind that you shall definitely achieve this but by fair means, where you don't inflict any pain on others. Needs & demands are your birth rights** and you should work smart to achieve them, you should learn skills to achieve them, you should commit yourself to achieve them, you should give your 100% to achieve them but never by betraying others. Finally you must accept the outcome, if you succeed celebrate and make another bigger goal and if you fail, celebrate & learn from the experience and challenge yourself to give another try but never give up in life. **But I don't understand why go in depression or become aggressive and make your life miserable. There is no other option!** You have to be happy and joyous all the time to maintain a positive energy field. Analyse what went wrong and give another try but for god sake don't make sadness your habit, it sucks and kills your precious present and future.

YOU) before moving forward, please answer some questions, i am little bit confused.

ME) Oh! You are confused. I am also confused. But I tell you, you being confused looks good because confusion only happens when you think and thinking for solution is the only way towards clarity. I am sure that even if I am unable to answer your questions, your own thinking, focused mind shall find answers to all your questions. I am happy that you have already started thinking so early in this book, to make you think is the prime focus and purpose of this book as it is only you who can understand yourself best and only you who can give best solution to self. I may have forgotten many things and you asking some questions here actually making my work easy. So I love you my dear REAL YOU for this. Please ask whatever you want to ask, I shall be highly obliged to answer you back but please ask at the end of the book and till then I will try to ensure that all the questions on your mind are taken care of.

YOU) Okay sir, but just one question please?

ME) Okay! Granted! Go ahead.

YOU) I have been reading all this with great interest and it's just amazing, the information and truth about life science. I have observed one thing in life that **most of us are attracted to negativity easily** and people find it difficult to stay in a positive state of mind. Please throw some light on it.

ME) who told you that it's difficult to stay in a positive state of mind? It is difficult for those who do not understand life and its various laws on which this universe is running. Once you know who you are, what your powers are and how you can control and use those powers, the difficult becomes easy. The problem is that most of the people do not want to understand self, life and universe.

See, our mind is attracted towards negativity out of fear of any threat to you. Mind loves you and wants to protect you, save you from any adversity, although it's a different issue that a mind with lower consciousness does not understand or differentiate between real and illusionary fear/threat. **But one thing is sure that mind is attracted to negativity only out of love for**

positivity. Mind always loves to be positive, happy but you, the boss have not trained your child (mind) well, haven't guided it well. Show your mind the right path, the right focus and it shall bring into your presence whatever you want.

Mind has forgotten positivity because it has witnessed negativity more than positivity and mind learns what it sees, listens and feels. See for centuries, humans have been exploited by some elite people. People have very bad experiences of fraud, violence, slavery, prejudice, bias etc. so their memory is full of bad experiences & negative beliefs and even many good people after bad experiences have resorted to negativity in the form of revenge, hate, envy etc. This is how most people's mind became negative and being negative became a common psyche. **Common beliefs developed overtime are "Do not trust anybody", "Be careful, he/she will ditch you", "Life is very difficult", etc.**

You just need to commit yourself to choose your forgotten nature of love, affection, trust, faith, gratitude, happiness, kindness etc. which will make your personal space positive, leading to good feelings flowing on to others making them positive also and those positive people will also spread positive feelings of love, this way positivity will multiply and spread like a virus. This way positivity will become a common phenomenon.

More and more people are now fed up of all the negativity and want to change the world towards positivity. **You being the reader of this book so far means that you are attracted to positivity more than negativity and wants to change/improve yourself.** So it is wrong to say that your mind is attracted to negativity, mind always want to be positive but a conditioned mind, out of compulsion resort to negativity. Positivity is in your nature and everybody wants to live their nature.

You must have seen that nowadays, there are bombardment of people teaching about life science, universe, consciousness and all secrets of universe which are no secrets any more. And I believe with everybody's effort and with a helping and caring attitude towards each other, the day is not far off when positivity will become a common phenomenon or you can say the consciousness/awareness of common people will rise immensely to make this world a heaven to live in. Then even the negative people who are very few will become positive.

3.8 I DON'T BELIEVE
ME: What? Please clarify what you don't believe?
YOU: There are many books, motivational speakers, and people talking about thoughts leading to things. They may be right but I don't believe as my mind is not clear on this.

ME) Okay don't believe what can I do about your belief, it's your choice.

YOU) Sir, people are spending a lot of time, energy and money in understanding how to live a quality life but not many able to change their life positively. My humble request to you is to make it **clear once and for all about the role of thoughts, emotions and mindset (the word you have used many times).** For me I don't believe that all my thoughts are manifested in my life and I think all the readers also agree with that. This question is tearing my mind apart, requested you to please help on this.

ME) I am impressed that you don't want to blindly believe anything. Please make this your attitude and habit for life, don't believe anybody and anything unless and until you experience that thing or you are satisfied with answers. I shall try my level best here to bring about much needed clarity on this.

Let's begin.

This is what you are saying that nobody in life thinks of miseries, nobody thinks about accidents, diseases, poor relations, poor economic conditions, so how come? These have been manifested in the life of people when nobody thought about it. **So saying that it is only thoughts that are being manifested is wrong to believe.**

Yes, my dear REAL YOU, I fully agree with you on that but still there are a lot of ifs and buts to it. I will make it simple for you. Let's understand thoughts from a deeper perspective **(I.P. thought process).**

See all the results in your life are the results of your actions and thoughts are directions to your actions. If you are taking unfocussed actions without awareness, you are going to manifest unexpected results which you have never thought of. **For example, while driving a vehicle or any machine, accidents happen when the focus of the driver/operator is somewhere else,** he/she was not thinking of the accident but his/her mind was somewhere else, not present. The action went wrong which manifested accident and an unexpected result. **Your thought was to reach your destination safely and didn't ever think about the accident but still manifested an accident. You are right, all thoughts are not manifested or manifest partly or exactly opposite of what you thought.**

As the focus of mind was elsewhere which lead to wrong action and finally the accident, an unexpected result, **so it is the focus of your mind which manifests or tears apart thought. An emotionally disturbed mind is not able to focus in the present moment and thus, the action goes wrong leading to wrong unexpected results.**

Same way, you eating an unhealthy/unnatural food on regular basis cause diseases in you. You thinking and believing yourself to be healthy is not going to be manifested if your actions are contrasting to your thoughts & beliefs. For healthy living, you need to understand and practice healthy food and healthy lifestyle. So, even if your thoughts are healthy but your actions are unhealthy, **in that case or any case your actions shall always win over your thoughts.**

Also all your thoughts are not manifested in your life as every person in life gets on an average of 60,000 thoughts per day. These thoughts are on various issues, contrasting and your mind keep on swaying from one thought to another, sometimes think of success and sometimes failure, sometimes become fearful, sometimes confident **but ultimately, the thought that you give your emotions to, focus upon, choose, believe and act upon consistently, persistently and relentlessly with full focus is going to be manifested in your life.**

Not all the thoughts but the processed/final thoughts on which you take action are going to be manifested in your life. **When we talk of thoughts determining your reality, it means your mindset and not the individual thoughts.** There are two types of thoughts **(I. P. thought process):-**

1) **I----Initial raw thoughts or first information report(FIR)**
2) **P---Processed thoughts or final understanding, final decisions and actions**

We experience so many varied thoughts, contrasting thoughts every time, so how can all thoughts become reality on the screen of life? We all process numerous, varied contrasting thoughts on all issues and reach a final conclusion on which we decide and act. **And your mindset is your overall understanding, perception, decision and action** and not the raw thoughts/ideas which are popping each & every second in your mind. **Two persons may have same situations, the initial thoughts might be same but the refined understanding and decision making is the mindset which differentiates and gives different results in life.** There may be temporary negative emotions associated with raw initial thoughts but the final processed thoughts determine the energy field/aura of a person and thus destiny of a person is not in temporary, initial raw thoughts but the final processed thoughts is called his mindset.

WHAT IS A MINDSET? It is a set of beliefs, values, perspectives and memories which determine the overall attitude, behaviour, and habits in life. And the beliefs/values/perceptions of a person are dependent upon his consciousness which is dependent upon his awareness, which is dependent upon his conscious presence. And it is your conscious presence which connects with your omnipotent eternal reality; the source of your life. Your conscious presence enhances the energy in your personal space, making it positive and leading to a **positive mindset** which is aligned with the truth, where all your values, beliefs, perceptions, decisions, actions, reactions, attitude and behaviour are guided by the divine, making your life a joyous journey.

A negative mindset, beliefs, values and perceptions are processed by an unfocused mind, not present in the present moment; a mind not connected to **THE REAL YOU** are invariably away from the truth leading to wrong attitude/behaviour/actions resulting to miseries in life.

A person with positive mindset has steady emotions, is focused in the present moment, is able to maintain positive energy field and is always connected to the source of life. This makes him understand the truth without any bias, align his/her decisions and actions with the truth and accept the outcome no matter what. A positive mind set is also a **flexible mind** which is open to new information, wants to learn new things, is receptive to other, listen others and decides based upon the truth and not based upon some beliefs. A person with positive mindset believes in the freedom of self/others, is not influenced by others, easily forgives self/others, love self/others, respect self/others and accept others. A real, forward looking person focuses on solutions having immense faith/confidence in self/almighty. A positive mind is an open mind, an optimistic mind which is able to attract and grab endless opportunities offered by the present moment.

A person with negative mindset has disturbed emotions, focused in past problems or future worries or both thus, not able to maintain a positive energy field/aura, so he/she is always disconnected from the source of life. He is not able to see the truth as it is, his/her decisions and actions are biased, away from the truth and thus attract undesired results in his/her life. A negative mindset is also a rigid mind which is not open to new information/ideas, does not want to listen to others, thinks himself right and wants to prove others wrong, disrespects others, hate others, envy others, rejects others, wants to control others, don't forgive others, always thinking about the past & future with worry, anxiety and fear dominant in his mind. A negative mind is a closed and pessimistic mind, closing the door to the endless opportunities that the present moment offers.

More on initial/raw and processed/final thoughts is explained in vertical alignment section 6.2 of PART B of this book and it is going to be a very exciting journey for you, my dear real you.

NOW YOU HAVE ALREADY UNDERSTOOD UNIVERSAL SPACE, YOUR PERSONAL SPACE COMPROMISING OF YOUR BODY, MIND/CHAKRAS, THOUGHTS, EMOTIONS AND BELIEFS, IT WILL NOW BE VERY EASY FOR YOU TO UNDERSTAND YOUR PHYSICAL LIFE, YOUR NEEDS & WANTS AND RELATIONS.

THEN WE WILL MOVE TO PART B & C OF THE BOOK FOR ULTIMATE SOLUTION, HOW TO STRENGTHEN THE CONNECTION WITH YOUR ROOTS AND TO MAKE YOUR MIND & BODY HIGHLY CONSCIOUS/ENERGETIC/SUPER INTELLIGENT IN ORDER TO FIND SOLUTION TO ALL YOUR PROBLEMS, TO FIND MEANING, PURPOSE, PASSION, JOY, PEACE AND PROSPERITY IN LIFE.

4.0 YOUR PHYSICAL LIFE

4.1 LIFE
4.2 NEEDS & WANTS
4.3 RELATIONS
4.4 HOW RELATIONS & LIFE BECAME PROBLEMATIC
4.5 THE SUMMARY OF PHYSICAL LIFE

4.1 LIFE

Let's understand your physical life once and for all. We have a physical body made up of organs which are made of tissues which are made of cells. **All organs of your body are working day and night continuously without you having any control over it.** Like the process/functioning of your breathing, digestion, pumping of heart etc. **are predetermined, pre-coded and they are working on their own, the same way in every human. It works in a similar way the earth is rotating and revolving based on some predefined laws and principles.** The very functioning of your physical organs makes your body alive. The very presence of numerous thoughts makes mind alive. Although, the mind & body are working on their own they need energy to function properly and that energy is available in the form of air, water, food etc. **So, we as a mind & body is a system which gets input energy from the outside and excrete faeces, urine, sweat and air out of our system.** So, a constant give and take is taking place between your body system (personal space) and with other systems of the universe (universal space). **Once the give and take ends the very functioning of organs stop and thus, stops the life.** A body system (personal space) without a process of give and take becomes a dead system, a dead body which is similar to a business becoming a dead business once the give and take stops. *SO FOR ANYTHING TO BE ALIVE, A CONSTANT GIVE AND TAKE IS A MUST---THE LAW OF LIFE. FOR GIVE AND TAKE ACTION IS A MUST. SO, ACTION/MOVEMENT IS LIFE. NO ACTION MEANS NO GIVE AND TAKE AND THEREFORE, NO LIFE.*

      The very action of anything/something attracts energy; life energy. The non-action repulses life energy. And it is the attraction of energy which makes them valuable & attractive. **The rotation and revolution of planet earth gives rise to its electromagnetic, gravitational energies, making it suitable for life to sustain.** The moment the earth stops rotating and revolving, it shall lose its energies and thus, becomes unsuitable for life to happen. **Similarly, physical movement/action/exercise of our body attracts energies/raises your energies, making it healthy, attractive and valuable.** The more physical work you do, the more energy you attract and the healthier you become. A person may not work physically but his life still goes on as vital organs are working constantly, providing him the much needed energy to survive. **The right thought process attracts natural energy, an intelligence making your mind healthy and source of success, happiness, growth for self and others.** The in-active physical body or non-thinking or wrong thinking mind or all creates resistance inside you which hinders the flow of life energy, making your energy field low/negative, leading to unhealthy body & mind devoid of natural life energy and thus, attract miseries in life. **Once the energy field becomes zero, the life has left your body; a dead body.** That is why a dead body is not called by the name of the person it belonged to, but just body as it has lost its energy/name/fame/source. Now, it's just a body identity without consciousness. A live person is identified by his/her work, name, fame and consciousness but a dead body is merely a body.

Although, we see one body but actually, there are three dimensions of life; physical, mental and spiritual. **Physical body** needs food, air, water etc. **Mind** has psychological needs and **spiritual thrives on giving.** Everybody is working day and night, either to fulfil their physical, psychological, spiritual or all needs, nothing else. Non-fulfilment of needs due to any reason is a problem and cause failure but fulfilment of needs is a success.

Nobody in this universe is perfect and encounters problems/challenges in their life. Having and encountering problems is an opportunity to learn new skills and practice those skills in order to overcome that problem. The more problem one has in their life, the more is the opportunity to learn, understand and become master of life or any other areas of life. **So, having problems is a blessing in disguise, an opportunity to grow in life.**

Mind & body are the tools given by God to experience life which needs energy to function and to get that energy, we need to use mind & body only; amazing! Isn't it a self-sustaining system! To fulfil the needs & wants of life, we need to act which is based on your perceptions and decisions. **PDA (PERCEPTION, DECISION, ACTION), the three core karmas of life decides the results in your life.** Wrong PDA leads to wrong results and the right PDA leads to right results. The quality of life is dependent upon the quality of PDA, which is dependent upon the quality of health, of your mind & body which is further dependent upon the presence of cosmic energy in your personal space. **The degree/percentage of the presence of cosmic energy is dependent upon your choice of thoughts, emotions, breathing pattern, food, water etc. which ultimately determines the quality of life.**

For a complete experience of life, you should be fully aware of all the three dimensions of your existence---physical, psychological, spiritual. Spiritual energy being the source of life creates, maintains and destroys life. If you are living a saddened life or experiencing miseries in your life, the only cause is emotional disturbance or less energy in your personal space that leads to disconnection with your source and disconnection from source means losing your guide, an intelligence which knows everything about your life and knows the right path of your life. To regain that lost connection, you need to choose a spiritual way of life, a spiritual attitude for joy, bliss, love, gratitude, happiness, acceptance, conscious presence, celebration and forgiveness in your life.

LEADING A SPIRITUAL PATH OF LIFE IS ONLY THING IN LIFE THAT IS IN YOUR CONTROL, EVERYTHING ELSE IS BEYOND YOUR CONTROL AND YOU SHOULD NOT WORRY ABOUT ANYTHING THAT IS NOT IN YOUR CONTROL.
Please answer the following questions
Q1. Is your birth under your control? Yes/No
Q2. Is your death under your control? Yes/No
Q3. Do you control the functioning of your vital organs? Yes/No
Q4. Are your Relations under your control? Do you choose your family or other people whom you meet in your life or do you choose the circumstances in your life? To some extent, you may choose what people stay or not in your life but are the people and circumstances in your control? Yes/No

And I know the answer to above, and the answer for all is NO, a big NO. If you are not able to control the above, then what is left for you to control? And most of us are trying to control what is beyond our control. **Isn't it foolish on our part as we are wasting our time and energy to control which can never be controlled by us.**

So now the big question is, what is in our control and how to control it in a better way for better life or in other words what change we can bring about in self to understand what to control or what not to control and how to control what we can control?
The things that are in our control are as follows:

1) The quality, quantity, frequency and timing of food that we eat, the quality of air that we breathe-in (determined by our breathing pattern), the quality, quantity and timing of water that we drink, all determines the quality of energy in our personal space and thus, the quality of mind & body.

2) The final thoughts that we choose (PDA) and not the thoughts that we experience determines our destiny.

3) It is not the situation itself but the response to the situation which is in our control and determines the outcome of a situation.

Life is all about choice and your choice is the input which is directly proportional to the output in your life. If you are getting wrong results in life, you need to change the input that is in your control and not to be disturbed or perturbed by the things that are not in your control.

So, life is all about maintaining healthy body & mind for responding to situations in a right way, nothing else. Once you are able to master it, you shall experience heaven on earth. *Hell and heaven are the results of your own KARMA (PDA), nothing else.*

Life is about the journey and not the destination, life keeps on moving forward, there is no end point. Once we achieve something, a new need or desire rises in our mind again, we work for it and achieve it. If it fails, we work on it again, to achieve it. One life ends, another starts. The death of a physical body only means a new life with a new body, **so life keeps on moving, there is no final point or destination.** If it is so, life is just about living the moment, as there is no end point or destination. We always forgot to enjoy the moment in search of destination which never arrives; this is the only cause of unhappiness in life. The moments we are fully focussed, in every thought and actions of ours are the most happy and productive moments of life; rest moments are just for passing/wasting of time.

IN SHORT, THIS IS WHAT PHYSICAL LIFE IS: Life thrives on needs & wants. When we have needs & wants, we also encounter problems and face challenges. To overcome challenges, to solve problems, we need the right usage of mind & body and also need help from others, for which we need to form and maintain good relations in life. Overcoming challenges is a success and not able to solve a problem is failure. Once you succeed, a higher new need arises in your mind, for which again you need to act. This way, you are kept busy in life, you encounter newer, mysterious, uncertain situations in life and **understanding & practicing right response to those situations is the most important skill/karma in life.** Life is full of action; no action, no life is the most important and very basic understanding of life.

Needs, action, give or take, relations, problems, challenges, success & failure are all parts of life and without them, there is no life. This whole book is about life; understanding life and bringing about a positive change in life so as to experience a better life, to set your life on natural path.
Let's move to your needs and wants.

4.2 NEEDS & WANTS

Having physical life means physical body which needs energy to sustain life. And the energy comes from food, water, air etc. The lack of these gives rise to needs & wants. *Something you lack makes you dependent upon others to fulfil that lack;* the law of duality, a universal law that exists in physical and mental world **is cause of all physical & emotional needs and thus, cause of attraction between opposites.** *It is this law of nature that is the essence of diversity of life.* No life is complete in it-self and thus, needs help of others to meet their natural needs & wants to sustain life.

When you see something in others which you don't have, you are naturally attracted towards them. For example, a student is attracted towards a teacher from whom he/she can learn and attain knowledge. So student having low knowledge or no knowledge is attracted towards a teacher having greater knowledge. **Male and female having different physical body** have varying degree of emotions is the cause of natural attraction for each other, as both fulfil each other's emotional needs and thus complete each other.

We are taking oxygen from plants and giving carbon-dioxide in return**, we need oxygen and they need Co_2. So, life can never exist in isolation and that is why the physical forms of plants & animals are different, having different needs & wants, different roles where one becomes source to other and other becomes source to others and/or each other and so on. **The natural food chains, where a smaller animal** is eaten by a bigger one, is the essence of life and very important to sustain the balance of the whole universe. All animals are both prey and predator; prey to a bigger animal and predator of a smaller animal. Cat is prey to a Dog and predator of a mouse.

Can you think of any life, whether its plants, animals or humans or all, on planet earth which does not depend upon others to fulfil their needs and wants????? **Needs make you imperfect as perfect does not have any needs. Thus, the nature of physical life is imperfection**; it depends upon others to meet needs. **Perfection is the nature of the divine**; complete in itself and not dependent on others.

Human needs, wants & desires can be categorized in to three types; 1) Physical needs 2) Emotional needs 3) Spiritual needs. Fulfilment of physical needs (basic needs) is a must to survive life, because fulfilment or non-fulfilment of emotional needs (desires) makes us happy or sad but it has nothing to do with survival of life.

So what are your needs and are these common to everybody? Yes, your needs are the same, like everybody needs food and water for survival but wants & desires can be different depending upon one's socio-economic status and level of contentment and status of one's conscious enlightenment (Knowledge about self and life). As one eats food at a small restaurant but other eats at a big 5 star hotel, some are happy with a small, simple house but some want big, luxurious house. Everybody wants **significance/importance**. This is an emotional need common to everybody but we can survive and live without the fulfilment of this need. Non-fulfilment of emotional needs give psychological pain but non-fulfilment of physical needs leads to physical pain and eventually, death.

A). PHYSICAL NEEDS- It is the 1st need of life (needs of our body) like food, water, breathing, sleep, excretion, physical intimacy and security are basic human needs and must for everybody for survival, but here wants (means) can be different, like some eat vegetarian food and some eat non-vegetarian food, but air and water are common needs and at the same time, fulfilled through same means. So at a physical level, needs and wants are almost the same. This is the basic human need or basic need for every living organism to sustain life. The pain of any physical ailment or non-fulfilment of hunger gives a similar degree of pain to all, irrespective of their socioeconomic conditions.

A healthy body is a source of real happiness, irrespective of any age/time. Without a healthy body, nobody can enjoy and experience life to the fullest and thus, the prime focus of all must be to fulfil the body needs of quality like food, water, air etc. in order to maintain a healthy body and experience a quality life.

B) PSYCHOLOGICAL- The 2nd need of life are emotional needs like security of profession & finances, significance/importance, friendship, family, physical intimacy, love & connection, material possessions. This is also a common need to every human but the means (medium to fulfil needs) can be different. E.g. some get money from business, some get money from a job. Also, degree of contentment or fulfilment of needs may vary for example, some are happy with 1,000 dollars and on the other hand, some are not even happy with 20,000 dollars.

Also, with the passage of time, the **fulfilled desire loses its value** and this leads to a generation of new desire, something bigger than the first one in terms of size, value etc. **For e.g., when we buy a motorcycle, we clean it regularly** for the first few days (we value it), then we just clean the handle and the seat, then, only the seat and afterwards, we lose interest in it (loss of value in our eyes) and a new desire is born in our mind to buy a car now. If new desire is fulfilled, then we become happy and if not, the non-fulfilment of desire gives pain. The motorcycle, which was once a source of happiness now, is not a source of happiness but fulfilment of new desire now will give happiness and further when that new desire is fulfilled again, a new desire for something bigger engulfs our mind. **Meaning, it is the nature of our mind or it is our psychology that once a source of happiness or excitement over a period of time loses charm, value and hence, happiness from materialistic things is not permanent and is the cause of disturbance in our mind & emotions.**

It is not that having desires for materialistic things is bad. **Materialistic things, wealth, importance, name & fame are food to your mind.** Mind should be given its food and rewarded based on its work, like we give salary to employees on the basis of their work/their input. Giving either excess or low to the mind shall corrupt the mind and it may choose the wrong path. Like, if you give extra salary/undeserved amount to your employees, they will lose value of it and most likely become irresponsible towards their job or if you give low salary/low amount, they shall indulge in corrupt practices which ultimately harm you.

You can say to your mind, if you want more, you need to work more, perform more, work hard & smart and earn yourself what you deserve but not by unfair means or by ditching others or by inflicting pain on others. Your mind will be guided by *THE REAL YOU,* as you being the boss and not the mind. **Too much attachment to something/anything** may cause you to choose unfair means, which is bound to give pain sooner or later. Show your mind the right path and you shall achieve anything. **So, detach yourself from**

all the desires. It simply means do not choose the wrong path to gain something. If you are not able to achieve something by fair means, you should remain centred, balanced in your mind, feel proud of your value system and keep on trying with a never give up attitude to ultimately achieve your dreams/desires/wishes and not by some unfair means.

C) SPIRITUAL NEEDS- Ultimate purpose & way of life (needs of soul): Self-realization/actualization, respect for others, morality, creativity, acceptance of facts, no bias or prejudice, gratitude, kindness, joy, unconditional love, ability to deal with worst of situations & people, feeling of oneness with the whole Universe is what we call spiritual way of life. Actions of spiritual people are not driven by mind but by their true nature, in fact they control their mind and not vice-versa. Their emotions are steady; they have learned and mastered the art of controlling their emotions. **The fulfilment of this need gives real happiness, joy and peace of mind. At this state of consciousness, there is complete contentment and acceptance of life.** This is a need for everybody but a very few reach this level of consciousness. Animals spend their whole life fulfilling just their physical needs. Most of the world population spend their whole life fulfilling their physical and emotional needs, but only a few elite, lucky one reach a level of consciousness where they realize their full potential, where they are able to understand their reality, get to know and fulfil the real purpose of life. These people go beyond their body & mind and meet their real self. We, as human race are lucky to have a big size brain to fully utilize mind to go beyond, to transcend mind only to find **THE REAL YOU**. When our body, mind and soul are fully synchronized, harmonized all your needs & wants (physical, emotional, and spiritual), they are fulfilled easily in an effortless manner. There is no feeling of lack, no effect of unpleasant people or situations, complete acceptance of physical reality, ego is dissolved and the feeling of deep serenity and peace-**a state of complete bliss**. People at this state of consciousness celebrate life, help/contribute for the wellbeing of society. **These people believe in giving and the more they give, the more comes back to them**. For them, the treasure of knowledge, peace, contentment, joy, and prosperity keeps on increasing. This is the only way of life, natural path of life, life on its soul path; an automatic path to love, peace, joy, happiness, success & growth in life.

Once a physical need of a human is secured, he works for fulfilment of his material needs and once he tastes all materialism, his mind moves towards spirituality where he loves helping others by giving what he has. This is all natural and automatic; embedded in the software of human mind by God. You can also correlate this to the life of a common man. **When born, every child's** parent priority is physical development and growth. **When he becomes young** (physically & mentally strong), another need becomes more prevalent in his life and that is the fulfilment of **emotional needs**---need for physical intimacy, need for material gains, name and fame. **And when he becomes**

older, he becomes responsible towards others; takes care of his family, works day & night to fulfil their needs **(spiritual needs)**. He is returning what he got during childhood and young age from his parents/others/society back to his family/parents/society. This way, a life keeps on moving effortlessly, where a systematic give & take keeps on taking place in the society.

A TABLE DEPICTING RELATIONSHIP BETWEEN DIFFERENT KINDS OF NEEDS TO BIOLOGICAL STATUS TO ECONOMIC STATUS TO LEVEL OF CONSCIOUSNESS

THREE DIFFERENT STAGES OF NEED FULFILLMENT	LIFE FORM/BIO LOGICAL STATUS	ECONOMIC STATUS AT DIFFERENT STAGES OF NEED FULFILLMENT	EMOTIONAL PATTERN AT DIFFERENT STAGES OF NEED FULLFILLMENT	LEVEL OF CONSCIOUSNES S AT DIFFERENT STAGES
PHYSICAL	Animals & Humans	Poor and low income people spend their whole life meeting out their physical needs and to some extent their emotional needs	Anger, hatred, Jealousy, Frequent Physical fights, negative emotions highest as compared to other levels	1ST BASIC – Weak mind--- Decisions based on needs of body
EMOTIONAL	Humans require fulfilment of both physical and emotional needs	Middle Class people spend their life fulfilling their physical and emotional needs	Seek approval of others, Not able to Accept the facts, Fulfilment of need gives pleasure and non-fulfilment gives pain, Mix of negative and positive emotions. People may resort to unfair means	2ND MEDIUM- Weak to Medium mind. Decisions based on emotional needs which can be biased
SPIRITIUAL	Some Humans rise above physical and emotional needs to fulfil their spiritual needs.	Higher middle to upper class people having full security of physical and emotional need, rise above to next level of consciousness to fulfil their spiritual needs.	Gratitude, Kindness, Happiness, Inner peace, acceptance of facts, they have risen above pain and pleasure, contribute to society, celebrate life, Maximum Positive emotions and a very few temporary negative emotions	3RD HIGHEST- Mind guided by nature/real you... a Spiritual mind. Decisions at this level are based upon truth, unbiased.

Source: Meet the Real You Copyright Chetan Bansal

Needs are needs and shall always be a part of your life. Needs can't be zero. The quantity and frequency of your needs may change with changes in your body & mind or it may vary from person to person. Some needs may become fully extinct from your existence at some point of time and it may rise again in future; you never know. When you have a body, you will always have body needs. When you have mind, you will always have emotional needs, **when you are a spirit, you always love to GIVE as spirituality thrives on GIVING; giving is a spiritual need. Fulfilment of spiritual need thrives on giving unconditionally and not asking for anything in return.**

Happiness is dependent upon fulfilment of needs which keeps on changing due to dynamism/polarity/duality of life, leading to both failures and successes in life. Leading a spiritual way of life ensures fulfilment of all your physical, emotional & materialistic needs in an effortless manner. The higher power is spirituality which knows solutions to all your problems and guides your life all the way to a blissful & joyous journey.

The above three forms of needs discussed can be further classified into **Six Preinstalled/Default Psychological Needs (PPN)** or we can say six preinstalled software of human mind. These are as follows:

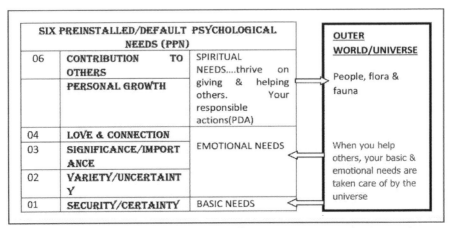

Source: Meet the Real You **Copyright:** Chetan Bansal

Like mobile phone manufacturers install some default applications in the phone, the same way our own manufacturer has preinstalled the above mentioned 6 needs/requirements in us which when fulfilled, shall give us a fulfilling life, otherwise we feel some kind of lack or void in life. **The understanding of these default needs shall help us in understanding and deciding what is right or wrong for us** or what is good or bad for us or more precisely, what is fulfilling or void for us and ultimately, what makes us happy and joyous. Various decisions in life can be taken by analysing these preinstalled needs pertaining to any particular situation/area of our life. **For example, we can easily analyse physical health, professional health, relationship health status with this PPN scan** and can decide what kind of change is required for betterment. It helps us immensely in taking personal decisions.

The use of PPN as analysing and deciding tool in any or all life situations shall help you in taking righteous decisions, always setting you on right path of life. **You will understand this in detail in PART-B (DECISION MAKING Techniques) of this book.**

As humans we have needs which can be met by the help of others. **The very basis of all relations is fulfilment of needs.** Moreover, human emotions are directly related to the quality of relations with other humans. And emotion is energy, if negative, it causes disturbance in mind and if positive, it gives peace of mind. So, to positively charge your mind & body with positive emotions, we need to maintain good relations. For that, we must understand the very basics of human relations; **what are human relations, importance of human relations, why problems in relations and how to make them harmonious?**

4.3 RELATIONS

Connecting with others at a physical, emotional, mental or spiritual levels or one/two/three/all of them is what we call a "relation", having only purpose of fulfilling your physical, emotional and spiritual needs. When we connect and start exchange of some thoughts/ideas/information or things or all, it is called a relation. The quality of the relationship is dependent upon the quality of the connection which is dependent upon the quality of the communication between two or more people involved. The problems in relations are due to miscommunications which results in disharmony and disconnection.

    And once, there is a disconnection, the give & take ends or it becomes unwanted, leading to non-fulfilment of needs & wants or dissatisfaction sets in relations. This leads to problems in one's emotion. The presence of other is causing a loss of energy (sadness, anger, frustration, hate) instead of increase in energy (happiness, joy, love, trust). **The goal & purpose of all relationships is to increase the energy through fulfilment of needs & wants. This increase in energy is what we call good feelings or happiness.** So, **EITHER** I need to mend the relationship by changing the attitude of self or other person or both **OR** change the relationship itself. If I don't do that, my life is going to be miserable as due to disturbance in emotions, I am losing my life energy/vital energy and with that making my mind & body defective and once my mind & body becomes defective, so that defect becomes my karma [wrong perceptions, decisions, actions (PDA)] which manifest miseries in my life.

"The ship of relations sails smoothly only when the rowing of ship by two or more sailors on board is in the same direction, having same speed and same frequency. Otherwise, there would be only wastage of time & energy of all on board, without any movement towards the natural goal & purpose of joyous, fruitful journey"
    -Chetan Bansal

Or in other words, it needs complete cooperation and coordination among all involved in a relationship. The more is the degree of cooperation and coordination, the better is the relationship and hence, we get the desired results. Let us understand the most important aspect of life; ***RELATIONSHIPS.***

4.3.1 HOW RELATIONSHIPS ARE FORMED; UNIVERSAL LAW OF DUALITY/POLARITY WHICH CAUSES ATTRACTION AND REPULSION IN RELATIONSHIP?

All humans are born with the same needs--physical, emotional and spiritual. **There is duality at physical** existence; Polarity: Male and female. **There is duality at emotional** level (love & hate) but **at the spiritual level, everything is one**, no duality. Spirituality is our very nature and we all thrive to find and live our nature. And for that, duality needs to be balanced. It needs to merge in to one. But all people have emotions, skills, talent, material things in different degrees; I have something in higher degree which the other has in lesser degree, which I want to give to the other and other wants to take from me with just one purpose of experiencing and balancing duality. The whole life, humans spend to fulfil their needs & wants for the ultimate purpose of experiencing and living their nature by balancing duality to achieve oneness; the ultimate source of joy beyond happiness. **This is the very backbone of all relationships between the two or many no. of people. Giving & taking is a natural phenomenon and basis on which the life thrives.**

When anything becomes excess in life, we give it back to others, to the needy ones and when anything reduces in our life, we try and acquire that from the universe (from nature, people etc.). This way, we balance our needs and wants. Balancing is universal in nature. So, in order to achieve balance, we need to fulfil our lack and the only medium is others. **So, connecting with others is nothing but relations. It is our karma to give and share what we have in excess and work to acquire what we lack.** See yourself and around, everybody is working day and night to fulfil their needs & wants, to achieve balance in their life but only through relations with others.

Say for example, the giver (mathematics teacher) having more knowledge wants to impart the knowledge to the seeker (mathematics student); they form a **student–teacher relationship**. See, the subject is same, "mathematics" where the degree/percentage of knowledge of mathematics varies among student and teacher; **this is the duality of knowledge.** Duality is the law of nature. Duality exists in the physical world. The duality of masculine and feminine, the duality of good and bad, heat and cold, energy and matter prevails in the physical world only. **In spiritual world, there is no concept of duality or polarity.** Polarity happens in physical world only; negative & positive poles of magnet, negative & positive wires of electricity, feminine & masculine etc. **Same way men and women have duality in their physical body and in emotions, but they are same spiritually.** This is only due to feminine and masculine physical nature that men and women are attracted to each other. **Polarity means same thing but in different degrees/percentages.** Like hot and cold are of same nature, the only difference is having different degrees of same nature. **Hot is less cold and cold is less hot.** So, heat wants to experience cold as it does not have cold and cold wants to experience heat as it does not have it. **That is why they attract & complete each other and**

magnifies their experience of existence. They are not opposite but different degrees of same nature.

Feminine, emotional qualities are love, care, patience, intuition. Masculine qualities are energy, self-reliance, logic. Males have all the latent qualities of a female but to a lesser degree as compared to female. Same way, females have all the latent qualities of a male but to a lesser degree as compared to male. Male want to experience feminine qualities and female wants to experience masculine qualities. That is why men and women are attracted to each other and comes close to each other in order to experience the more of the opposite qualities, qualities which they have but in a lesser degree. **While attracting, a subtle energy circuit is formed at the physical, emotional and spiritual level which makes both of them experience each other's qualities. This balances their emotions, leading to mental compatibility between them.**

All relationships are formed to fulfil either physical or emotional or spiritual or all of your needs. **It's a reality that all relations thrive on the principle of give & take.** Once give & take stops, relationship may end or one wants to give and other does not want to take or one is demanding and the other would not want to give, then also relationship ends.

Some relations may end physically, means the related persons are not sharing their personal time and space but they are connected spiritually, they are connected through their heart. These relations are beyond time & space and are truly spiritual, means that they are permanently connected through their spiritual vibrations. This is a true, loving relationship where both want to see the other person happy. True romantic relations are the examples of these relations.

4.3.2 POLARITY IN NATURE, MALE & FEMALE CAUSES ATTRACTION, CONNECTION AND THUS LEADS, TO CREATION

When we relate and connect the two opposite wires, **one positive hot wire** (means having current in it) and **other negative cold wire** (means having no current in it), both wires experience each other qualities of opposite extreme degrees resulting in balance in their qualities. The temperature and current of hot and cold wire becomes the same and they lose their originality of hot and cold, there is no difference in them. **The attraction and connection of the two extremes result in the formation of a circuit of current (electric current) which can be used to run light bulbs, air fan etc.**

Have you ever witnessed the **sunset or sunrise or both**, the beauty of sky speaks for itself. It is a meeting point of day with night or vice-versa.

"The meeting point of two extremes is where the beauty and creativity of life is"
  -Chetan Bansal

Same way humans, animals and plants are created by nature in two opposite life forms, namely male & female, having masculine & feminine qualities. This duality/polarity is the basis of reproductive system where there is a merger of two opposite energies having identical nature and upon balance of these opposite energy causes the creation of new energy called life; out of natural attraction of two opposites of same nature but varying qualities which we call love. This is the nature's way for continuity of life. **We, being a part of nature, it is our foremost duty (karma) of life, to give birth and nurture life so as to maintain continuity of life.**

When two opposites meet, they give birth to a new life, a gift of nature out of their natural attraction/love. This is an involuntary, natural, automatic love out of their nature having no control over it; that is why we call these involuntary natural relations. We, the creation of God suddenly realize and experience the power of creation within us; a moment of proud, joy, love, happiness, blessings and celebration is difficult to explain. **Then for the whole life the unconditional love** and nurture of child becomes our prime responsibility, where we are ready to sacrifice most of our needs as parents. **This spiritual need of giving without expectations** is embedded in our mind by nature to ensure continuity of life. **So we are doing nothing consciously, all is happening automatically; every action and response of ours is being controlled by nature.**

We, as real beings love not asking or taking from others but we enjoy giving; our nature is of giving and helping others without conditions. If at any point of life due to disturbance in mind ego sets in which clouds our nature of unconditional love & giving, then the focus of mind shifts from giving to asking, taking and even snatching from others; that is when relations and life becomes problematic.

Relationships magnify the experience of our life by balancing emotions, meaning that we experience and feel those emotions as well which we have in lesser degree. It gives the complete experience of all positive emotions of nature. Duality leads to love & attraction and love is the source for all the creation in this world.

Nature derives its creative power from love. By love, happiness increases which increases the cosmic power within us and that cosmic energy **gives immense inner strength & creative power which further leads to personal growth and success in every area of your life viz. HWRC.** Love completes the person in every respect and aspect of life, leading to a peace of mind and once the mind is at peace, it becomes a creative mind, a helping mind and contributes to the well-being of others. **This is how personal growth of an individual leads to a happy and prosperous society.** This is all natural and automatic result of love.

True love has the power to heal, even deadly diseases and there are many instances in history where the people have been cured of incurable disease just by getting immense love and care in their relationships. Thus, having good relations is the key to your success and personal growth. **THE MOST IMPORTANT POINT HERE IS TO UNDERSTAND THAT WE ARE GETTING SUCCESS, GROWTH AND HAPPINESS FROM THE INCREASE IN COSMIC ENERGY IN OUR PERSONAL SPACE AND THE ENERGY WE ARE GETTING IS THROUGH GOOD-LOVING RELATIONS. BUT THE BIG QUESTION IS, CAN WE GET THAT COSMIC ENERGY FROM OTHER SOURCES ALSO?** This shall become clearer as the book progresses.

4.3.3 TYPES OF RELATIONSHIPS

Almost all relations are natural, automatic and involuntary, where the creation of relationship was not under your control and decided by nature. Although, the creation of relationship happened through nature but the quality of these relationships is decided by your quality of giving/response/dealing/action (Your Karma) which determines the quality of receiving in relations (Results/fruits) and thus, the quality of your life viz. success and happiness in your life.

Everybody has relationships but the happier ones, the luckier ones know how to deal with these relationships. People deal and interact with their relations in a different way based on their varying degree of consciousness and perception that determines varying degree of success in relations. **There are three types of relations:**
1) RELATIONS WITH MIND & BODY OF SELF
2) RELATIONSHIP WITH OTHER LIVING AND NON-LIVING FORMS IN THE UNIVERSE
3) RELATIONS WITH OTHER HUMANS

1). RELATIONS WITH MIND & BODY OF SELF (NATURAL, AUTOMATIC, INVOLUNTARY) as you do not choose your mind and body consciously, but this relationship is decided by super intelligence of nature. **The relationship with your mind & body is life-long.** Once the physical life ends, so does the relationship with physical body ends but your mind is always a part of your soul and never part ways with you. Once you enter your new life, you get a new physical body but the mind remains the same as of previous life.

Your mind & body thrives upon energy. For you to achieve success in the outer world, it depends upon the degree of control that you exercise over your mind & body. The best way to control your mind & body is by treating them with eternal life energy which will increase the energy field/aura of your personal space, leading to a healthy physical body and highly conscious/super intelligent mind. Choosing right thoughts, natural food, right water intake habits, and natural breathing patterns is the best way to increase the energy & consciousness of your mind & body. A highly conscious mind leads to righteous PDA, further leading to attraction of righteous people & situations in life and thus, a happy life.

The difference with different people is having varying degree consciousness of same mind leading to different karma and thus, different results in life.

2) RELATIONSHIP WITH OTHER FORMS OF LIVING AND NON-LIVING THINGS IN THE UNIVERSE (NATURAL, AUTOMATIC, INVOLUNTARY).

You are naturally related to air, water, soil, planets, sun and moon from which you get the energy to grow and maintain your mind & body. We humans have either knowingly or unknowingly polluted the air, soil and water by our irresponsible acts towards nature. Whatever you give to nature, it comes back to you multiplied. The food from polluted soil, the water from polluted water bodies and the air from polluted air enters our mind & body, making them unnatural, defective and prone to many diseases, makes life miserable.

This relationship is also life long and this relationship is not about individual karma, **but joint karma of masses/majority of people.** If the majority of people are acting in an irresponsible way towards nature, the results are borne by everybody, even the people with responsible actions. So it is very important to spread awareness among masses about their actions toward nature and its impact on their own life. This give and take with universe is life long and we all must practice focussed and aware giving to the nature in order to get quality results from nature for a quality life.

3) RELATIONS WITH OTHER HUMANS

3A). SOME HUMAN RELATIONS ARE INVOLUNTARY BLOOD RELATIONS LIKE PARENTS, BROTHER OR SISTER.

Relationship between parents and a child is the most natural relationship and this is a true relationship of unconditional love, where parents love, nurture and care for their children without any expectation in return or they expect only the well-being of their child. The dynamics of this relationship is simple and whatever little changes this relationship witness, one thing remains constant that both parents and children want each other to be happy all the time.

Relationships with your brother, sisters or with other relatives of your family may or may not be strong and its strength depends upon the fulfilment of your psychological needs. The more is the fulfilment of needs, the stronger is the bond of relationship; the lesser is the fulfilment of needs, the lesser is the bond or it may just be a formal relationship where you just meet at family gatherings and the presence or absence of anybody does not mean anything to you or does not matter to you.

3B). SOME HUMAN RELATIONS ARE VOLUNTARY MADE OUT OF LOVE FOR THE FULFILMENT OF PSYCHOLOGICAL NEEDS LIKE FRIENDSHIP, ROMANTIC OR MARRIAGE.

But again, this is also an involuntary relationship. We might think that we have chosen our friends, life partner etc. but it is actually your karma, your energy vibrations that has chosen all your relations. We shall understand the amazing law of karma in PART-B of this book.

3C). SOME HUMAN RELATIONSHIPS ARE VOLUNTARY, "FINANCIAL AND CONTRACTUAL", which is formed to gain profits in monetary terms like **business relations,** where one supplies the goods or services or both in exchange for money.

Employee-Employer: Where the employee gives his time and presence to accomplish some job/work for the employer and employer gives salary in return. When the employee is not able to fulfil his job responsibilities or the employee chooses another company with a better salary or better working conditions or both, this relation ends.

Educational institutions-student: You take education and give money in return, once you complete your education, the relationship ends or if the student is not satisfied with the quality of education, he leaves and joins the new educational institution.

Medical facilities: You take medical facilities and give money in return, once you get the required treatment, the relationship ends or if the patient does not get the required treatment, he/she shifts to another hospital or if the hospital does not have the required infrastructure to treat patient's illness, they shift the patient to another hospital which has better desired health facilities.

The time duration of every relationship is limited to the time of fulfilment of needs. So, some relations are temporary and some are long term or even lifelong, depending upon the bond you developed in a particular relationship. Sometimes you meet somebody as your colleague in office, school mate, college mate or business partner or business associate or any type of relationship, but you also develop an emotional bond with each other and become friends or become business partners or become life partners. **So you converted a short-term relationship into a long-term or life long relationship depending upon your liking and understanding with others.**

The purpose of any contractual relationship is the very backbone of a relationship. The moment you stop getting what you were supposed to get from a relationship, the relationship goes haywire or comes to a dead end. Like you started a business for a profit and now if profits are not coming or you are incurring losses, you will definitely stop that business or business relationship **because the basic purpose of relationship is no more alive now, it's dead. And once the need/purpose of relationship is dead, the relationship is also dead. This is how all contractual relationship works.** If employee does not get the salary, if student does not get the education, if a supplier does not get his payment, if an employee gets better job somewhere else; the relationship ends.

The strength of relationships! *Be it any relationship, the more is the interdependence on each other for fulfilment of your physical, materialistic,* *emotional and spiritual needs, the stronger is the relationship.* It's a reality that all relations are need-based. EVEN IF WE LOVE SOMEBODY UNCONDITIONALLY WITHOUT EXPECTING ANYTHING IN RETURN, WE ARE STILL FULFILLING OUR NEED FOR LOVE. We love, care, respect and fulfil the needs & wants of the special person in life even if the other person is not giving anything in return, **why? Because** you feel it's your responsibility to help the other person, **you get happiness by helping them, and also because you feel connected to them.** Then, what you are getting, my dear friend? **You are fulfilling your spiritual need and your spiritual nature is to love unconditionally without expectations.** You just want the other person to be happy because the happiness of other person gives you happiness. So you are getting happiness which is your spiritual need, the highest need of life. Parents have this unconditional love for their children, even if children don't love and respect their parents. **Real friendship bonds and real marriage relationships are governed by unconditional love** for each other where they just want to see the other person happy and does not expect anything in return; they unconditionally trust, respect, accept and does not blame but understand each other and even help in personal growth of each other. **Can this attitude be the solution for all relationship problems? Probably yes! We need to understand, learn and practice that.**

Fulfilling emotional needs like respect and care, along with contractual needs is always a boon to a relationship and creates a strong bond beyond times. In business relations like employee-employer, if a person gets more than the contract, relationship becomes stronger, and if less, the relationship becomes sore and ultimately vanishes. **For example, if an employee gets respect, importance in his job**, his emotional needs are fulfilled and that employee in return to that respect will naturally and sincerely work more for the company, which further will help in the increased profits and growth of the company. **Again, in return the company can give promotion**, increment in the salary to sincere and hardworking people which can further strengthen the bond between the employee and the employer. Even if for some reason the employee leaves the organization, the employer will always remember them for their love, care and respect towards him. **These are timeless bonds beyond any contracts. That is why it is very important to respect everybody that you meet in your life, irrespective of his/her colour, caste, creed, religion and socio-economic status in order to create a timeless bond.** You never know which person will come handy in your life at any point of time, so you should always be helpful, humble and down to earth in your attitude towards others for a better, fulfilling and happy life.

MARRIAGE IS THE MOST IMPORTANT RELATIONSHIP IN HUMAN LIFE.

It is the relationship which fulfils all of your needs; **physical, emotional and spiritual.** Having a harmonious marriage is must for a happy, joyous and successful life. Marriage, though contractual relationship but is the base of all blood relations, **so we can call MARRIAGE the most natural/divine relationship which serves the divine purpose of creation, nurture of life and hence continuity of life on planet earth.**

The purpose of marriage is to fulfil all your physical, emotional, spiritual needs and fulfil the purpose of continuity of life. The more the needs are being fulfilled on a regular basis, the stronger becomes the bond. Spiritual responsibility for continuity of life by giving birth to life and nurturing that life is our prime responsibility. **Spiritual need is amazing, being a need which thrives on giving.** The basic fundamental of spirituality is to give unconditionally and the amazing fact about it is that it gives immense happiness; actually it fulfils the voids in our life. **Sexuality is also a part of spiritual need** where both involved give love to each other which give birth to a new life and that life is a gift to the giver/givers which bestows immense happiness or more appropriately something more than happiness, "bliss" to both the parents. Amazing, isn't it!

Marriage although, is a contractual relationship but it is the foundation of all blood relations. So, this becomes the most important relationship or the supreme of all relations or father of all relations in life. Happiness in this relationship determines the happiness of whole family like children, grandparents etc. **So choosing a right partner is very important but more important is living a harmonious relationship with your partner** and the only way to harmonious relations is by giving respect and fulfilling all your responsibilities towards each other.

If anything goes haywire in your marriage, you can restore harmony by understanding and working on your relations like when **your physical health weakens**, you work upon your health, get medical treatment and become healthy again. **But the bitter truth of today's world is that most of the marriages are ending in divorce as people don't want to understand the problems and work upon them.** And most of the times when these divorced people remarry another person, they face the same problems that they faced in their previous marriage and again end up in divorce. Most of the times, it's an issue of trust and the other times, it's the misunderstanding due to miscommunication which further creates an illusionary mistrust that causes emotional disturbances, making you take wrong decisions in haste. **And in most of the cases, people regret in future.** Okay, I understand your pain but if there is some problem, you need to give some time and some space before jumping to conclusions. **You must need to understand the dynamics of driving the car because changing that car won't make you a perfect driver.**

The only solution to good, timeless relations is your capability of understanding and handling the other person in the most compassionate way and for that, first you need to understand your true-self, your relations, your life, and your problems to re-develop harmony in relations. **It is your mind operating from a lower consciousness which has caused problems** and the only solution is your conscious presence, your connection to your *REAL*

YOU, a higher power above mind to activate natural intelligence, clear perspective, right decisions and right actions for a timeless bond which is not dependent upon or affected by any situation; situations which are temporary & dependent upon time. **Understand, learn, practice and make spiritual attitude your way of life to regain harmony in your relations, and everything you desire in your life is discussed in PART-B OF THIS BOOK.**

HOW RELATIONSHIPS BECOME PROBLEMATIC OR WHAT CAUSES REPULSION IN RELATIONSHIPS?

Opposite attract and the same repulse, so when different or opposite qualities of same nature gets changed to the same degree or the differences in degree becomes less prominent, they repel each other. **When the voltage of a hot wire becomes very high that the cold wire is not able to bear; the cold wire melts away and the circuit is broken.** This is a typical case of suppression of one by other. When one person in relationship becomes very dominating, the other fears loss of his/her original nature and thus, runs away from the relation. Only thick wires can bear the high power voltage and one person being weak emotionally cannot bear the high volt aggression of the other person. **And when the voltage of hot wire is too low,** there is not enough energy for the cold wire to receive, which does not satisfy the needs of cold wire; hence the flow of energy, chances of attraction are low and thus, the chances of creation are also very low. **When the degrees of two opposite became same or nearly same, they lose attraction and repulse each other**.

THIS IS HOW REPULSION OCCURS:-
1). BOREDOM DUE TO TOO MUCH OF CLOSENESS. When too much closeness happens, the hot wire starts to lose its heat to the cold wire and/or vice versa, so they repel to retain their originality, after all everybody loves their originality. **Same happens with men and women, after too much of closeness, they lose their originality** or you can say, when men experience too much of femininity or women experience too much of masculinity, they fear the loss of their originality or they are bored of too much experience of other quality and want something new in their experience. **Boredom has set in your relations.** That is also the reason that after a long relationship, your attraction for each other reduces and you repel. **Then is the time to create a time gap between the relations, so as to get back the original attraction.**

2). MEN LOSE HIS MASCULINITY OR WOMEN LOSE HER FEMININITY OVER A PERIOD OF TIME DUE TO CHANGES IN THEIR BODY. Men are not able to give their masculinity to women and women are not able to give femininity to men. In other words, their degree of nature becomes same and hence they repel each other.

3). ONE OF THEM LOSES THEIR NATURE OF FEMININITY/MASCULINITY. Then one is not able to fulfil the need of other. So again, there is no attraction.

In all the above three cases, they are not able to complete each other or in other words, the give & take in a relationship has ended or there is no duality left in them or they have become same, thus leading to repulsion. **E.g. Men being aggressive** and full of energy shall always be attracted to women who are soft, loving and caring but when men becomes soft and women are also soft, their duality ends and with that ends the attraction; so they repel. **Similarly, when women become very aggressive** and men by nature are aggressive, their duality ends. So this will cause ego clash, leading to unnecessary, frequent fights & quarrels between them; so they repel or the relationship ends. **Same way, two men with equal power cannot be friends**, there has to be a certain degree of difference in their power for a relationship to exist. Two men in same profession with almost same professional skills and qualities become competitors but can't be friends. They can only become friends once they rise above the concept of duality and show respect & love for each other out of their spiritual nature. **This shows us that end of duality or becoming same cause repulsion in need based relationships but timeless bonds are beyond duality and needs, which thrive on unconditional love for each other.**

THE MAIN CAUSE OF PROBLEMS IN RELATIONSHIPS IS YOUR DYNAMIC DUAL MIND WHICH KEEPS ON CHANGING WITH CHANGING TIMES.

_DUALITY AFFECTS YOUR RELATIONS IN 2 WAYS:-

1). DUE TO DUALITY IN MIND & BODY, PEOPLE HAVE VARYING DEGREE OF ENERGY & CONSCIOUSNESS WHICH LEADS TO VARYING DEGREE OF PERCEPTIONS, BELIEFS AND OPINIONS. We must understand, value, respect and appreciate the differences of physical forms, perceptions, beliefs, skills, profession, colour, caste, creed, race of different people as differences are the source of fulfilment of your needs and thus, the very basis on which life thrive. But we always try to prove our beliefs right and of others wrong. You are not accepting or approving or appreciating the views of others, making them feel disrespectful. This causes a dispute. It is very difficult to change mind of self and you are thinking of changing the mind of somebody else. If you want to change something, then change your own attitude and learn to understand and accept people as they are. Ask yourself; don't you want people to accept you as you are? If yes, why not do the same with others?

2). ALSO, THE BELIEFS & PERCEPTIONS OF PEOPLE KEEP ON CHANGING WITH CHANGE IN THEIR ENERGY FIELD CAUSED BY

1) Change in time due to change in planetary movements which bring about the changes in your energy field and thus body & mindset. Your needs & wants keep on changing with age.
2) Due to the influence of different people & situations having different energy fields, your mindset (thought process) changes leading to change in your decisions/actions.

3) Due to the influence of different places having different energy fields. You must have noticed, at some places you get positive feelings and some negative bringing about the change in your mood & behaviour. And you don't know the reason; the only reason is different energy field of different places.

All the above factors change the energy field, mindset and thus needs of a person. This happens with everybody, you can check this on yourself. As your mind & body keeps on changing, so does your needs & wants. That is why, once some need which is a priority with both of you is now not a priority with the both of you or for one of you. **Changes in needs & wants of a person may change your opposite qualities, to become same, causing repulsion** and most of the times this is the only reason for problems in relations. **And how the opposite qualities became same or nearly same** is due to change in emotions caused by change in mind that has changed due to change in physical bodies, caused by change in energies. And the energies change due to change in time which changes due to change in movement of planets and various astral bodies. And the change in astral bodies has changed the degree or percentage of energies of one's mind & body, thus effecting the change in needs & wants. **How change in needs & wants bring about the repulsion?** This change in need & want makes the other person incapable of fulfilling the new need and/or change in one's emotions may make them incapable of fulfilling the need of the other. So once a thriving relationship, where a natural attraction and natural give & take was taking place has now become dull, non-attractive or repulsive.

Changes happen in your mind, body and needs. You always want a loving & flourishing relationship and you really want to revive the relationship but the constant blaming, complaining and tagging your acts as intentional by the other person makes you withdraw from a worsening relationship. But are you at the receiving end or are you treating the other person like this? You **must understand and respect that the changes can happen with the others too and you should not develop a blaming attitude towards them.** Remember, most of the times, it is not the intentions but the uncontrolled changes in mind due to changes in time can cause problems in relations/life. **Change is life, everything in life keeps on changing.** If the time has caused some problem in your relations/life, you just need to understand, trust, love, respect self and the other and with patience & faith, the same time will give you the solution at the right time.

4.4 HOW RELATIONS & LIFE BECAME PROBLEMATIC
WITH SELF, OTHERS AND UNIVERSE

NOT GIVING IN A RELATIONSHIP OR TOO MUCH OF EXPECTATIONS FROM OTHERS IS THE REASON FOR NON-FULFILMENT OF SELF NEEDS & WANTS AND

HENCE, PROBLEMATIC RELATIONS CAUSED BY A MIND WITH LOWER CONSCIOUSNESS.

The problems in relations start not when we stop getting from a relationship but when we stop giving in a relationship. *To get, we need to give first; a simple law of need fulfilment.*

Spiritual need thrives on *GIVING* out of love without expectations.

Physical & emotional need thrives upon *RECEIVING*.

So, a person has both natural qualities of GIVING and RECEIVING. When a person stops giving, his/her receiving of physical and emotional needs stop which is the cause of pain & miseries. **Fulfilling physical & emotional needs of others is the cause of real happiness and it is only giving on which life thrives. If you stop giving or have undue expectations** which the other is incapable of fulfilling, it is going to make your relations problematic and life of all involved miserable.

The truth about physical and emotional needs is that their intensity and frequency changes with changing times. Need based relations are always like this, they can never be permanent, but are dynamic. Unaware of this truth, people upon non-fulfilment of self needs & wants feel that their trust has been broken, they have been used & manipulated, starts doubting the intentions of the other person, blaming the other person, wants to teach a lesson to the other person, wants to prove the other wrong and self as right and **ultimately, intentionally stops fulfilling the needs of the other person.** They do not want to listen and understand the other person. **Sooner or later, the other person feels unaccepted, disrespected** and even he/she intentionally stops giving to the other person. **Or the person was about to come back in normal relationship** but didn't due to the negative attitude and behaviour of the other person. **Whatever may be the reason, non-fulfilment of needs devalues the person, the respect for each other goes away, with respect goes the communication and with communication goes the love, care & affection and misunderstanding takes over the space of relations.**

The disagreements and fights are part of all relations but it is all balanced by understanding, love, care and empathy. If you can't balance your disagreements with understanding, you do not have the right to be happy. But if the people involved are rigid, do not want to listen to others, think themselves as right and others wrong, then your relationship space witnesses more fights than love. **Slowly and steadily, over a period of time frequent, intense fight become more prominent and value & respect for each other goes away. Then constant anger, frustration, judgements, control, emotional reactions are the only emotions left in a relationship.** Communication is taking place from the level of mind and not from the level of heart. Both of you or all involved have become emotionally disturbed, immensely negative and lost all of your energy & consciousness; a super intelligence of life. A negative space/negative environment only attracts more negativity, and therefore, attracting more miseries in your life.

Soon, negative emotions take over the space of the relationship and once these negative emotions become more prominent, more negativity becomes a part of this relation. Your mind forgets the positive qualities/good deeds of the other person and only reminds all the past bad experiences with that person. **The mind focus is now only on the few negative qualities of the other person and expands that negativity exponentially.** Your mind is filled only with negativity about the other person, making you react unreasonably in an aggressive manner on every act and behaviour of other. If the other person is also negative or having low consciousness, he/she also react in an aggressive manner. **This give & take of aggression keeps on taking place unless it reaches a peak from where silence takes over. Again, a slightest of irritation spark the heated exchanges, you two have now become totally unconscious, unaware of your actions.** Your perception/intelligence has been clouded by negative emotions where you can only take blunder decisions. Human untrained/unaware mind who does not know how to deal with this challenging situation, breaks down the communication, creates a wall between the two; ego sets in and thinks of ending the relationship as a permanent solution.

You become either **overtly depressive or overtly aggressive: Overtly depressive**--to fulfil your lacking needs, you resort to drugs or may even choose suicide. Drugs are unnatural chemicals which gives you a temporary high. The need for drugs have risen because the production of natural biochemical (hormones) have been hindered/blocked due to low vital energy/*prana Shakti (power)* due to negative emotions created attitude of internal resistance in response to the outside situation. Drugs harm your physical body over a period of time, making your hormonal system defective. So bio-chemicals are not being released and you become too much dependent upon drugs for your happiness which is nothing but addiction. **Overtly aggressive**--people may resort to physical or verbal abuse/violence or if it is about marriage, they may choose divorce or in severe cases, may even choose to kill/murder the other involved.

You have become negative, the other person has become negative or one of you is negative. The meeting of two negatives lead to decrease in energy and disturbance of mind. Mind loses its peace, creativity, love and once that happens, all negativity engulfs your mind; anger, hatred, blame, verbal abuse and heated exchanges. All in all, emotional disturbances have become your way of life/relations which not only harms you but your family and everybody involved. **Even you are not able to take care of your health, wealth, job/career/profession** making your life a complete misery. **Ego sets in, you separate yourself from the other**, you view the other as different, you are not able to accept and forgive them as you fear repetition of past problems.

Your nature is being clouded by disturbed emotions, leading to wrong karma (PDA) that further deteriorates your relations and your mind, making your life more miserable. You chose the relation for happiness and now the same relation has become the source of miseries. **This is the time to understand life/relations from a broader perspective in order to find solutions.** Do not haste into decisions, give some space and time to yourself and to the other person.

You have become weak, emotionally and mentally; fragile. This is the time when negative people with vested interests may come in your life, influencing you to take the wrong decisions. These people will pretend to be your friends but in real, they are not and have come in your life just to gain something from you. If you listen to them and act on their advice, it can create an irreversible damage in your relations/life. So be very careful about anybody's advice in those difficult times. **Do not share your problems with anybody/everybody but only with expert psychologists and some very close friends** who really care about you; want to help you by realising and correcting your mistakes.

THE EFFECT OF HARMONY, DISHARMONY IN YOUR RELATIONS/TEAM WORK BE IT ANY, VOLUNTARY OR INVOLUNTARY.

When two negatives meet, the result is -1-1= -11, lowest degree of coordination and cooperation; going down in life.

When one negative meets one positive, the result is 1-1=0, one is cooperative but the other is not, your energies/your hard work is being wasted and sooner you shall go down, do not get disturbed by negativity of the other person, help them become positive again for the benefit of both or all involved.

And

When two positives meet, the result is 1+1=11, highest level of degree of cooperation and coordination, even your small effort is fetching you many fold positive results. Keep it up; you are on the right track.

DUE TO YOUR NEGATIVE ATTITUDE YOU HAVE MANIFESTED PROBLEMATIC RELATIONS WITH OTHER HUMANS, MOTHER NATURE, YOUR OWN MIND & BODY AND PROFESSIONAL RELATIONS

Not only your relations with spouse, parents, children, brother and sisters are in stray but a negative mindset, an emotional, disturbed mind can only manifest bad relations with everybody else, be it professional or with nature or with wealth. **As an emotional disturbance means bad relations with your own mind & body which makes your personal space negative.** And a negative space only attracts negativity, nothing else.

1) We have created bad relations with the nature, why? Because we are not valuing, respecting nature, we have polluted it knowingly or unknowingly and it is coming back to us in the form of natural calamities and diseases.

2) We have bad relationship with our body because we are giving it polluted air/water/food. We are feeding it with chemically processed food. We have made our body lethargic by choosing unhealthy life style. What came back from the body are just physical & mental diseases.

3) We have bad relationship with our mind as we are not giving our mind the right guidance, right understanding. We have shifted its focus on negative emotions; we have shifted its focus on problems instead of solutions. Mind is your child, it needs your guidance but instead you have been acting based upon the raw assumptions, unprocessed thoughts of your mind leading to wrong perception, wrong decisions and wrong actions which attract miseries in life.

4) You have bad relations with other humans and other life forms, parents, spouse, children, friends etc., plants, animals, planets, moon, sun as you are not respecting and valuing them; they have always fulfilled your needs and instead of being grateful to them, you are busy finding faults in them.

5) You are not giving your focus and time to your profession, you are not giving 100% in your planning and execution and you blame that you do not get the right salary or you do not get the right profits or you are not able to produce the right products/services for your clients.

So **you have problems everywhere** due to your own wrong actions as you do not understand what is right or wrong. This further creates wrong results and miseries in life, creating more emotional disturbances in life. **Wow! Great! You are lucky, god has thrown you an opportunity to understand, learn and grow in life.** Let's be grateful to him.

WHO IS TO BE BLAMED FOR PROBLEMS IN RELATIONS AND LIFE? WELL! IRRESPONSIBLE/UNAWARE ACTIONS OF HUMAN MIND COMING FROM LOWER CONSCIOUSNESS IS TO BE BLAMED.

The real problem with humans is their mind, a mind which can be very **destructive if operating at lower consciousness or very constructive if operating at higher consciousness or a mind with medium consciousness which is neither very destructive nor creative but somewhere in between.** During the life time of a person it keeps of swaying between lower to higher consciousness and thus is sometimes problematic and sometimes amazingly constructive at its best. This gives rise to all sadness and happiness in life.

On the other hand, nature had no choice or its consciousness is of highest level which is predetermined, making all the actions of nature spiritual. They only give without expectations and hence do not suffer in life like sun, earth etc. They do not have emotions and thus can't lose their energy, power, value and are always on the right path of giving, without any expectations. **They have no duality of mind and thus the only choice they have is to give/serve others exactly with same amount of quality and precision every time, without any variations.**

Same way, animals do not have a much choice, their needs are simple and basic. Their only actions are to feed their body with food, water, sex and sleep. These are the basic needs of body which they fulfil easily. They do not have the mind to think beyond these needs and thus, do not have big desires, so their problems are also few.

A human mind highly evolved has been bestowed with so many creative powers but the same powers become destructive for self, other humans, animals, plants and the mother nature if the consciousness of mind becomes defective. The very powers of the mind makes the humans feel very powerful and supreme, which might make them greedy, diverting them away from the path of truth/nature. **They want to conquer and control everything, taking wrong actions without any care, respect and responsibility towards others.** They are not aware of the fact that whatever they give comes back to them even multiplied and their irresponsible actions manifest in miseries.

So miseries in human life is due to their unaware actions and much desired happiness comes with responsible/right actions and for that, first action should be to raise energy & consciousness to manifest all success in life. *THAT IS WHY, A HUMAN MIND AT HIGHER CONSCIOUSNESS IS YOUR BEST FRIEND AND AT LOWER CONSCIOUSNESS IS YOUR WORST ENEMY. So, having a big size brain can be a boon or a bane, depending upon your conscious choice. The varying degree of consciousness of humans is the cause of varying degree of success while animals on the other hand have near same degree of consciousness and thus, their life patterns are almost same.*

HOW COME MINDSET/PERSONAL SPACE BECAME NEGATIVE OR UNCONSCIOUS?

This does not happen in one day. When you were born, you were completely natural, full of energy and full of life. Once you started growing up, you were exposed to various people around you like your parents, family, school, friends, neighbours etc. Human mind subconsciously absorb attitude, actions and behaviours of people whom so ever it comes in contact with. As most of the people are not aware about the truth of life, they developed negative behaviour/attitude over a period of time which you also absorbed subconsciously. **You absorbed negative/disempowering beliefs, habits from the people & situations in your life.** So, they are to be blamed. **It is not that they taught you negativity intentionally but they just shared their views, opinions and beliefs with you to the best of their knowledge.** They are also unhappy in their life and you have absorbed the perfect recipe for unhappiness/miseries from them unknowingly. It has happened slowly and steadily over a period of time. You were not aware of your thoughts, emotions, actions & reactions and your unawareness have made you what you are today. You absorbed unconscious state of others subconsciously and became unconscious yourself and your continuous unconscious actions made you more unconscious, leading to all the negativity and miseries. **Ultimately, your unawareness is to be blamed.** Same happens with the other person they are also unaware of what is right or wrong. **So blame the unaware mind of you and others which is same and not different.**

Physical life thrives upon GIVE AND TAKE. And to get, you must give first and that too it a manner which is useful for the other and not in a manner which you think is right. **If everybody conditions his/her mind to give only after receiving, then how would anyone get his/her needs fulfilled.** This attitude is conditional and not based on your nature of giving. This attitude hinders the natural give and take cycle and thus, hinders the quality of relationships/life; only attract miseries in life. **If the other person has stopped giving, it's your responsibility to rise above your needs and continue giving.** The other person might have become incapable of giving due to any reason but if you are capable of giving and still choose not to as you want your expectations to be met first, you have lost your natural intelligence, natural love and negativity has clouded your nature. **Then, you are to be blamed. If the other person also has the same attitude, both of you are to be blamed.**

But if you dig deep, it is only you who is to be blamed for any or all problems in all of your relations and thus, life. Your thought process, your own mind is to be blamed and not the other person.** You do not know how to control and manage your thoughts & emotions. **If the people & situations are able to create disturbance in you, it clearly indicates that you are weak, mentally & emotionally** and any disturbance/problem outside your body is affecting you negatively. The emotional disturbance makes you incapable of performing your responsibilities, incapable of dealing with difficult life situations and you have lost the power to give.

When this can happen with you, the same can happen with others too. So, they need your understanding and support but you being disturbed yourself become incapable of understanding, helping and supporting others. You can't give the other person and the other is also not giving you then who will give to the both of you? Needs of both is not being fulfilled and how can a relationship thrive without fulfilment of needs? Both have become weak, have nothing to offer but only demand, you have lost value in the eyes of other; puts away the other person.

You think that the other person is creating problems deliberately. Your expectations are not being met. But I ask you a simple question, are you able to meet all expectations from yourself, is your mind listening to you or under your control? And if not, your own relationship with your mind & body is not perfect and you are expecting a perfect relationship with other humans who are also a slave of their mind & body. **When you do not understand yourself, how can you understand other people?** A person always attracts people & situations which are aligned to his/her mindset or a person always gets what he/she deserves based upon their karma/actions. So if you are not happy in life, only you to be blamed and not others.

The very non-fulfilment of your needs cause disturbances in your emotions, leading to unconscious mind & body devoid of positive energy. The focus of your mind has shifted to others; you want to control, change, take revenge, hate and you are angry on others; keep on thinking about others. This has filled your mind with all the negativity and a negative mind can never give you solutions, growth and prosperity.

Your intelligence has been hijacked by your negative emotions, making your PDA defective, biased, unreal, and away from the truth, leading to miseries in life. Physical and emotional needs are always fulfilled by others and to get ours need fulfilled, we need to have good relations with others. **And good relation means the act of giving to the other has to be perfect, exactly the way the other wants and not the way you think is right or comfortable with.** The key is to understand the other person; his/her needs, exactly the way they are without any bias. Unaware of the truth, you have stopped giving or your act of giving is wrong or not up to the mark or up to the satisfaction of others. So your relationships with your own mind & body, other people, flora & fauna, nature, and universe has been corrupted due to your unawareness and you expect a right reward from them, isn't it foolish on your part?

Till now you have corrupted your mind & body by wrong attitude towards life and created internal disharmony. Your unhealthy mind & body's unfocussed/unaware actions has led to wrong results in your job/career, you have wasted your hard-earned money on unnecessary expenses, your life has become directionless, without any clue/clarity about what is right or wrong, you created disharmony with nature, with other people and has thus, attracted negative results in your life. So boss, only you are to be blamed. And unaware of your own wrong actions, you are blaming others.

My dear, become aware of your actions, your responses and you will come to know that your own actions taken in the past has manifested your present situations. It's high time if you understand this. This is going to be the most amazing day of your life, a new you is born, my dear **REAL YOU**. Now, you just need to analyse your wrong actions and change your action/response in your present moment, to manifest the desired situations in future. It is only your response to the situation which determines the outcome of the situation, so respond wisely to make yourself lucky. **Understand your wrong actions/karma and bring about a right change in your actions/karma to get the desired output.**

Once you change your response to the situation, you will be able to control the situation. You will be able to transform the negative situation to the positive one or a negative relation to the positive one.

WHOSE RESPONSIBILITY IS TO MEND THE RELATIONSHIP?

The other may or may not take a step forward depending upon their state of mind but you should take a responsibility to heal/mend the relationship, irrespective of the choice of the other person. As life of many is involved, you being the **REAL YOU** should step forward and make a move towards positivity. After all, life is all about you, your actions have created problematic situation, and so for the sake of your own happiness, you should take the right step. If others want to change, improve or not, let them decide, it's their karma. Help them if they choose life, if they choose positivity but you have to choose life, irrespective of their choice. The problem is that people don't want to accept their problems, think themselves as right and do not want to change. **A rigid mind is the cause of all problems in life. In life, all of us face problems and challenges but the luckier ones are those who are flexible in mind;** wants to know the truth about problems, focus on solutions to learn and improve upon their thoughts and actions. And you reading this proves that you are the *REAL YOU,* a flexible mind, a keen learner of life who wants to grow in life, who wants to come out of their shell and expand his/her limits and explore what is beyond your present consciousness.

SO WHAT IS THE SOLUTION FOR ALL YOUR RELATIONS; WITH SELF, OTHERS, AND UNIVERSE?

Before jumping to conclusions and taking decisions in haste, you must first understand yourself; mind, needs & wants and your nature. This shall help you find & realize your true nature and also help you understand the other person in a better way. Give some time and space to the other person, you become who you are and let them become who they are. Always keep the communication alive from the level of your heart (nature) and not from the level of your mind (disturbed emotions). All in all, you need to be fully focussed, consciously present in all your relations to understand, perceive, decide and act in a way that is beneficial for everyone involved.

As physical and emotional needs keep on changing with changing times, it brings about changes in your body & mind, so the intensity and satisfaction of these relations also keeps on changing with changing time. **So dealing with these relations from a level of mind can never be a solution,** as mind also keeps on changing, it can never understand the differences in opinions, beliefs and perceptions. **A problem of mind can only be solved by a higher power called nature which is universal & permanent**; a super intelligence which knows and understands everything about you and your life.

You were focusing on mediums; other people & situations whom diverted the focus of your mind, influenced your mind, diverting you from your natural path of life. **What you want in your life; happiness, joy, bliss, pleasure which can only be possible once you change your focus on to yourself; growth in energy and consciousness, to make your PDA truthful for successful life.**

You need to first manage your own mind; thoughts and emotions. The best way is to rise above your emotional disturbance is to make yourself powerful and strong again; a person who is not perturbed by any of the unwanted people & situations, a person who is not dependent upon others, instead is capable of fulfilling the needs of others without any expectations. If others are not loving, appreciating and accepting you, it is your duty to accept, love and appreciate yourself; why depend upon others?

Your mind thrives upon love, acceptance, approval and appreciation for it does not matter who does it, either you or the other person.
        -Chetan Bansal

BEST WAY TO DEAL WITH ALL YOUR RELATIONS AND THUS, LIFE.
When you understand, accept, respect, help and love yourself and others unconditionally, a need based relation is transmuted to a spiritual/timeless relation, a source of permanent peace and bliss. **Giving without expectations makes you valuable and attractive again** and you automatically get back the respect, love, care and affection. Your raised vibrations/emotions not only heals you but also heals the other person, activates the nature of the other person and once both of your nature is restored to normal, relationship is also restored to normal.

        Once this nature, a source of life becomes dominant in you, all your needs, be it physical, emotional or spiritual are being taken care of by the nature/universe. So, let's live all your relations from a spiritual space/supernatural space/super intelligent space higher than your mind and it shall take care of you.

        After understanding the importance of your relations with your own mind & body, with other humans, with plants, animals, the whole universe, the changes you need to bring about in yourself and the ultimate solution by practicing spiritual way of life, you shall easily be able to maintain harmony within, with others and once that happens, life becomes easy, effortless and fruitful.

        In the rarest of cases, even after living a relationship with attitude of spirituality, you will come to know that you two are separate like water and oil and you may need to part ways. But the irony today is that people have made rarest common out of their ignorance and lack of awareness.

        For all your practical understanding and actions regarding mending your relations with yourself and others are covered in PART-B & C of this book; converting an unconscious/negative mind to a conscious/positive/spiritual mind.

4.5 THE SUMMARY OF PHYSICAL LIFE

The 7 chakras/minds are different manifestations of one's universal consciousness which are the source of your physical body and thus, life. These chakras give rise to all the needs, the intelligence and courage to take actions to fulfil those needs. Whatever problems, be it in any area of life viz. physical, mental, relations, job/career/profession one faces in one's life is due to wrong PDA, due to lower consciousness, due to disconnection with the source, due to imbalance in the chakras. And the only solution to all problems is balancing of chakras which raises your consciousness, establishes strong connection with the source leading to truthful/righteous PDA (the 3 core karmas of your life) and hence desired results in life. Before understanding that connection, just go through the summary of your physical life.

1) Your physical life is due to the presence of your mind & body. The source of mind & body is universal consciousness/energy. The more is the quantity of energy in your mind & body, the better is your natural intelligence and thus, a better life. The differences in the life of people are due to differences in energy/consciousness, nothing else.

2) And your mind & body have duality of energy (lower consciousness to higher consciousness). Daily mind & body activity consumes energy, reducing your energy levels and thus, you need energy refuelling on a daily basis.

3) Non-fulfilment of your needs (physical, emotional and spiritual) is a problem and causes sadness. And fulfilment of need is success and cause of happiness.

4) Physical and emotional needs are fulfilled from other/external sources. The spiritual need thrives on action of giving, where you help others achieve their physical & emotional needs. When you give & help others, your physical & emotional needs are taken care of by the universe.

5) Life in universe is in different forms (biodiversity) like plants, animals, and people with varying mindset having different skills, professions etc. only due to varying energy & consciousness. The very differences make all life forms valuable for each other, as they fulfil each other's needs.

6) Having good relations with others determine the quality of our need fulfilment and thus, the quality of life. All relations thrive on give and take. **To get what we need, we need to give first; a simple law of life.** You only get what you give. Choice is yours, what you want; give love to get love or give hate to get hate.

7) Problem is that we want everything but do not want to give anything. Wrong giving or no giving is the cause of wrong getting or wrong results in life. So, if results in life are not good, only your act of giving is to be blamed, not others.

8) We have polluted the nature; air, water, soil which comes back in the form of polluted air, water and food makes our mind & body unnatural/corrupt. **We have polluted the mind of self & others** by an attitude of undue uncontrollable anger, hate, blame, complain, suppression, control and envy which disturbs the energy field/emotions of self and others.

9) This creates lack of energy in our personal space, making mind & body negative/unconscious/devoid of life energy and disconnected with the source. All the physical & mental diseases and life issues/problems are due to low energy/consciousness. If the energy of personal space becomes zero then physical life ends.

10) Negativity attracts more negativity like all dirty places attract various rats and disease causing microbes, a dirty society attracts bad elements, a dirty physical body attracts various microbes. **Your personal space has become**

negative; perceives, decides and acts negatively which attracts negative people & situations in your life, making your life miserable and you unlucky.

11) You have become weak physically, emotionally and mentally and thus, lost the capability to act/respond in the right way. Losing the capacity to act/respond is the only source of miseries in life. Wrong or no or less actions/giving will invariably attract wrong results. Your value has gone down in your own eyes and in the eyes of others which puts away the positive people & situations from your life. **So you have to become valuable again by making your personal space positive.**

12) The only way to make your **personal space positive is by removing all negativity, by raising your vibrations/**energy/consciousness, by strengthening the connection with the source of life.

13) Connection with the source of your life ensures the right perspective/clarity without any bias, right decisions and right actions for happiness of all, ensuring positive results/situations in your life.

14) Once we create a positive space, a positive environment, all negativity automatically runs away, making space for positivity to flourish. A positive space manifests unexpected positive results in life, making you lucky.

15) It is the **foremost karma** of life, to make your life a happy and prosperous life. And that can be possible by fulfilling all your needs which can only be fulfilled through righteous karma.

16) Right karma comes automatically from your nature and for your right karma, your foremost karma is to get connected to your source of life which was, is and shall always be present in you.

17) This is how to change your life and make yourself lucky.

To connect with your **REALITY/REAL YOU,** you need to enhance your energy field; **A) by raising your vibrations** or B) **you need to remove all negativity from your personal space** (removal of toxins in your body and removal of negative emotions & disempowering beliefs from your mind). Doing one of them shall ensure reconnection but doing both of them shall ensure very fast results. We are going to understand many ways of removing negativity and enhancing positivity in your personal space, to get back, to reconnect with the **REAL YOU** in **PART B & C of this book**.

NOW IS THE TIME TO UNDERSTAND THE SYSTEMATIC PLAN (REAL TOOLS & TECHNIQUES) IN CHAPTER 5.0 OF THIS BOOK, A RECIPE TO MEET YOUR FORGOTTEN, OMNIPOTENT, ETERNAL REALITY, THE REAL YOU in order to fulfil your personal space with energy/consciousness, to activate an AUTOMATIC/NATURAL PATH OF LIFE, a purposeful life making you a magnet for effortless manifestation of happiness, success, joy in each and every moment of your life that IS WAITING TO BE BROUGHT IN TO YOUR CONSCIOUS PRESENCE, MY DEAR REAL YOU.

5.0 A RECIPE TO MEET THE REAL YOU

USING YOUR MIND & BODY TO RAISE YOUR ENERGY & CONSCIOUSNESS

Fulfil the Purpose of your life; personal growth from Lower conscious to Higher conscious, Awakening the soul within.

THE SYSTEM FOR SELF REALISATION, SELF EMPOWERMENT, PERSONAL GROWTH & SUCCESS; A RECIPE TO MEET THE REAL YOU: This is the system we shall be mastering in *PART B and PART C* of this book in a very easy, effortless way to gift you the *REAL YOU*.

RAISE YOUR VIBES TO RAISE YOUR LIFE
⇩
POSITIVE CHANGES IN FABP (FOOD & WATER, ATTITUDE & FOCUS, BREATHING PATTERN, PHYSICAL BODY POSTURE LANGUAGE & VOICE)
⇩
INCREASE IN LIFE ENERGY, BALANCE IN LIFE ENERGY-GETTING CONNECTED TO THE REAL YOU, INCREASE IN YOUR CONSCIOUSNESS.....
⇩
DEVELOPMENT OF PHYSICAL & EMOTIONAL STRENGTH, LIFE ON AUTOMATIC PATH, FIND & LIVE A PURPOSEFUL, PASSIONATE LIFE. POSITIVE CHANGES IN MINDSET (PERCEPTION, BELIEFS, DECISIONS, ACTIONS, HABITS), ATTRACTION OF POSITIVE PEOPLE & SITUATIONS IN LIFE
⇩
HAPPY & JOYOUS LIFE (ULTIMATE PATH)-DESIRE AND QUEST OF EVERY HUMAN AND SUCCESS & GROWTH IN ALL AREAS OF LIFE VIZ. HEALTH, WEALTH, RELATIONS, CAREER

Source: Meet the Real You Copyright: Chetan Bansal

See in the PART-A of this book, we understood various laws of nature, Universal space, our real identity, our personal space comprising of thoughts, emotions, beliefs, needs & wants, relations, mind, and how mind unable to handle difficult life situations became disturbed and thus lost connection with the source of life. We came to know that difference between two people is just varying degrees of consciousness/awareness though having the same mind. In quest to enhance the quality of life for self & others, this understanding was very important without which we could not have gone into deeper roots/depths to find solutions to all your problems, to live a meaningful, purposeful and joyous journey.

WHAT IS IN YOUR CONTROL AND WHAT IS NOT?

The quality of your physical life is determined by the choices you have; the things that you can control and change in your life. **Birth, death, the functioning of your body organs, needs & wants are all universal, predetermined, natural & automatic without you having any control over it**. Your birth & death does not cause of any miseries or do not pose any problems as all this happens in your unconscious state where you are not aware of anything. **The people & situations in life to some extent are also predetermined.** So we don't have much choice in life as everything is almost predetermined and not in our control. The things that you cannot control can never be the cause of problems in life. **The real problem is wrong results in life which are directly proportional to your actions or your response to the people & situations** which are definitely under your control and **in life you must focus only on what you can control and leave every other thing to almighty.**

The results in your life are the result of your decisions & actions which are the result of your perception which is dependent upon your consciousness dependent upon the energy field/aura which is dependent upon your emotions (energy in motion). **So to control your actions/response/reactions and thus life you need to control your energy** and controlling your energy is your conscious choice, but how? **See the changes in the planetary positions/movements** changes the energy field of the universe which affects the energy field of the personal space. Negative changes in the energy field disturb your emotions leading to a low energy field leading to disconnection with the source. Disconnection with source reduces your consciousness/intelligence leading to wrong/biased PDA and thus wrong results in life. **But the planetary movement is also not in your control and thus you cannot control your PDA & life.**

No! You can control your energy field/aura and thus your intelligence leading to right PDA and right results in life irrespective of changes in planetary positions, but how? See your consciousness is dependent upon the positive energy field of your personal space and **if you can somehow maintain the positive energy field of your personal space then your life becomes timeless which is not affected by the change in time or planetary movements. Your personal space comprises of physical body & chakras/mind made up of 5 elements of life air, water, fire, earth, and space.** If we can somehow maintain the balance of these 5 elements we can maintain the energy field and thus consciousness, but how? See we are getting these 5 elements from these inputs; **F** (food & water), **A** (attitude & focus), **B** (Breathing pattern), **P** (physical body postures, language & voice). **If we choose righteous/natural/spiritual FABP** we can maintain the balance of 5 elements and thus energy field. **These are the inputs to our body & mind which controls the results/output in life.**

So the first & foremost response/giving/karma of life **is to maintain your positive energy field/life energy by balancing the 5 elements of life by**

choosing righteous FABP which is always under your control. Choosing righteous FABP will raise your energy vibrations strengthening the connection with your omnipotent eternal reality; *THE REAL YOU*. Connection with *THE REAL YOU* enhances the life energy/aura leading to the activation of higher faculties of the mind; divine guidance, intuition, logical abilities, attraction of opportunities etc. leading to right perception/decisions/actions and thus success & growth in each & every area of life viz. health, wealth, relations, career/job/profession (HWRC).

THE FIRST GIVING OF LIFE, GIVE YOURSELF THE BEST GIFT OF LIFE,"THE REAL YOU"

Everybody wants to live a happy, prosperous and successful life. And why not it is our birth right, and we should aspire for that but only aspiring won't give you the desired results. You have to *GIVE* your best to be able to live on the natural path of your life. *GIVING* is the highest level of your psychological need, and this is the only need which can give you the highest level of happiness or more appropriately the joy & bliss much above the happiness. *Helping self/others out of love is the best and only giving which activates the highest level of happiness in life. GIVING*, a virtue of your *REAL BEING* is explained in detail in *SPIRITUAL ATTITUDE (kindness)* in this **PART-B** of this book only.

Life thrives on the action based on the exchange of give & take only. And giving is the first step of any exchange, for any **action** and thus **receiving** to take place, and thus, life to happen. If *GIVING* stops, life stops. If *GIVING* is not up to the mark the **receiving/results** are also not up to the mark. You only get what you give. The quality of output is directly proportional to the quality of the input. Many people are not aware of what to give, how to give, to get exactly what they want. But you are lucky my dear *REAL YOU*, you will now get to learn and master the skills for *GIVING* in the perfect way to get exactly what you want i.e. happiness, success, growth in all areas of your life viz. health, wealth, relations, career/job/profession (HWRC).

See most of us has this misconception or disempowering beliefs that I am unlucky, I am incapable, this is impossible for me, I am not able to do it and I get all the problems, these thoughts keep on bombarding our mind when we face problems or fail in something or the other or when we fail on a regular basis or face difficult situations on and off or on regular basis or when we see people fail around us and even more when people around us keep on cursing life, keep on saying life is difficult, we think that we are unlucky, or that we have been destined for misery. **But how many of us care to find the cause of the problems/situations that we are in,** is it someone else or only we are responsible? What mistakes led to this situation and now how to change, handle and go about it to change our life and situations positively or how can we and/or how to create our own luck? We think people who are successful, are born lucky and we attribute their success to their luck. Okay, I fully agree that people who are successful and happy are lucky people. *But do* *you know the definition of luck? How they got lucky? Well, the luck is in your magic box and the magic box is in your hand, whether you make it lucky or unlucky, the choice is always yours.* The lucky people either never allowed their magic box to become a misery box or they converted their misery box back to the magic box by working hard and smart.

Most of the people want to know the magic trick for success in the outer world, achieving material things, big name, and fame but how many try to know the tools, want to sharpen the tools, fuel the tools without which no external achievement is possible. **And yes, I am talking about your own mind, body and energies, your personal space; the *MAGIC BOX* of your existence** which is the source of super natural intelligence, courage, skill, determination, imagination, ideas and righteous PDA for living a purposeful, successful and happy life, even in difficult times.

The **energetic/highly conscious, personal space** is what we call a *MAGIC BOX* and a **personal space devoid of energy & consciousness** is what we call a *MISERY BOX*. So, the magic is in the life energy and the thoughts & actions of a magic box are highly super intelligent, leading to happy & successful results and miserable results are caused by unaware/biased thoughts & actions of the misery box. You gave wrong inputs to your magic box, corrupted it, lost connection with its source and became a miserable box. The input that you gave was garbage, the output you are getting is garbage and in the process, your box became the store-house of garbage. Pardon me; if you didn't like it but I have picked this word 'garbage' from GIGO (Garbage in Garbage out, the principle on which a computer works). But sir, not only computer but everything in this universe works on the principle of GIGO. **Your unaware, wrong choices, decisions and habits** have converted your magic box to a misery box, making you unlucky. Amazing! Isn't it? God gave you a magic box and you made it a misery box. **The first & foremost skill of life is to make yourself lucky again by converting your misery box back to a magic box** by super charging your mind & body with life energy in order to gift yourself the natural, powerful, stronger and valuable you; *THE REAL YOU*, a person who is useful, not only to self but to the society as well.

THE MIND IS A CARRIER OF MEMORY and the mind of every person carries with itself, their own beliefs through which they perceive life that determines their decisions, actions, habits, attitude and behaviour which ultimately determines the quality of their physical life. **If the mind is full of garbage/disempowering beliefs, it is only going to manifest garbage in your life.** The people, circumstances and the socio-economic environment that you are in or you were till now in your life have made up your beliefs and perceptions. Different people have different experiences and circumstances, so the mind of people carries different beliefs and so does their perceptions which are different, given the same situation. **So, the influence/experience of outside people & situations determined your beliefs, state of mind and thus, determine the definition of right or wrong in life.** That definition of right or wrong is different for different regions, societies, countries and religions which creates a cloud of confusion and thus, causes dispute/misery in life. Everybody claims to be right in his/her own perspective but no one is sure because if they are sure, why would they suffer or are unhappy in life or why would they want to prove themselves right and others wrong? **I do not know who is right or who is wrong** but one thing is sure that your happiness & success is dependent upon your state of mind, which is dependent upon the consciousness of your box and not the box of others. So from now on, focus upon your own box and do not depend upon the box of anybody else, whomsoever he/she may be.

The **definition of right and wrong for unlucky people** is determined by other people **but a lucky person trusts** his own awareness & consciousness to arrive at all his decisions, not others. So, today is the day to take back the charge of your life by raising your energy & consciousness, to connect with *THE REAL YOU* and make yourself lucky.

My dear *REAL YOU*, if you are not getting what you want in your life or you are living a life of misery, it clearly indicates that consciousness of your mind is low and the only cause of low consciousness is that your mind is being controlled by the outside people & situations which have passed on disempowering beliefs to you and you accepted them as it is, without filtering through your conscious presence that converted your magic box to a misery box, leading to wrong PDA and thus, wrong results in your life.

AND THE BEST THING ABOUT LIFE IS THAT YOU CAN CHANGE YOUR LIFE POSITIVELY ANYTIME, IRRESPECTIVE OF YOUR AGE, SKIN COLOUR, CASTE, CREED, RELIGION, REGION AND COUNTRY; IT IS JUST YOUR CONSCIOUS CHOICE, DO IT RIGHT NOW AND THE WHOLE WORLD WILL BE YOURS. You do not have to go anywhere, all knowledge; every power to understand, correct and create your life is within you. So close your eyes, dive inside, *MEET THE REAL YOU* and become lucky.

The **degree/percentage of luck is directly proportional to the level of energy & consciousness.** People who seem to be luckier than you are just having a high level of energy, leading to more strong connection and thus, higher consciousness. And the best & only way to increase your energy is by controlling your thoughts & emotions in order to achieve a peaceful/stable state of mind, by choosing **righteous FABP.**

LUCK: DIFFERENT PEOPLE THOUGH HAVE SAME MIND BUT DIFFERENT LEVEL OF CONSCIOUSNESS AND THUS DIFFERENT KARMA (BELEIFS & PERCEPTIONS, DECISIONS AND ACTIONS) FOR THE GIVEN SAME SITUATION LEADING TO DIFFERENT RESULTS IN LIFE.

THE DEGREE OF YOUR LUCK

IS DIRECTLY PROPORTIONAL TO

THE DEGREE OF YOUR CONSCIOUSNESS OR

DEGREE OF CONTROL OVER YOUR MIND OR

DEGREE OF CONTROL OVER YOUR EMOTIONS OR

DEGREE OF CALMNESS OF YOUR MIND

WHAT CONSTITUTES LUCK OR HOW THE INCREASE IN ENERGY ENHANCES YOUR LUCK?

See, the 7 chakras/minds contain all the codes/software for a happy, joyous, prosperous & successful life. These codes have been corrupted due to accumulation of negative emotions, beliefs and impressions in your chakras/mind through your wrong karmas of past life and this life. Choosing high energy vibrations through righteous FABP is like an antivirus which cleans all accumulated negative impressions, be it of past and this life from your mind/chakras, making your mind and code to work at its natural best, leading to rise in natural intelligence/consciousness by:-

1). Making **each & every cell of your body healthy, energetic & vibrant** and thus, a healthy body & mind devoid of any disease.

2). Shows you the **hidden talents and purposes** of your life.

3). Activates your **3rd eye/intuitive powers**, removes disempowering beliefs, enhances your memory, logical abilities and activates truthful perception in you, leading to righteous decisions & actions for right results in life.

4). It not only **attracts righteous people & situations** in your life, but also removes negative people & situations from your life for fulfilling all your needs and thus, success & growth in all areas of your life.

5). It also gives you the **courage, determination, strength & power**, to be able to follow the path of truth where you become valuable and helpful, not only for self but to the others also.

Once you raise your energy vibrations, the all above attributes of luck are automatic in your life where everything that is needed to you come towards you in an effortless way rather than you chasing and what more you want in order to become lucky. We will understand more about luck and destiny in Chapter 7.0 of this book.

GOOD LUCK! LUCK IS WAITING FOR YOU TO REAVEAL ITS MYSTERIES TO YOU, TO BECOME THE PART OF YOU, TO LIVE THROUGH YOU. SO, THE FIRST, FOREMOST, MOST AND THE ONLY IMPORTANT STEP; THE FIRST GIVING OF YOUR LIFE TO CONTROL YOUR DESTINY OR TO MAKE YOURSELF LUCKY OR TO SET YOUR LIFE ON THE RIGHT PATH, BY RAISING THE CONSCIOUSNESS OF YOUR MIND BY JUST GIFTING YOURSELF THE REAL YOU AND THE REST IS ALL AUTOMATIC.

THE FIRST STEP A BIG LEAP

A SIMPLE SYSTEM ON HOW TO CONTROL LIFE TO ACTIVATE LUCK; **Understand the system, how it works?** This is going to be the most exciting and the greatest knowledge a man has to know about the dynamics of life, to know about the source of life, to know about the tools and techniques available with us, to get the real connection with source, to fulfil the very purpose of life. Life is amazing and mysterious at the same time. The more you learn about life, universe and its guiding principles, the easier and enjoyable life becomes and more mysteries of the life unfold. You will always want to know more and the more you know, the more you come to know that you don't know anything. Just keep living your life, the only key to live life is to be always connected to your source and then, the real communication happens within you and when there is inner communication, there is life, there is happiness, there are solutions, there is everything for life to happen the way it has been designed by the almighty.

THIS IS HOW TO CONTROL LIFE BY CONTROLLING YOUR ENERGY, RAISE YOUR VIBES IN ORDER TO RAISE YOUR LIFE.

We have been talking about energy, energy, and energy. See these are our roots, this is the ultimate truth and this is what we are. The decrease or increase of energy in your life determines the quality of your life. Low energy is the cause of all problems and high energy is the one and only permanent solution to all your problems. And you are reading this book, to gain knowledge about self, life, and universe just to solve all your problems, by mastering your mind, thoughts & emotions and thus, life.

SEE WHAT YOU ARE GIVING AS INPUT TO YOUR MIND & BODY DETERMINES THE QUALITY OF YOUR CELLS, BIOCHEMICALS, THOUGHTS AND EMOTIONS WHICH DETERMINES YOUR ENERGY FIELD/AURA THAT FURTHER DETERMINES YOUR MINDSET AND YOUR MINDSET DETERMINES THE OUTPUT IN YOUR LIFE. When you know that, you are just a manifestation of one universal consciousness and the source of this consciousness is within you, that your life energy which maintains and sustains life is also manifested in different forms of chakras, cells and organs. And these cells and chakras are made up of **five elements: Air, Water, Fire, Earth and Space** which maintains working and functioning of your mind & body. You are continuously getting these five elements from the universe in the form of **food, water, air, vision, sound and feelings.** *SEE, THESE ARE INPUT TO YOUR BODY AND YOU HAVE THE POWER TO CHOOSE THE QUALITY, DEGREE AND FREQUENCY OF THESE INPUTS.*

ELEMENTS OF LIFE	SOURCE OF ELEMENTS	
Air	Breathing pattern, Attitude & focus	*THIS IS THE MOST BASIC SCIENTIFIC AND ONLY WAY TO CONTROL/CHANGE YOUR LIFE POSITIVELY*
Water	Water, Attitude & focus	
Fire	Food, Attitude & focus	
Earth	Food, Attitude & focus	
Space	Energies, Emotions, Thoughts dependent upon your attitude & focus	*MUST BE FOREMOST KARMA OF YOUR LIFE*

Source: Meet the Real You **Copyright:** Chetan Bansal

THE SOURCE OF 5 ELEMENTS OF LIFE I.E. FABP are always under your control; **4 Powerful Changing Agents, FABP ('Food & water, 'Attitude &**

focus, 'Breathing pattern, 'Physical body posture language & voice (PPLV)). **The food that you eat contains Earth, Fire and Water element.** You can surely control the quality, quantity and nature of your food that you eat. **Water that you drink contains water element.** You can surely control the quality, quantity, timing and the nature of liquids that you drink. **Air you breathe contains oxygen which is an air element.** You control the quality, quantity of air that you breathe in by choosing the right/natural breathing pattern which is deep, long & slow and by controlling the air pollution. **And your Inner Space**, your degree of consciousness depends upon the quality of perception of information that you get from what you see, listen and feel through your five senses. You can never control what you see and listen but you can always control what you feel, believe and perceive about the information. *IT IS NOT THAT THE INFORMATION YOU ARE GETTING FROM OUTER WORLD MATTERS BUT WHAT MATTERS IS HOW YOU INTERPRET & PERCEIVE THAT INFORMATION.* **For example, one son after seeing the miseries of his drunken father chose never to drink in his life, the other son became addicted to drinking and the third one chooses to drink as a variety or on occasions in limited quantities.** So, it is processed thoughts (PDA) which determines your energy & consciousness and is always under your control.

Your very own unaware, negative choices of FABP corrupted your cells & personal space which took you towards the negative side of life. You were not aware what to control and how to control for positively changing your life but now, when the destiny has knocked your door, make a full advantage of the opportunity that life has thrown on you; *MEET THE REAL YOU* by choosing the right FABP that balances the 5 elements of life, thus, making your mind & body highly energetic & conscious.

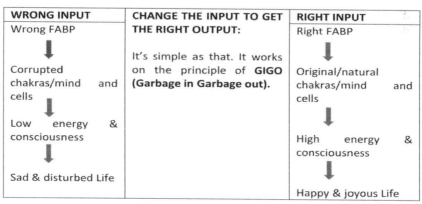

WRONG INPUT	CHANGE THE INPUT TO GET	RIGHT INPUT
Wrong FABP ⬇	**THE RIGHT OUTPUT:**	Right FABP ⬇
Corrupted chakras/mind and cells ⬇	It's simple as that. It works on the principle of **GIGO (Garbage in Garbage out).**	Original/natural chakras/mind and cells ⬇
Low energy & consciousness ⬇		High energy & consciousness ⬇
Sad & disturbed Life		Happy & joyous Life

Source: Meet the Real You Copyright Chetan Bansal

SO THE FIRST ACTION/GIVING/RESPONSE OF LIFE IS TO ENHANCE THE DEGREE OF ENERGY & CONSCIOUSNESS OF YOUR MIND & BODY WHICH IS ALWAYS UNDER YOUR CONTROL BY CHOOSING THE RIGHT FABP TO TAP THE SOURCE ENERGY.

A PRACTICAL SYSTEM TO BRING ABOUT POSITIVE CHANGES IN LIFE

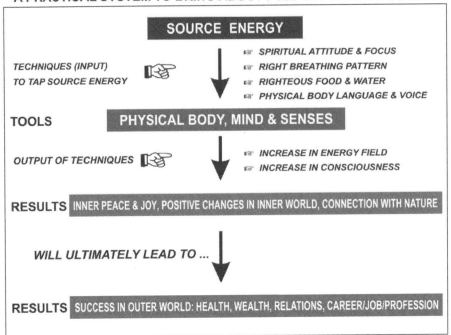

SOURCE ENERGY

TECHNIQUES (INPUT)
TO TAP SOURCE ENERGY

☞ SPIRITUAL ATTITUDE & FOCUS
☞ RIGHT BREATHING PATTERN
☞ RIGHTEOUS FOOD & WATER
☞ PHYSICAL BODY LANGUAGE & VOICE

TOOLS — PHYSICAL BODY, MIND & SENSES

OUTPUT OF TECHNIQUES

☞ INCREASE IN ENERGY FIELD
☞ INCREASE IN CONSCIOUSNESS

RESULTS — INNER PEACE & JOY, POSITIVE CHANGES IN INNER WORLD, CONNECTION WITH NATURE

WILL ULTIMATELY LEAD TO ...

RESULTS — SUCCESS IN OUTER WORLD: HEALTH, WEALTH, RELATIONS, CAREER/JOB/PROFESSION

Source: Meet the Real You Copyright: Chetan Bansal

Mind, body and senses are tools in your hand to experience joy, happiness, success & growth in all areas of life viz. health, wealth, relations, and career/profession/job. It is your foremost duty (karma) to maintain and sharpen these tools on a regular basis by treating them with the source energy and this source energy can be tapped through righteous FABP. Choosing right FABP will change your life positively, from being miserable to flourishing, from being on Wrong journey to Righteous, purposeful life and ultimately to the Path of Self-realization; **THE REAL YOU.** You just need to give your time & energy to these techniques and with regular practice you shall become the master of your life, the creator of your own life, where the destiny comes in your own hands. **Then you shall be able to direct the steering of your life to the path and destination of your choice, a choice of your inner voice, a choice of your soul.**

The permanent use of righteous FABP connects us with the source energy which makes our mind, body and senses energetic, vibrant, sharp and super intelligent, leading to perfection in PDA and thus, desired results in life. **Now the choice is yours,** whether you want to live life or curse life, whether you want to sit idle or want to do something, whether you want to repent life or live life, whether you want to change, manage and control your life situations or be controlled by external situations/circumstances, whether you want to control your mind, body and senses or be controlled by them, whether you want to help, support or contribute to the growth of others or be dependent on others, whether you want to become a solution to problems or a problem to others.

There is nothing called destiny for those who know how to change or create their life. Choice is yours; life is calling you, waiting for you to live through you and to live for you. Come on, get up, it's now or never, you are reborn my dear **REAL YOU**. Forget what ever happened in your past, it is an illusion, just a reference point and can't determine your future. *The future is in your present actions, HAVE FAITH IN YOURSELF, START MOVING AHEAD IN LIFE, MEET THE REAL YOU, BECOME THE REAL YOU,* TAKE CONTROL OF THE STEERING OF YOUR LIFE AND *FULFIL PURPOSE OF YOUR LIFE; PERSONAL GROWTH FROM LOWER CONSCIOUS TO HIGHER CONSCIOUS BY AWAKENING THE SOUL WITHIN.*

NOW TO MAKE YOU LUCKY, TO CONTROL THE STEERING OF YOUR LIFE, TO BECOME THE SKILLFUL DRIVER OF YOUR LIFE IN ORDER TO ENJOY THE JOURNEY CALLED LIFE, we will understand righteous FABP to align with the source in Part B and Part C of this book.

PART B: UNCONSCIOUS TO SUPERCONSCIOUS MIND

6.0 SPIRITUAL PATH, ATTITUDE AND WOW FOCUS
A: *RIGHTEOUS ATTITUDE & FOCUS, where you practice Acceptance, Focus in present moment, Faith/belief in self/almighty, Gratitude, Happiness, Kindness, Unconditional love, forgiveness, and celebration to align with the source.*

7.0 LAW OF LUCK/DESTINY/KARMA: Perception, decisions and actions

PART C: RAISING ENERGY & CONSCIOUSNESS THROUGH PHYSIOLOGY
8.0 FUELLING YOUR BODY
Through righteous F B P

MEET THE REAL YOU

A Recipe to Find Meaning and Purpose of Life; Master Emotions and Focus; Raise Prana Energy; Awaken Conscious; Enhance Love, Joy, Success, Growth and Happiness in Life

PART B: UNCONSCIOUS TO SUPERCONSCIOUS MIND

Attitude & wow focus to raise your consciousness and energy field

TWO CHAPTERS
6.0 Spiritual Path, Attitude and Wow Focus
7.0 Activating Your Luck

Mastering your thoughts & emotions through attitude & focus to strengthen the connection and arrive at truthful/unbiased perceptions, decisions and actions

Enhancing the degree of your Spiritual Quotient (SQ), Intelligence Quotient (IQ), Happiness Quotient (HQ), Emotional Quotient (EQ), and Relationship Quotient (RQ)

6.0 SPIRITUAL PATH, ATTITUDE AND WOW FOCUS

RAISING VIBRATIONS OF YOUR MIND; LET'S DIVE INSIDE--THE REAL PATH OF LIFE--SPIRITUAL PATH, DIVINE CALLING, MEET THE REAL YOU--GETTING CONNECTED TO YOUR SOUL

Living a life with spiritual attitude strengthens the connection with your roots/source. **The beauty of life is in your roots/source and once connected,** you will be able to find solutions in all areas of your life, be it health, wealth, relations, job/career/profession by converting a unconscious/disturbed/negative mind to a positive/conscious/super-conscious/super-intelligent mind that is **charged by a natural medicine called cosmic energy; the source of life.**

Many of us are alien to the word 'spirituality', we think it is not for us or it is meant for some enlightened seers or to live spiritually, we need to leave this materialistic world. If you think so, you are not right. You are spiritual, I am spiritual, and we are all spiritual. In fact, every living organism on this planet is spiritual. It is the very source of our existence and is alive in us at each and every moment of life. The only thing is that we do not understand spirituality. That is why we feel alien to this world. We think spirituality and materialistic world can't exist together or we cannot be spiritual while living in this materialistic world. But the truth is just the opposite and that is, spirituality is the basis of all success in this materialistic world, means to be successful in this physical life and to enjoy this materialistic life, we need to have strong spiritual connection. Spirituality is the source of your physical life. The strength of your spirit is dependent upon the presence of cosmic energy. The more is the presence of cosmic energy in you, the more is the connection, communication, cooperation, coordination and synchronization of your mind, body and soul. When this happens, your soul/nature becomes your guide of life leading to righteous PDA and right results in life. Low energy in your personal space leads to the disconnection with your natural guide and thus, a miserable life.

SO LET'S UNDERSTAND SPIRITUAL SPACE: A SPACE ABOVE MIND

"A problem of disturbed mind (devoid of energy & consciousness, having low frequency vibrations) can never be solved by the mind. A higher place of spiritual space, having high frequency vibrations can only heal the disturbed mind."
-Chetan Bansal

A Universal/spiritual space above mind having highest frequency vibrations, a divine super conscious space which in itself is nothing but creates, contains and maintains everything. Everything exists in this universal space (outer space), all planets, stars, galaxies, all exist in space the same way your spiritual space creates, contains and maintains your physical body & mind. Your spiritual space is an extension of the Universal space and thus, connected to each other.

"Space is nothing yet everything exists in space. Without space, there can be nothing. For everything to exist needs space, nothingness is the space to everything"
         -Chetan Bansal

The time and space of past & future is a psychological time and it belongs to mind. The mind constantly feeds on past & future to survive which causes emotional disturbances and thus, loses connection with the spiritual space. **The present time & space** is the space between the past and the future which is nothing but a spiritual space, leading to death of disturbed emotions & overthinking mind and marks the rise of super-conscious mind. Spiritual space is a space of silence which silences the disturbance of mind.

ROLE OF SPIRITUAL SPACE/BENEFITS OF CONNECTION WITH SPIRITUAL SPACE/IMPORTANCE OF SPIRITUAL SPACE

The benefits of connection with spiritual space, you have already read 6 pages earlier in chapter 5.0 under the heading "WHAT CONSTITUTES LUCK OR HOW THE INCREASE IN ENERGY ENHANCES YOUR LUCK". Let's explore it a little deeper.

      A spiritual space is a super intelligence beyond the imagination of logical mind, it is your natural power extension of universal consciousness and knows everything about your past, present and future, **knows all your likes and dislikes,** it not only knows what is good or bad for you, it exactly knows what is needed for you or most appropriate for you, it knows the very purpose and path of your life. **Whenever life poses you with some kind of unpleasant situation or challenge or problem, there is a bigger divine purpose for your benefit only.** It just wants you to see the truth as it is and put your best foot forward without being perturbed by the situation. It wants you to accept the challenge, learn new skills, find opportunities in problematic situations and not give up or run away from the situations.

      It is a power which removes all hurdles from your life, prevents and escapes problematic situations/places/projects from your life. Many a times people experience something like this, **they wanted to visit a particular place** and missed the train or flight or any other means of transport and some accident happen saving them from the disaster. They were initially regretting, missing the place/event but on knowing the eventuality, they thanked God. **Someone decided to start a new business,** but somehow he was not able to and regretted but he thanked the almighty after some time, when he found that Government had levied huge taxes on that business, making it unprofitable.

It shows and gives you all the energy to fulfil the very purpose of your life, for which you are born with an inbuilt natural talent. Living on purposeful path fills all the voids in life. Many people, even after having good money, health or relations or all are unhappy in their life because they are not living a purposeful life. **The people who have found and are living or lived a purposeful life are the people who have been responsible for great inventions, discoveries and are great leaders** who have revolutionized this world for the overall welfare of society. **The biggest purpose of your life is to live a happy & joyous life and that can be only possible by an attitude of giving, helping and unconditional love for self/others.**

Spiritual space gives natural/higher dimension to your values, highest level of consciousness where you value humanity, love, compassion, empathy, etc. The focus of your value shifts from "I, me and mine" to "We". From this state of consciousness, you don't see I, you and others separate but only a creation of the same source. This creates harmony within and with others leading to good relations and ultimately, fulfilment of your needs, making your life easy & effortless.

It is a source of all intuitive powers. All the **thoughts and ideas** come in mind. But have you ever wondered, are thoughts & ideas created in mind or are just communicated to your mind? **Yes my dear friends, all thoughts/ideas come to your mind from a universal /spiritual space but** then what is the role of mind? **Mind gives form to the thoughts/ideas or you can say mind conceptualizes the ideas**. For example, I have written this book from the thoughts & ideas that I attracted in my mind but used logical mind to present the same in a reader friendly way. **The connecting link between your mind and the spiritual/universal space is the third eye which is located between your eye brows.**

The word focus is very important. Where ever is the focus of your mind, ideas /thoughts about that thing is brought into your mind from that universal/spiritual space through your third eye. **People with high focus/concentration power a**re able to find solutions to their problems perfectly and are able to understand complex phenomena very fast only through this third eye, in conjugation with the mind. Strong focus converts the normal mind to a super intelligent mind by connecting it with a spiritual/universal space; the super intelligence of nature. So, in order to become super intelligent, you just need to control the **focus of mind.**

FOCUS- We all need to master, to control the mind.

Just remember this one thing that will solve all problems, whether big or small and bring all success in your life i.e. *FOCUS OF MIND*. Whatever we focus upon is expanded in life. When you focus on solution, solution expands. Solution being positive in nature enhances your energy by connecting with spiritual space that gives solutions. **When you focus on**

problem, problem expands. Problem being negative in nature causes disturbance in emotions, leading to depletion of energy which disconnects with your spiritual space, leading to more problems in life. **If you focus on negativity or lack in others or worry a lot, etc.,** you attract all that negativity in your life.

SHIFTING YOUR FOCUS FROM: **Problems to solutions, non-acceptance to acceptance, past & future worry/anxiety to present moment, feeling of lack to feeling of content, doubt to faith, from hate to love etc. will increase your energy connecting with your spiritual space, leading to a cool & calm, super conscious mind.**

What happens in emergency situations? Whenever there is an emergency of any kind, the overthinking mind automatically stops and focus of mind shifts to the present moment, where you take fast & best actions to save yourself. Then, the mind is not thinking about past or future but is fully focussed on the present moment which is an emergency situation where your spiritual space/nature wants to save you. You are not perturbed by the mind which does not allow you to act in normal conditions, **for example, you are not feeling well and reluctant to walk fast** but as soon as a dog starts to run towards you, you will definitely run very fast, to protect yourself. **If some terrorist comes with a gun in his hand**, you will run like anything and may even climb walls as high as 10 feet to save your life or you may decide to fight the terrorist being a do or die situation. Whenever you face any do or die situation, your natural, super intelligence space acts very fast and uses your mind & body to activate the impossible action in you. This is how miracles happen in life, **through Space which uses your mind & body only to produce out of the box solutions.**

A typical difference between mind (lower consciousness) and spiritual space or mind with higher consciousness
--Mind says it is impossible; space says anything is possible.
--Minds sits, think, think, worry, worry; space says think, act and achieve.
--Mind will say how; space will say take the best of action now and I will take care of how.
--Mind brings sadness and fear; space brings joy and cheer.
--Mind says there are problems; space says that problems are opportunities.
--Mind says it's over; space says let's start anew.
--Mind says you are week; space proves you are strong.
--Mind gives doubt; space gives faith.
--Mind is logical; space is miracle beyond all logic.
--Mind has intellect; space is super intelligence of nature beyond all limits.
--Mind is a seat house of all negative emotions; space converts negative emotions to positive ones, super charges the mind with cosmic energy, guides it to perfection--it is like a father rescuing the unaware child.

So a connection with the spiritual space is where the solution to all problems lies and that connection is only possible by increasing the cosmic energy in the personal space, as that will convert our unconscious mind to conscious mind; a super conscious mind, an intelligent mind beyond the imagination of logical overthinking mind. So the **big question is, how to get connected with the spiritual space, what are the connectors?** We need to find the connectors and then work on those connectors to establish the much desired connection for a happy, joyful and prosperous journey called life. And for that, we need to increase our energy field and at the same time, need to protect the depletion of same but only through attitude & focus.

ATTITUDE OR MINDSET OF LIFE: *WHAT IS THE ATTITUDE OR MINDSET OF YOUR LIFE? The way you think, feel, perceive, believe, and act upon in your life and life situations is your attitude or mindset of life.*
The path of your life, guided by your soul is the spiritual path which is activated by the spiritual attitude. And there are various spiritual connectors or attitude which enhances cosmic energy in your personal space, leading to a connection with your spiritual space like **Focus in the Present moment, Acceptance of life as it comes to you or take life as it comes to you with zero resistance, focus on the attitude of gratitude, happiness, kindness, unconditional love, forgiveness, celebration and faith in self/god, leading to a path** of all success & happiness in life.

The path of your life guided by disturbed emotions and influenced by negative people & situations is an unnatural path, leading to a miserable life. **The opposite of spiritual connectors are dis-connectors** like non-acceptance, doubt, hate, blame, rudeness, disrespect, sadness which depletes our vital/cosmic energy leading to disconnection, a perfect recipe for miserable life.

The above spiritual attitude/connectors are nothing but the nature of your spirit and the best way to align with your source. So in life, it is very important to understand roots, work on it and align with it to activate your super natural intelligence and thus, find a real success in all areas of our life viz. HWRC. **Are you ready to start your journey?**

Let's begin. Who is stopping you? No body. Choice is yours, and you have already chosen it. Life is waiting for you to unravel the mysteries of life, to find and live the purpose of your life.

SPIRITUAL ATTITUDE OF LIFE; FOR CONNECTION WITH SPIRITUAL SPACE
Spirituality is the acceptance of life as it comes to you; the acceptance of reality as it is posing zero resistance to the present moment, to be at peace in each & every situation of life, to accept good & bad alike but never means

that you approve bad, to take right, unbiased actions in order to improve the quality of life, of self and others, to have respect and unconditional love for everybody, to take responsibility of everything that happens in your life, to give your 100% each & every time, to forgive self and others, and to have faith in acts of god or acts which are beyond your control.

It is realizing the fact that the present situation is the outcome of the past karma, analysing that past action, understanding what went wrong or right, taking responsibility by yourself and not blaming others, learning from your mistakes, not to repeat them ever in life and taking the right action today for a better present and a brighter future. It is the learning and evolving in life, to say yes to life, to accept every challenge and to see the opportunity in every challenge of life...

SPIRITUALITY gives you the wisdom, to be able to see the truth as it is and intelligence & courage to take the righteous action, to bring about the right change in any situation which is under your control and strength to bear the situation/reality which is beyond your control.

LET'S UNDERSTAND A SPIRITUAL ATTITUDE THROUGH AN EXAMPLE

Let's suppose you are driving a car on a highway. Think of it as your journey of life, where **you are the consciousness** and **car is your physical body**. Now you are driving very smoothly, there are no problems in life; you increased the speed of your car. Then suddenly, a speed breaker came on your way, you immediately applied brakes and there were some jerks felt by you & your body (car) which can be correlated to the emotional & physical pains in life. Now, you slowed down the car so as to save yourself and car from certain outside circumstance/situation over which you have no control, but you had control over yourself and you did the wise thing by slowing down the car in order to save yourself from a possible outside threat which if you have not done, could have resulted in a serious injury or even death. Now, after crossing the breaker you again accelerated the vehicle.

Now after covering some distance, a rough patch of road came your way and now again wisely, you slowed down and now you couldn't speed up again as the road ahead is still rough and it does look a very long patch that refuses to end. **Now you have to drive patiently, bearing some jerks (pains in life)** on the rough road and you can only wish for, hope for with faith that this rough patch shall end fast and smooth road will come again. Again, it is not under your control, you can only hope for, you have to take action according to the present situation of the road and your only wise action is to drive cautiously and slowly, you can't speed up based on your past memory/experience of good road or expectation of good road in future. **This rough patch only came on your journey to make you learn patience in the present moment and faith in future.** This also taught you that no matter what your mind thinks or wish for you, you have only one wise option, to take action only based on reality of your present situation/circumstances. You have to act according to the present time and space in which you are in. **The only**

one action in this present moment is to drive slowly on the same road or choose another way/road, but you need to wait till you find the new road and when you find the new road, how can you predict that the new road will be better than the present one? That will be a tough choice and decision about the unknown zone of the future. **But you can't deny the condition of the present road or you can't predict the condition of the new road which you have chosen or want to choose in order to change your path and hope of better journey.** Here, you just have to take your own decision, you may ask some people, the passer byes about the condition of the new road but the credit and debit of choosing the new road goes to you only. You can't blame the others for guiding you wrong for the new road. The decision is only yours. And a decision of a spirited person is based on intuitions which are always right.

Suppose you choose the new road (you took a risk) in the hope of a **better road,** for better journey and it actually turns out to be a better road; a successful decision. **But what if the new road is even worse than the previous one, is it a success or failure**? It looks like failure at the moment but in the long run, it may prove otherwise. The scenario here is a worse road, a new worst experience and you being shaken by it, what is the purpose? The purpose of your spirit/nature here is to develop more life skills, like patience in you, it wants you to renew the road or it wants you to learn, to ride on rough roads, to make you a better driver of life, a strong person who is not perturbed by the challenges of life but actually love challenges.

When rough road (rough patch in life) comes, you have 3 choices: 1) **Cry about the bad condition of road** and stop the car, life is stopped; **2) Accept the road as it is and take action according to the situation of the road,** slow down the speed of the car and cross that rough patch patiently, with hope and faith of a better road ahead; or **3) Cross that road patiently and guide others** with your experience about the condition of the road. You can send information and suggestion to the road department so that they can repair the road to make a smooth ride/journey for the new comers. This way, with your experience you can help others and contribute to the well-being of others. **This is how our society, world have developed over a period of time, everybody has contributed for the growth of society in some way or other.**

Now some big mountain came your way, what will you do? **Choice 1)** Stop and think it's impossible for you to cross that mountain, **2)** Think of different possible ways to cross the mountain. Like Build a tunnel, it requires time, energy, and hard work but that's the only option for a true spirited person, the real you who loves challenges. For this, you need to meet new people, develop relations with them, develop a team, use coordination and cooperation skills, develop skills to manage people as a big task of building tunnel, you will need people from all walks of life; engineers, contractors, workers, financers, your only job is to manage the people to put everything in the right place. This way, you learned new skills leading to your personal growth and at the same time contribute to the welfare of the society.

Isn't it the best way to live life? Take life as it comes to you, accept whatever is offered by nature, take it as challenge, learn new skills, make new goals, accomplish new goals and enjoy each & every moment of your life. It does not mean that you won't feel the heat, you might feel frustrated or hopeless or may feel like giving up, but my dear friend, **THE REAL YOU** inside will always inspire you to fight and come out victorious & successful. **THE REAL YOU** will give you faith, confidence and self-belief in each & every moment of your life but for that, you just need to do one thing, *"KEEP ON MOVING FORWARD IN LIFE WITH A POSITIVE ATTITUDE, KEEP YOUR VIBRATIONS HIGH & STRONG THROUGH FAITH, BELIEF, AND PATIENCE, A DIVINE HAND WILL ALWAYS BE THERE ON YOU."*

SEE, FOR RIGHTEOUS RESULTS, WE MUST HAVE RIGHTEOUS PDA AND FOR THAT, A CONNECTION TO YOUR SPIRITUAL SPACE THROUGH SPIRITUAL ATTITUDE IS A MUST. SO BEFORE UNDERSTANDING ABOUT THE RIGHT KARMA (PDA, the 3 core karmas of your life), FIRST, WE MUST UNDERSTAND THE ART & SCIENCE OF CONNECTION WITH YOUR ETERNAL REALITY "THE REAL YOU ON REAL PATH OF LIFE THROUGH THE REAL ATTITUDE OF LIFE" TO BRING BACK YOUR LIFE ON YOUR NATURAL PATH, A PATH OF REAL HAPPINESS AND BLISS.

LIVING SOUL PATH THROUGH SPIRITUAL ATTITUDE

SPIRITUAL ATTITUDE

To develop a pure, spiritual attitude, you must follow and live some laws of spirituality. Wrong perception, interpretation, understanding of life situations & people around you invokes negative feelings & emotions in you, which in turn depletes your vital energy making your mind, body and spirit weak leading to various physical & mental illness. This ultimately derails you from the spiritual path of life. The following attitudes and principles shall immediately set you on the right path; the path of pure/God energy, of happiness and absolute bliss by increasing the cosmic energy (food of your soul) in your personal space.

Observe children to regain your nature, to regain your spiritual path. A child always lives his nature. This is what a child does:

1) He has full faith & trust in god/self: He gracefully surrenders himself to you without any fear and accepts everything; he will eat, drink, and wear whatever is given to him. When you throw him up in air and then catch him back, he does not resist/fear but enjoys it having full trust over you.

2) He keeps on playing: A natural player & celebrator, irrespective of any situation around him, even injuries don't bother him.

3) He keeps on taking action, keeps on trying, keeps on experimenting, keep on taking objects in mouth, keep on touching, throwing objects, he just keeps on doing something or the other. He is not worrying about the result of his actions but just enjoying every action of his.

4) He even fights, expresses his anger, cries but all is temporary, forgets and forgive immediately and naturally.

5) He is very kind, helps others, plays with others, and does not differentiate between rich and poor.

6) He is always enthusiastic, energetic, happy, and joyous characterized by a natural smile on the face.

7) He does everything with his full focus.

You don't have to go anywhere to learn the natural way of life, a spiritual way of life. Just observe the children around you and once you understand your nature, it becomes very easy for you to understand life of others as nature of all is same and universal.

Now let's understand spiritual attitude (a real diamond) which is your nature but somehow you have forgotten it. It will immediately set you on your natural path of life far, far away from the disturbed state of mind. Not even far, it is relinquishing that the disturbed mind identifies and transforms the disturbed mind to a super conscious state of mind.

6.1 ACCEPTANCE
TAKE LIFE AS IT COMES TO YOU/ACCEPTANCE OF PEOPLE & SITUATIONS AS THEY ARE WITH ZERO RESISTANCE: Unconscious state to super-conscious state

#1 TRUTH OF LIFE: Every person has their own set of beliefs/values/perceptions/opinions as all have varying degree of energy/consciousness. So likes, dislikes, decisions & actions and hence, soul path of every person is different. Also the mindset of people keep on changing with changing times caused by changes in the planetary positions, which changes the energy and thus, mindset of a person.

Everybody wants to live life their own way and at the same time, wants acceptance from others. Ask yourself; don't you expect this from yourself and others? **ACCEPTANCE FOR YOUR SELF** *is to live life guided by your inner voice and not under the influence of others.* **ACCEPTANCE FOR OTHERS** *is to let them live their life the way they want without any control.*
If you can understand this truth about life, 95% of problems will get solved. So you have to **understand and accept this truth, align your decisions and**

actions with this truth. **95% of problems in life are related to either you trying to control/change others or others trying to control/change you and nobody wants to accept each other.**

But what we forget is that everybody has their own life path and the sequence of events/situations in everybody's life is determined by their soul path. The events/situations might look difficult but each & every situation has a purpose and happens for your good & growth. But people don't accept the changes in their life, they resist change, they fear change and don't want to break their comfort zone. Accepting everything coming in life is the only path to success, growth and salvation from the miseries of life.

Non-acceptance of reality of self is the cause of resistance. Most of the times, we know the reality but a person with low consciousness decides on the basis of fear & greed. And once, we do not decide on the basis of truth, we lose our soul path and thus, attract miseries in our life. **A simple example for this could be that most of us know it is our unhealthy eating habits and no/less physical activity that has made us obese/unhealthy,** but still we choose to live with that unhealthy lifestyle. Over a period of time, health gets worse, making life miserable. The only thing is that we don't want to come out of our comfort zone under too much influence of taste buds and thus, do not want to align habits with truth. This is a simple non-acceptance of truth and thus, a miserable life. You have manifested an unhealthy body but it is an opportunity to understand about your health and changing it to get healthy, change to set your life back on natural path but your non-acceptance, due to attachment with comfort didn't allow you to take a wise decision.

Non-acceptance of the reality of others is the cause of resistance. An unaware mind of you and others try to control the life of each other, this creates resistance, either in you or others or all, leading to the disconnection from your nature, source of life and thus, a problematic life. **People & situations appear unwanted because you don't accept them as they are leading to resistance inside you.** An emotional, disturbed state of mind caused by unwanted people & situations is what we call resistance. There is internal resistance caused by non-acceptance of reality. You feel the urge to blame others, you want to change others, you want to control others, you want to prove yourself right & others wrong but they reject and resist your opinion/suggestions. This causes an emotional disturbance, an internal resistance in you. You think yourself to be perfect, who is not ready to change self but want to change everybody else. This sets you on an unnatural path of life caused by the disturbed state of mind. You lose connection with your nature where your state of mind is expressed in anger, hate, envy, jealously, ignorance and rudeness.

Non-acceptance leads to an emotional disturbance (resistance) leading to all problems in life. As internal resistance reduces, the flow of energy current in your personal space leads to reduction in energy field/aura which shall only result in you being disturbed mentally, emotionally and physically, followed by an unhealthy body & mind. An unhealthy mind or mind with low energy or low consciousness activates biased PDA and thus, wrong results in your life. So the situation outside was wrong/undesirable/painful and that was not enough, you created internal resistance, converted your magic box to a miserable box manifesting further miseries in life.

GOING FROM UNNATURAL PATH OF LIFE TO YOUR SOUL PATH BY ACCEPTANCE

Spirituality is living life as it comes to you; it is the acceptance of life as it comes to you. Doing so can only put your life on soul path. Living on the path of your soul is spirituality. Whatever is happening in your life and coming in your life is guided by your soul path and for your own good. Your soul path wants you to succeed and grow in every area of life but your non-acceptance of the situation puts away the right path. **But the problem is that we fear change, we do not accept change, we resist change**; for most of the people, this is the lifelong problem as the path they choose is invariably guided by fear, greed & comfort of mind which does not allow them to accept and live the truth, leading to an unnatural path and miseries in life.

ACCEPTANCE IS SEEING THE SITUATION AS IT IS, WITHOUT ANY BIAS. To be able to rise above all fear, greed and comfort of mind, it shall help us in understanding & perceiving life/self/people from a higher space without any bias, to be able to take righteous decisions & actions for right results in life. The best would be to accept whatever is happening in your life, pose zero resistance & surrender to the reality of the present moment. This gives you the intelligence to see the truth of the present moment as it is where you are able to understand what you can change and what you cannot and then put your best foot forward with a never give up attitude in order to change what you can.

ACCEPTANCE IS NOT TO CONTROL BUT ACCEPT WHATEVER IS HAPPENING IN YOUR LIFE UNCONDITIONALLY. Acceptance is to accept self, unconditionally. Many situations in your life are beyond your control and the only intelligent choice you have is just acceptance. All natural processes of life are beyond your control like birth, death, ageing and resisting them is like moving away from the truth; a recipe for misery, nothing else. **Like, if you have become old**, your hair might have turned grey, and your face might have developed wrinkles as it is a natural phenomenon which you can't reverse. The best would be to accept it without any sadness or without any urge to reverse it, as practically it won't be possible. Resisting it or trying to reverse it is only going to create sadness and frustration in you. This way, your unnatural desire of reliving your past by becoming physically young again will not only make you miss the colours of your present moment/age, but also the low energy created by your sadness/resistance that shall also speed up your aging thus, creating more wrinkles on your face. The best is to enjoy each and every moment of your life, each and every colour of your life maintaining your happy state of mind.

ACCEPTANCE IS NOT TO CONTROL BUT ACCEPT OTHERS UNCONDITIONALLY. You don't feel the urge to blame/control/change or to prove the other wrong. You just accept that there are differences in opinions/beliefs/perceptions of different people; it does not mean that one is right or other is wrong. Everybody is right in his/her own perspective. When you understand this, you take decisions accordingly, where you choose people in your life wisely, who are aligned with you and where you don't have the option to choose, you just accept the people as they are. You understand that you are with wrong people and you need to remove them from your life or you are with right people but you are not managing them right, you were trying to control them or you were expecting too much from them, so you need to change your approach/attitude towards them. **For example**, your child wanted to be a Lawyer but you didn't respect & accept his decision and you forced him to become a Doctor. And now, when he/she failed the medical exams, you are blaming your child. You didn't accept the fact that every person/soul has their own path; they are the best judges of their life. What you think is right might not be right for others. You did not accept your child's decision, you did not give him the freedom to live his life the way he wanted, may be you wanted to enforce your own unfulfilled dreams upon him. So, acceptance is to give freedom to live people by their own choices and not to control/change their ideas/beliefs. What you can do is just support & guide them but the final decision has to be taken by the life of the concerned.

ACCEPT PEOPLE & SITUATIONS AS THEY ARE OR ACCEPTING THE LIFE AS IT COMES TO YOU MEANS to accept the reality/truth of the moment as it is without any bias. **ACCEPTANCE DOES NOT MEAN THE APPROVAL OF SITUATION IN THE PRESENT MOMENT** which might be painful to you or others or all. **It just means approving the presence of the situation** that it is there, already happened and can't be reversed. **It is accepting the fact that the outside situation or people are not in your control but what is in your control is the response to the situation and that should be your only focus.** Responding to the situation in most responsible way is the only way to deal with each & every moment of life/whole life, to get the right outcome from the situation, nothing else.

ACCEPTANCE WITH ZERO RESISTANCE MEANS not creating any disturbance in your own emotions or not to get perturbed by any of the situations or not to get affected by any of the situations. It is to maintain your cool & calm mind in each & every situation of your life.

ACCEPTANCE WITH SURRENDER is the same as to accept the truth or surrender to the truthfulness/reality of the situation in the present moment so that it shall not be able to disturb you emotionally, as emotional disturbances leads to disconnection from the source. A cool & calm mind, stable mind, a conscious and energetic mind has all the natural power and the capacity to deal with any of the adversities of life. So surrender to the almighty/**REAL YOU** for the connection and real solutions in real life.

ACCEPTANCE MEANS TO FIND OUT THE CAUSE OF THE SITUATION: 1) Was it **due to your own actions** of past or **2)** due to **actions of somebody else** to whom you are related or **3) due to the majority action** of your family/society/country or world as a whole **4)** or **any reason which was beyond the control** of anybody? You may have been part of that on a major basis or may not but the situation created by those actions also affected you. **ACCEPTANCE MEANS TO PUT YOUR BEST FOOT** forward, to bring about the required change in the situation. So let's understand your best of actions/responses in the above said 4 causes.

1). WHEN THE PRESENT SITUATION IS THE OUTCOME OF YOUR INDIVIDUAL KARMA/ACTION, 95% of your life situations are the outcome of your own actions/karma/responses, so life is all about bringing a right change in your own karma (PDA) for a better present and future. **For example,** you need to accept the truth about you being poor in material wealth. You need to find out about your non-action or wrong actions or both which didn't allow you to become rich. You need to search for new ways to make yourself rich, take action on it to achieve your goal but never to become sad, depressed or make resistance your way of life, even if you fail every time, you just have to accept everything in your life. All in all, your unaware actions lead to your present moment, so you need to forgive yourself for your past mistakes and you need to accept yourself unconditionally to change yourself positively. **Same way, others also want acceptance from your side, are you ready for that?** Acceptance and forgiveness is the highest virtue of mankind. As the book progresses, we shall understand deeper aspects of unconditional love, acceptance, forgiveness and kindness for a fulfilling natural life.

2). WHEN THE PRESENT SITUATION IS THE OUTCOME OF ACTIONS TAKEN BY SOMEBODY ELSE, then you need to make them understand the causes and help them to take corrective actions. **But if you dig deep, it was only your non-action which gave approval for actions by others** that resulted in the situation today. If you already knew that their action was wrong, then the question arises, why did you allow that person to take that wrong action **or** you were not aware yourself that the action of the related person was right or wrong? Whatever may be the reason, either you were not aware yourself or you were weak to stop them, the responsibility of the result lies with you. Now you have to make yourself powerful and strong by accepting your own mistake and stop the other person from repeating the mistake and at the same time, correcting the mistake. If you took decisions/actions under the guidance/influence of somebody else, only you are to be blamed.

3). WHEN THE PRESENT SITUATION IS THE OUTCOME OF THE MAJORITY ACTION OF YOUR FAMILY/SOCIETY/COUNTRY OR WORLD AS A WHOLE. **For example, a lot of crimes taking place in your society** are obviously due to the mismanagement of the Governing bodies; their rules & regulations, their actions were not up to the mark and though, you are a part of the society, but not part of the governing body. So you have to accept the situations of crime, you don't have to make yourself emotionally disturbed by the situation, but you have to resist the wrong actions of the bad elements and you don't have to surrender to bad elements. You have to bring about the change in the Govt. policies or their way of working or bring about the change in the Govt. itself by increasing the awareness of masses. But for that, you need to understand the truth, accept the presence of bad elements and wrong governance, maintaining cool & calm and to respond in the best possible way in order to bring about the required changes so that these things don't happen in future.

4). WHEN THE PRESENT SITUATION IS BEYOND THE CONTROL OF ANYBODY, like the death of someone or natural calamity such as earth quake, thunderstorms, floods etc. on which nobody has any control, you just need to accept the situation, both internally and externally. The only action here is to pray, take actions to control the damages and keep moving forward in life. Situation in your present moment is your destiny beyond your control and the only thing in your control is your karma/actions/responses. And your job is to control and act on what you can change and forget about what you cannot. For example, your height is a result of your destiny and divine planning and your body weight is the result of your karma. Any natural calamity is a result of higher divine planning beyond your control and what you can do is heal the injured people and reconstruct the damaged properties. The only truth and knowledge is that "anything or everything is possible in life". The only thing that is in your control is to keep learning from the happenings, keep growing your knowledge, keep growing your awareness, keep doing good karma and leave the rest to nature/universe/god.

Whatever the situation may be or whatever may be the cause, your first action is not to create any internal resistance so as to make yourself strong, powerful who is capable of taking the best of the actions as per in need of the hour. **The best way to deal with any of the people & situations is FTIPP that is explained in the FORGIVENESS section 6.8 of this book.**

SO ACCEPTANCE IS,
Acceptance is seeing the situation as it is, without any bias.
Acceptance is to accept yourself as you are without conditions.
Acceptance is not to control others but to accept people & situations as they are without conditions.
Acceptance is acceptance of presence of situation and not approval of the situation.
Acceptance is to understand the cause which created the situation.
Acceptance is accepting responsibility for the outcome and not blaming others.

Acceptance is not to get perturbed by the situation without any internal resistance so as to activate the right actions/responses which are as per the need of the hour and not as per your comfort to bring about the required changes in the situation.

PURPOSE OF SITUATIONS, BE IT GOOD OR BAD

Situation is a situation, whether good or bad but having some purposes. **Some situations can never be changed**, it is the truth and the only choice you have is to accept it like the death of a near and dear, loss of limb etc. These situations are irreversible, not in your control and accepting it gives you the immense power & strength, develops faith & patience in you. **Some situations can be changed**, they are reversible and under your control. Like you might have become poor economically or you might have become unhealthy physically or mentally, or you might have developed bad relations or all. This is all due to reduction in your consciousness, because of the impact of negative or difficult times on your mind. Your disturbed mind's PDA went wrong, manifesting those problematic situations in your present. So for the right results you need to correct your PDA, nothing else.

Whatever may be the situation, it is meant for your personal growth but only if you want to make use of it. **Every situation, whether bad or good, poses some opportunities** for you to find and tap but only if you want to. Make use of every situation to understand life; learn from life, learn from your mistakes, correct your mistakes, develop life skills and convert all situations into opportunities. The situation might have come to develop some skills in you for you to be able to effectively deal with future situations/events. So, all the situations have some purposes but to meet these purposes, you need to be flexible, open minded and this can only be possible by an attitude of acceptance. The only purpose of any situation is to make you wise, strong, powerful, intelligent and valuable or may have come to change your life path which was on the wrong path. **Actually, all difficult situations are blessings in disguise** but for that, you need to accept the pain associated with the situation, it is a gift by nature as it wants you to grow and evolve in life.

The ultimate truth of the life is, "Whatever happened and is happening and shall happen is for good and for a cause, it is beyond your control, it is beyond your imagination, you cannot imagine the divine script and planning which is for a higher purpose." So, accepting all situations gracefully is the only intelligent option you have and resisting it is the cause of all misery. So accept the truth and align your PDA with truth for right results in your life.

WHAT ACCEPTANCE DOES TO YOU?

ACCEPTANCE, SURRENDER, ZERO RESISTANCE is the perfect formula to stay away from negative emotions, maintain cool & calm mind and maintain your energy & consciousness for much needed connection with the *REAL YOU,* **for**

perfect PDA in each & every moment of your life. It activates your natural path of life where you become a powerhouse of energy, expressing yourself **through** faith & belief in self/almighty, love, gratitude, kindness, happiness, forgiveness and celebration which gives you the much needed energy, confidence, courage, patience and intelligence to deal with all the situations, be it any. **Acceptance will give you the strength** to bear the situation which you cannot change, will give the courage and wisdom to take the appropriate required action, wisdom to change what needs to be changed. **Acceptance helps you to see the opportunity in every situation**. See, life is always full of opportunities, even if there are worst of situations, there are some opportunities hidden in that. So keep your mind, eyes and ears open, be flexible and always be ready to grab the opportunity. **Acceptance activates your third eye**, the seat house of all intuitive/creative powers having solution to all of your problems. **Acceptance not only activates your intelligence but at the same time, gives you the courage** to take righteous decisions and actions for right results. With right results comes the real success and happiness in the outer world.

When you start to take life as it comes to you, you will always feel contended, happy and at peace of mind in each & every moment of your life. And when your mind is at peace, your energy enhances that intensifies your spiritual connection, which further enhances your intelligence, leading to perfection in your thoughts, ideas, perceptions, decisions, behaviour and action as all are guided and directed by your soul which is much more intelligent than your mind. You become a source of happiness, not only to self but others also. You become your own Guru (Teacher), solving all problems of self and others; a real solution man in the community. **On the other hand, if you try to resist the situation,** you will definitely lose your peace of mind & intelligence, leading to wrong PDA & wrong results in life.

Acceptance gives you immense strength where you become an ocean of deep calmness, where no adversities in the outer physical world will be able to shake you; instead every unwanted situation makes you stronger and responsible. There may be a ripple which is superficial and temporary but that stone (unwanted situation) which produced a ripple on your outer layer of existence is not strong enough to impact you on the inside.

An emotional, disturbed state of mind depletes vital energy that creates disharmony in the mind, body and soul leading to all miseries in life. **The very purpose of spiritual practice of acceptance is to connect with your nature, is to develop a cool & calm mind,** a mind free of emotional disturbances, a mind which is not affected by the outside situations, which is able to see the truth as it is and takes the most appropriate action as per in need of the hour or demand of the situation. If you are able to live each & every moment of your life this way, you will be able to maintain a healthy mind & body leading to a perfect, natural life away from all emotional disturbances and thus, far, far away from miseries in physical life.

But how to develop an attitude of acceptance, zero resistance and surrender when the situations in life are contrasting and adverse? It might be very difficult as many of you have tried many times but the only secret is practice, practice and practice in your real life situations. To make it easy for you, I can give you a formula but again, you need to apply that formula in your life on a regular basis. And that formula is living your life consciously where you are fully focused on solutions and your actions in the present moment. **But again, you will think how to focus in present moment** and again, I give you a magic formula for this and **that formula is WOW, to make your life WOW.** Let's understand the *PRESENT MOMENT LIVING or VERTICAL ALIGNMENT*, how to practice a conscious way of life through WOW in next section of this book.

YOU) Can anyone achieve 100% degree of acceptance?
ME) No! Yes! Actually it all depends on you; your desire to understand, learn and practice the real science of life. The more you understand and practice in your real life situations, the greater becomes the degree of your acceptance. But, as you are humans having a duality in mind, there might be some situations which invoke disturbances in your emotions, where you might get angry or feel sad or jealous or any other negative thoughts or emotions may engulf your mind. **But again the solution lies in acceptance of even your negative emotions.** The acceptance of negative emotions of self or others or all shall raise your conscious presence and no negativity can withstand your conscious presence. **Acceptance of anything or everything, negative or positive dissolves all negativity & resistance and marks the dawn of light in your life.**

6.2 VERTICAL ALIGNMENT, I.P. THOUGHTs AND WOW

LIVING WITH CONSCIOUS PRESENCE OR LIVING WITH FOCUS IN PRESENT MOMENT OR PRESENT MOMENT LIVING OR VERTICAL ALIGNMENT; Unconscious state to conscious state

PRESENT MOMENT LIVING (PML) OR MORE APPROPRIATELY, VERTICAL ALIGNMENT simply means focus of mind in the present moment which converts a disturbed mind to a peaceful mind, leading to a connection with your source. It simply means the mind that is not disturbed by the past or worried about the future. It does not mean a non-thinking mind but a mind with full focus on present thoughts & actions leading to not only perfection but reduction in time of your work. Focus in the present moment raises your energy, consciousness (intelligence) and thus, awareness (knowledge) through activation of the 3rd eye which ultimately results in enhancement of intuition, creative power, memory, logical abilities and righteous PDA for better & brighter present and future.

When we talk about mind, we are invariably talking about thoughts & emotions and controlling your mind invariably means controlling your thoughts & emotions which can only be controlled by bringing the focus of mind in the present moment. We have already understood about thoughts & emotions in PART-A of this book but we need to understand deeper aspects of thoughts & emotions, to be able to control them and thus, mind and ultimately, your life.

Living in the present moment does not mean zero thoughts or no thoughts. It simply means that you are not getting thoughts which causes emotional disturbance in you like making you sad, angry, fearful, anxious, egoistic, overconfident, etc. These negative/biased thoughts only come when the focus of your mind is in the past or future where you are not aligned to the reality. **Focus of mind in the present moment ensures** deep insight into the work in hand, leading to truthful, transparent and unbiased clarity, understanding and perception about the work. So living in the present moment does not mean zero thoughts but thoughts of perfection at your work in hand. **On the other hand, thoughts from past & future** most likely result in negative emotions, leading to a biased PDA in the present moment; a perfect recipe for disaster. *"SIMPLY, YOUR CONSCIOUS FOCUS IN THE PRESENT MOMENT ENSURES THOUGHTS & EMOTIONS ARE COMING FROM HIGHER CONSCIOUSNESS LEADS TO A TRANSPARENT/TRUTHFUL PDA AND YOUR FOCUS IN PAST OR FUTURE ENSURES THOUGHTS & EMOTIONS COMING FROM LOWER CONSCIOUSNESS LEADS TO A BIASED PDA"*

But before understanding the thoughts & emotions and various techniques to control them, to control the focus of your mind, we must first understand the morphology of your personal space **through metamorphic model of your mind, time, body, real you, spiritual space and divine space.**

147

UNDERSTANDING THE CONNECTION OF MIND, REAL TIME (PRESENT), PSYCHOLOGICAL TIME (PAST, FUTURE), REAL YOU AND UNIVERSAL DIVINE POWERS through a metamorphic model MBS

DIVINE POWERS: The source of life, super consciousness, eternal omnipotent energy having highest frequency vibrations of love, passion, gratitude, happiness, forgiveness and celebration. It has no duality.

REAL YOU: The super conscious child of divine, eternal omnipotent energy having same frequency as that of Universal divine powers. **The real you and divine powers are always connected to each other**. It also has no duality.

YOUR CONSCIOUS MIND has the power of thoughts which are nothing but energy vibrations having frequencies. The duality of mind is due to the different frequencies of different thoughts. **Thoughts having high frequency energy vibrations** of love, gratitude, happiness, kindness, forgiveness, celebration and acceptance connects with the source; *REAL YOU* **and divine powers.** This source energy makes the mind & body perfectly healthy, natural, powerful, and intelligent beyond all logics, leading to perfect PDA and desired results in life. **The thoughts of low frequency vibrations** of undue anger, undue fear, hatred, envy and jealousy **clouds the subconscious mind** which weakens or cuts the connection with the *REAL YOU* leading to low energy and consciousness. The subconscious has lost its natural guide and attracts negative people & situations in life. Due to lower consciousness, mind comes under the influence of negative people & situations and hence gets corrupted leading to biased/defective PDA. Due to duality of mind, the thoughts keep on swaying from negative to positive to negative, thus, resulting in different karmas (PDA) at different point of time and thus, different results/situations in life. *THE ROLE OF CONSCIOUS MIND IS TO UNDERSTAND THIS VERY NATURE OF MIND, RISE ABOVE THE NEGATIVE THOUGHTS/LOWER CONSCIOUSNESS AND CHOOSE A HIGHER CONSCIOUSNESS FOR A HAPPY, PROSPEROUS AND PURPOSEFUL LIFE.*

PAST AND FUTURE TIMES (PSYCHOLOGICAL TIME) is a time of past which we have already experienced and future time which mind imagines. Mind always feeds on the past & future times and takes us away from life which is only in the present times/moment. Past and future are illusions of mind which constantly takes away your focus from present, precious moment, the only place for real action. And for action to be perfect it requires your full focus & energy but your focus on past or future or both creates scatter/division of energy in past, present and future. **Low presence of energy** in your present thoughts & actions lead to disconnection with the source, leading to lower consciousness/intelligence, leading to lower awareness/knowledge, leading to imperfection in your present decisions and actions resulting in imperfect or undesired results.

Past is nothing but memory and future can be anything but imagination. Both past and future times are in the mind. The mind lose its existence in the absence of past & future, **the very focus of your mind in the present moment marks the death of past & future (psychological times) and hence, the death of the mind operating from the memory or beliefs or lower consciousness.**

When a person is not able to fulfil his needs and wants, faces too much problems or unable to solve his/her problems, then the conscious mind has a tendency to focus too much on the past problems and fearing the repetition of past problems in future also. This creates an emotion of fear, sadness, anger and anxiety in the person. The emotions having low frequency vibrations disconnect from the present moment. Present moment is where the life is, a real time for real action and a real connection with the source of life happens here. If the negative thinking and emotions become a pattern, it clouds the subconscious disconnecting with its source of energy/light; *THE REAL YOU.*

PRESENT TIME AND SPACE is the present moment which belongs to your spiritual space. Life is in the present moment. It is absolutely necessary to have an attitude of faith in self/god, gratitude, happiness, kindness, unconditional love, forgiving, and celebration in the present moment to establish connection with the source. This enhances your energy field & consciousness leading to happy and joyous journey. Life is not in past, it is not in future, it is in now, the real moments of life, being fully focussed in the present makes your moment joyous and highly productive, rest all moments are just passing of time. So your conscious presence in the present moment is absolutely necessary to live every moment, moment by moment, by just focusing on the present moment, without being disturbed by past and future worries or problems. This connects you with your spiritual space, a space which causes perfection in your present actions of planning and execution for a better present and future. **A gap between mind activity is a where the divine space is present,** having solution to all your problems, having all the super intelligence for you to lead a happy, prosperous and purposeful life.

CLOCK TIME- Time calibrated and divided into units of seconds, minutes and hours on the basis of rotations of planet earth about its axis. It takes 24 hours for the earth to complete one rotation about its own axis which constitutes a one single day and so on. Clock time has been created by humans for their convenience to record events, to memorize past events, to set time limits for some actions/goals to achieve in future, to analyse performance, to compete with each other but it has nothing to do with life which is in the present moment. **Time is a creation of mind which always wants to analyse and compete with others.** But for life which is in the present moment, there is only one time and that is now. See for plants, animals, stars and planet etc., in fact the whole universe, there is no such thing as time, they are just living the moment, fulfilling the needs and purpose of their life.

CONNECTION OF LEFT, RIGHT, MID BRAIN & VERTEBRAE WITH THE PAST, FUTURE AND PRESENT TIMES

If you observe your brain, the left side of your brain is a store house of past memory and the right side of your brain is related to your future. The centre of your brain & vertebrae is connected to the *PRESENT MOMENT, REAL TIME, REAL YOU, and the DIVINE POWERS.* That is why you must have heard many people talking about mid brain activation. It is actually an activation of the third eye which connects your mind with the universal, divine powers for the activation of your intuitive/creative powers. **The centre of the brain is where there are minimal thoughts or your thoughts are focused on just one issue or intuitive thoughts coming from the divine space.** In meditation practice, we focus on the area between the eyebrows of both eyes, a place where the 3rd eye is located for connection with all the divine powers in the universe.

When someone focuses on the left side of brain, he/she gets connected to past. And when someone focuses on the right side of the brain, he/she is either dreaming or imagining future. This is the universal truth about all humans. NEED A PROOF OF THIS EXPERIMENT YOURSELF: Stand in front of the mirror and **start thinking about some incidence of your past,** to your amaze you will witness your eyes moving towards the left side of your brain. **Same way, if you start imagining about your future,** to your amaze you will witness your eyes moving towards your right brain. **Same way, if you somehow focus, observe the mirror in front of you**, your eyes will remain at the centre. When you start observing the things in front of you or your thoughts & emotions inside you, it means you are fully focused in the present moment. This enhances your energy, connects you with the universal divine powers activating the highest level/degree of intelligence, intuitive powers in you.

EXPERIMENT WITH OTHERS: You can even observe the eyes of any person whom you interact with. For example, ask him to describe the building (entry gate colour, design, no of rooms, furniture in rooms etc.) of his office or any other place he is well versed with. To your amaze, you will observe his/her eyes moving towards left while he is describing the each and every detail of that building. You ask him to visualize about his future, for example, ask him to describe what he will do if he becomes a prime minister of the country, again while describing his future, his eyeballs will move towards the right.

DIVINE POWERS, REAL YOU, FOCUS OF CONSCIOUS MIND IN PRESENT AND YOUR BODY ARE ALL VERTICALLY ALIGNED: Think of your brain and vertebrae, they are vertically aligned. All your energy chakras, endocrine glands and nerves are situated along your vertebrate and the mid brain. **Where there is focus, there is energy.** That is why when your focus is in the present moment, the cosmic energy movement starts happening vertically, energizing your all energy chakras, endocrine glands, body cells and mind, making them perfectly healthy, natural and intelligent. That is why only we the humans out of all living beings have the advantage of a big size brain and vertical vertebrae where movement of energy and consciousness happens just by **FOCUS OF YOUR CONSCIOUS MIND IN THE PRESENT MOMENT OR WORK IN HAND OR FOCUSING ON THE POSITIVE EMOTIONS OR ALL.** It's just a matter of choice, once your mind knows about how to get the optimum life energy.

PAST, FUTURE, AND MIND ARE HORIZONTALLY ALIGNED: The left and right brain are aligned horizontally. When the mind is constantly thinking about the past or future or both, there is a horizontal movement of energy from left to right to left and this way, the chakras, nerves and the endocrine system of your body, along the vertebrae does not get the required energy leading to lower energy field in your personal space and thus, an unhealthy body & mind having a lower consciousness.

MOVING FROM HORIZONTAL ALIGNMENT TO VERTICAL ALIGNMENT
JUST OBSERVE THE FIG. MBS 1, MBS 2, MBS 3 AND MBS 3a METAMORPHIC MODEL SHOWING CONNECTION OF MIND, TIME AND UNIVERSAL POWERS, TO GET A DEEPER UNDERSTANDING ON HOW MIND BECOMES NEGATIVE, DISCONNECTED FROM SOURCE AND HOW TO BRING BACK THE LOST CONNECTION

People whose mind is mostly occupied with past memories and future worries are aligned horizontally and disconnected with the present space. These people have a weak, emotionally disturbed mind & a body devoid of energy. A monkey mind that is not able to focus on present work and keeps on jumping from past to future, one issue to another, one problem to another; constantly thinking about things and issues which are not relevant anymore in the present times. Constant thinking about negative past experiences bring anger & sadness and future causes anxiety & fear leading to formation of clouds of negative emotions over your subconscious mind. This leads to decrease in vital energy in your chakras, vertebrae, endocrine system, nervous system and ultimately, cells of your body leading to an unhealthy mind & body. This leads to the disconnection with the higher self (space), which means losing your natural guide leading to wrong PDA which results in failure & misery instead of hard work and efforts. This creates more anger, frustration and sadness whose intensity will keep on increasing, unless and until we come out of this constant mind activity of past & future and learn to give space between the mind activity; learning to still the mind.
Also, **by too much thinking about the past or future, we are just wasting/killing our present, precious time** either not taking any action or doing unfocussed action. This way, you consume more time in your work which is also not up to the mark. An emotionally disturbed mind due to constant mind activity feels low and disconnected, unfocused in thoughts & actions, leading to wrong/biased PDA and thus miserable present and future.

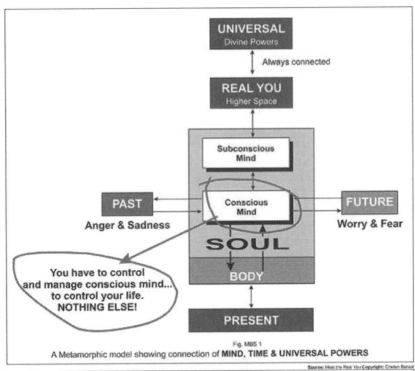

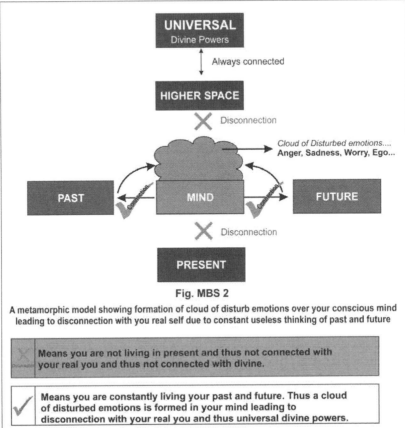

Fig. MBS 1

A Metamorphic model showing connection of MIND, TIME & UNIVERSAL POWERS

Fig. MBS 2

A metamorphic model showing formation of cloud of disturb emotions over your conscious mind leading to disconnection with you real self due to constant useless thinking of past and future

Means you are not living in present and thus not connected with your real you and thus not connected with divine.

Means you are constantly living your past and future. Thus a cloud of disturbed emotions is formed in your mind leading to disconnection with your real you and thus universal divine powers.

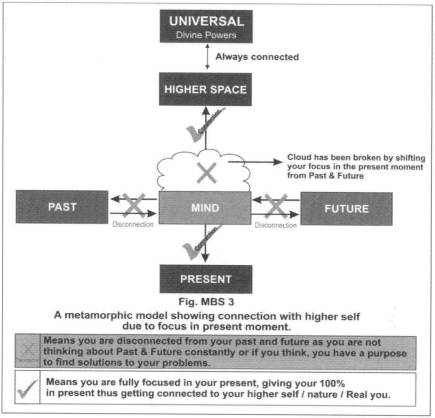

Fig. MBS 3

A metamorphic model showing connection with higher self
due to focus in present moment.

Means you are disconnected from your past and future as you are not
thinking about Past & Future constantly or if you think, you have a purpose
to find solutions to your problems.

Means you are fully focused in your present, giving your 100%
in present thus getting connected to your higher self / nature / Real you.

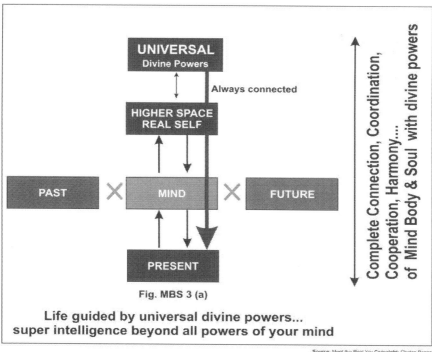

Fig. MBS 3 (a)

Life guided by universal divine powers...
super intelligence beyond all powers of your mind

Constant thinking of past problems creates same negative vibes which results in same negative actions & behaviour in present which leads to same types of problems which we experienced in the past. Thus, we are creating our future on the same past patterns by giving our focus to our negative past. This way, many people keep on replicating their past, in present and future. Frustrated with this, they lose connection with life, negativity becomes their set pattern of life and a belief is developed in them, **"Why me? Why is this being done to me? Why do I always attract negative people & situations? My life is a curse. I am unlucky." Thinking about the past won't change it** but understanding how the past became problematic and now how not to repeat the same mistakes is the only intelligent choice you have. **Same way, fearing the future** won't fetch you any desired results but a planning and action with your conscious cool & calm mind will take you towards your goal.

Bring back your focus on the present moment breaks the cloud of negative emotions, but the big question is how? Regular watching and observing of your thoughts & emotions is enough to bring back your focus in the present. **Focusing on your present aligns you vertically, charging your vertebrae, chakras, nervous system, endocrine system and body cells with life energy/source energy.** This leads to a complete harmony of vibes of mind, body, soul and energies making them work as one unit with the highest level of coordination and cooperation. The energy coming from the divine space super charges your mind & body which makes your mind extremely conscious and body perfectly healthy. Only a conscious mind can plan and give 100% in his actions in the present moment; a perfect recipe for a happy, successful and prosperous life.

Make it your regular habit to watch your thoughts & emotions, to maintain steady emotions, cool & calm, conscious mind and thus, vertically aligned. Vertical alignment sends a light of positive energy from higher self which strikes & breaks the cloud of ego over your chakras/subconscious, leading to complete removal of darkness. Once connected, all your actions, reactions, decisions, attitude, behaviour, beliefs, habits, goals, and purpose of life are guided by divine light where a mere intention with less effort will bring in required circumstances in your real life for manifestation of desired results; a real divine planning/blessings.

We all know the **importance of focus and must have** experienced that when we are not focused, we are not able to concentrate on even some very easy tasks in hand and on the other hand, when we are focused while doing even some difficult tasks, we are able to complete it, not only fast but also with perfection. **To change your life, the only secret formula is to bring back your focus in the present moment which connects with your eternal reality leading to perfection in PDA and thus, desired results in life.** So think positive, act positive and live in now to make your life wow through a best formula, WOW to enhance your focus and connection. We will understand about WOW in this section of this book only.

Exercise: Think any of your past experiences when you completed very difficult task with speed and accuracy. Also, think of any easy task which you were not able to complete in time due to disturbance in mind or unfocussed mind. **Write down**

Your   one   experience   of   focussed work_____

_____

_____

_____

_____

Your   one   experience   of   unfocussed work_____

_____

_____

_____

_____

So, you must understand the importance of living in the present, no worries for future and no regrets of past. Whatever happened can't be reversed, just use your experience to learn from your past mistakes, correct them, do not need to worry about future, just be in the present, giving your 100% focus in planning & actions and your future will automatically yield you desired results.

YOU) People want to relive their past or keep memorizing their good past or dream for better future but are never happy about their present or think their present is not good, why?

ME) *See, these are the people whose mind is not focussed in the present moment. They are not happy about their present moment and their focus of mind invariably goes in past good memories or future imagination of miracles.*

They want to relive their past because when their past was their present, they were not focussed in that moment and missed the enjoyment, fun and **opportunities of that moment**. They did not value that past moment then and now, they want to relive that moment which will never come back. You valuing your past (lost moment) can't give you any value rather, it's killing your present, precious moment where again, you will miss the focussed planning & action, again leading to wrong results.

And once you will lose this present moment, in future you would again like to relive your past (this present moment). Commonly, this is why people in college say that their school life was good and after college, their mind says my college days were good and when we become old, our childhood was good and so on. **But they will somehow find some reason to**

be unhappy about their present. See, it is not bad to relive your past good memories in your present, but just don't make it your habit or don't miss the precious present moments or do not limit your past memories as your best memories, who know that this moment will become your best memory till now and future might witness even better moments.

Same way, your mind will also keep on saying to you that future magical moments are coming in your life. But to create that magical, desirous life focus and persistence in thoughts, planning & actions are required in your present moment. Mere thinking of good future without right action/karma in present moment won't manifest it and if it were so, then your present would have been good, also as you dreamt in your past moments. So thinking, dreaming of a good future is good but it will become reality only if you align your dreams with your karma (righteous perception, emotions, actions).

The best way to live life is to be fully focussed in the present moment where you will have no regrets in life or you won't have the urge to relive your past or haste in to your future. Present moment is a gift of God and accepting the gift is experiencing peace, bliss, happiness, success and growth in life.

YOU) What about some people talking about going to future times or past times? I mean, many people talk of physically travelling to past or future?

ME) Good question. The answer is a simple No! A BIG No!

Yes, you can go to your past and future but only through your mind. **But physically, it is not possible.** Life is in now, there is no such thing as past and future for real physical life. Mind is a very powerful asset. It is a store-house of all information of past or we can even know about anything which has already happened in someone else's life or we can even see the live telecast of any incident happening at a distant place, only through the 3rd eye. But for that, a very sharp focus mind is required which can hear, feel and watch anything happening anywhere in the universe. Even the present vibrations of all people, intentions are present in the present space and the future can be seen by your mind by interpreting the same. But again for that a strong, focussed, sharp mind is required and it requires immense rigorous practice to master that skill. **So, anybody saying that a man can time travel physically is not possible** but possible virtually in your mind through self-meditation or by someone helping you through hypnotism.

I think, for a simple man like me, I use my mind to go to my past (past means this life, past does not only mean previous life) to analyse what went wrong in my life or what mistakes I have done which I don't have to repeat, I go to the past to enjoy my past happy memories. I visualize my future which I want to become or manifest in my life. So all in all, I use my mind to improve myself and my life situations.

Mind is an excellent tool, use it to go in the past and enjoy your pleasant memories, go to your past memories for some references, go to the future to see and feel your dreams getting fulfilled. Use your mind to plan and execute your goals. But never let your mind generate negative emotions in you or if generated, kill those negative emotions with your conscious presence. And please, do not bother about time travelling to past or future. If you are not excited about your present life, you can never enjoy your past or future.

YOU) Sir, I have understood that changing the focus of my mind from past & future's psychological times to the present space of divine is where life is but when I try to focus my mind on the present, it does not happen, somehow my mind goes to the past and future.

ME) yes, it will go to past & future but with practice, you can reduce the frequency of your focus going into past and future. It is the nature of mind to become sad and fearful, as it wants to protect you but it does not has the intelligence to assess the truthfulness of any situation as it cannot differentiate between illusion and reality. It is your job to show the right path to your mind by making your mind highly conscious through your focus in the present moment and not getting disturbed by any situation.

Forget about your focus in the present moment, **the simple solution** is to never allow any situation disturb you emotionally, meaning, no situation should be able to make you sad, fearful, angry, egoistic, depressive or aggressive, as all these emotions drain energy from your personal space, leading to low energy in your mind & body. Maintaining steady emotions is the way of presence in the present moment and connection with your omnipotent reality.

YOU) But sir, how can it be possible as I am not a super human and some situations will definitely disturb me?

ME) Okay! I agree and I understand that it can happen, but it should be temporary and you can choose to come out of that negative state of mind consciously as your mind is now aware about the bad effects of negative emotions on your physical body and life (refer **3.6 EFFECT OF THOUGHTS, EMOTIONS AND BELIEFS ON YOUR PERSONAL SPACE AND LIFE)**. Do not worry, now your aware mind will automatically choose happy state of mind sooner as it knows the impact of negative thoughts & emotions on your life. That is the power of awareness about self, mind, life and universe which has risen already within you, through you.

YOU) But sir, my knowledge & awareness about thoughts & emotions is still limited. Please explain it further, give some deep insights.

ME) you are making life difficult for me. But I will try to make it more insightful for you. I think I must ask some questions to you for me to understand your level of understanding and thus, give specific answers to you. So are you ready?

YOU) Yes, Sir.   **ME) Can you explain internal resistance?**

YOU) Resistance in any electrical circuit reduces/hinders the flow of current, the same way, internal resistance is like resisting the flow of current of life energy in personal space. The resistance is an emotional disturbance which reduces the flow of energy, depletes vital energy/life energy and it all happens due to too much worrying/thinking. This reduces the energy field/aura leading to an unhealthy mind & body devoid of energy.

Emotional disturbance=internal resistance

ME) Very good, so how can we stay away from internal resistance when the situations are difficult and testing in our life?

YOU) as the situation already happened, we can't reverse it. As the situation is either due to our own past actions or something which is beyond our control. The best I can do now is to ignore, accept, pray and rise above the situation if it is beyond my control or I have to act in the best, possible way for situations I can change/control. And for that, I have to understand the situation with 100% clarity, decide and act as per the truth for the best results. **When my focus shifts from crying to finding solution for the problem,** there is no space for any internal resistance or negative emotion.

ME) WOW! You are absorbing the concepts of life science perfectly. I am happy that I have made you understand exactly the way I wanted to. Now tell, what happens in an emotionally disturbance state of mind and emotionally stable state of mind?

YOU) Emotional disturbed state of mind: Sir, imagine a battery of mobile phone having low energy or no energy, the phone does not work properly or do not work at all. Same way, low energy in your personal space (mind & body) leads to a defective and an unhealthy mind & body which does not work the way it has been designed for. And when the working of mind & body becomes defective so are the undesirable actions and miserable results in life. **And low energy is due to emotional disturbances caused by too much focus of the mind in past & future's psychological times.** The energy is spread in the past & future times away from present space & time. This is the horizontal alignment where there is very less energy in personal present space.

   Emotionally stable state of mind: Same way, imagine battery of a mobile fully charged, the phone works perfectly the way it has been designed. Same way, a body with full energy acts, behaves and responds its natural way, leading to perfect results and happiness in life. The high energy is either due to our conscious focus in the present moment or not getting perturbed or disturbed by any/all situations in life. **The energy is spread vertically right from the bottom of your vertebrae to the centre and whole of your brain charging all the chakras, endocrine glands, nerves, and each & every cell of your body.** This activates super natural intelligence, creativity and intuition leading to truthful PDA and desired results.

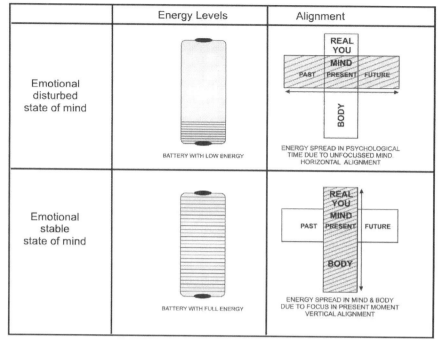

	Energy Levels	Alignment
Emotional disturbed state of mind	BATTERY WITH LOW ENERGY	ENERGY SPREAD IN PSYCHOLOGICAL TIME DUE TO UNFOCUSSED MIND. HORIZONTAL ALIGNMENT
Emotional stable state of mind	BATTERY WITH FULL ENERGY	ENERGY SPREAD IN MIND & BODY DUE TO FOCUS IN PRESENT MOMENT VERTICAL ALIGNMENT

Source: Meet the Real You **Copyright** Chetan Bansal

FOCUSED MIND	UNFOCUSED MIND
-FOCUS IN PRESENT MOMENT -FOCUS ON SOLUTION -CHOOSE NOT TO GET DISTRUBED BY SITUATIONS -ACCEPTANCE OF PREESENCE OF SITUATION/PEOPLE EXACTLY THE WAY THEY ARE ⇩ VERTICAL ALIGNMENT ⇩ OPTIMUM LIFE ENERGY IN PERSONAL SPACE ⇩ LIFE ON ITS NATURAL PATH GUIDED BY SUPER CONSCIOUS MIND	-TOO MUCH FOCUS IN PAST/FUTURE -FOCUS ON WORRY -ALLOWING SITUATIONS TO DISTURB -NON ACCEPTANCE ⇩ HORIZONTAL ALIGNMENT ⇩ LOW ENERGY IN PERSONAL SPACE ⇩ LIFE ON UNNATURAL PATH GUIDED BY DISTURBED/UNCONCIOUS MIND

Source: Meet the Real You **Copyright** Chetan Bansal

ME) Wow boss, you have explained wonderfully. Now kindly explain thoughts & emotions associated with acceptance and non-acceptance, and their impact on your life.

YOU) Sir, you answer it please.

ME) Okay! See, there are situations in life, some to our liking and some not. And we have a habit of resisting situations, we don't like and accept the situations we like. Or in other words, the thoughts & emotions associated with acceptance makes us happy which enhances our energy and thoughts & emotions associated with non-acceptance makes us sad which reduces our energy.

But the real fact is that whatever the situation is, whether we like it or not, it is there being truthful and inevitable. So, choosing non-acceptance about something which is there but we don't like is the cause of emotional pain & drain. This even clouds your natural intelligence which has the capability to change the situation positively. **This non-acceptance of reality is what I call negative or pessimistic or biased thinking because it drains your energy.**

But choosing acceptance of something that we don't like is the cause of emotional strength and activation of super natural intelligence, to convert the undesirable situation into a desirable one. **This acceptance of reality is what I call positive or optimistic or truthful thinking because it enhances our energy.**

Being optimistic and positive does not mean that you expect everything to be your way but you accept whatever life poses you, you accept the truth as it is, you take any/every problem as challenge, you take responsibility of your life, you take righteous actions. And all these thoughts and attitude will help in maintaining your cool, calm and balanced state of mind. This means you have faith, patience and belief in yourself which will always keep you positively charged. And you being positively charged means your vibrations are of high frequency which connects & synchronizes with your omnipotent, eternal reality. Once that happens, you are on your soul path; a natural path of life.

Many people misunderstand the concept of positive thinking. They think positive thinking is away from reality but for me, it is to accept reality as it is. Means that when you accept something, even which is not to your liking, you are not moved by it negatively and you remain in a balanced state of mind which gives you the intelligence to deal with the situation in the most responsible way. Non-acceptance creates internal disharmony and disturbance in mind which leads to losing your natural intelligence further leading to diminished ability to respond in a responsible way. And once the responsibility diminishes, so diminishes the happiness in life. **What positive/truthful thinking does** is that it generates thoughts & emotions of faith/belief in self, of patience, acceptance and unconditional love which charges you with energy/life energy/cosmic energy/energy of high frequency vibrations. Positive thinking comes from acceptance of reality which always keeps you high on energy.

What negative/biased thinking does is that it generates negative emotions of hatred, envy, jealousy, undue anger, ego, overconfidence, fear, resentment etc. which depletes life energy in you. Negative/biased thinking comes from non-acceptance/resistance of reality which reduces your energy.

Acceptance of reality----steady emotions----Thoughts of solution, of responsible actions---positive results in life. **Non acceptance of reality**----

internal resistance, disturbed emotions----Thoughts of worry, anxiety, frustration, undue anger-----further misery in life.

Let's understand the effects of positive thoughts & emotions associated with acceptance and effects of negative thoughts & emotions associated with non-acceptance on life situations.

SITUATION: "I want to marry Riya but her parents are against our marriage."
Fearful thought/Negative thought due to non-acceptance of reality: And thus, I have this constant fear that her parents shall be a big trouble and won't allow this marriage to become reality. This thought creates worry & anxiety in me and if this emotion becomes dominant in me, it won't allow me to act in a responsible/intelligent way, I will lose my confidence and hence, I won't even try to talk and convince to her parents.

Optimistic thought/Positive thought due to acceptance of reality: I want to marry Riya and I know her parents are against this marriage. I accept this truth. I have a faith & belief in self/almighty my marriage with Riya is bound to happen. Now, my focus here is to find out the reason as for why her parents are against me, talk to them, figure out and sort out the problem.

So I went to their house, talked to them, tried to convince them but they still said no to me. I was feeling uncomfortable, angry but I didn't lose my calm in front of them and came back to my house, still thinking about what is the way out.

Now I know her parents are adamant but still my persistent thought should be an optimistic one because that would keep my vibrations high and when my vibrations are high, it shall definitely create some situation to make this marriage come true. It is not that I will always feel good, sometimes fearful, pessimistic thought may come to my mind due to some unwanted circumstances or incidences, but I should accept them as well. At that time I should think that it's just a temporary passing thought and I must consciously change my focus to an optimistic thought. The key is to just believe in want you want and not be perturbed by temporary negative thoughts caused by a contrasting situation. And keep on taking action in the direction of your goal.

And you know why a persistent optimistic thought? A positive thought brings about positive results, as positive thoughts give us positive emotions of faith, belief and confidence which in turn makes our vibrations of high frequency that impacts our actions and behaviour positively, thus, attracting positive results in our life by attracting positive people and situations of high frequency or transforming the erstwhile negative person to positive or by removing negative people & situations from our life.

The law of energy vibrations is working each and every second of our life. We always attract what we always think or think most of the times. If we think of blessings, our life becomes easy and full of happiness and if we always think of problems, our life becomes problematic. So, acceptance is the

key to maintain high energy vibrations, to understand the truth, to align our decisions & actions with the truth and keep on taking actions as per the need of the hour and not as per our comfort or liking. **The good news is that we always have the power to change our thoughts, from negative to positive no matter what**, we always have the power to choose and today I take oath and the oath is,

"I choose to be happy & joyous each & every moment of my life, no matter what, I choose to value and love myself, I choose to accept life, people, and situations as they are, I choose to give my best in all my thoughts & actions, I am happy with everything, every situation."

ME) kindly explain, "Choose not to get disturbed by situations".

YOU) Whatever happens outside of me in my physical life is not under my control or what other people think & act is out of my control but what happens inside me is always in my control and I should never allow any outside disturbance to disturb me internally. I choose to accept life, challenge life, keep on learning and growing in life, always say yes to life and never give up in life. This is my conscious choice and nobody or no situation can take away my conscious choice from me.

ME) and what you think, do you have any other choice?

YOU) No sir, the only intelligent choice I have is to choose only positive thoughts & actions for the benefit of self or others or all to maintain my energy field and witness positive results in my life. Due to the presence of undesirable situations in my life today, if I choose emotional disturbance, my present actions shall go wrong leading to further miseries in my life.

ME) I am speech less, in short you have explained everything. Okay, now tell me the difference between thoughts and emotions.

YOU) Sir, both are energies but thought is a stable energy, an idea, a belief, a perspective about something and when the thought starts moving, it becomes emotion; energy in motion. Emotion, if positive enhances my energy field/aura and if emotions are negative, it simple means an emotion which reduces my energy field/aura.

ME) what are positive and negative emotions?

YOU) EMOTIONS/REACTIONS COMING FROM LOWER CONSCIOUSNESS/MIND (PSYCHOLOGICAL TIME) are of low frequency which further decreases energy and thus, leading to a low or negative energy field are negative emotions. Examples are fear, greed, non-acceptance, anxiety, undue anger, over-confidence, hate, envy, etc.
EMOTIONS COMING FROM HIGHER CONSCIOUSNESS/NATURE/REAL YOU/PRESENT TIME are of high frequency which further increases energy and

thus, leads to high or positive energy field. Examples are faith, acceptance, love, gratitude, kindness, celebration, forgiveness etc.

ME) so, what you think? What is more powerful, a thought without emotion or a thought with emotions?

YOU) Obviously! A thought with an emotion is more powerful than a thought without emotions, as emotions draw my focus/attention to believe/perceive/decide and finally take action. An emotion has an impact on my energy field, as it either enhances or reduces my life energy.

And the thoughts which are not able to invoke any emotions in me, meaning those thoughts does not attract my attention and when something does not attract my attention/focus, it fades away very fast from my mind and does not become any belief/perception/decision and action in my life. It was just a passing thought which came in to my focus and went away without any impact on my life.

If the emotion is wrong, it gives wrong direction to my life and if the emotion was right, it gives the right direction to my life. But whatever was the emotion, it was due to my thought. So, having right thought is the key to right emotion and thus, right PDA and right results in my life.

ME) NOW LISTEN CAREFULLY, THIS IS VERY IMPORTANT FOR YOU TO UNDERSTAND. "**YOU ARE ALMOST RIGHT HERE, BUT YOU CANNOT BLAME THE THOUGHT FOR YOUR EMOTION. IT IS YOUR INTELLIGENT CHOICE WHICH REJECTS OR ACCEPTS THE THOUGHTS AND ALLOWS OR DISALLOW THEM TO BECOME EMOTIONS. SO, IF YOUR INTELLIGENCE IS NOT WORKING PROPERLY, IT MEANS YOU ARE NOT ATTENTIVE OR FOCUSSED IN ALL YOUR THOUGHTS & ACTIONS, YOU MIGHT END UP GIVING EMOTIONS TO THE WRONG THOUGHTS AND WHEN THAT HAPPENS YOUR PDA AND HENCE, RESULTS WILL GO WRONG.**"

SEE, THERE ARE TWO TYPES OF THOUGHTS (I.P. thought process)
INITIAL TO PROCESSED (I.P.) THOGHTS
RAW THOUGHTS/FIRST INFORMATION REPORT/INITIAL THOUGHTS are instant/initial thoughts or reactions to the situation that we are in. These types of thoughts are always based on what looks apparent which may or may not be true. **The FIR needs to be processed through intelligence of higher faculties to arrive at FINAL THOUGHTS/PROCESSED THOUGHTS.** The final thoughts are our perceptions/decisions/actions which determine the outcome in life.

See, you will invariably get **wrong/illusionary/biased thoughts** of fear or greed as your mind is not intelligent enough to see the truth of the situation as it is, without any bias. You need to filter all your thoughts or thoughts of others who try to convince and influence you, *GIVING YOUR CONSCIOUS PRESENCE BY WATCHING, OBSERVING, WITNESSING* (WOW **technique** to activate your super natural intelligence) *YOUR THOUGHTS &*

ACTIONS AND SHOW YOUR MIND THE TRUTH. It is your duty to guide your mind, show it the right path and the job of your mind is to manifest anything/everything directed by your conscious choice. If you give wrong input to your mind, the output will also be wrong. Your mind works on the principle of **GIGO (Garbage in, Garbage out)**. So, you need to control the input and give the right input/guidance to your mind for right results in your life.

Mind is like a child with less knowledge/awareness and it is the duty of the **father with high knowledge/awareness** to guide the child. Once the child gets the direction, they start working in that direction with full focus and energy. So mind/child can never be blamed for wrong results but the guide/father of child/mind is to be blamed. In case of your mind, your consciousness is to be blamed. **It is your duty to activate your higher consciousness by watching/observing/witnessing every thought of your mind,** to filter out wrong thoughts and absorb right thoughts.

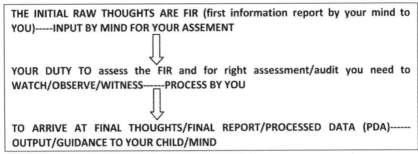

I.P. THOUGHT PROCESS (INITIAL TO PROCESSED THOUGHT THROUGH FILTERS OF WOW

THE INITIAL RAW THOUGHTS ARE FIR (first information report by your mind to YOU)-----INPUT BY MIND FOR YOUR ASSEMENT

YOUR DUTY TO assess the FIR and for right assessment/audit you need to WATCH/OBSERVE/WITNESS------PROCESS BY YOU

TO ARRIVE AT FINAL THOUGHTS/FINAL REPORT/PROCESSED DATA (PDA)------OUTPUT/GUIDANCE TO YOUR CHILD/MIND

Source: Meet the Real You Copyright Chetan Bansal

Let your **NATURE/THE REAL YOU** be the judge and not your reactive, disturbed mind. Nature is a space higher than mind. It is far more intelligent than your disturbed mind. *Like, a criminal is not judged on the basis of FIR by police or by the opinions of the parties involved as they are most likely to be biased, a further deep investigation by intelligence agencies (Mind focussed on solutions) is required for a Judgment to be passed by a Judge (Nature) who is unbiased and not related to the parties.*

Once a final judgment is passed by higher faculties (mind observing in the present moment), these FINAL THOUGHTS get the energy (Fuel) to travel to your subconscious and get stored there. Beliefs/perceptions/decisions are nothing but the emotion stored in subconscious mind. Now, this **PD (perception/decision)** becomes the action in your life and if this PD is wrong, then your **conscious choice is to be blamed** and not the thoughts by your mind.

THIS IS HOW A WRONG BELIEF/PERCEPTION BECOMES A MEMORY IN YOUR SUBCONSCIOUS, THROUGH A CLOUD OF POSITIVE & NEGATIVE EMOTION:

There are 2 situations in your life, either GOOD as perceived by you or BAD as perceived by you.

Situation 1 GOOD: This is what happens when your life situations are good, your mind perceives your present and future to be good also as mind always perceives based on experiences/beliefs/memories, irrespective of the truth. So, under the influence of success & happiness, it might miss the truth of the present times/situations which might require some corrective plans, decisions and actions for successful results in future also.

Situation 2 BAD: When your life situations are bad, undesirable, and painful to you, your mind perceives your present and future to be bad also, as mind always perceives based on memory/beliefs/experiences, irrespective of the truth. So it might miss some opportunity to succeed as it is engulfed in a deep state of sadness. And when you are in a negative state of mind, you lose your ability to see the truth. You invariably witness negative processed thoughts where your mind says everything is finished with no solutions to your problems.

The light in your life has been clouded by your emotions, either positive or negative leading to a biased PDA and hence, wrong results in life. **So the initial thoughts** can be positive which creates an illusion of only success & happiness in life or **your initial thoughts are negative** which creates an illusion of only failure & misery or your thoughts might keep on swaying from positive to negative to positive, irrespective of any reality or truth. These types of thoughts either make your understanding/perception/decision/action wrong or may not allow you to take action at all.

Whatever may be your thoughts, it may look negative or positive or balanced to you and the best way to deal with your thoughts is to give your conscious presence on all your thoughts to arrive at truthful balanced final thoughts, PDA. Make it your habit to watch, observe and witness (WOW) your thoughts. Giving your conscious presence to your thoughts align you vertically leading to the flow of super intelligent life energy in your vertebrae, brain activating your natural intelligence which shows you the truth of what to do, and how to do in the best way for the best of results.

RAW INITIAL THOUGHTS--------FILTERED THROUGH CONSCIOUS FOCUS (WOW)------STEADY EMOTION/VERTICAL ALIGNMENT-------ACTIVATES SUPER INTELLIGENCE------TRUTHFUL FINAL THOUGHTS PDA-----RIGHT RESULTS IN LIFE

RAW INITIAL THOUGHTS--------FILTERED THROUGH PSYCHOLOGICAL SPACE/MEMORY/BELIEFS------EMOTIONAL DISTRUBANCE/HORIZONTAL ALIGNMENT-------LOWER CONSCIOUSNESS-------BIASED FINAL THOUGHTS PDA-------WRONG RESULTS

YOU) Sir, I have listened & read in many books and blogs that positive thinking is the way to success & happiness and here you are, saying that positive thinking can lead to a biased PDA and thus, wrong results in life. Kindly throw some more light on it.

ME) Yes, positive thinking if takes away your focus from the present space is of no use. I have already told you, forget about thoughts being negative or positive, just give your focus on all your thoughts to find the truth of any thoughts/information coming in your presence, as your presence ensures life energy in your vertebrae & brain ensures working of your super natural intelligence all the time, whether you are thinking negatively or positively, does not matter. **What matters are your final thoughts, your perception/decisions/actions and for truthful PDA, the KEY is your focus in the present moment.**

YOU) Sir, does it mean that I should never go to my past memory or should I never imagine/dream about my future as that would lead to a horizontal alignment and thus, no energy in vertebrae which will lead to a biased PDA?

ME) No I am not saying that, you can and you should go to your past memories and even dream/imagine about your future but never allow any thought, either from past or future to disturb you emotionally. **Ensuring a steady emotion shall ensure vertical alignment** which shall even show the truth about your past memories, leading to the removal of negative beliefs/memories from your mind. It shall help you to find the mistakes of your past and the same intelligence shall also shows you the real dreams/purposes of your life for which you have come on this planet. This way, it shall put your life back on your original, natural path designed for you.

YOU) Sir, does that mean going to the past and future is not overthinking?

ME) Forget going to past or future, just remember this, any thinking which disturbs you emotionally is overthinking and any thinking which guides you towards solutions, to your problems is right/balanced thinking. And always remember, whatever you are doing, either thinking or taking any action or doing both, maintain your focus in the present moment, to maintain your energy and never allow any situation to disturb you. So, thinking for solutions are always good and thinking that leads to worry/anxiety are always bad.

YOU) Sir, this is really exciting, to know the depths of my mind; thoughts & emotions to control my mind and thus, life.

ME) I assure you one thing that by the time you end this book you will become the master of your thoughts & emotions and all your confusions/myths about your life/mind/thoughts/emotions/beliefs will be broken. I have tried to write this book in such a way that if something does not become clear to you in PART-A of this book, it will become clear in PART-B and if not in PART-B, then it will definitely become clear in PART-C Or, if you are still not clear about something/anything, WOW focus is always there with you.

YOU) Sir, please correct me if I am wrong, the above discussion means that not all thoughts but the *FINAL PROCESSED THOUGHTS* are under my control and to control them, I need to maintain steady emotions so as to maintain eternal energy in my personal space. *RAW INITIAL THOUGHTS* are the reaction of mind to the situation which is not under my control. So, I cannot stop initial thoughts; they will come, let them come and my only job is not to get disturbed by them or overwhelmed by them. I can just give my conscious presence to them by watching, observing and witnessing them. This ensures complete focus on my thoughts leading to the removal of negative/irrelevant thoughts from my mind and perfection & clarity in my *FINAL PROCESSED THOUGHTS (PDA).* This also gives an insight that all thoughts are not manifested in my life but only **the final processed thoughts** that I choose, focus upon, decide upon, gives my time & energy are manifested in my life and rest all have is no impact on my life.

The life energy is the root of my life which creates & maintains my life and the absence of it ends life. So maintaining that energy in me ensures strong roots and when roots are strong, the whole tree, branches and fruits shall be strong, powerful, healthy, happy and joyous. And to maintain that energy, I just need to control and manage my emotions, by giving my full focus through watching, observing and witnessing all my initial thoughts, emotions and beliefs, to convert them to useful, truthful, righteous information (processed thoughts) for the final action.

ME) Brilliant! My *DEAR REAL YOU*, I am now 100% sure that you will always use your presence and no situation will ever be able to influence you or disturb you emotionally.

Now understand the most important skill/technique for a vertical alignment, for real connection with *THE REAL YOU/CREATOR/GURU* inside you, to activate truthful PDA in each & every moment of your life. **"WOW TECHNIQUE"** to control/check/correct/audit your **INITIAL RAW THOUGHTS**, to arrive at truthful **FINAL PROCESSED THOUGHTS** (PDA) BY STEADYING YOUR EMOTIONS OR TO ALIGN YOURSELF VERTICALLY OR FOR THE PRESENT MOMENT LIVING OR FOR THE SPIRITUAL WAY OF LIFE OR TO FIND and live the TRUTH.

To help convert a disturbed mind into a peaceful mind or for bringing the mind back to the present moment along with practicing the attitude of acceptance of life as it comes to you, we must practice some present moment living techniques. The purpose of all spiritual practices is to achieve permanent peace of mind through present moment living. Here are some practical techniques to bring the mind back to the present moment, to connect with a space above mind; a natural space, divine space, spiritual space for a perfectly healthy body and a positive/realistic/conscious mind.

Let us understand spiritual techniques to increase your energy vibrations and thus, consciousness; very powerful mind power techniques to **MEET THE REAL YOU,** to enhance your life skills, to set you on path of happiness, success & growth.

TECHNIQUE FOR VERTICAL ALIGNMENT OR FOR CONVERTING A DISTURBED MIND TO A SUPERCONSCIOUS MIND

1) AND THE ONLY ONE: FOCUS/DHYANA/MEDITATION USING "WOW" TECHNIQUE

WOW FOCUS technique is the father of all mind power and spiritual techniques. All other techniques are derivative of WOW only. So if you can learn, practice and master WOW, then your life will surely become WOW. Let's start.

Unfocussed mind keeps on jumping from past to future to present, one issue to another without your permission. This way, your focus in the present moment is less which means less energy that reduces your energy, consciousness and super natural intelligence leading to wrong/biased PDA and miserable results in life. The more is the time of focus on something, the more is the connection which leads to more awareness, clarity, understanding and perception about that thing, further leading to righteous decisions, actions and results in life. Thus, you need to develop laser sharp conscious focus, we all know the importance of focus but the big question is, how to develop that laser sharp focus i.e. WOW.

WOW (WATCH/OBSERVE/WITNESS) TO LASER SHARP FOCUS

Meditation is just Dhyana or focus. **Watching, observing and witnessing (WOW)** is a process of Dhyana/focus leading to increase in the degree of your focus. The more you WOW, the sharper and stronger become the Dhyana/focus.

Broadly speaking, there are two types of meditation/focus:
See, this is very simple in your present moment, you have **YOUR INNER WORLD** of thoughts, emotions and feelings and **YOUR OUTER WORLD** where you have some job, work to do or you need to tackle some people & situations.
Internal meditation- Watching, observing and witnessing your thoughts, emotions, feelings, body parts, breath is internal meditation. WOW increases your energy leading to a connection with your source that leads to increase in

your consciousness and awareness. We will understand the scientific basis, process and benefits of internal meditation in PART C of this book only.

External Meditation- Watching, observing, and witnessing, giving your full focus to your job/work/people/situations in your life is external meditation which establishes a sharp connection with your work/people/situations, leading to perfection & clarity in your awareness, which further leads to righteous PDA and thus, desired results in life.

WOW is just **watching, observing and witnessing your thoughts, emotions, job, work, people & situations around you without any emotional disturbances of over excitement, anger, fear, greed, anxiety etc. Watching and observing is giving your focus (Dhyana),** enhances your connection with the spiritual space. **Witnessing is something as simple as just observing without being involved in action.** A witness is always an observer of the agreement, action of the third parties. He is not involved in any way, neither as an actor nor as an advisor nor his feelings/emotions involved. He is unperturbed by the actions of the third parties, fully detached from them, just observing the situation/people/third parties. Witnessing is like choosing not to be affected emotionally by any or all thoughts & actions of yours and others.

What WOW does? It enhances your focus, your conscious presence, steadies your emotions and thus, enhances clarity where you are able to perceive the truth as it is, without any bias leading to a right appropriate action/response and not an emotional reaction. All in all, this activates the highest level of PDA leading to righteous results in life.

How WOW works? Think of somebody with a defective vision, has a blurring vision as images do not focus on his retina. Corrective glasses help focus images on retina leading to a crystal clear vision. Glasses helped him to view the objects clearly, exactly as they are. **Same way, when you watch, observe and witness something/anything, your focus becomes razor sharp which gives clarity about that thing, person or situation.** See, when you WOW something, your focus enhances leading to high energy vibrations, which further leads to the connection with that thing and connection gives clarity about that thing. Then you are able to view, hear, understand and feel the situations/people as they are, without any bias. **So for clarity, you need energy, for which you need focus which comes from WOW. Understand the flow chart of WOW, leading to more focus, energy, awareness, clarity, and transparency.**

WOW TECHNIQUE TO DEVELOP LASER SHARP FOCUS

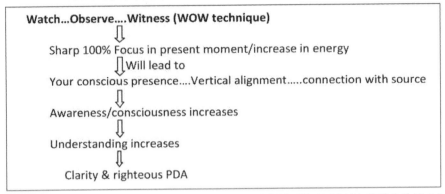

Do you perceive life situations through awareness or beliefs? If, through beliefs your perception might be biased and thus, a miserable life. **Remember, a belief is based on past memories and awareness is based on the present moment.**

INTERNAL MEDITATION PRACTICE

Meditation is like bringing the focus of mind from many to one; many thoughts on varied issues to one issue. This enhanced focus of mind increases the energy of your mind leading to a vertical alignment and thus, enhancing your natural intelligence setting your life on automatic/natural/successful path of life.

Breathing plays an important role in your practice of focus/Dhyana/Meditation. So if you know how to breathe, you can easily meditate and you reading this book confirm that you are breathing but may be not in the right way or disturbances in your emotions have distorted your breathing pattern and you are not aware about it. Don't worry! I will not only make you aware of that but also give you the techniques to correct your breathing pattern, to control your emotions but all that in **PART C of this book.**

The purpose of all meditation practices is to bring your focus in the present moment, a process to calm your mind. **Internal Meditation is for everybody; for you, me and all of us**. It is a simple process to control, guide and enhance the consciousness of your mind, by connecting with the source of life, *THE REAL YOU.* **A simple practice of internal WOW meditation using your mind & body where you give your full focus/attention to your thoughts & emotions** will align you vertically. When alone, give your full focus onto yourself as if you are the only and the best person in your life, at least give 30 minutes to yourself everyday where you practice internal meditation.

A simple act of ANTAR DHAYANA/INTERNAL MEDITATION (focus) will increase your awareness (knowledge), making you SAYANA/conscious (intelligent) by connecting with your source of life. Internal meditation, when done on a regular/consistent basis **will** bring your mind to the present moment, increase self-awareness by showing your likes & dislikes, hidden talents, passions, purposes of life, remove all negative thoughts/emotions/beliefs from your mind/body/soul, enhances physical well-being by balancing all your chakras/hormones/glands, will make you emotionally/mentally/spiritually stronger where trust, faith, love, care, happiness, gratitude, kindness, celebration shall become your attitude of life. Where all your actions, reactions, decisions, perceptions, beliefs, and habits shall be guided by the God power sitting inside you so that you can find solutions to your problems, fulfil your dreams & purposes leading to a meaningful life where you witness success & growth in all areas of life viz. HWRC thus **enhancing your overall happiness quotient in your life**.

Mind & body are excellent tools given by nature to experience and enjoy life, but the problem is that we are not aware about the tools & techniques, to make them efficient or utilise them to their full potential. So we do hit and trail which gives wrong & undesired results in life. Meditation helps in activating the powers of your mind & body, by treating them with the source of life.

The physical technique of meditation, to instantly raise your energy vibrations is practiced **by focusing on your breath, the third eye, vertebrae** and you will understand it in PART C of this book.

EXTERNAL MEDITATION PRACTICE

Watching, observing, witnessing the real physical world (people, situations, and your actions) in your real present space is a simple technique of external meditation. Practicing WOW in your routines will make your every action easy, effortless and successful. Most problems or majority of your problems, say about 99% of your problems are due to your mind not being present in your thoughts & actions. Rest 1% problem are not in your control and you should not worry about them. Your responsibility is to enhance the quality of PDA for desired results in life but that can be only possible through WOW focus in each & every action of yours.

This is how to follow, practice "WOW" meditation in your daily life: Give your full focus; watch/observe/witness every action/job of yours whether eating, bathing, studying, driving, doing your professional job etc. and never allow your mind to be somewhere else. This will keep you connected with your eternal reality, leading to steady emotions, leading to truthful perception, righteous decisions and development of hand, eye, foot, complete body and mind coordination for perfection in actions. This helps you to complete your work in optimum time with ultimate precision, perfection and quality. With regular practice of WOW, your perfection about everything you do will keep on increasing, making you a skilful master. The more is the focus, the faster is the speed of learning and mastery. We will understand about developing skilful action (WOW FOR SKILL DEVELOPMENT) in section 7.3 of this book only.

PRACTICING WOW FOCUS FOR ENHANCING LIFE SKILLS
A) RELINQUISHING NEGATIVE THOUGHTS & EMOTIONS, "WOW" TECHNIQUE
A1) "WOW" TO SOLVE PROBLEMS
A2) CONSCIOUSLY CREATE A GAP BETWEEN MIND ACTIVITY THROUGH "WOW"
A3) BALANCING YOUR THOUGHTS THROUGH FOCUS/ AWARENESS/CONSCIOUS PRESENCE:
A4) ALWAYS FEEL GOOD: CHOOSE/FOCUS ON POSITIVE EMOTIONS
B) "WOW" FOR LOVE & COMMUNICATION- SEC 6.4
C) "WOW" FOR ACTIVATION OF HIGHER FACULTIES OF MIND TO RELINQUISH DISEMPOWERING BELIEFS AND ACTIVATING RIGHTEOUS PDA- SEC 7.1
D) "WOW" FOR SKILL DEVELOPMENT- SEC 7.3

A) RELINQUISHING NEGATIVE THOUGHTS & EMOTIONS, "WOW" TECHNIQUE

A1). WOW TO SOLVE PROBLEMS

When we encounter problem for which we don't have any solution, **our emotions** of anger, pain, sadness, fear, anxiety and frustration take over our personal space. We start repenting the situation and blame others for the situation. This forms a cloud of disturbed emotions over our real intelligence leading to confusions, opaqueness, and misunderstandings. The biased perception and decision of an emotionally disturbed mind leads to wrong actions, further leading to more miseries and nothing seems to work in a right manner. Life has become hell due to our own negligence, non-awareness of self and others.

We worry too much about the problem which further creates disturbance in mind. **Shifting the focus of mind on solutions** is the real solution to all problems, be it any. Focusing on the solution is the only intelligent choice you have, instead of thinking why it has happened, you must focus on how it has happened and what best you can do to bring about the required change and if you can't do anything about it, leave it to the almighty and just pray for the best. To practice this, a cool & calm mind is required to control negative thoughts & emotions, but how?

A simple solution is "WOW". **Watch, observe and witness your thoughts & emotions steadies your emotions,** will automatically shift your focus from problem to solutions, also shows you the root cause of the problem, how it happened, how it can be changed now, what immediate actions you need to take to reduce the problem, and finally to eradicate the problem from the roots so that it can never happen in future. Not only that, you will also be able to see and tap the hidden opportunities that are always intrinsic part of the problems be it any. All in all, your conscious presence through WOW will prove the statement right, "Blessing in disguise".

A2) CONSCIOUSLY CREATE A GAP BETWEEN MIND ACTIVITY USING "WOW" FOR A VERTICAL ALIGNMENT OR how to deal with arguments and emotional reaction of self and others (heated exchanges) by creating a time gap between the mind activity. **Wait for a while, listen to the other and then respond but don't react.**

Means stop your mind from thinking for a moment or two; make it silent. If you can break the continuity of your mind, you get connected to a spiritual space, a real space, a super intelligent processor; your conscious presence. A human mind feeds on past & future, means it needs psychological time to survive. Remember, the past & future are psychological times and present is the time of your super intelligent nature. Creating a gap of conscious silence marks the death of mind where focus shifts from past or future or both to PRESENT. And this is what we want for a peaceful, non-reactive mind. **The silence of mind activates response instead of a reaction.** Response comes from the word responsibility, your ability to respond in the most appropriate manner as per the need of the hour. **Responsibility= Response + ability.**

<u>Let us understand Reaction:</u>

If you have read chemistry, you must be aware that when two chemicals meet, a reaction happens which changes the chemical and physical properties of original chemical, meaning the original chemicals lose their originality and they become something new due to interaction with each other.

Chemical A + Chemical B = Chemical C

Both A and B lost their originality and became C.

Same way if you are facing wrath/emotional outburst of someone else and if you allow their negative energy to mingle/synchronize/align with your thoughts, your emotions change which in turn changes your biochemistry leading to the change in the original nature of your body cells causing physical health issues and at the same time, your nature/behaviour of love, compassion, and empathy changes to hate, anger, frustration and you also start reacting from a disturbed state of mind. **A mind has unknowingly caught the negative energy of the other, a reaction has happened where you lost your original nature and start reacting from a disturbed mind.**

But you also have a choice, to create a gap in the mind activity by

1). Pausing your negative thoughts consciously, either by silencing your mind or maintaining coolness & calmness in your mind.

2). Ignoring the emotional outburst of an unconscious person. You know that the other person is behaving in such a way as he is himself disturbed or he/she does not know the truth. The unconscious state may have become a permanent feature of the other person due to wrong understanding, interpretation and perception of life & life situations. All in all, they are unconscious of what they are doing and their mind is under the influence of negative emotions.

Watching, observing and witnessing the people and their behaviour brings your focus back in the present moment thereby, helping you maintain your cool & calm, help you in understanding the cause of behaviour of the other person, activates right response/intelligence to deal with the other person. This will not allow mixing/reaction with negative energy of the other in you and thus, protects your original nature. Moreover your WOW also calms, heals and silences the other person.

Reaction comes from a space of conditioned mind or beliefs based on misinterpretations of past memory and impressions where the other person tags you the culprit, like **"you abused me, ruined my life or betrayed me".** Well, that may be true but mostly, it's not. Whatever may be the reality, whether the other person is carrying the truth or illusion in his memory, a slightest of irritation or problem activates that past painful memory leading to over-reactive emotional outbursts on to you, a poor you. If you yourself are unconscious/unaware, you also react aggressively making the other more reactive and a series of negative action-reaction between you and the other starts. Frequent emotional reactions are the major cause of problems in relations and thus, almost all areas of life.

People who have a habit of reacting immediately without understanding the truth suffer from biased perception which leads to misunderstandings. Misunderstandings lead to negative emotions causing reactive behaviour, verbal abuse and may result in physical violence which leads to disconnection with people. Once disconnected, communication goes and nobody will listen to you, even if you are right as you have activated bad feelings/dislike for you in the other person. **The only solution is responding with a cool & calm mind,** we must learn the art of dealing with people & situations in the most understanding, loving and caring way which requires immense **silence and patience.**

Reacting aggressively, even when you know that the other person is biased, have vested interest, and trying to fool you is foolish on your part. We cannot change the other person as they have their own set of core beliefs, opinions, perceptions and habits. Trying to change the other person from a lower space of mind (aggressive reaction) will only result in disputes and fights. But rarely, if the situation demands us to react aggressively, we must but anger should always be in our control. **We will understand how to use anger in happiness in section 6.4 of this book.**

The other person may or may not change positively, but it is our duty/karma to protect the consciousness (intelligence) of our mind by bringing the focus in the present moment and the easiest way to do that is "WOW". WOW connects with your spiritual space, by creating a gap or silencing your mind, gives you the strength & intelligence to listen, understand and to respond/communicate without hurting the feelings of the other person. In 95% cases, your positive response also cools & calms down the other person, activates his/her spiritual space where sooner or later, he/she also starts responding. This attitude of positive response is where the solution to all problems and disputes lie.

SS MIND: RS TO SS (REACTIVE SAD MIND TO SILENT SMILING MIND).
You always have a choice, to convert your RS mind to SS mind by choosing inner & eternal silence and smile. It is like a SS (stainless steel) which is not affected/rusted by outside atmosphere as compared to RS (raw steel) which is rusted by the atmosphere. Here in case of your mind, the choice is yours, to not to get affected by difficult situations outside, by choosing a best response i.e. SS (Silence & smile). A silent & smiling mind is unperturbed by any of the circumstances and is able to maintain its originality, it's cool & calm nature away from all disturbance and noise but all through WOW conscious presence.

A3) BALANCING YOUR THOUGHTS & EMOTIONS THROUGH WOW FOCUS; YOUR CONSCIOUS PRESENCE:

So many thoughts are knocking on your mind continuously but you need to process all to filter out unwanted/irrational/irrelevant thoughts, to arrive at final choice/thoughts. Life is not about controlling the flow of thoughts but to filter thoughts through a conscious presence.

Thoughts are thoughts, neither positive nor negative; it is just the perception of your mind. BOTH negative and positive thoughts are good for us. Positive thoughts give confidence but excess can give overconfidence and ego, where a person may deviate from the truth leading to failures. A little of negative thoughts help us in good analysis & understanding of life and situations, a little concern or caution to help in decisions but excess of negative thoughts are always irrational and gives depression. Both positive & negative takes us away from the reality and balance in both brings back us to reality. **So, we need to balance both with awareness and increase of consciousness.** And the best way to do that is to **watch, observe and witness** your thoughts which will show us the truth, removing clouds of confusion making your vision crystal clear, leading to righteous actions and desired results in life. **WOW all your thoughts to remove all negativity/darkness from your mind as no negativity, either of yours or others or all can't withstand your conscious presence.**

A4) ALWAYS FEEL GOOD, CHOOSE/FOCUS ON POSITIVE EMOTIONS

ALWAYS FEEL GOOD, ALWAYS BELIEVE GOOD, ALWAYS ACT GOOD TO RAISE YOUR VIBRATIONS, TO RAISE YOUR CONSCIOUS PRESENCE AND THUS, LIFE.
The simple trick is to have positive/optimistic/truthful thoughts: **Tremendous no. of thoughts, wide variety of thoughts sometimes negative, sometimes positive, sometimes from past, from future, from present situation keep on bombarding mind. It is the universal fact that every person on an average gets almost 60,000 thoughts every day. 60K! Isn't it amazing!** Some thoughts invoke a positive emotion that enhances your energy and some negative

emotions deplete your energy. It is very difficult to control the flow of thoughts; the best would be to control the feelings. Either we feel bad or we feel good but never both. If we are feeling bad, we would invariably attract negative thoughts and if we are feeling good, we would only have positive thoughts and it can't be vice-versa. The best way to control your thoughts is by feeling good all the time and the best way to feel good all the time is by doing things that makes you happy.

The good feelings/happiness come from the spiritual way of life where you choose acceptance, conscious presence, faith in self/almighty, Gratitude, Happiness, Kindness, Forgiveness, Unconditional love, celebration; where you pursue your hobbies like listening to music, dance, watching favourite movie, playing your favourite sport, travelling; anything that makes you feel happy.

This is the only way to raise your energy vibrations, to raise your consciousness, to raise your awareness, to arrive at a truthful PDA and finally, desired results in life.

FORMULA FOR RIGHTEOUS THOUGHTS: AFG-ABG-AAG
(ALWAYS FEEL GOOD, ALWAYS BELIEVE GOOD, ALWAYS ACT GOOD)

A	B	C
Input of conscious mind	**Effect of conscious feeling in our subconscious mind**	**Output results in our life**
Persistently feel, believe, act only good in your life	Makes our subconscious and energy field positive	Happy, prosperous, successful life
Our focus must be on column 'A'(Conscious mind) only to automatically take care of 'B' and 'C' .	Vertical alignment activating 3rd eye for effortless life	Purposeful life/life on its natural path

Source: Meet the Real You **Copyright** Chetan Bansal

Feeling good---Positive vibes of high energy & frequency
Feeling bad---Negative vibes of low energy & frequency
Formula for right/positive/optimistic/balanced thinking is "AFG—ABG---AAG"
ALWAYS FEEL GOOD--ALWAYS BELIEVE GOOD--ALWAYS ACT GOOD.

This should be your conscious choice and if you have any problem choosing this, WOW is always there to automatically activate **"AFG—ABG---AAG" in you. WOW takes you towards** right thoughts, beliefs and actions which are always aligned with the truth.

Always remember that the results, happiness, success and failure in your life are dependent on your 3 core karmas which are dependent on the focus of your mind.

THE SECRET TO RIGHT PERCEPTION IS FOCUS, THE SECRET TO RIGHT ACTION IS PRACTICE WITH FOCUS, THE SECRET TO RIGHT RESULT IS PATIENCE WITH FOCUS, *BADI KAMAL KI CHEEZ HAI YEH FOCUS, SAMBHAL KAR RAKHNA, KHO MAAT DENA ISKO*

(means the focus is an amazing tool to success, always keep it with you, never part with it as parting with it means inviting miseries in life)

YOU) Sir, please explain the difference between consciousness and awareness.

ME) Look boss, don't try to audit the words, just understand the feeling and the meaningful message associated with it. Since that you have asked, I will try to explain it to you.

Energy is the source of life and increase in the energy leads to increased **consciousness (intelligence) of your mind** which leads to **increase in awareness (knowledge) of mind** about self, others, life, universe or anything/everything you focus upon. **The secret to increase in the energy** is your conscious presence, meaning focus in the present moment and the secret to conscious presence is WOW which ultimately leads to increase in your awareness. **The more is the energy,** the more is the consciousness and better is the awareness. Better awareness always means understanding the truth as it is, without any bias, aligning your decisions & actions with the truth for better results in life. So, increase in awareness is the only recipe for success, peace, prosperity and harmony in life, nothing else. **The real science to control your thoughts & emotions is very simple and that is WOW focus.** When you watch/observe/witness your thoughts, your focus energises your thoughts. Energy being divine light transcends and converts negative thoughts to positive ones. It is like cleaning the mind of negative, unaware thoughts with your laser sharp focus, like a laser light is used to kill diseased cells from your body.

When you give your conscious presence to your thoughts & emotions, it steadies your emotions, connects with your spiritual space raising your energy and consciousness where the focus of your mind automatically shifts from problems to solutions, from what you lack to what you want, from non-action to action, from irresponsible action to responsible action, where you keep on doing your karma consistently, persistently with purity of intentions and what more you want to become lucky.

YOU) How to find whether mind is in the present moment/cool & calm/focused or roaming in past/future/disturbed/unfocussed?

ME) *Badi jaldi sayanee ho gayee tusi* **(very fast you have adopted WOW and became intelligent). Wow! I loved this question of yours.** See, the slightest of irritation means that mind is disturbed/unfocussed, either it is angry about something which has happened in the past or it is fearful about the future. When the mind is in the present moment, it will always be cool & calm and above all focussed, doing exactly what is required to be done in the moment.

YOU) Does it mean that after practicing WOW, I will never become irritated and negative in my behaviour?
ME) Yes, only if you are always aligned vertically or focussed in the moment. But as this is life, it is not possible to be vertically aligned always. Some situations might make you lose your cool & calm, you may forget WOW and may react negatively. The only option is to regain your consciousness, consciously by practicing WOW and once you do that, you will be aligned vertically. The key here is to keep on practicing WOW, with more practice, the frequency of negativity or irritation will reduce in your life. Life is never absolute but comparative. Nobody is perfect in this world and you must focus on increasing the degree of your conscious presence with every passing moment.

6.3 FAITH & BELIEF

FAITH & BELIEF IN GOD/SELF: Fear to Confidence, Insecurity to Security and Worry/anxiety to Peace/Bliss.

"Having faith and belief in oneself/god is the biggest source of strength and inspiration in life."
      -Chetan Bansal

To live a life of truth, a life on your soul path, you need to accept people and situations as they are, without any resistance. But for that you need to have full faith and belief in the acts of god/nature. The biggest knowledge of life is **"whatever happened, happening or will happen is bound to happen, it is beyond your control, fear and worry is useless and acceptance is the only intelligent choice".**

Everything happens for a cause and problems come and go by it-self. You have successfully overcome so many problems in your life. Many times, you have faced frightening/terrible situations where you lost all hope but some divine help in the form of miracles saved you, same way your present problems shall also disappear with time, depending upon your faith & belief which activates righteous PDA in you. If you have the confidence to deal with the situation, then there is no problem. And if the problem is not in your action zone, you just need have faith/belief in almighty, **your karma here is to pray, trust his plans, do your best and maintain patience.** The results of the situations may not be as you expected but surely it is for your good. Only this attitude of acceptance with full faith and belief in self/almighty is a perfect recipe which transmutes all fears/insecurity to confidence/security and all worry & anxiety to peace and bliss.

"Why worry & fear, he who has given life will also take care of it."
    -Chetan Bansal

Having full faith & belief in God/Self means surrender with zero resistance! But how do we surrender, it is very difficult to surrender. Kindly help!
See, people do not surrender because of fear. Faith & belief in self/almighty is the only way to surrender and relinquish all your fears. Let us first understand the fear which is fundamentally of two types, **1) Real Fear & 2) Illusionary/psychological fear.**

REAL FEAR VERSUS ILLUSIONARY FEAR
Real fear is physical in nature like, if you do not know swimming and **you directly jump in a deep pool of water,** it is a real fear/threat that has a very high probability of resulting in disaster. **Fear of being burnt by a burning candle** or any type of fire, the fear of **falling from height** if you are standing on the edge of a building and the fear of **accident if you do not know driving;** these are all real fears and naturally inbuilt within you to protect your life/existence.
The real fears can be overcome by practicing some precautions and learning new skills. For example, learning and practicing driving from an expert professional will make you a perfect driver and your fear of driving a vehicle will transmute to the confidence where driving will become a child's play for you. You need to plan, make strategies, make systems, take calculative risks to secure yourself and overcome real fears.

    Illusionary fears are psychological in nature, being a creation of your fearful mind. All psychological fears belong to future like fear of stage, fear of death and fear of losing all your money etc. without any logic. **Illusionary fears are just creation of your disturbed mind influenced by some sort of negative news about some dreadful incidences. For example, if an earthquake occurs** at some place away from you and you listen and watched all the tragedy in news, the negative news will create fear in your mind where your mind will keep on imagining the same tragedy happening with you. Till you keep watching, hearing the negative news, your mind will remain in the grip of fear which will keep on imagining the tragedy happening with you. **The only way out of a psychological fear is to shift the focus of mind somewhere else or stop listening to the news.** If you think earthquake is going to happen at your place, then I think you should move to some other safer place but do you or anybody know any place which is 100% safe from earthquake. If yes, then why fear and if not, what is the use of fear? Nothing is guaranteed in life, if earthquake is meant to occur at your place, it won't inform you in advance and you have no option but to face the eventuality. For taking life as it comes to you, for acceptance of present needs immense **faith & belief in self and acts of God. Just remember, control/change what you can with your 100% focus and surrender to the almighty what you cannot**.

So what you can do for them? Bless and pray for the people and place where that tragedy happened. Help them by contributing clothes, food, medicines etc. Choosing a helpful action will activate your omnipotent reality which will automatically remove all fears of your mind. **What you can do for yourself?** You can take some precautions; make some earthquake safe zones at your home and offices so that in case of eventuality, you can reduce the damage or are able to fully protect yourself. But for the sake of God and your own happiness, do not live in that fear which has not happened in reality with you. You are generating vibrations of fear which takes away your focus from the precious present leading to unfocussed thoughts & actions which might lead to wrong results like if you are driving a vehicle, your unfocussed mind might manifest an accident. So relinquish the fear to live with faith and confidence, no matter what, for your own good and happiness.

Once a friend of mine asked me, "Chetan *Yaar (friend)*, I have travelled so many times on aeroplane, but I always fear it will crash which does not allow me to enjoy my journey." I asked him, how many times you have travelled on aeroplane. He said approx. 30-35 times means he was a frequent flyer. So I asked him, how many times it actually crashed. He said," What are you talking? If it had crashed even a single time, I would have not been there in front of you." **Exactly, that is what I was trying to make you realize, you always feared it to crash and it never crashed and you still fear, isn't it foolish?** Something deeper touched him and he became silent for a while. I told him it's true that in case of any eventuality, there is no second chance but have you observed that so many flights are flying from every corner of the world on a daily basis and how many actually crashed; negligible. Airplane being a high tech product, it is very rare for it to crash but the risk will always be there. I told him it is normal to fear; it happens with everyone, even the frequent flyers, pilots and air hostess. **It is okay to have fear but it is foolish to carry that fear throughout the flight.** Your fear cannot control the destiny of flight, even the pilot does not have much control over the emergency situation but the quality of flying machines are very good and proven. Your worry has nothing to do with the safety of flights. **Have full faith and belief in god/self because "when he has sent you on flight, he will also take care of your safety"**. Same way in life, we should not feel insecure, when nature has given us life it will also take care of it. **So next time when a fearful thought comes to your mind, smile at it and say to your mind, "My dear mind, you can't create fear in me now, just relax and help me enjoy my journey".** I said to my friend that the nature of mind is to create fear only to protect your life but it needs your conscious light to understand the truth in order to come out of that illusionary fear and enjoy the journey called life.

Understand the fear of mind, if it is relevant/real, take action on it and if it is irrelevant/illusionary leave it as it is. Enjoy your journey, do not waste your precious journey worrying about issues beyond your control and if some emergency situation happens, do what best you can do to save your life.

WE CAN OVERCOME ALL PSYCHOLOGICAL FEARS by negating/ignoring our fearful thoughts and by taking actions against fears. And that can be only possible when we have full faith and belief in self/god. **Let us understand this in context of two major psychological fears which keeps us on back foot in life,** blocking our growth and prosperity: **1) Fear of death and 2) Fear of future.** Let's see how to relinquish these fears and live a life full of faith, belief, confidence, peace and prosperity.

1). RELINQUISH FEAR OF DEATH: I know that I am nothing, I don't know anything, my knowledge is limited, I am just a small pebble in the vast ocean of this universe and I am a puppet in the hands of the supreme creator of this Universe. He has created this universe out of love and he has decided my birth, life path and death, then what is there for me to worry. You should know that it's not your death but the death of your physical body. You are the energy that keeps on changing form but can never be destroyed and nobody has the power to kill you. This awareness is enough to rise above all fears in life. That supreme power is the creator of your and everybody's life. That every problem, every situation, every person, every gain & loss in your life have been determined by him. *Your only job/action/responsibility/concern is to just accept every challenge that life poses you, take best of actions and keep on learning, understanding and living life with a happy state of mind, rest everything is beyond your control and you should not worry about.*

You must understand that life and death are not in your control. Ask yourself, did you control your birth and did you know anything about your birth before your birth? No! You came to know about your existence only after 3-4 years of your life when you gained some consciousness in this physical world. So if you cannot control your birth, how can you control your death? **Have you ever thought what happens after death; a complete rest, eradication of all problems in your life. To understand this, just observe your sleep,** in sleep you are in complete rest, lose consciousness and forget all problems. Only when you wake up, your consciousness comes back and so did your body, mind, the people, situations and the problems associated with your life. So it is the consciousness which witness life and pains/problems associated with life. Death is a complete loss of consciousness, physical life and thus, eradication of all worry, anxiety, fear and problems in life. **I always say we are reborn after every sleep. The only difference between sleep and death is that** when we wake up from sleep, we are reborn with the same physical body, same relations and almost same life situations which we left before sleep but after death, we get a new physical body, new relations, and new life situations. So death is good; it relinquishes your old, worn out body, old relations, all problems and a new beginning of a new life. So, why should we fear death in life?

But what we should fear is an unhealthy life, a bedridden miserable life waiting to die every moment which is nothing but an experience of hell in life. This is the real pain for the person and his near & dear ones, alike the real problem which we must fear and do something about. **So what can we do; 1) We must maintain a healthy mind & body,** the amazing tools through which you experience life, to be able to enjoy your life by following a healthy life style, by choosing righteous **FAPB** which is always under your control; **2) Another real fear is concern about financial security of my family and for that, life insurance policy is always there.** And always remember, everyone including your near & dears have their own life covered by divine security, so why worry for them, the Almighty will take care of them. **So, don't fear death which is in future unknown zone, let it be mystery, it is not in your control and never fear something which is beyond your control. Life is in now, live now, enjoy now, celebrate now and let the fear die its own death.**

2). RELINQUISH FEAR OF FAILURE

I cannot do it, I am incapable, it's impossible for me are all outcomes of the beliefs developed in you based on your past bad experiences or opinions of others about you or both. This makes your mindset negative, a fearful state of mind which does not allow you to take action and you don't even have the confidence to try. Self-belief has taken a jolt; you keep on fearing failure in your mind that does not allow you to be fully present & focussed in your actions leading to wrong results in life. See, the results are not in your hands but the input actions and your karma is to give your 100% in actions and your first action/choice is to relinquish all fears, be it any.

Why fear failure, will it give you desired results? Surely not! What if failure happens, analyse what worst could happen, take precautions and safety measures to guard against it. **A word of caution**, if the fear is real in nature, like a situation of life or death is involved or a situation of huge financial risk, it is always better to take calculative risks and avoid blind risks to avoid severe loss. **For example, if you are investing in some new business,** invest only that percentage of your total wealth which you can afford to lose, means your normal lifestyle is unaffected and you can earn back your incurred loss from your old running business or job within a short span of time. **Just an insight for you to understand and not something to be followed exactly the same way.**

Why fear anything if your thoughts, intentions and actions are right for the benefit of all. If someone has wrong intentions for somebody or he is planning to gain by giving pain/loss to others, only then it's a real fear and all other fears are illusion of your mind.

Why worry/fear what others will say? Let them say whatever they want to say, it should not be your concern, people have a habit of criticizing irrespective of it if you fail or succeed, they do not know about your life, your skills, dreams, desires and your hidden powers/talents. **Normally, when people say that "you cannot do it", they invariably believe and mean that "they cannot do it, so how can you do it?"** Never believe what others say about you, their beliefs and opinions are based on their understanding and perception of their own life situations which has nothing to do with your life. Believe only in what you think is right for you, so focus on your own beliefs, perceptions, actions and goals but not on what others think about you. Even if you fail, you should accept your failure and always believe in self/almighty, a best attitude to relinquish all your fears. Developing such high faith/belief/confidence in self is the biggest success and source of immense happiness in life and the **best answer to your critics. Failures are good and help me learn, understand and grow in life. My belief mantra, "Everything that has happened, is happening right now and everything that will happen in future in my life is for my own good and is helping me grow in life".**

HOW TO PRACTICE FAITH & BELIEF IN SELF/ALMIGHTY IN REALITY TO TRANSMUTE FEAR INTO CONFIDENCE

Whenever some fear arises in your mind be it a fear of some people or situation or both, what can you do? Your first step is the acceptance and addressing of fear which is present in your mind. Second, you should have faith & belief that you can easily conquer that fear, third, you must act with full focus and good intentions; this is enough to conquer all your fears. WOW your fearful thoughts to understand the cause of fear and the right action to remove fear from your mind. This will also make you understand whether the fear is real or psychological.

If real, think, decide and take the best action possible with full focus. **For example,** if you have to jump from a building without any precautions and safety measures, obviously your decision is a big no. And if you have to jump with some safety rope and belts tied to you under the guidance of some experts and you have been watching other people doing these jumps successfully, then I think it is safe and now it's just a question of conquering your psychological fear. You can try this activity but only if you have passion for it, if you are comfortable with it. But if you are uncomfortable with it, does not want to do, choose not to do even if others persuade you. But if you want to do meaning your inner voice is strongly in favour of it, go and do it and do not listen to others.

If the fear is psychologically mind driven, then take action against it to rise above that fear. Ask your mind to give the best solution to it, be fully present in the moment, to give your 100% in action without worrying about the result. Let's understand with an example of an **Experience of past failure in particular activity that creates permanent fear of that activity.** Someone was excellent and brilliant in his subject of speech, tried speech for the first time and failed, the only reason for failure was just his psychological stage fear. That first bad experience has created such deep fear in his psyche that he is not even thinking to speak again on stage. **But someone somehow convinced him to give it another try and he agreed, don't you think this was his first victory over fear?** But the moment he reached near the stage, his mind reminds him of that failure; the picture, images, sound of that moment of failure comes in front of his eyes. Anxiety sets in, making him shiver and he is not able to move his body towards the stage. **So what can he do?** "Taking action against fear is the best way to conquer your fears." He should fight his fears by creating a thought, **"I can do it. I can do it. It's easy for me, easy for me."** He should not only say that but should also make an instant move towards the stage and without thinking should start speaking his heart out. Once he starts, soon the butterflies in his stomach will vanish making him comfortable and once the speech progresses, he will become more confident. Now, next time he will have less fear and with repeated stage exposures, his fear will permanently vanish and speaking on stage will become **'like a child's play for him'. That one moment of decision, of taking action against his fears transmuted his fear into confidence.**

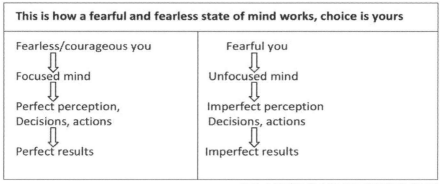

Source: Meet the Real You Copyright Chetan Bansal

What is the difference between a successful person and a person who failed? The successful person believes in his goals/dreams/desires and **has the courage to take action and thus, succeeds.** And **an unsuccessful person** has a fearful mindset; worry and doubts his goals, **does not take action** or is not fully present in his actions and thus, fails invariably. You being fully present or focussed in all your actions being the only mantra and the foremost karma for success & happiness in life and rest everything else is temporary and illusions of mind. Even the god salutes and help such a person achieve success in life.

Sometimes I do fear. How to regain my lost confidence?

See, sometimes some situations makes us fearful and it is absolutely normal to be fearful. You must have witnessed many good players losing their form and thus, confidence. If big players who are mentally & physically strong can't avoid fear, then anybody can become fearful in difficult moments of life.

Constant fearful state of mind can dent your confidence deeply and we must do something to regain our confidence, but how?

The best technique here is **1)** *try to remember and recall some incident or time period of your past when you were at the peak of your confidence.* *Visualize that confident moment with your full focus; what were your thoughts, actions, behaviour at that moment of time. Repeat this mind exercise again and again, with more repetitions you will yourself witness your confidence coming back.* **2)** Shift your focus from result to performance, bring about a change in your physiology; straighten up your body, walk & talk with confidence, consciously make your voice loud & clear and soon your confidence will be back. Even if you are fearful, act as if you are confident and you will definitely become confident.

SELF BELIEF

A belief involves the feeling of certainty about something. **"A faith or a strong feeling that it is bound to happen."** **My constant thought and belief is,** "My writings are of best quality, for the benefit of society and will definitely bring about positive changes in people and society as whole". One person with a strong belief can achieve anything irrespective of his present reality. **For example, if someone is poor, uneducated** but has a strong belief that one day he will become very rich, then definitely he will. It is only the belief that determines the outcomes in your lives. Whether you believe you can or cannot, you are always right. Whatever you believe in will always be manifested in life, if you believe life is easy, it is easy, if struggle then it is struggle, in either of the cases you are always right.

How does belief work? Belief gives you the focus, thoughts, ideas, resources, skills, will, time, energy, determination, courage and power to take action, to make belief become a reality on the screen of life. So in life, it is very important to believe in self for the fulfilment of dreams, desires and wishes in order to live a happy and prosperous life. We can use beliefs to **1) Create your intended reality, 2) as an energy medicine to cure many physical & mental diseases.**

1). SELF-BELIEF FOR CREATING YOUR INTENDED REALITY

This is how beliefs work subconsciously. Why beliefs control your life or why you get results according to your beliefs; the reason is that *whatever you believe in, you have a strong faith in it and you believe it to be true without any doubt. Your mind, body, thoughts, emotions are in total harmony with the belief and are on the same wavelength emitting energy of the same frequency. This leads to the highest level of coordination and cooperation within your mind, body and soul leading to perfection in all your actions, reactions, decisions, attitude, behaviour and perceptions which are in line or in tune to your beliefs making them manifest on the screen of your life in an easy and effortless way.*

THOUGHT + EMOTION = ATTRACTION OF OPPORTUNITIES BY SUBCONSCIOUS
THOUGHT + EMOTION = EFFORTLESS PERFECT CONSCIOUS ACTION GUIDED BY SUBCONSCIOUS.
EFFORTLESS PERFECT CONSCIOUS ACTION GUIDED BY SUBCONSCIOUS = DESIRED RESULT
So this way, by giving a strong, synchronized emotion to your desire/thought, you can attract that desire on the screen of your physical life. Synchronisation means your body, Conscious Mind, Subconscious mind all believe in the same thought/Idea. Anything that is passed on to your subconscious mind through your conscious mind in the most affirmative faithful way shall always be honoured by the subconscious.

But there are certain exceptions for belief to manifest on the screen of your physical life.

1). It must be real. If I believe that I can fly one day without any machine, then that belief can never become true as our body physics is not suitable to flying. That belief can only come true if in my next life, I become a bird.

2). Belief works only on self and not others. If others do not agree with your belief, then it won't work for them. **For example,** if you believe that your child will become a doctor and your child does not want to, he might try to become a doctor on your persistence but due to his lack of interest/belief, his actions won't be focussed and most likely, he is going to fail.

3). Beliefs not complemented by actions. For anything to manifest on screen life needs action. Although belief is a direction for action, if you do not take action, your belief won't be manifested at all. Non-action or unfocussed action for your goal means that **you don't have strong emotion/desire/belief for your goal,** some where there is disharmony in your mind, body and soul about the belief. **If you really believe something the action is automatic, effortless and perfect without you having any control over it.**

4). Belief against nature or humanity may become true but they are bound to manifest destruction and miseries in life, not only for others but for self. A child's mind is a fresh mind without any beliefs, if he/she is being given the training of terrorism, they might become a terrorist and the cause of destruction & misery for all.

5). Beliefs under the influence of others don't work. Most people on seeing the success of others set their goals for the same profession or somebody else convinces you about pursuing some profession which might misguide you either for their vested interest or they themselves are unaware of the truth. And everybody today knows the formula for success; **Believe in, believe in, believe in and just keep believing.** Oh my God if there is so much effort required to believe then imagine how much effort will be required in your actions. **The truth is that if beliefs are not aligned to your mind, body**

and soul, then sooner or later belief will diminish deactivating actions for your goal and thus, wasting your lot of time, energy and effort only to manifest frustration. Goals under the influence of others or not coming from your inner being require a lot of effort from your side both in belief & action. What works is an effortless natural belief for a goal coming from the source, so your first step must be getting connected to your inner being, *THE REAL YOU,* your natural *GURU* **(Teacher)** who will automatically give you the purpose, passion, goals and also the belief to fulfil the same.

2). BELIEFS CAN BE USED AS ENERGY MEDICINE TO CURE MANY PHYSICAL & MENTAL DISEASES.

In a **hypnotic state of mind** (a state of mind where a hypnotherapist can directly talk/suggest to the subconscious of a person), if hypnotherapist suggests that it's very cold and your body is shivering, the body will start shivering even if the room temperature is hot, say around 38 degree Celsius. **See, what mattered here is belief and not the reality**. Reality here is that it's "very hot" but the belief of a subconscious mind in the hypnotic state is that it's "very cold". So, mind does what it has been told, to be true even if it's not real. So once a belief is developed in the mind, mind will always work according to that belief irrespective of whether the belief is real or imaginary, true or false. Remember, a belief will not change the outside temperature which in real is 38 degree but it will change the temperature of your body to make it shiver. **So, belief works on your mind & body but it does not have the power to change the reality of outside situations.**

There is a term called the **Placebo effect**, a belief which is commonly used by many doctors/healers to heal the patient psychologically. In that case, it is not the medicine but the belief that cures the patient. Suppose someone visits a doctor for a minor ailment. Most patients have a belief system that **"Medicines are necessary for the cure of any ailment". Doctor knows that this ailment does not need any medication but he/she still gives the medicine to satisfy the psychology of the patient. Most of the times, it is the belief and not the medicine which cures the patient,** so he gives simple tablets with zero medicine in it that acts as placebo and heals the patient.

Frequency vibrations of belief and faith bring about what kind of changes in you?

The frequency vibrations of faith and belief in self/god are very high positive energy which connects with your nature/spiritual space, enhances your energy and consciousness, activating righteous karma in you leading to righteous results in life. And frequency vibrations of fear activates wrong karma not allowing you to take action, forces you to sit idle and worry a lot. The choice is yours, what you want to choose, either faith or fear.

A *Real you* is unperturbed by external situations and keep on doing his/her karma being fully present in the present, with full faith/belief in self/almighty. **The best security in life is not having huge wealth but in having full faith & belief in self/god, a divine security.**

Faith and belief in self/God (high frequency vibrations)----Energy increases----- activation/balancing of 7 chakras/mind----activation of hormones (biochemical)-----healthy body & highly conscious mind----connection with real you-----righteous awareness, righteous thoughts (righteous perception/belief/values/decisions)-----righteous actions/behaviour----righteous results and success/growth/happiness in all areas of life.

6.4 GRATITUDE & COMMUNICATION

Complain/ungrateful/thankless to gratitude/appreciation/thanks, Ineffective to effective communication

To be Grateful/Thankful to Almighty, Universe, Parents, Teachers/Gurus, Relatives, Friends, everybody/anybody whether known or unknown to me whether living or non-living is the source of immense energy and the way of my life.
      -Chetan Bansal

See, whatever you have got in this life could not have been possible without the help of others.
-Your body belongs to the planet earth made up of 5 elements air, water, fire, space and earth.
-Your mind /soul belong to the almighty God.
-You were born and brought up by parents.
-Your spouse is sharing your responsibilities, caring & loving you unconditionally.
-Nature is giving you air, water, food, solar energy, space to live.
-Your teachers gave you knowledge and education.
-You are getting clothes, medicine, doctors, drivers, vehicles, hotels, restaurants to fulfil all your needs and the list is endless.

Have you ever felt thankful to anybody or have you ever appreciated the effort of anybody? The whole universe is giving and fulfilling your each & every need in life but are we thankful/grateful or instead we blame and complain?
 Pause: Imagine your life in isolation; is it possible and obviously no, then why we forget to be thankful and grateful for everything that we have?
Where is our focus? Are we focusing on lack in life or happy about everything that we have in life? Are we finding faults in others or are we appreciating the good deeds/habits of others? **Whatever we focus on is expanded in life**. Focusing on lack enhances lack and being grateful for what we have maintains happiness in life. We are always on the lookout for fulfilling new dreams and desires, in the process, we forget appreciating and valuing what we have and ultimately may lose it. **Whatever we value, feel grateful about, feel happy about, feeling thankful about something in life always increases in life.** This is the basic law of life which we must understand to enjoy life. When your focus is on gratitude, more situations of gratitude are manifested in your life.
        Let's understand with an example. When we appreciate the good work of our employees the percentage of good/quality work by them increases. On the other hand, if we keep blaming and complaining about some mistakes by them, the percentage of mistakes increases. See if your

employee is not skilful or suitable for the job, get him trained, recheck his work, support him in bad times, appreciate the good work in him, appreciate his improvements, and be grateful that he is doing good job for you. Everybody makes mistakes, no matter how skilful they are. If he/she is not improving, better to remove them from the job and not create unnecessary negativity in his and your mind. When you are grateful to god that you have got good employees, you appreciate their good work, the good work performance of your employee increases and your vibrations of gratitude will attract more good performing new employees.

Human mind and nature is universal, so for any or all of your relations, be it your parents, teachers, spouse, friends etc., always be grateful/thankful to them for whatever they have done for you. Always believe they are doing best from their side. They are not perfect, you are not perfect, and you cannot fulfil all the expectations of others, so how can they fulfil yours? See and appreciate their intentions, efforts and the improvements.

Hating and envying rich people are like indirectly hating money or pushing away the money from us. We can never get/attract/manifest anything in our life which we hate. The mantra for attracting money and wealth is being grateful for whatever money you have, appreciating the rich and their good actions to earn money.

If someone is a struggling actor and learning in the academy, he should appreciate the good acting skills of his colleagues, doing this will also attract good acting skills in him. Some people hate/envy good acts of their colleagues being appreciated by others. The vibrations of hate and envy will only attract more situations of hate & envy where he will never be able to manifest good acting skills and appreciation from others. Appreciating the good acting skills in others help him sublimely absorb good acting skills of others, this is how vibrations attract like vibrations. **Appreciating the good in others help you by 1)** making your energy field positive, making your thoughts and actions positive **2)** attract good qualities of others making you skilful also. This is what is needed for excellence and thus, appreciation from others. The best way to learn good habits and skills from successful, talented people is by appreciating them and not by hating or envying them.

GRATITUDE ENHANCES YOUR COMMUNICATION: INEFFECTIVE TO EFFECTIVE COMMUNICATION

GRATITUDE $\Longrightarrow$ COMMUNICATION $\Longrightarrow$ LOVE & CONNECTION $\Longrightarrow$ SUCCESS & GROWTH

When you say thanks or appreciate anybody, he/she feels being loved and is naturally attracted towards you and would love to listen and talk to you. Isn't it happens this way? Think yourself!

Being grateful means not only saying thanks verbally but your emotions, feelings and body language also communicate the same to the other. The other person will feel the instant love & connection and communication happens through soul. **A word of caution:** The real connection will only happen if you are thankful, not only verbally but your vibrations are also of the same frequency, means you also mean the same from your heart, it's natural and not artificial. **A thank or appreciation at a superficial level is meaningless** which only creates more negativity. So say thanks, appreciate only if it is coming from the inside. **The best would be to train your inside to appreciate the good in everybody without any bias.** A truly spirited person will always appreciate the good deeds of everybody/anybody without any bias.

Gratitude is an instant connector which instantly establishes connection with your spiritual space/nature and nature of the other person. Gratitude is the fastest connector in relations. The energy vibrations of gratitude bring about instant happiness in relations. It increases connection and once connection is established, communication happens in an effective manner. The people who practice gratitude and are in a habit of using the word "thanks filled with emotions and a smiling face" are the people whose communication skills are excellent. They are the people who are able to convince others in the most loving and compassionate way.

Complain and blame causes emotional disturbances leading to noise which causes miscommunication. Gratitude not only calms the mind but also enhances the happiness quotient, a mind free of emotional disturbances and you are able to listen & understand the other person. Not only that, the vibrations of gratitude synchronizes your mind, body, soul blossoming love everywhere, leading to soul to soul communication. **A person with an attitude of gratitude** will always have a soft tone, sweet voice, is a good listener, respond with love & compassion which constitutes effective communication. **A thankless/ungrateful person's** voice and tone is rude, they react instantly, are bad listeners, have complaining attitude leading to bad relations with others. **Observe people around you and to your amaze, you will find this to be true**.

Only a person with good communication skills can establish right connection with other people. Right connection means effective communication which leads to good relations. And happiness, success and growth come through good relations only, nothing else. See a good author, speaker, manager, politician or someone whose job is to deal with numerous number of people needs to have good communication skills, to deal with them in the most effective and loving manner.

LET'S UNDERSTAND THIS WITH A TYPICAL RELATIONSHIP TIMELINE

See, two people will always have some differences of opinions, perceptions, habits, attitude, and behaviour etc. initially in love relations, okay we will talk about marriage. Initially when the marriage is new, both people appreciate the good in each other, are thankful to god for getting such a good spouse. They focus more on good in each other and value each other. They know each other's lack/problem but do not focus much on them. There communication was excellent; they listen to each other, have compassion for each other, they respond to each other in the most loving and compassionate way. **Somehow after sometime, I don't know, god knows for whatever reasons**, one or the other or both focus somehow shifts from what they like in the other to what they dislike in other and starts complaining about it and soon that complaining becomes their habit and he/she forgets to appreciate about the good in other. **The vibrations of complaints will start attracting and manifesting more complaining situations in relationship**. This is how love goes away and complain becomes a permanent feature of relation. With frequent complaints, the tone of a person becomes rude, harsh and he/she does not want to listen to the other, does not want to understand the other and reacts in an abusive way. Ultimately, the communication breaks leading to all types of misunderstandings where sooner or later, love is transmuted to hate.

So if we want loving, fulfilling relationship we should focus more on gratitude, appreciation and complain less. Complaining, blaming is a mind activity, a mind which wants to prove him-self right and others wrong, which wants to control others leading to the rise of ego in between the two. *The only secret to good relations with others is to appreciate the good in other, focus on the good in other, ignore what you dislike in other and communicate your dislikes with empathy and compassion without hurting the feelings of other.*

Same way if you are grateful to almighty, you will always remain connected to him where you get everything that you need in an easy and effortless way. Be grateful/thank the nature/universe/god for whatever you have and for everything that you want to achieve in life. If you like present situation, be thankful and even be more thankful if you do not like the present situation because these difficult situations help develop some life skills which will help you change your life, in a way it is a divine plan for all the success and growth in your life.

THE VIBRATION OF GRATITUDE BRINGS MORE POSITIVITY AND GROWTH IN YOUR LIFE.

The frequency vibrations of gratitude are very high positive energy vibrations which connect with your nature/spiritual space. What it does is it not only converts your negative mindset to positive one but also the mindset of people with whom you interact with. **On the other hand, frequency vibrations of complain** activates your egoistic mindset leading to disturbed relations with others and attract more lack in life.

A *REAL YOU* chooses & practices gratitude over complain, is **unperturbed by external situations,** maintains his cool & calm, taking righteous decisions and actions being fully focussed in the present. The best way to grow in your life is by learning from your mistakes and correcting them but not by blaming others. The more problems you have in life, the more you will learn and grow in life. So be grateful to everything in life be it problems, lack and for everything you have in life. Be grateful, be grateful and just being grateful is the best formula for all the success & happiness in life.

Gratitude (high frequency vibrations)-----energy increases----- activation/balancing of 7 chakras/mind----activation of hormones (biochemical)-----healthy body & highly conscious mind----connection with real you-----right communication skills----righteous thoughts (righteous perception, belief, values, decisions)-----righteous actions/behaviour---- righteous results------Success/growth/happiness for you. Practice it in your real life for continuous 40 days to experience it. Any knowledge is incomplete without experience. And only practical experiences enhance knowledge and gives desired results.

YOU) why complaining or blaming does not work or it makes things worse?

ME) **When you complain and blame, you activate negative feelings/emotions in the other person which disturbs his mind.** A disturbed mind can never work perfectly or can even stop working. The memory, perception, decisions and actions of the emotionally disturbed people becomes defective as his/her focus shifts from work to worry/anxiety/fear/hate etc. Now if you are complaining and blaming somebody/anybody, either unknowingly or knowingly, you are attracting wrong actions/reactions/behaviour from them.

The choice is yours, whether you want solution or you want to aggravate the problem. Say for example, your employee has a habit of forgetting task/works given to him or not doing them perfectly. **You rudely, repeatedly keep on complaining & blaming, is not able to correct him and instead is aggravating the problem.** The problem is that you have created emotional disturbance in the mind of your employee which is not allowing him to work efficiently in a negative environment of blame/complain. **The only solution is to work and correct your own attitude of blame and complain to remove disturbances in the mind of your employee**. For that, you must start communicating with them in a loving & caring manner, by making them comfortable, with an attitude to help them by making them understand what needs to be done and how it needs to be done. Like, **"please complete this work now which I told you yesterday, you may have forgotten, thanks"** or **"I know you are busy in other work but please do this first, it's a priority, thanks"** or by motivating them that **"you look disturbed, is there something bothering you, can I help you in some way?"** etc. This enhances the energy of the other person, he feel loved, accepted and will automatically give his best, even his/her memory will increase and in future also, he will always complete the work with perfection and on time.

YOU) Sir, I have understood about gratitude leading to love and communication. Please clarify more on developing effective communication skills.
ME) let's understand a secret to good relations, WOW FOR EFFECTIVE COMMUNICATION AND LOVE.

"Nature has given two ears, two eyes and one tongue, so listen and watch more and speak less. This is the secret to developing perfect communication skills, nothing else."

OBSERVE YOUR SENSES TO UNDERSTAND COMMUNICATION

Two eyes--------Watch more, INPUT DEVICE
Two ears--------Listen more, INPUT DEVICE
One Tongue----Speak less.......OUTPUT DEVICE
4 input devices and 1 output device clearly indicates that nature wants you to listen 80% and just speak 20%

When with somebody/anybody give your full attention to that person as if that person is the best person in your life. Just watch, observe and witness the person you are with, listen to them completely with patience, without interrupting with a cool & calm mind. This will establish a perfect connection with that person. Your understanding, perception and clarity about that person will increase and become perfect with time leading to the right response from your side and thus, good relations with them. Let's understand further.

STEPS OF EFFECTIVE COMMUNICATION
STEP 1 - INPUT: Listen and watch first because eye and ear are **Input devices**, so use them first
⇩
STEP 2 - PROCESS: Process the information in brain using your conscious presence
⇩
STEP 3 - OUTPUT: Then speak, respond in a specific manner with a cool & calm mind having control over your emotions.

Do not try to give output without processing the input through your conscious presence as it can, it may or most likely lead to an emotional disturbance and thus, misunderstanding which leads to miscommunication and bad relations.

Benefits of Step 1 and step 2: Listening first and processing afterwards:
1). Listening to someone with full focus, patience and cool & calm mind makes the other person feel important, where he/she feels the instant connection with you and would love to speak to you more.

2). The more you listen and observe with your complete focus, the more you understand the person; his/her mindset, real needs and issues, understanding level, opinions, beliefs and perceptions etc. This way, it will give you an insight on how to deal with that person in the most effective way.

Step 3- Respond with a cool & calm mind
1) Talk to them in the most loving and compassionate manner.
2) Appreciate their good deeds.
3) Talk in a language they easily understand and are comfortable with.
4) Any disagreements with them shall be respected. The communication has to be constructive with the intent of finding a solution and not with the intent of proving yourself right and the others wrong.
5) Do not criticize them or verbally abuse them or argue with them. This leads to an instant disconnection, putting away the other person or the noise of arguments and abuse leading to the miscommunication which ultimately ends up in unnecessary disputes and fights.
6) Maintain a good eye contact for an effective focus.
7) Keep a smiling face to avoid your own emotional disturbance.
8) Maintain a positive body language to make the other person feel good in your company.

70% of communication happens through body language. Verbal communication is only 30% and all humans being super intelligent understand the body language of others subconsciously. If they have to believe in words or body language, humans will always believe in body language, as body language never lies. Body language is a language of feelings & emotions and which the mind perceives instantly.

Universe understands the language of feelings and emotions, your feelings are instantly observed by others, by plants and animals, by everything in the universe; they may not understand your spoken language but they surely understand your body language. **Alive person is characterised by live energy field which means a working mind & body characterised by thoughts & feelings which are always expressed through emotions. And body language is nothing but expression of emotions. You can choose not to speak verbally but can never stop your body language which is communicating your emotions constantly. So, you can never stop your communication which is happening through your body language.**

You can easily understand the feelings & emotions of others by observing their body language. And the best way to understand what actually the other is saying or hiding or both can only be possible when you are fully focussed on the other person interpreting and correlating both their words & body language.

You observing, listening and responding the other person through your conscious presence by practicing WOW is the best way to establish a wonderful connection with the other person, leading to effective communication and flow of love in between. And where there is love, there is energy and where there is energy, there is happiness, so there shall be no scope and space for negativity.

The most successful people in this world are people who have good communication skills. Your communication skill is the gateway for connection and love with other people. Nobody in this universe can achieve success alone but needs people for help which requires good relations that comes from effective communication but only through WOW. Practice it to master it; the only secret to effective communication is your conscious presence through "WOW".

6.5 HAPPINESS & ANGER

Happiness is external and limited, **PEACE** is internal & eternal: From Sadness to Happiness, Anger to Peace

HAPPINESS **is external and limited.** It is dependent upon situations outside, it is limited to the amount of success in the outer world defined by the rules of the outer world **but *PEACE* is internal & eternal,** a higher state above mind and your conscious choice irrespective of the outside situations. **So, happiness is a conscious choice, to remain at peace irrespective of any success or failure in life.**

A human unconscious mind always looks for happiness in fulfilment of his/her needs & wants or material desires. When the need & want or desire of a person is fulfilled, they feel excited and happy. Non-fulfilment of needs & wants make a person feel sad & unhappy. This is how human psychology works. For ages, human beings have been confined in this cycle of happiness and sadness, if situations are to their liking they feel happy, otherwise sad. This is the reason that nobody has been able to adhere to happiness for a long time/whole life irrespective of their social, political, financial position. Happiness has nothing to do with money or power, **everybody/anybody who has not conquered his/her mind has faced and experienced the miseries of mind leading to all unhappiness in life**. People have been aspiring for a permanent happiness in their life as human mind does not like sadness and would always want to be happy & successful just to satisfy their ego. **It means happiness is temporary and chasing anything temporary is not an intelligent choice**. It is the state of mind which keeps on changing with changes in outside situations in life. So, something that is temporary is illusion, is limited and can't be your reality. **Your nature is to be**

calm, composed, peaceful and energetic in all situations of life. So, an internal peace is eternal, **permanent** and not dependent upon fulfilment of desires, wants and satisfaction of ego in life. If happiness is what you aspire for, choose to be happy right now, choose to adhere to it permanently as it is just an illusion of mind and we humans are perfect in creating illusions of mind, so who stops you to create this illusion of happiness in your mind? See, how easy it is to manifest happiness in life, just your conscious choice.

See the nature of mind is duality which keeps on changing with changing times. So, a mind will always have varying degree of happiness, sadness depending upon the varying degree of success and failure in life which keeps changing with changing time. So the only solution is to adhere to your nature which is permanent, timeless, state of complete peace and bliss.

NOW, LET US TRY TO UNDERSTAND WHAT IS REAL AND UNREAL HAPPINESS IN REAL LIFE WITH EXAMPLES OF SAME SOURCE, BECOMING BOTH CAUSE OF HAPPINESS AND UNHAPPINESS WITH THE CHANGE IN TIME/SITUATIONS.

See, hunger creates a desire of eating within you and upon eating food, you feel happy and satisfied. Now, if you over eat the same food, it causes indigestion and uneasiness in your stomach and body as a whole. **The same food that gave you happiness when you were hungry became the source of unhappiness, discomfort and disease when your stomach was full.**

In relationships commonly this happens, once the physical needs or emotional needs is fulfilled, boredom sets in, you are no longer attracted to the other person, love goes away, and unhappiness sets in. Change in love/happiness with changing times with the same person. So, a love dependent on need fulfilment which was the source of immense happiness when need was being fulfilled has now become a source of unhappiness when the needs are not being fulfilled.

A FINE BALANCE IS REQUIRED FOR HAPPINESS IN ALL AREAS OF YOUR LIFE, WHETHER IT'S HEALTH, WEALTH, RELATIONS, JOB/CARRIER/PROFESSION.

For example, in your love life, if you always say yes to the demands of your loved ones even when the demands are undue just to gain some favour from them, make them happy, satisfy their ego irrespective right or wrong, soon they will start demanding things beyond your reach or something which is out of your comfort zone or something which is not real need or just a waste of money, they start to take undue advantage of you; the love which was once flourishing becomes a source of unhappiness for you. **Be it your child, spouse, friend or anybody, you need to draw a fine line between what you can do or what you cannot or what is normal to expect or abnormal to expect in a relationship.** And when you stop saying yes to them for their undue demands, they will start saying no to you, even for the needs which are normal to expect in a relationship which they can easily fulfil. They do this to manipulate you, to get their undue needs fulfilled from you, a kind of blackmail and conditional in love. This leads to disputes and problems in relations. And to get back, the happiness in relations you need to balance, sort out and understand each other, strike a right balance between what is normal or abnormal to expect in a relationship. If both of you are cooperative and understanding, soon relationship becomes normal and a source of happiness for the both of you, a timeless relationship not dependent upon need fulfilment but based on love, care and understanding.

Same way, if you are giving too much of your time to your job or career and neglecting your health or relations or hobbies or all, soon that job or career will become a source of unhappiness for you. Too much focus on health, neglecting other areas of life like wealth or relations can also become a source of unhappiness for you. **So, a balance in all vital areas of your life like health, wealth, relations, and job/career/profession is must for a happy life.** A fine balance is needed to let them remain a source of happiness for you. **Less or excess, both are poisonous and becomes a source of unhappiness.** Right quantity and quality is needed for that same source of happiness, to remain a source of happiness and not turn into a source of unhappiness.

ONCE YOU ACHIEVE SOMETHING, THE DESIRE GOES AWAY AND GOES AWAY THE HAPPINESS WITH THAT. A man wanted to speed up his travelling had a desire for a bicycle, bought a bicycle, he was very happy on buying that cycle and is a very proud owner who daily cleans & washes that cycle himself, proudly drives that cycle. It gives him a sense of superiority that he is one of the few who owns a cycle in his community. Now after some time, the cycle is with everybody, it's very common to have a cycle. The same cycle now does not give him the same pride and thus, happiness. He wants something new to show his superiority over others. **Good news! Motorcycle has come in the market** and a new desire has risen to buy the motorcycle. Again, motorcycle will become a common phenomenon which will steal his happiness. **Now, a car will come then some luxury car,** the desire will keep on changing, increasing, and it's endless. Once something that gave happiness, now no longer is the source of happiness and instead, it has become a source of unhappiness.

So, is it bad to desire something/anything? The big answer is No! It is natural to desire for new things. But for that a smart work, hard work and a fair practice to earn money is required but still, if you don't succeed, can you still maintain your happiness? If yes, good! Great! Nobody can steal your happiness. The only mantra for **real success & happiness is to keep** doing your karma, taking right action or changing action to fulfil of your desire but with purity of intentions. **See, the desire for fulfilment of needs & wants is**

natural, normal, your birth right and the foremost karma of your life for which you must keep on working hard & smart.

LET'S UNDERSTAND 4 UNIVERSAL NEEDS TO UNDERSTAND REAL HAPPINESS IN LIFE.

1). Body needs for fulfilment of food, water and oxygen which is a real need for a life to sustain. If the person is not getting these needs fulfilled, then it's the cause of **real unhappiness and pain**. Skip food and water for say 2 days to experience real pain or real unhappiness. Close your mouth and block your nose for a second or two, you will come to know what real sadness or real pain or real unhappiness is. Go and beg for food, sleep on roadside without any clothes on chilly nights. Go and spend a day in slums full of garbage. Then, you will come to know what is real pain or real unhappiness.

But have you ever noticed that this basic need of food for everybody is being fulfilled, irrespective of their socio-economical, educational status. Even the animals get their food. All creatures are able to fulfil this need and want. But the difference is in the way their basic need is being fulfilled. Some live in big houses, some in huts, some on roads, some eat at 5-star hotel, some eat at streets, some beg for food. Some live in unhealthy and unhygienic conditions, a source of disease and real pain. So the basic need fulfilment of good healthy food, clean and hygienic homes for healthy body is must for real happiness. So maintaining a healthy body is the source of real happiness as it is through your physical body you experience life.

2). Emotional needs, that comes from **satisfaction of ego, approval, acceptance, appreciation, love by others.** Maintaining good relations is the key to your emotional needs, as emotions are fuel for life which expands and enhances experience of life. Good relations with people and your own mind is the source of fulfilment of all your emotional needs which comes from unconditional love or love without any attachment or helping and giving in relations. We must act in a responsible manner in all our relations doing everything/anything that is right and not do choose any irresponsible/wrong action, even if others do not approve/appreciate it. Doing something which is wrong to please others to gain something from them shall give only temporary happiness and permanent disturbance in mind. Doing good karma can give you permanent peace a state higher than happiness of mind.

Achievement of some materialistic needs like having big business, big house, luxurious food, branded goods, all in all a luxurious lifestyle, big name (being famous), powerful position of influence over others also gives an emotional high. But what if these materialistic needs are not being met, **you tried very hard to achieve them but couldn't or you lost all your material wealth, can you still maintain your inner peace or can you accept the unexpected in life?** If yes, your attitude of life is completely natural/spiritual and it is this attitude which is a source of fulfilment of all your needs and thus, much desired success and happiness in life.

The real you is unperturbed by any outside situations, keep on doing his karma to improve/change his/her life towards positivity invariably chooses peace of mind, for them happiness is not dependent upon situations outside but a conscious choice.

3). Personal growth gives real happiness. If you are an open mind who keeps on learning and growing in life, if you are taking action to learn something new, to achieve something new, to create something new, then happiness is not your conscious choice but you are the choice of happiness in life.

4). Contribution to others/society gives real happiness. When you are helping others, doing something for the benefit of self/others or society as a whole for uplifting the standard of life or for happiness of others, then your happiness button is permanently switched on.

A natural happiness comes when we rise above ego and connect to our nature where acceptance of truth, living in present moment, underlying faith & belief in self and acts of almighty, gratitude, kindness, unconditional love, forgiveness, celebration becomes our permanent attitude of life.

So why are you sad? Now you know what will give you real happiness. Wakeup, stand up, change your attitude, do what is required and change your focus from unreal happiness to real happiness or from happiness to permanent peace and bliss. **But hey! Don't hate sadness, it is a gift from God,** it has come in your life to realise & correct you mistakes, to enhance your life skills, to give something unexpectedly amazing and beautiful. LET'S SEE HOW? **FOR THAT YOU NEED TO UNDERSTAND SADNESS/HAPPINESS FROM A BROADER PERSPECTIVE, A REAL SPIRITUAL PERSPECTIVE, A BETTER UNDERSTANDING IS ALWAYS THE KEY TO BETTER DECISIONS, ACTIONS AND BETTER RESULTS IN LIFE.**

UNHAPPINESS & FAILURE LEADS TO SUCCESS, GROWTH & HAPPINESS

Even unhappiness/failure is good and built-in part of your mind with an ultimate divine purpose to spread peace, prosperity, happiness, success & growth. **Let's see how.**

When you achieve something, happiness comes but after sometime your mind gets bored, unhappiness sets in and wants something new to become happy again. So you think of achieving & creating something else or improving on something that you already possess. *It means this nature of mind of getting bored, unhappy is the cause for creation of something new, for improvement and growth.* So, unhappiness is good, being part of your mind which keeps you think and act for improvement/growth/creation in life. So next time, enjoy your sadness/unhappiness as it is a sign of some growth in your life. *Happiness is the mark of some achievement and unhappiness is indication that it's time for a new creation or improvement or growth or all.*

So if you want growth and happiness in your life, you have to accept sadness & happiness alike.

If you become contend & comfortable with your level of success or becomes overtly depressive with failure/unhappiness, your urge/motivation for improvement goes which makes your life dull and inactive. Once action stops, life stops, it leads to depletion of energy and emotional disturbance leading to all kinds of miseries in life. So action is a must to improve for success, growth and real happiness. That is why unhappiness or sadness or boredom is inbuilt in your life for you to keep on taking actions in life. With actions comes new challenges and with new challenges comes the new opportunities, leading to new creations & growth in life. Life will keep on happening through actions, challenges, opportunities, failure and success, keeping you busy otherwise, life will become dull and boring. So, unhappiness is good and is the cause of your success, growth and happiness in life but for that you need to choose peace and cool & calm of your mind.

THERE IS NO WAY TO HAPPINESS BUT HAPPINESS IS THE WAY ITSELF

Happiness is your conscious choice; it's a journey and not a destination. Always choose to be happy now and always, don't wait for some situation or some achievement, don't depend on somebody/anybody for your happiness. In life, there will always be reasons/circumstances to be happy and unhappy both. A human untrained/unaware mind always chooses unhappiness and is more attracted towards negativity. But it is not the fault of the mind as it does not have the intelligence to make a conscious choice, you being a master of your mind, it is your duty to make it more conscious, aware and thus, intelligent to make right choices in life.

A sad mind becomes emotionally weak, losing its connection with the source leading to wrong PDA and wrong results in life or the problem remains unsolved. With problems remaining unsolved, sadness will become a permanent feature of your life. So choosing sadness will only manifest sadness in life. **Tell your mind that to tackle problems & challenges, you have to be cool & calm and choose peace over all negative emotions.** This develops immense emotional strength connecting with the source leading to rise in consciousness, awareness and with that, activation of righteous PDA for right results in life. That is why happiness is the only way to be happy and choosing it is the most intelligent choice.

But why my present life situation is difficult? Remember, your present situation is due to your past karma/actions/vibrations which were wrong or biased and it manifested the present bad situation. It clearly indicates that you were practicing the vibrations of lack, sadness and unhappiness which lead to wrong/biased past karma/action. Now if you again continue to feel and practice the lack, it will manifest more lack into your life. This way, your life/situations won't change and happiness will remain a dream for you.

To change your life /situations, you must choose to be happy now and always. If you wait, you will keep on waiting and chasing happiness but will never be able to grab it. Choosing happiness connects with the spiritual space which will guide you to solve all your problems, overcome all challenges, achieve your goals, fulfils your dreams, desires and wishes. So choose a higher frequency of peace & happiness over a lower frequency of lack & sadness to raise your life. Experience it to believe it.

YOU) Okay! I agree but still I am not able to maintain my happiness. I have tried many a times but I have failed, again and again. How can I be happy?
ME) See, it is your mind which becomes happy on achieving success or becomes sad, angry or frustrated if failure happens. That is all right, your mind is designed like that. There is nothing wrong in being feeling sad, angry or frustrated. **But I mean for how long you will hold on to these negative emotions, they are a part of life but should only be given temporary space in life**. The only purpose of these negative emotions is to make you understand life science and your karma is to transmute those emotions to meet a bigger power, a spiritual space and divine light above the darkness of a disturbed mind. **Actually, negative situations and emotions are divine plan, to force you to rise above your problems, to find solution to your problems.**

It is difficult to practice positive vibrations when your state of mind is negative, but there is no choice, we have to do it, it is the only solution. See, this difficult time in your life is a time of uncertainty, an unknown zone which is causing much fear & anxiety in your life. I understand you may have tried very hard for something but you still failed, so either that thing is not meant for you or your approach is not right. In either of the cases, **you need to surrender and just allow your spiritual space to take control of your life by practicing acceptance and conscious presence.** Then, you will get everything that is needed to make you happy much more beyond your imagination or it will give you permanent peace which is much better than dip and rise cycle of happiness and sadness.

So my dear **REAL YOU,** make a choice which is more intelligent, sensible and forget your difficulties, even surrender your difficulties to your source, he will make everything easy for you. So being happy and at peace is the only and the most easy choice you have.

NOW LET'S SEE HOW TO TRANSMUTE SADNESS, ANGER TO A PEACEFUL, and COOL & CALM MIND. When we are talking of happiness, does it mean that we will never get angry, definitely we will. But the big question is whether your anger is responsible/due and causing some good change or irrational/undue and creating problems. But for some, anger has become a permanent feature of their life, making them a source of repetitive sadness, mental & physical torture for self and others. Their acceptance level is almost negligible and the slightest of irritation makes them angry or they become angry on very small, irrelevant issues. So, anger needs to be corrected or managed or deleted or all and if left unattended can ruin the life of all concerned. A little of anger or anger as medicine or anger for some solution is always right but excess of it is always poison and killer of life! Being angry all the time or most of the time depletes vital energy leading to more emotions of anger, hatred, jealousy which in turn bring about negative biochemical changes leading to various physical & mental diseases. Not only that, it negatively impacts your perception, decision, action and behaviour leading to problems in almost all areas of life i.e. HWRC. Others may or may not get affected by your anger but surely it is a real slow poison for you.

So anger is a negative emotion that must be deleted completely from your psyche. NO, it is a very good emotion but only if it is used as a medicine to deal with bad elements or to find solution to a problem. The **key here is the right usage of anger for right purpose, for right duration.** We should not become a tool of anger but use anger as a tool.

So, a balanced anger is the sensible requirement, but most of the time or most people complain that they are not able to control their anger. This is not true, it is a lie and I don't agree with this. By stating that, you can't control your anger, you are just fooling yourself. **Don't worry, I will prove it right here** and you shall appreciate it to be true. See, anger comes when something unexpected happens which you don't like, don't expect, something not digestible which you think is totally wrong. You may be right in your own perspective but someone who has done that act has only done it because he thought that it to be right, otherwise, why would he do this? I agree with your reaction, it's natural for all humans to react towards an unexpectedly wrong thing/act/deed. So, anger is natural but whether you choose anger or not is just your conscious choice. But we practice bias as we sometimes choose response and other times we choose undue, indiscriminate anger. But why do we discriminate? See, we express anger only at weak people or on people whom we think are safe to get angry upon as they won't be able to confront us. **Take for example, when we feel angry** towards our father, boss, teacher or seniors **(people whom we fear or value or respect), then we suppress our anger. But when we feel angry** towards our juniors, children, spouse etc. **(people who fear us or respect us or value us), then we express our anger at different degrees depending upon the value we assign to the other person. So, we are subconsciously and consciously choosing our anger as per the strength and weakness of others irrespective of what is right or wrong but we are not realising this.** *NOW THAT THE REALISATION HAS COME, I AM SURE YOU WILL ONLY CHOOSE TO RESPOND IN A COOL & CALM MANNER IRRESPECTIVE OF THE OTHER PERSON BEING STRONGER OR WEAKER THAN YOU.* **If you want to get angry, get angry on everybody without any bias when expressing anger.** Yeah! You should have this much guts, if you think you are strong, powerful angry men or women. *"If you are strong then why practice and indiscriminate anger and if you are weak, then why get angry, don't you want to safeguard your beautiful teeth?"*

SEE IN ANGER, people use bad language, harsh tone and even become physically violent which invariably wreck/break even the strongest of bonds between the two people. **A little of disputes, fights and anger sometimes are all part of all relations but if it becomes a regular practice, then people feel unaccepted and disrespected leading to the development of permanent dislike for the other person, an irreversible damage.** And that bond can be between a child/parent, husband/wife, friends, business ties etc. and can wreck your whole life within seconds.

Even the most violent acts, crimes happen in just a moment of anger where a person becomes a tool of his emotion of lethal anger. Most people repent that moment and described their own action as involuntary, means that they did not wanted to act in such extremely violent manner but they were not able to control their devil anger.

See, this is where we need to learn to manage negative and uncontrollable emotions like anger which can be so damaging and can wreck your whole life. 90% of our relationship problems are due to uncontrollable anger. The reason being is that we do not accept the unexpected from the other person. We must learn to accept the unexpected, many a times, something unexpected happens which is not intentional but situational beyond the control or understanding of the other. Who knows why it happened which you never wanted to happen. Have you asked the other person why it happened or have you tried to understand the situation or your untrained mind just latched on to the opportunity to showcase its power. *My dear mind, relations are precious being the only key to happiness or the biggest source of happiness in life.* And for good relations, we need to practice attitude of acceptance, respect, empathy and compassion, nothing else.

So take an oath from now on, you will never get angry no matter what and instead of getting angry, what you can do is think of possible solutions, try to understand the situation and act upon it in the most responsible way, taking care of feelings of all concerned including you but for god sake, for the sake of others, your own sake, your own mental peace, please don't get angry. **Please give me a reason to be angry,** you get angry on something that has already happened which you can't change, so why get angry? **If you are right,** then why get angry? **If you are wrong,** then you don't have the right to be angry. **Anger causes physical and mental ailments**, so why get angry? **Anger breaks human relations,** so why get angry? If you don't like somebody or something, why get angry, better to stay away from them. **When required make conscious anger, use it as a tool but never become a tool of anger.**

NOW WHAT IS THE SOLUTION: So the big question is how to manage and stay away from undue anger and ultimately delete undue anger from your life. Let's understand in steps.

STEP/STAGE 1: Make a commitment to yourself that you won't make anger your habit, no matter what and to help you, there are some techniques which will delete indiscriminate anger from your life. Even if there is strong urge to express your anger, you must express it in the most responsible way. Use these techniques to deactivate your mind activity.

PAUSE TECHNIQUE: At the time of unpleasant situation, do not react immediately with disturbed emotions but pause for some seconds by silencing your tongue and mind both. This breaks the pattern of emotional disturbance and thus, silences your mind.

WOW: Watch, observe, and witness (WOW) your thoughts, emotions, people and situations make your mind silent, leading to deactivation of your emotionally disturbed mind, rise in your consciousness and thus, natural intelligence which leads to an automatic, righteous response as per the need of the situation without any bias.

ACCEPT EVERYTHING: Realize that life is full of uncertainties, you can't control people & situations, try to understand the situation, to accept the difference of opinions/perspectives of people which are inevitable due to different degree of consciousness of people. This realization will help you understand that unpleasant situations are a part of everybody's life irrespective of your financial, social or economic status, it does not matter whether you are beggar or king, so why get angry and unnecessarily burden yourself.

FOCUS ON SOLUTION RATHER THAN FOCUSING ON PROBLEM: Cursing the problem, why it happened and why me. Instead, focus on how it happened, to find out the real cause and now what is the best solution and taking the best action.

SPEAK LESS AND LISTEN MORE: Speak less or don't speak anything, better to be silent even if the situation is provoking, leave the place if possible but don't react. Only respond when you and other person have cooled down and are ready to listen and understand each other.

You have already understood all the above techniques in detail in Sec 6.2 of this book only.

REVERSE COUNTING: Oldest, simplest and most effective technique, reverse counting from 7 to 1 i.e. 7, 6, 5, 4, 3, 2, 1. Reverse counting is uncommon for your mind and requires a lot of effort. This changes the focus of your mind from anger or breaks the pattern of disturbed emotions. When mind encounters any uncommon its focus changes and impetus to a negative impulse/emotion breaks.

WHAT IF THE OTHER PERSON IS EXPRESSING ANGER: Even if the other person expressing anger, we need maintain our cool & calm. When someone keeps getting angry even on small issues, he or she has some deep pain inside, some unresolved issue which are constantly causing anger in that person. Getting angry with that person not only aggravates the anger of the other person but also disturbs your mind. Then, both of your vital energies are drained leading to expansion of negativity. This state of disturbed emotions can only aggravate problems and can never be a solution to any problem, be it any. **Only a highly positively charged battery can recharge or heal a negative person. The other person** can only be changed by love, care and compassion but if the other person is still adamant and do not want to change then it is not your responsibility to change that person but never infect yourself with their disease. Your responsibility is to convert your disturbed mind to a peaceful mind, maintain cool & calm and always remember it's foolish to get angry with an ignorant person. You will get to know the **FTIPP technique,** to deal with any type of people/situations in your life in **FORGIVENESS section of this book.**

STAGE 2: Miraculously within a short span of time, through regular practice of above techniques, through conscious choice and through understanding, anger will leave your presence permanently or you can say that you mastered the art of using anger in a controlled manner. **Now, you are at peace from the inside, even the most difficult situations are not able to shake you.** Also, to your amaze, you will find that unpleasant people & situations have left your life or those same people are now pleasant with you.

Now, you have mastered your thoughts & emotions leading to mastery in the art of managing even the most difficult people & situations with love, care and compassion. Now, no more unpleasant people and situations are encountered in your life or if encountered, they are under your control; it does not aggravate as it used to be earlier. The only reason, when you consciously choose to be at peace no matter what the life offers you, whether pleasant or unpleasant, your vibes have becomes positive permanently leading to truthful PDA and right results in your life.

OTHER TECHNIQUES AT HELP
Vertical alignment has been already discussed, deep breathing, regular meditation, plant based diet, physical exercise, physiology of your body, all helps steady your emotions and thus, find your inner peace permanently; are recipes for all the success & growth in life which are all covered in this book.

ONE IMPORTANT FACT, good people become angry on the wrong deeds of bad elements in the society. If you are that angry truthful man or women then listen carefully, do not waste your energy by getting angry, instead use that energy to bring about a change in your own attitude, to bring about a change in society, learn good communication skills and learn the art of handling bad people/situations in a cool & calm manner. Although you are right being truthful but your undue anger may land you in troubles. Nobody will listen to you even if they want to because your anger, your expression of truth in a violent manner shall be felt, read by others as threat and not something as truth or for their benefit. Even your angry attitude will be misused by bad people to prove you wrong because those so-called bad people are very good at managing their emotions, will exploit your emotion of anger, to bend the reality and to prove you guilty. So, if you want to show the truth to others, you need to learn the art of managing your anger, so that you can kill the demons of society by your conscious mind which is never possible by your disturbed emotions. *ALSO READ F-TIPP ON HOW TO DEAL WITH PEOPLE & SITUATIONS IN FORGIVENESS SECTION 6.8*

ALWAYS REMEMBER! CHANGE YOUR VIBES TO CHANGE YOUR LIFE. Use anger as a tool but never become a tool of anger and make peace your habit to achieve success, happiness and growth. So whatever the life situations offer you, choose happiness, if the situation is to your liking and if it is to your disliking, feel happier about it that a challenge has been thrown at you, accept the challenge, learn new skills, grow in life and achieve success.

Happiness (high frequency vibrations)-----Energy increases----- activation/balancing of 7 chakras/mind----activation of hormones (biochemical)-----healthy body & highly conscious mind----cool & calm mind- ---connection with real you-----Righteous awareness/thoughts (righteous perception, belief, values, decisions)-----righteous actions/behaviour---- righteous results------Success/growth/happiness for you. Practice it in your real life situations for continuous 40 days to experience it. Any knowledge is incomplete without experience. And only practical experiences enhance knowledge and gives desired results.

6.6 KINDNESS
Unkind to kind, Selfish to Generous

Kindness is the greatest virtue of mankind, it being the highest manifestation of love. The strongest positive energy having the highest frequency vibrations is what kindness is. **The act of giving unconditionally without any expectations with the only intention of helping someone in need is the real kindness.**

There is no use/purpose/value of life if we are not kind to self/others. It is our foremost divine responsibility pre-programmed by god in our mind but somehow we have forgotten this virtue, we have lost connection with it. Being kind and generous is a sure way to peace & bliss much above happiness. Material things can give you only temporary happiness but a small act/attitude of kindness is a sure way to permanent smile forever in your life. Nothing can replace an act of kindness.

If you can bring smile on the faces of others, then you have truly mastered the art of life. If you have a helping & caring attitude, can feel and heal the pain of others, then you have truly understood the depths of life and even if you are illiterate, you are far better than a highly educated person who is unkind. Kindness does not mean that you have to give big bucks for charity. Even small acts of kindness on a regular basis shall bring about a permanent smile in your life.

To give and contribute is to live. Somebody said giving is your responsibility but it is not, then what is it? It is just your nature. Then, why to make big fuss, **'responsibility'** looks like a burden something that is being enforced upon. Actually, it is very easy and natural for us to give. *MY REAL ME* loves to give but giving should never be enforced.

When we enforce giving, it generates a sense of fear among people and a fearful person deviates away from the nature, it being suppressed by a fearful mind where they choose not to give. Only a comfortable, fearless and happy mind can help and give others out of natural love & affection. That is why it is difficult to get taxes from people when there are tough/strict laws, rules, regulation and more so when there are rude/egoist/corrupt law abiding officials.

Whenever we help somebody/anybody in some way or the other it gives us a feeling of happiness, peace and something more which can't be defined in words but can only be felt by heart. We can start contributing to the society right now by following some small acts of giving/kindness.

a) Help somebody financially.
b) Uplift the morale of depressed person.
c) Keep your environment clean and green.
d) Obey traffic rules.
e) Instead of selling your old clothes and goods, give them for free to the people in need.
f) Talk to people from lower income groups like security guards, cleaners etc., appreciate their work, respect them, make them feel important, listen to their problems and help them the way you can.
g) Give your full focus, attention, hard work, and 100% in actions related to your job, career, work, relationships, and health.
h) When you see someone in pain physical or mental, bless them with the grace of god. Praying for others, blessing them with health, wealth, peace, prosperity is like experiencing the grace of god within.

All the acts of kindness should be from the bottom of your heart without any expectations in return for you to feel the real zeal of happiness. And the above are some examples but you can always help others in whatever way you can, without compromising on your own happiness.

YOU) what to expect in return after giving?
ME) Only give, help whatever you can do comfortably without compromising on your happiness, feelings, and comfort. Give only what you are comfortable with. Sometimes, people give too much and then repent. That is of no use. It will make your vibrations negative/low or you energy will deplete. The basic purpose of giving is to help you connect with your nature, to make you happy. If by some act you feel unhappy, better no to do it or avoid it, a fine balance is required. If you give only to get something in return having expectations, then, my dear friend better not to give. Give only what you can give comfortably, without any expectation, only with the intention of helping someone and if it makes you happy.

YOU) how much should I give to help others?
ME) Help to meet out someone's basic needs or for emergency needs and do not give to fulfil luxuries. For example, if your child asks for 20k dollars for buying a car and you can't afford it, you should say no to it and god forbid if someone in your family is seriously ill and needed the same amount of money (20k dollars), you should somehow/anyhow arrange for it as it's a question of life and death.

If some beggar asks for huge money, give him/her food or enough money to satisfy his stomach. If you give excess to someone, they will become corrupt. They won't value the money, they won't work hard which is needed to earn that money. **Your responsibility/nature is to help them fulfil their basic needs** and even help them find some job or give them job. Let them work hard and earn them their own money to fulfil their materialistic/luxurious needs.

YOU) whom to give or what is the priority of giving?
ME) You can help everybody/anybody in need, the decision and choice is always yours only but still this is what I feel should be your priority of giving. Everything starts from self. **The first thing that people forget is when we talk of giving, it starts only with you**. Your first priority is you, the core is you and everything starts with you, so first you need to give to your mind & body to make yourself strong, powerful and valuable. Once you become that, you can easily help others. Giving others simply means fulfilling their basic and emotional needs like food, shelter, clothing, appreciation, listen to them with love, care and empathy etc. Giving is contagious, once you start to give unconditionally, people also start to give unconditionally, this way the whole world can become spiritual where they will realise & practice their nature of giving & helping others out of love. Once it happens, this world can witness a real heaven on earth. Oh! I was telling you the priority and just lost in my words. **By the way the sequence of giving should be like this,**
So your **first** priority is you.
Second are your immediate family (spouse, parents, children etc.).

Third are your relatives and friends.

Fourth priority is your business contacts, job contacts, colleagues etc.

Fifth is your society, anybody in need whether known or unknown to you.

SEQUENCE OF GIVING/HELPING

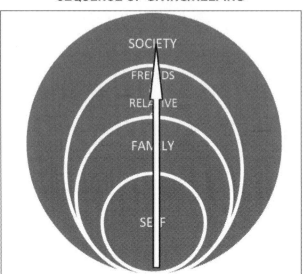

When I say that the first priority is me only, it does not mean that it's about only I, me and myself, it is the understanding and practicing the fact that you needs to empower yourself first before giving to others or in other words, only a powerful person can help others.

PEOPLE TALK OF SOCIAL SECURITY BUT LET ME TELL YOU, START CONTRIBUTING TO THE LIFE OF OTHERS TO GET THE SUPREME SECURITY; "DIVINE SECURITY". When you give, you get blessings which always take care of your life, help you in each & every moment and each & every problem of your life. The best security which even helps when all other doors are closed and when all hopes are lost. *DIVINE SECURITY WORKS 24/7/365/WHOLE LIFE/THIS LIFE/ALL LIVES.*

Whatever you give to others comes back to you. This is the law of nature. The vibrations of your acts of gratitude, happiness and kindness makes your energy field/aura positive, leading to a positive mindset (truthful PDA), healthy physical body, activation of intuitive powers, attraction of positive situations & people, all result of divine blessings effecting miracles in your life. **This is what I call GHK (Gratitude, Happiness and Kindness) your way of life, the #1Formula for a fulfilling life.** What GHK does is, it totally harmonises your mind, body and soul making you a power house of energy, an unshakable you, connects with your omnipotent reality.

Kindness (high frequency vibrations)-----Energy increases----- activation/balancing of 7 chakras/mind----activation of hormones (biochemical)-----healthy body & highly conscious mind----cool & calm mind-

---connection with real you-----Righteous awareness/thoughts (righteous perception, belief, values, decisions)-----righteous actions and behaviour----righteous results------Success/growth/happiness for you. Practice it in your real life situations for continuous 40 days to experience it. Any knowledge is incomplete without experience. And only practical experiences enhance knowledge and gives desired results.

6.7 BHAKTI YOG

Unconditional love: Hate, attachment to love/Passion

WHAT IS REAL LOVE: When we are ready to help others, give our precious time & energy for the benefit of others without expecting anything in return. When our focus is hard work, giving 100% in every action, every time in all areas of life viz. HWRC without being too much attached to the result, then it is the love & passion without any expectations or conditions; a true love for life.

IN RELATIONS, UNCONDITIONAL LOVE is when you let your related person live their life their own way; giving them the freedom of choice & time, you just help & guide them but do not try to control them. It is normal to expect your physical & emotional needs being fulfilled from them but you don't enforce your demands on them, you do not burden them with your expectations or you do not burden them by expecting what they are incapable of giving. When you help and contribute to their growth just to make them happy, then your love for that person is real, natural, and unconditional.

And what about the fulfilment of your needs & wants from a relationship; See, it is normal to have expectations in relations but the simple law of life is **'to get something, you must first give something'**. This is not a give & take relationship but a natural law. By giving first is not something conditional, it just means that by nature, you are a giver and when you adhere to your nature of giving, you automatically get your needs & wants fulfilled through the nature of the related person/ universe. But if you impose conditions, in return the other person will also impose conditions.

The more the conditions in any relationship, be it family, business or any other relationship, the shorter is the life span of relation. The only condition in love should be no conditions but only love which automatically fulfils your needs & wants. More conditions mean more fear which means doubt and insecurity. And any relationship based on fear, doubt and insecurity is not a natural relationship and sooner or later it's going to create a dispute and ultimately develops cracks in relationships.

UNCONDITIONAL LOVE FOR YOUR PHYSICAL AND MENTAL HEALTH is when you choose and practice natural, spiritual and righteous food & water intake habits, righteous physical activity, natural breathing pattern, focussed way of life and the right amount of sleep etc. If you respect your body, you are ready to give your 100% focus to it, meaning you love it. If you ignore your body, means you are not taking care of it, it will invariably lead to disease.

UNCONDITIONAL LOVE FOR YOUR JOB/CARRIER: If you love your job, you work for it even overtime with your full focus without expectations of instant pay increments or financial gains. Your focus is on performance & excellence in your work which is the perfect recipe for success and on the other hand, if a person imposes so many conditions & restrictions that he will not work overtime, not do any work out of scope of his present job and needs instant increments/extra bucks for any extra work. **Surely everybody wants extra bucks for extra work** but don't you think that if you impose so many conditions before doing any job, then your boss may say no to you, being burdened by your conditions. This is your loss but not the loss of your boss and he will soon find another person. **You have lost an opportunity to grow and learn new job/skill.** On the other hand, your boss loves his work so somehow, sooner or later he will find another suitable, passionate person who loves work. So these two people will grow and you will envy & hate their growth. **Big bucks are bound to come when you accept, welcome and work unconditionally.** The best would be to say yes to extra work which means new opportunities to learn new skills and growth. Once you provide results, your company will definitely give bonuses and increments to you as everybody/anybody wants to retain a good employee. And even if they don't give any increment to you, their competitors are not only ready but they are desperate to have an employee like you. So, you have everything to gain but for that, you must love your work unconditionally to make yourself valuable, a person who is an asset to anybody/everybody.

LOVE GIVES RISE TO FOCUSSED ACTION WHICH GUARANTEE SUCCESS.

RESPECT	LOVE	100% FOCUS IN ACTION	SUCCESS

HATE AND IGNORANCE GIVES RISE TO INACTION OR UNFOCUSSED ACTION
OR INVOLUNTARY ACTION WHICH GUARANTEE FAILURE

DISRESPECT	IGNORANCE	UNFOCUSSED ACTIONS	FAILURE

Source: Meet the Real You **Copyright:** Chetan Bansal

SOME PEOPLE MISUNDERSTAND UNCONDITIONAL LOVE. Unconditional love does not mean that you accept and approve every deed of the other person to make them happy. If the other person is doing something wrong, if he/she is on the wrong path, then it is your duty to help them correct themselves. Unconditional love does not mean saying yes every time to your loved ones. *When it comes to deeds & action of a related person, acceptance means to accept what has already happened, forgive for that act which was out of ignorance or was not intentional but it does not mean approval for the next time.* If repeated next time, it shall be dealt with *F-TIPP* (explained in forgiveness section).

If something has to be a no, it has to be a no, if something is against humanity or nature or against the well-being of self/others or all, then it has to be a "NO". What will you do if your body becomes unhealthy; you will definitely get it medically treated to make it normal again, even if the medical treatment is painful or expensive and you will never ignore the disease. **What does it mean? It means that you love your body and hate the physical disease present in it** and you are ready to **undergo even a painful treatment**

213

to get rid of your disease. **In the same way, you love the sinner but hate the sin and you may have to take strong actions against the sinner to get him/her rid of their sin.** Your actions may seem rude or painful in short term but eventually in a long run, they would realize that it was meant for their good and even if they don't realize, you should be happy that you have acted with utmost responsibility. **When parents scold their child**, they do it out of their love as they want to see them on the path of success, so their anger is to prevent the children from some wrong deed/action.

BHAKTI YOG: This says human nature is to give & love unconditionally. So, real *bhakti* (worship) of god is to help and love self/others, without any conditions. To love the creation of God equally without any bias is *Bhakti Yog*. We must first love & help self to become happy, as happiness activates our nature of love and help for others.

People misunderstand *Bhakti* as religion. Real *Bhakti* is not forcing anybody to worship any religion which has been created by humans, the real *Bhakti* is to love & worship God and its creation; all humans, plants, animals, stars, planets, water, air, earth, fire and everything about nature, without any discrimination or bias. The real *Bhakti* is to respect the beliefs and religion of everybody/anybody.

We have a responsibility towards nature for maintaining the nature as it is by respecting, loving and valuing the nature. And we have been doing the opposite; we have polluted, destroyed and created imbalance in nature which is totally against our nature of *Bhakti*. Going against your nature is like becoming your own enemies. So, realising and living your nature of love, care, respect for nature is what we call *bhakti* yoga or unconditional love. If you can't respect others or your love and respect is biased based on caste, creed, religion, sex, race, social status, economic status etc., then there is no use of your education, better to remain uneducated then to practice bias towards nature and its creation. If you worship some religion but disrespect humans, are rude towards others, hate others, then my dear friend, you do not understand religion. The only religion is love; love for other humans, flora, fauna and the whole creation in this universe, a *Bhakti Yoga*.

Love is the basis of all creation in this world. When two opposites meet, creation happens and why two opposites meet, they are attracted towards each other, they complete each other, and they fulfil each other's lack. So, love happens to fulfil your need which in turn causes creation in this world. Love is the cause of your existence and existence of everybody on this planet. Love is responsible for the continuity of life, without love there can be no existence or no life.

Bhakti **means love but doesn't mean any religious practice. Religion is a part of *bhakti* but is not complete *bhakti* in itself.** There are various religions in this world. **People with same beliefs and values make their own religion.** *'Religion is nothing but a set of common beliefs, values and certain rituals being practiced with only one intent and the purpose of finding a* *god's grace for oneself or experiencing god in one's self'.* All religious teachings are the same that god is one, we all are children of god but the ways and rituals of worshipping god is different. **Real God is in the form of people, if we cannot love people who are present in front of us, who can be seen with the naked eye, touched, felt, can we really love God whom no one has seen?** God is in me, in you, in everybody, in everything, everywhere, god is love; so love yourself and everybody else to feel, believe and experience God within you. **This is the real *bhakti* (Love) which will give you ultimate *Shakti* (Power) to experience the power of God within you.**

UNCONDITIONAL LOVE VS ATTACHMENT

Attachment means to focus too much on your own needs & wants but not the source (related person) of your need fulfilment; you are attached not to the source of your need fulfilment but the need itself. In attachment to get your need fulfilled, you do anything/everything irrespective of it being right or wrong where you even try to control/manipulate other people (source of your needs) for your own gains, even by inflicting pain on them. Your love for the other person is only till he/she keeps fulfilling your needs. Once a need fulfilment stops from the other person, the love for the other person transmutes to hate where people even resort to physical & verbal abuse. That is not a natural, loving relationship but a conditional relationship where you just want your own gains, without any concern for the other person.

This will create negative energies in the other person. The pain created by your selfish act in the other person will ultimately come back to you, making your energy field negative and life hell. So if you really love somebody, you can't hurt them or if the other person is hurting you, it means you both do not accept/respect each other or you are not able to fulfil each other's needs & wants simply because you both focus on getting from the other and has forgotten to give to the other. Once the natural give & take stops, the so-called love which is nothing but an attachment is transmuted to hate.

The only solution to transmute hate to love is to accept the other person as they are, without any bias, allow the other to live life their own way, give them the freedom of space & time where you are ready to help them, without any expectations in return out of your pure love & affection. **Detachment does not mean that you do not have needs & wants**, it simply means you are not addicted to your needs & wants, you also take care of the needs & wants of others, that you do not believe in fulfilling your needs & wants at the cost of others, in detachment, you want to create a win-win situation for both where needs & wants of each other are taken care of, without any pain to anyone.

Attachment is like loving to your needs & wants and not the related person (source of your needs & wants). You are addicted to the other person as long as your own needs are being fulfilled by him/her. Your focus is on taking from others and not on giving to others. **This leads to a mismatch of give & take cycle of life/relations** and once give & take is out of balance or stops, problems are inevitable in relations. **In detachment,** you need to detach from your needs & wants and instead focus on fulfilling the needs & wants of the other person. *The simple law of life is to get something, you must give first*. Once your focus goes on giving, you will automatically get what you need. **Always remember giving is input and receiving is output** and you should only focus on your input karma. **Spiritual person always focus on input and never worry about the output**. Spirituality is like detaching your focus from the results and attaching yourself with your karma/actions.

    Same way, when your focus is result and you are not focusing on your action/planning/execution about the work your performance downgrades due to your attachment with results. You want good results, so your focus is results and you have forgotten your action which is the cause for result. If you love your work unconditionally, then your focus will be 100% in your action and performance and when your focus is performance, you are not attached to the results.

    SO, THE REAL LOVE IS IN GIVING YOUR BEST TO GET THE BEST. And to give your best is caring at its best and for caring in a responsible way, you need to understand, value, and respect the source of your needs & wants. The more you understand your health/wealth/relations/job/career/profession, the more you focus on your input action which ultimately manifests desired output results.

    For right understanding, you need to connect and communicate effectively. And for effective communication, you need to master the art of WOW, watching, observing, witnessing, listening more and responding in the most responsible manner but only after understanding. **For example, to understand anybody, you need to listen and observe them to find out about their likes & dislikes, their expectations from you.** Only then you need to act/respond to fulfil your responsibilities towards them. You need to communicate about what is easy for you to give and what you cannot. The more you communicate with them in the most caring & loving manner, the more they will understand, respect, value and connect with you leading to a fulfilling relationship where love flows from both sides. **Same way, the more you understand, respect and value your work/profession,** the more will be your hard work/effort and better will be the results. **Same way, the more you understand, respect and value your mind & body,** the more will be your effort towards maintaining their health which actually makes your mind & body healthy.

    Love (high frequency vibrations)-----Energy increases-----activation/balancing of 7 chakras/mind----activation of hormones (biochemical)-----healthy body & highly conscious mind----cool & calm mind----connection with real you-----Righteous awareness/thoughts (righteous perception, belief, values, decisions)-----righteous actions and behaviour----righteous results------Success/growth/happiness for you. Practice it in your real life situations for continuous 40 days to experience it. Any knowledge is incomplete without experience. And only practical experiences enhance knowledge and gives desired results.

YOU) How to find what you are passionate or madly in love about?
ME) if you are attached to your comfort, you won't work hard to achieve something or anything. It means you love your comfort more and your work less. When you love something so deeply that you forget all your comfort, work tirelessly, relentlessly for long hours, then it is nothing but only passion. If you are passionate about something, you work for it irrespective of the results and without any expectations in return. This is the real love/passion where you even love the hardships associated with your passionate work.

The energy vibrations of love & passion are vibrations of the highest frequency which sets up path for your success at the speed of light. So, anything that you are madly in love with, are passionate about is manifested very fast in your life. Love/passion synchronizes your mind, body, soul and energies leading to the highest level of coordination and cooperation within all your cells, tissues, organs, body, mind, and emotions, leading to righteous PDA and perfect results in life. Synchronization of mind, body, soul with energies is the only secret to guaranteed success & peak performance and secret to synchronization is love & passion.

YOU) How to find, whether you love somebody or not?
ME) the simple answer is that, if you respect the other person without any conditions, you invariably love that person. If you respect someone even if he/she do not fulfil your needs & wants, then it's real love.

When someone stops respecting and loving someone once the need fulfilment stops, it is a clear case of love being conditional, temporary and situational; a typical case where the attitude of the person changes, he/she becomes rude leading to disrespect, disconnection and loss of love which was actually never there.

It is not wrong to expect the fulfilment of your needs & wants as life itself means needs & wants. Two people entering a relation only for the fulfilment of their respective needs is nothing wrong and all natural. Changes in time changes the mind and hence, needs & wants which makes a person incapable of fulfilling the needs of the related person, this causes emotional pain but you rise above your pains and tries to understand & help the other person. You are still responsible, respecting, caring and loving the other person. **This is the highest form of respect, a pure love.**

YOU) How to get respect and love from others?
ME) most people have one urge i.e. to control the life of others, wanting acceptance, approval and appreciation from others without any conditions but do not want to do the same for others. This is pure hypocrisy and the first & foremost cause of all misery in life.

No two human beings can ever be the same. All have different beliefs, opinions and perceptions. **The only formula of love is Acceptance, Approval and Appreciation (AAA)**. Non-acceptance is resistance and friction. Acceptance means love, approval means more love and appreciation means the highest degree of love. That is AAA formula for love.

Would you like a person who does not listen to you, don't want to understand you, who wait for an opportunity to find a fault in you, criticize and supress you? Same way, nobody will like you if you behave the same as above. Differences in opinions/beliefs are natural and are the very base of all human relationships. We must use difference in opinions/beliefs to arrive at a better decision & actions, using and combining the intelligence of all but never to aggravate disputes and problems. Make a magic combination 1+1= 11 and do not allow it to become a misery combination -1-1= -11.

If you can accept, approve and appreciate yourself, why not others? Accept them as they are, listen to them, understand them, respect their feelings and opinions, help them overcome their mistakes, support them in their bad times, have love and compassion from them. Let them decide and live their life their own way; give freedom of space and time to them. Just one sentence, "when needed, I am always there for you". Only this is the recipe to get respect and love from others, nothing else.

6.8 FORGIVENESS AND FTIPP
Hurt to Peace, Blaming/Complaining/Revenge to Forgiveness

"Forgiving is the greatest virtue of mankind, an act that proves the presence of divine in each & every life"
   -Chetan Bansal

Whenever we encounter something unexpected in life, it causes a pain/hurt in mind, disturbing our emotions. A weaker mind is not able to accept the presence of situation and illusions, as it is the end of life. The real truth of life is that everything/anything that happens in life is the outcome of your own actions taken in the past. You may have done something which was not appropriate/reasonable/out of ignorance, but resulted in a painful situation today. The acts of the person who inflicted pain on you may have been intentional or unintentional and you never know why or how they have acted in an irresponsible manner. But an unaware/emotionally weaker mind does not understand the dynamics of life and invariably blames the act of the other person as intentional with a purpose of causing pain in you. **You may be right but most of the times, it is the unintentional, unaware action of the self/other person.** Whatever may be the reason, the situation has already happened and you don't have to make it worse by choosing an emotionally disturbed state of mind or you don't have to carry that burden lifelong, cursing/blaming self/others. **You need to mend the situation and for that, the first step would be to mend your own mind by releasing the hurt through a simple, sensible act of forgiveness.**

Forgiveness is nothing but relinquishing all the hurt & pain from your personal space which has made each & every cell of your body defective, unnatural and the source of misery in life. Forgiveness releases all the negative energies of pain, anger, hurt, frustration, hate and envy stored in your each & every cell of the body to make your personal space vibrant/energetic, full of life.

Whenever you get hurt due to any action of anybody, it gets stored in your subconscious or in deep memory and if not released early, it becomes a permanent memory in each and every cell of your body. This makes your subconscious defective/unnatural and corrupts the natural coding of success & happiness leading to wrong PDA and wrong results in life. So, we need to remove all the hurt & pain to make your mind & body perfectly natural and effective again like we remove viruses from computer using antiviruses. Forgiveness is the most effective natural antivirus present which can only be activated by your conscious choice.

REASONS FOR HURTING SITUATIONS IN LIFE: All the people & situations are only attracted in your life based on your past actions/karma of this life or previous life or bad karma of masses or due to non-action or wrong action in the present space & time.

HURTING PEOPLE DUE TO PAST KARMA: People like parents, children, spouse, business partner etc. are in your present life based on your karma of previous life. These people have come in your life due to some pendency in karmic accounts like:

---With some, you have the pendency of revenge or somebody owed something to you.

---Somebody did something wrong to you in previous life or you did wrong to them and they have come in your present life so as to balance out.

---Somebody needs your help in their evolution and understanding of life.

---Somebody came in your life to help you learn and grow in life.

HURTING SITUATION DUE TO NON-PRESENCE: For example, a road accident can happen due to your mind not present or wandering somewhere else. It is a typical example of wrong action in present space & time.

HURTING SITUATIONS DUE TO NON-ACTIONS/WRONG ACTIONS OF MASSES: Say for example rape, robbery, theft, terrorism can only happen due to non-actions or wrong actions of masses where the laws of the land are weak and people do not raise their voice against the bad elements in society. This leads to the growth of bad elements in the society and innocent people become victims.

But if you dig deep, you will always find the one cause of all problems i.e. your own karma (thoughts, emotions, perception, decisions, and actions taken by you in the past or present). All people and circumstances in your life are the outcome of your own karmic vibrations (mindset/PDA), **so we cannot blame the other person**. Even if you have done something under the influence of somebody else even then you are to be blames as the final decision and action was only yours. The other person may have mala fide intentions but was successful in influencing you to gain something from you but the final decision was always yours. It means your PDA was wrong as your intelligence was clouded due to your negative emotions. So ultimately the cause of your hurt is only you, it clearly means that you need to work on your consciousness, understanding, and perception not only to correct present hurting situations but to avoid future hurting situations.

You can blame the other person but will it be of any use? They are what they are. They are also the product of their own past karma/impressions. If something is wrong with them, it is their karma to correct themselves and not yours. This does not mean that you are giving a clean chit to bad elements/criminals but a strong message to all, to wake up and raise their voice against all the evils in the society. Your karma is to stay away from the people with mala fide intentions, give them a chance to correct themselves, forgive them for your own peace of mind, bless them with wisdom, kindness, and love for humanity but if they are stubborn, adamant and keep on repeating crimes, inhuman acts, they need to be taught a lesson in a language they understand it best, be it of violence. **A truly divine/spiritual person will never think twice to use violence if it is the only option left to end violence/crimes/evils in society.**

IN CLOSE RELATIONS, if consistent, persistent complain and blame hadn't changed the other person the way you wanted, so what is the use of your blame and complain? By repeated blaming the other person, you are creating unnecessary pain & hurt in self/others. So, it will be foolish to complain again and again if things are not changing your way. The best would be to understand the situation of the other person, help them in whatever way you can, have compassion and empathy for them. Forgive them, bless them and if the other person is not acting as per your expectations, it does not mean that you are right, it simply means that you both have different beliefs, perceptions, opinions and priorities. If the other person is fulfilling his/her responsibilities, is giving what needs to be given in a relationship, then you need to change yourself and not the other person. **But the big question is, who will decide who is right or who is wrong? The big answer is your conscious presence.** Let's see how? Your first step is to understand your own expectations; are they realistic, are you too much interfering in his/her personal space, is he/she is repeating the same mistakes again and again or is not improving himself/herself? **If they are improving,** it is good, **if they are not improving but have the intention of improving,** then you need to help them and **if they do not want to improve,** then you have a choice to remove yourself from their life. Whatever the case may be, forgiveness is a must for your better present and future.

See, **we attract all blood relations** like parents, brother, sister etc. based on previous life karma. All other relations like teachers, students, business partners, life partners, love relations etc. and be it any relation, all are the outcome of your past life or current life karma. If something is wrong in relationship, either you need to improve self or the other person needs to improve himself/herself or both need to improve. So whether you like it or not, you need to accept all your relations, if something is wrong or more precisely you dislike about the other person, the better way instead of blaming is to make them understand about your likes & dislikes in the most loving and compassionate way, forgive them, give them another chance and if they still repeat the same mistake, then either they are doing intentionally or did not understand your view point or are not capable of meeting your expectations or do not value you. Make them understand again and still they don't change, it your only choice that you can remove them from your life or if the situation is that you cannot remove them from your life, accept them but at all cost, forgive them for your own peace of mind. **Acceptance here does not mean that you approve their misdeeds** but you just accept them as they are and now you have dropped your desire to change them. **You may not accept them in your heart but you don't hate them either.** You pray for their wellbeing, you are taking care of your responsibilities but now, you do not have any expectations from them either. You neither hate nor like the other person but have empathy for them even if they are no more in your personal space and time.

Everybody is contributing to the growth of each other in many different ways, either by creating pleasant or unpleasant situations. If you can understand this principle of karmic account, you can understand each other well and help each other grow instead of leg pulling each other. Even if you had severe bad experiences with somebody close in your life, the best way to correct is to forgive them and more rightly forgive each other, understand each other and start anew. But for that, the consent and understanding on both parts is required.

If one is willing and the other does not want to, then it is better to get separated from each other. Even if the situation demands you both to live together, still you need to change yourself and forgive for the sake of your own peace and peace of other. If you still keep on fighting and blaming the other, you will never find peace entangled in karmic vicious cycles of distrust, misunderstandings, fear, anger, hurt, pain and miseries until & unless your awareness, wisdom, consciousness; your nature of love, care and understanding became more powerful than your ego and takes the control of your life. **Only forgiveness can release all negativity from your life by releasing you from the prison of your unconscious mind.**

In case you are not able to bear the other person or the presence of other person is hurting you again and again, better to get separated. But in case of separation, also forgiving each other is must. Forgiving and blessing the other person ("God give him wisdom, peace and happiness") ends the karmic account and you two shall not meet again to balance out the debit & credit of karmic accounts or even if you meet again in this life or next life, you can start afresh as there are no pending accounts. **So never leave any karmic account in your mind**, never give permanent space to the feelings of revenge and curse anybody. **Always end all disputes by forgiving the other person and by blessing them with happiness, peace and wisdom, so that you and the other person lead a happy life.** If you want peace, happiness and love in your life, bless the other person and if you want a curse in your life, curse the other person because whatever you are doing either cursing or blessing, it is being stored in your subconscious mind. If your subconscious stores vibrations of blessings, you will attract blissful situations or if it stores vibrations of curse you will attract curse in your life. **It means that you need to relinquish all hurt and pain through the act of forgiveness, to make your energy field/aura positive to attract blissful people & situations.** Otherwise, you will keep attracting those hurting people & situations in life.

So, do not spread the vibrations of hurt and curse. Everybody is human, everybody's nature is the same that is to give and love unconditionally, just beliefs & perceptions are different, they might be under the influence of their egoistic mind, under illusion, under some false identity, or they might be ignorant of the truth. So, they need help from your side. Even if you can't help them, at least forgive them and bless them with good karma. It is important to forgive which releases your subconscious mind of karmic account/impressions giving permanent peace in your life. When you don't carry any heavy baggage or let go off all grudges in your life only then you can live a blissful, purposeful, passionate life.

Releasing your mind of all negative emotions is true liberation, true salvation and forgiveness is the right tool for that salvation; a true liberation from the miseries of your mind can only be possible through forgiveness. So forgive everything, every person, forgive self, every situation, forgive irrespective of who is right or who is wrong, and forgive your past, present that is causing any pain/hurt or any type of negativity in your mind. Only then, your consciousness/awareness will arise leading to truthful PDA and right results in life. So forgive, forgive, forgive and keep on forgiving for your own peace of mind, to move ahead in life for opening new chapters in your life.

Unless you forgive, you will keep entangled in situations of blame, complain and hurt. **"JUST FORGIVE AND BLESS THE OTHER TO HAVE A BLISSFUL LIFE."** **Forgiveness (high frequency vibrations)-----Removal of all negativity enhances your energy-----activation/balancing of 7 chakras/mind---- activation of hormones (biochemical)-----healthy body & highly conscious mind----cool & calm mind----connection with real you-----Righteous awareness/thoughts (righteous perception, belief, values, decisions)----- righteous actions and behaviour----righteous results------ Success/growth/happiness for you.** Practice it in your real life situations for continuous 40 days to experience it. Any knowledge is incomplete without experience. And only practical experiences enhance knowledge and gives desired results.

YOU) How to deal with people who hurts you?
ME) FORGIVENESS! First you should know
a) Whether they have hurt you intentionally or
b) Their hurtful action was out of unawareness or lack of knowledge or some misunderstanding or it was just a temporary emotional outburst.

If the case is a), I have no place for people in my life who **repeatedly, intentionally hurt me** or are intentionally hurting others and are not willing to change themselves. I forgive them for my own peace of mind. I choose to be physically away from them. I will not be sharing my personal time and space with them. I choose to be at peace and not hurt by any of their actions. They have no control over my mind, thoughts, emotions and actions.

But my heart still blesses them with all the blessings of nature/God for them to become wise, nice and kind for self and others. And I bless them that they come out of their unconscious state and regain consciousness. They are what they are but only because they are carrying a huge baggage of some hurt or pain of some past experience inside them. They are carrying hurt so they are spreading hurt as a person gives only what he/she has. This is not their mistake, as their nature has been clouded by some unresolved issue, misunderstanding, or some hurt which has taken the shape of Ego, the big ego which is being reflected in their behaviour towards others. So, it will be foolish on my part to hate them. That will further enhance pain in them and they will spread more pain. I tried many times to make them realize their bad behaviour or tried to help them come out of their unconscious state but they are not able to overpower their ego. So, I choose to be away from them to protect my own mind but at the same time, I pray for them. **This is the only way to stop spreading of hate and pain.**

If the case is b), then my hurt is also temporary and it is my responsibility to make the other person understand my perspective, communicate my dislikes to them in the most loving and compassionate way, enhance the

level of communication, enhance the level of connection between the two of us so that these hurting situations are not repeated again.

I will also try this first in case of a) also. If this does not work and the other person becomes unbearable to me, then I have only one choice and that is to get separated from them.

YOU) how can I find that I have forgiven a person or situation completely or am I still carrying the baggage of hurt within me?

ME) the answer is very simple. Ask yourself, when you think of that person or that hurting situation, does it bring pain in you, does it invokes negative emotions in you, do you feel that hurt again? If yes, you have not forgiven the person or situation completely. It is still bothering you.

Practice forgiving again and again. Speak in your mind, **"Nobody or no situation is strong enough to bother/disturb me. I am strong than anybody/anything in this universe, I forgive them without any conditions. I forgive them even if they are not sorry for it. I bless them with happiness. Oh God! Thanks for making me such a strong and loving Human."**

If thinking about that hurting person or situation does not invoke any negative emotions in you or you are not affected in any way, remembering does not cause any unpleasant feeling in your mind and you still bless him/her for a happy life, then great! You have mastered the art of forgiving. You have developed a strong connection with **THE REAL YOU**.

YOU) But sir, how to find out the intentions of the other person, whether good or he/she is innocent or he/she has mala fide/bad intentions.

ME) why would you want to know that?

YOU) Because sir, if the intentions of the person are not bad, it means he/she is innocent and the hurting situation might be due to some misunderstanding or due to different perception or may be my perception is not right. Then I would like to remain in the relationship, find the cause and try to correct the cause.

ME) Wow, great! I am impressed. If you can develop such level of understanding, then my dear **REAL YOU**, you will never fail in life. And 99% of the times, it is an issue of perspectives/misunderstandings and not bad intention in human relations.

YOU) Thanks Sir!

ME) what if the other person is really having bad intentions?

YOU) I may decide to remove the person from my life.

ME) choice is always yours, nobody else can take a decision for you but whatever you may decide, forgiveness is a must in all cases or any of the cases. Now, this is how you find the real truth about the situation or person or both.

WOW: Watch, Observe and Witness the other person; his/her behaviour, actions, try to make them comfortable by choosing silence & peace so that they can speak their heart out, do not interrupt them while they speak or do not try to suppress anything while they speak even if they are using abusive language, give them complete freedom to speak and act. Soon you will be able to understand their mindset including their intentions. Are they innocent, ignorant, have bad intentions, the real truth will soon popup. Do not haste into such decisions involving humans and relations. Have some patience and let the time decide, let the awareness decide, let the nature decide. So observing, watching, listening the other person without any emotional reaction is the key to understand the other person. This will help you take the most appropriate decision. Just practice it to experience it.

YOU) IS CHANGING THE RELATIONSHIP THE RIGHT SOLUTION?

ME) *BEFORE CHANGING THE RELATIONSHIP, FIRST CHANGE YOU, MAYBE YOU ARE PROBLEMATIC AND NOT THE OTHER PERSON.* If by changing yourself positively, sync does not happen between the two of you, either you have not changed yourself perfectly, so try again or the other person is adamant, egoist or rigid. So what you can do, try to communicate your concerns with them and if nothing works, you can remove them from your life and I would not ask you to compromise on your happiness.

People change relations but does not want to change self. If something is wrong in your relations, if you are not getting what you want in your relationship, then it is because of your own thoughts, decisions and actions.

You must find your fault, work on them and bring about the positive changes in self. Doing this will also change the other person positively or more appropriately, synchronization happens between the two of you. This creates a balance in the give & take cycles in relations, where both of your will experience that whatever you give in relations comes back. Previously, you were giving hurt and manifesting hurt and now you are giving happiness and thus, manifesting happiness.

Even if after changing yourself positively, the other person is still not aligned with you, then your vibes are different. Then you have the right to change the relation **but first, it is your duty to understand and change self.** See, in many societies today, people are constantly changing their relations meaning they are never satisfied with any of their relations. It means that people are not able to align with anybody and even after changing so many relations, they are always blaming others. It proves that the fault is not with the other person but it is within self; limiting beliefs, negative behaviour, self-centred actions are activating wrong response from others and you think you are unlucky who is attracting same type of hurting people & situations, again and again. Really, you are unlucky but only you are to be blamed. Change yourself positively to attract positive response from others and thus, manifest long lasting, loving relationship.

Learn to drive the car and do not keep changing the car, changing the car won't make you a perfect driver but understanding the driving

systems and practicing on them shall make you a perfect driver. Then, no matter which car you drive, you are perfect at driving, there may be small adjustments which you need to make to drive different cars but the basic driving skills, systems and skills to handle them are the same. Same is with relations, in relations also, changing the relation won't work either, you need to understand your nature, nature of the other person, practice the art of connecting and synchronising with the other person.

YOU) But sir, give me something that I can remember and practice easily, on how to deal with people and situations? I think if I am able to handle people and situations, my 99.9% problems shall be solved.

ME) Amazing! You are very intelligent you seem to know everything, why are you asking me?

YOU) Sir, please tell me, why you are pulling my leg?

ME) Ok! Jokes apart, **finally some good TIP from my side.**

And That TIP is **F-TIPP.**

YOU) Hmmm! F-TIPP, *yeh kya hai* sir (what is this sir?)

ME) Step 1: "F" means forgiveness.

If step 1 does not work follow step 2

Step 2: "T" means talking/communicating your concerns.

If step 2 does not work follow step 3

Step 3: "I" Ignoring the other person or situation.

If step 3 does not work follow step 4

Step 4: "P" Punish the other person.

If step 4 does not work follow step 5

Step 5: "P" Pray if nothing works.

But the problem with people is that they go directly to step 3 or step 4. We must first use step 1 and step 2, as 99.9% problems solve here. For 0.01%, you may need to go to step 3 or step 4.

YOU) and what about step 5?

ME) it is simple but difficult to implement. If the situation is such that the other person is very important for you or for some bigger cause, you need to stay in the relationship, you have no other choice but to accept the person as it is and pray to God for the happiness of both of you. **Pray to God to give you the strength, power, courage, love, and kindness to deal with the other person, and above all, the strength to maintain your own cool & calm. For example,** you have children and your marriage is in question, then you need to bear each other at all cost for the happiness, present and future of your children who are totally dependent upon you both and need the joint presence of both of you. Any disharmony in the family can ruin the life of whole family. **Only a spiritual, emotionally strong person can rise above his/her likes and dislikes choosing step 5. *I admire, pray, wish and bless happiness, success and harmony to return in their relations who follow the step 5.***

6.9 POWER OF CELEBRATION
Dull to celebration

"Celebration is the very essence of life; celebration magnifies the experiences of life."
                    -Chetan Bansal

Life means celebration, so let's celebrate; play games, follow your hobbies, follow your passions. Celebration is the enjoyment through any activity/action. It is raising your vibrations through your senses by treating them with dance, singing, watching movies, going to parties, doing adventure activities, playing some sports, travelling, holidaying or anything which brings smile on your face, anything which you are passionate about or more precisely gives a feeling of high can be safely called an act of celebration of life. Celebrating each & every moment of your life is feeling happy about, enthusiastic about and curious about to experience the uncertainties of life, to explore the unwanted, to enjoy the moments of life even if it is to your disliking. When you can maintain cool & calm, when you are ready for any challenge, when you can maintain your enthusiasm for life, even in the worst moments/situations of life, it is the real celebration of life. Celebrate each & every moment of life, do not wait for any moment instead make every moment a celebration. **Celebration and playfulness is your nature and not celebrating is the major cause of dullness/voids in life.**

Remember when you were small children, you use to celebrate each & every moment, use to laugh at small things/incidents having immense enthusiasm in life. As and when you started growing older and older, you lost all enthusiasm and with that, your beautiful smiles. It is very important to laugh, smile and celebrate each & every achievement and incident in life. Laugh at yourself, your failures/mistakes, just laugh/smile/celebrate have good sense of humour, finding happiness/joy in every moment of your life. Whether you are alone or in group, always laugh and make others laugh. Laughter is the greatest medicine given by god, having the power to mend/correct/cure even the deadliest of diseases ever known in the history of mankind. It releases all negativity from your mind, brings it back to the present moment, a space of divine to set your life on happy/automatic/natural path of life. The more you celebrate the more energetic, magnetic and powerful you become and that is what is needed for a successful and happy life.

You have forgotten to celebrate and enjoy life instead you keep on worrying about problems and difficult situations in life. And you are not enjoying life waiting for your troubles/problems to end to celebrate life. **But my dear friend, that trouble-free moment never comes in life as once you**

overcome a problem, another is waiting to challenge your life. This is the truth of life which most people realize only in the last moments of their life. Then you will curse yourself, "Why have I wasted my life worrying instead I should have enjoyed all the times of my life irrespective of situations or problems or age? "So believe me challenges /problems will always be there in life, just start enjoying and celebrating each & every moment of life, then even the problems will look exciting and to your amaze, once this becomes your way/attitude of life, then your focus automatically shifts from worry to celebration, from cursing problem to solving problems in life.

Well, do you know the purpose of problems in your life? See, the problems are a part & parcel of your life conspired by the universe for you to become more skilful, physically, mentally and emotionally stronger in life. The more problems one faces in life, the stronger, skilful and powerful he becomes. I think this is a wonderful reason to celebrate problems in life. **Another reason:** Once you will solve a problem, it will never come back in your life or next time, it won't be a problem for you as you already know the solution to it. **So, you won't get a chance to celebrate your problem once it is solved.** Better celebrate your problem as and when it arises, having one thought in your mind, ***"Now I shall be learning something new, unknown to me, important for my future and for my personal growth"***. This one thought will bring back your peace of mind, smile, never give up attitude where you welcome problems with open arms and once your arms are open, problems become your friend and a friend always transmutes all problems to solutions. **Try this next time you face a problem to verify the truthfulness of this statement**.

We have a habit of delaying celebration, for example, when I will get admission in college I will celebrate then when we get admission we think to celebrate after getting the degree and when we get the degree, we think to celebrate after getting the job and you see that celebration time never arrives. We always think of achieving more & more and in the process forgot to celebrate & reward our each & every achievement. **This way, we will never be able to celebrate and if we are not celebrating life then what is the use, purpose and meaning of life? Remember, a life without celebration is a meaningless life.**

If you don't celebrate/enjoy the moment, delay your celebration then your life becomes dull & depressive. When you delay celebration, you forever miss the opportunity for that celebration which was only possible in that lost moment. Suppose you achieved something, obviously the feelings at that moment are very good/positive/high and that is the only right time/moment to celebrate. But somehow you decided to delay your celebration due to any reason, may be your mind wants to celebrate after achieving something bigger and better. **But when you achieve that something bigger by then, your feelings of previous achievement is already dull or there is no excitement left with that previous achievement. For example, when you bought the bicycle, you didn't celebrate and after buying the car,**

you have no value for the bicycle and you shall never be able to celebrate that moment of buying a cycle. Same is with your current achievement, as your mind would again want to delay it till you achieve something new/bigger and this way, you won't be able to celebrate any of the achievements/moments. **This makes your life dull where you will always dream of good future and carrying a residue of negative feelings of non-celebration of the past.** This residue of negative emotions, of non-celebration shall keep on increasing with every delay in celebration making you feel dull and unhappy all the time instead of all achievements. Also, as this life is full of ups & downs, in future you might fail or is not able to achieve your goal then also, you won't celebrate. **So, you delayed the celebration on success for the want of bigger success and on failure obviously you won't celebrate, so when will you celebrate and taste life.** This attitude creates void in your life where you lose motivation/enthusiasm for life. The only way to feel happy, excited, motivated in life is by celebrating your each & every moment, each & every achievement, each & every failure alike. The moments that you celebrate are your real life moments rest are just dates and passing of time.

Use celebration to strengthen relations and to end disputes. It is normal to have fights, quarrels, disputes and differences of opinion in relations but the best remedy or the best formula to maintain/enhance the strength of all relations is by celebrating together. **Celebrating together invokes positive feelings for each other.** When you celebrate together, the other person feels accepted by you, this dissolves all negative feelings and **you should always remember feelings always take higher space than logic in the human psyche.** When you have a problem in relationship normally communication stops, then there are 2 choices; **1) Either to keep the communication shut** which will ultimately end the relationship or worsen the problem in a relationship or choice, **2) Where you rise above the differences and celebrate together which ultimately invokes positive feelings in all involved in a relationship** and where there is a celebration, communication happens naturally leading to the flow of love in the air.

Never allow your life to become dull. The moment you feel dullness in your life, consciously choose celebration to raise your vibrations. Dullness will invoke negative emotions like depression/sadness in you will cause depletion of energy ultimately leading to various physical, mental ailments and thus, misery in life. It is okay sometimes to experience a few temporary moments of dullness but do not allow it to take permanent space in your mind. Choosing celebration is like connecting and communicating with your *REAL NATURE OF LOVE, leading to all positivity and happiness in life.*

Be fully focused and present in your celebration, just be your natural best without bothering what others think or say about you. As someone rightly said- Dance freely as if nobody is watching and sing as if nobody is listening. **Do whatever that makes you happy,** eat on roadsides if it makes you happy, go for shopping if it makes you happy (but beware of your pocket limits, laughs!), go to beauty salons, go for swimming, listen to your best songs, watch your favourite movie, watch comedy shows, enjoy your weekends, go for vacations a few times in a year, pursue your hobbies on a regular basis and do not delay, give a permanent space to your hobbies and celebration in your daily, weekly, monthly, yearly schedules. I mean celebrate life in whatever way you like that will make you happy and when you become happy you will always attract happiness in your life.

Take break from your work to pursue your hobbies on regular intervals, otherwise life will become dull for a simple reason, that your nature is to play, enjoy, celebrate and if you are only working all the time, when will you enjoy your life? Delaying on the pretext that you don't have enough money for celebration is like fooling yourself where you are missing the precious moments of your life only working, working and working without giving a gift of celebration to you. And obviously, we all are working to fulfil needs and a need to celebrate/enjoy is also our natural need. **Remember, work/profession is for you and you are not made for work/profession.** Work/profession is important but not at the cost of your life and learn to balance your life.

Come on my dear *REAL YOU*, let's start celebrating & enjoying each & every moment of your life, start finding happiness in every situation, **start rewarding yourself on your each achievement, be it small or big. Celebration** is your nature and the real way to connect with your lost nature, to find forgotten happiness, to fulfil all voids in your life.

So, make celebration your permanent attitude of life. **Celebration (high frequency vibrations)-----Energy increases-----activation/balancing of 7 chakras/mind----activation of hormones (biochemical)-----healthy body & highly conscious mind----cool & calm mind----connection with real you----- Righteous awareness/thoughts (righteous perception, belief, values, decisions)-----righteous actions and behaviour----righteous results------ Success/growth/happiness for you.** Practice it in your real life situations for continuous 40 days to experience it. Any knowledge is incomplete without experience. And only practical experiences enhance knowledge and gives desired results.

YOU) I don't have money or more precisely I have very less money to pursue my hobbies. I wanted to visit India, it's a great country having rich culture, beautiful heritage of monuments & buildings, rich in knowledge about life science and spirituality and it's a dream destination for me. I want to visit once and want to learn so much from there but the lack of money is not allowing me to go there. What to do?

ME) **See if you have a desire, there is always a way out.** You can budget your expenses; plan your tour, sit with some expert or you can yourself search on web like which hotel, it's not necessary that you stay in 5-star, you can choose 3 or 2-star or even you can stay in *Dharamshala* (free accommodation at religious places in India), plan & schedule travelling expenses (Air, Train, Bus) as per your budget. **Take it as a challenge, do not delay if you have a strong urge to go there now, plan now and actualize now**. There is always a possibility and to convert that possibility into certainty I am sure you will be able to find all possible ways within your pocket limits or you will be able to earn the required money for your tour in a short span of time. **Best of Luck, I can see you enjoying your holiday in India.** Remember, today you have strong feeling/emotion to visit India, it is an opportunity for you and if you delay it, you never know what will happen in future, you might get busy in some other work or your feeling might fade away. **Better to do anything/everything when you have a strong feeling for it, if not doing so it becomes a lost opportunity and takes the shape of a bad feeling/void for life. It is common for these people to state, "I never fulfilled my wish/dream in my life". If you are the one, don't repent what you missed in the past but start celebrating from now.**

****

You have just understood a spiritual attitude, an attitude to convert your unconscious mind back to the natural, super conscious mind. This attitude of *ACCEPTANCE, FOCUS IN THE PRESENT MOMENT, FAITH & BELIEF IN SELF/ALMIGHTY, GRATITUDE, HAPPINESS, KINDNESS, UNCONDITIONAL LOVE, FORGIVENESS, CELEBRATION* calms down your disturbed emotions, enhances your energy field/aura positively that activates your super natural intelligence leading to truthful/righteous perceptions, decisions and actions in your life.

It is only your PDA which determines the results in your life and to make yourself lucky, you just need to make your PDA righteous/truthful which can only be possible when your source becomes your guide. And the only way to connect with your source is by raising your vibes to the level of frequency of the source by practicing spiritual attitude of life, nothing else.

In practical terms, unlucky people keep on blaming others, try to control/change others, keep on worrying problems too much which clouds their natural intelligence leading to a biased PDA and hence, wrong results in life. They don't want to understand anything, have a rigid/negative mindset and are thus, stuck in life. **On the other hand, lucky ones** don't blame/control/change others but instead try to understand the life from a broader perspective, enhance their knowledge, consciousness, awareness, works on their own perception/decisions/actions, focus on solutions, have a flexible/positive mind-set and thus, are able to learn and grow in life.

Your present situations/life might be difficult or miserable as your past responses (PDA) was wrong but with spiritual attitude your emotions, PDA and thus, life situations start to change positively over a period of time.

Although the spiritual attitude makes a positive impact on your Mindset (beliefs, perception, decisions, actions), but you still need to understand and explore PDA along with real practical techniques to enhance the degree of your PDA in life, to make you more aware, conscious of what is right or wrong or how to practice right or avoid wrong in life to manifest happiness, joy and prosperity in physical realms of your life.

OUTPUT OF SPIRITUAL ATTITUDE: Righteous perception, righteous decisions, righteous actions AND ULTIMATELY RIGHT RESULTS IN LIFE.

See, the result of the spiritual attitude connects with your source where every action, reaction, decision, attitude, behaviour, habits, beliefs, and perceptions are guided by the divine. The REAL YOU/ Source/Spiritual space/Divine not only shows you the truth of life but also 1) gives you the intelligence to decide right 2) the courage, strength, confidence and skill to take actions right 3) the strength to accept success & failures alike.

Righteous perception & understanding-----see the truth without any bias.
Decide------On the basis of truth, decide to change what you can change or accept, what you cannot change which is beyond your control, leave it to the almighty.
Action------On the basis of truthful decisions, take action with full focus, confidence without any fears.
Result-------Accept the outcome irrespective of success or failure in life. In case of failure, check & correct your PDA for desired results in life. For a spirited person, results are always right as it is your input efforts which determine the output in life. So if it is not what expected, you need to change your input which is in your control, your action zone which determines results in life. For everything else, you don't need to worry and surrender to the mighty.

TRUTH VS RIGHT OR WRONG THROUGH THE EYES OF LIFE/HUMANITY/SPIRIT

Now what is Truth?

If some truth is against humanity, is it right or is it wrong? You should hide truth from others or not? We should always speak & practice truth or not? Or is there something higher than truth which we must follow & practice rather than blindly follow the truth irrespective of "if truth is harmful for me or others or everybody/anybody or all".

We hide many truths from others, we do many things in darkness or privacy, even if everybody knows about it like bathing, using washroom, acts of intimacy etc. **Why? It is because it invokes negative feelings and to staying away from negativity is more important than seeing the truth.** When I lie to protect somebody from a wrong person/bad element or lie for the benefit of some person, the society/humanity as a whole, is it truth or lie? Obviously, it's a lie but it is the question of saving the feeling/energy of a human rather than being truthful. **For example, if someone is facing some deadly diseases and that person believes me.** And I saying to him/her that you shall be healthy again soon can instil self-belief in her/him which can lead to healing of the disease. **So my words do not reflect the truth of the present situation but obviously it is something to create a truth for the good future of that person.** Life is just about creating your intended reality with your mind which works on illusion. **And it is my duty to make my mind believe the illusion I want to create for the betterment of me, you and all.** Life is just an illusion, a dream, so why not dream peace, happiness, prosperity, health for all? So can you yourself judge about what is real truth that you must follow in your life? For me, the thumb rule is this,

"Any truth/lie which is harmful to any individual or group of people or society as a whole is wrong karma or any truth/lie which is beneficial to individual or society as a whole without paining anyone is the right karma."

So, good karma/right karma is always a question for the benefit of me, you or all without any pain or harm to anybody and it is not about the truth or lie. Let us understand the real truth or more appropriately right karma that we must follow in life through the eyes of nature/humanity/love/life or more appropriately, through the *LAW OF DESTINY/LUCK/KARMA/LIFE in next section 7.0 along with various techniques to enhance the quality of your PDA (the 3 core karmas of your life).*

7.0 LAW OF DESTINY/LUCK

LAW OF DESTINY OR LUCK OR KARMA OR LIFE

Understanding right and wrong through the law of destiny or karma or life, Ultimate Gyan (knowledge) or understanding life through the eyes of nature.

What is Karma? Karma is a combination of your **intentions, thoughts, emotions, perceptions, decisions and actions**. All these are energy vibrations. A combination of all these energy vibrations determines all the outcomes in your life. The harmony in your intentions, thoughts, emotions and actions is must for a harmony in your life.

LET US FIRST UNDERSTAND ACTIONS THROUGH THE EYES OF LAW OF KARMA/DESTINY/LIFE/LUCK.
The law of karma states that **"Our every action shall always have equal and opposite reaction"**. In real terms, **"whatever we sow, we reap"**. Our present situations are the outcome of our past karma and whatever we are doing today will determine our future. It means yesterday's deed determines the present destiny and present deeds will determine future destiny.

Many people believe only in destiny, some in destiny & karma both and some only in karma, but **the matter of fact is that there is *NO DIFFERENCE BETWEEN DESTINY AND KARMA*, both are the same.** Karma is a source of destiny, karma is a cause and destiny is the result of karma. Both are inter-related and co-exist. You can't isolate karma and destiny. If karma is there, destiny shall be there and if destiny is there, karma is there. They shall lose their identity in the absence of each other. **So, either both exist or do not exist at all**.

See, **God/Universe created all humans with the same mind & body power, but with varying degree of consciousness (intelligence)** leading to varying degree of karma and hence, varying degree of successes/failures/paths/destiny/results in life. Some are poor, some are rich and some are super rich, some are healthy, some unhealthy and some in between, some have short life, some long and some in between and some have good relations, some bad and some average etc. **God gave all of us equal powers to write our own story & destiny**. He never differentiated like parents never differentiate and give their children everything in equality but still destiny of everyone is different only due to their different individual karma. **The only difference between individuals is the awareness due to the difference in their consciousness.** The aware ones have better karma to get better results and are the people with perfect destiny or luck. These people have understood, worked on their mind, body and soul; realized and developed their powers. **They are evolving their powers each & every second, each & every moment of their life and going further & further, in their quest to understand and improve the quality of life.**

You must be wondering that why some people are born rich or poor or some born healthy or some with disease etc. See, that is the result of the past life karma which manifests in present life. Your DNA decides about your body weight, height, complexion, brain capability, and thought process, etc. **And your DNA is nothing but a composition of your karmic vibrations/impressions** that controls your life. So your body, family, relations, profession and wealth are all decided by your past life karma.

If this is so, then nothing is in my control or can I change my destiny or not or my present situations won't change at all? See the present is already manifested and can't be changed as you can't reverse your past karma. And you don't even need to know about your past life karma, it's not important. **The important is to know how to change your present karma, to change your future destiny. Just accept the fact** that your present life situations are the outcome of your past karma. This awareness makes you accept people & situations in your life and accepting life is the first step to change your life positively. Acceptance raises your vibrations, aligns you vertically and brings your focus in the present moment; the best natural way for perfectly focused action/karma in the present moment is to write your own destiny. This will help you analyse your present situation and bring about the required changes in your present PDA for right results in life. You just need to take conscious decisions and actions to change your destiny and life. It may take time but with the purity of your intentions, consistent & persistent thoughts and actions, your intended reality will soon become a reality on the screen of physical life.

On the other hand, unlucky people do not want to understand self, life, universal laws, are rigid and keep on blaming destiny and others for problems in life. A person with such an attitude can never change their life positively to control their destiny and life. The only thing they need to do is synchronize/harmonize their mind, body and soul with nature. The rest would start happening in their life on an auto mode. The only problem is that they are not aligned with their nature which is the cause of all problems in their life. But my *DEAR REAL YOU,* you being the reader of this book till now proves that you have an open mind, want to understand life and change your destiny; means you are already lucky and I can see you transforming your life positively and the process has already started.

NOW LET'S UNDERSTAND THE LAW OF KARMA, THE LAW OF BIRTH/REBIRTH AND THE LAW OF BLESSINGS & CURSE WITH A SIMPLE EXAMPLE.

1st **life:** A man was born in a poor family. The family was just hand to mouth. Whatever they earned everyday was just enough to meet their daily food requirements. That man kept on working hard his whole life to meet his family basic daily needs and never went beyond that level. **Literacy and education was his dream which never became a reality.** One day in his old age, he died.

2ⁿᵈ life: Then, he was born again in a poor family but as compared to his last life, this family was literate and had enough money to get him educated. So in this life, although he worked hard for money but at the same time got educated. He completed a simple graduation, started working in some company at a low pay scale and earned enough to get his children educated and also bought a small house. **He always dreamt of becoming a big businessman,** but lacked confidence and resources. **During his whole life, he helped others in every possible way. He was always blessed by others due to his kind nature.** Again in his old age, he died.

3ʳᵈ life: Then in the next life, he was born in a medium-class salaried family. He educated himself in Engineering. Somehow, he met some good business people, developed partnerships with them and became a highly successful business person. During his growth, he faced many challenges but overcame all successfully. He worked hard, was sincere, kind-hearted and helped people in many ways. So, his constant karma of hard work, helping nature attracted blessings which helped him achieve all successes in his life. **But didn't know after becoming successful, his attitude towards life changed. Instead of becoming more humble and more kind to others, he became rude, arrogant and egoistic** leading to bad relations with all, including his family. **This negative vibes of his drew curse from others**, lost his happiness, fell ill and ultimately died.

4ᵗʰ life: Then in next life, he was born in a family having people with negative mindset, lower consciousness suffering from bias and ego. He suffered physical and verbal abuse in his family life. Fed up, he attempted suicide but someone saved him. Now, why was he saved and who saved him? His good karmic vibrations of his past life saved him through an intelligent, enlightened person. The early part of this life was a curse due to his bad deeds from his past life, just a lesson for him and now it's time for a positive transformation to live a blissful life. His karma chose that enlightened man as he needed some *Guru*/teacher to understand self, life and universe where his knowledge about life enhanced immensely and he used that knowledge to help others understand and grow in life. **He understood that the purpose of life is personal growth which can only be possible through self-realization** and that is only possible through increase in consciousness by choosing a spiritual way of life. Your purpose must be to keep moving up the ladder of knowledge/awareness in life and rest every success & happiness is automatic in life.

After acquiring such immense knowledge, practicing spiritual attitude and even spreading such knowledge among the masses will definitely attract huge blessings in life and surely, his next life will be king size, full of blessings. Yes, very true but even after such a blissful life, **one wrong deed/action** can attract a **very strong curse** in life where you will be thrown back to your starting point, **like in a game of snake and ladder**; one snake bites and you are thrown back many steps down, a waste of all your efforts and you need to start again. **So, wherever you are in your life today,** always be humble, help others and avoid any actions which will bring pain to others, to **collect blessing and stay away from the curse.** The crux is, **"Intentionally do not give pain to others or play with their feelings and don't harm someone for your own vested interests."**

Taking strong actions against bad elements does not account for bad **karma.** If someone did wrong to you, their karma shall take care of them and you should avoid entanglements with them. But if they keep on abusing you or causing harm to you, then it is your **responsibility is to protect yourself, raise voice against them** and if required, take strong action against them; **FTIPP.** This does not account for bad karma but actually, it is a good karma where you clean the society of bad elements.

BIRTH, RE-BIRTH, IS THERE ANY CONTINUITY OR IS THERE ANY CONNECTION?

Your past, present and future time & space are all connected and manifested through the vibes of karma, blessings and curse. The information about your past, present and future is stored in your subconscious and the universal mind in the form of karmic vibrations; intentions, emotions and actions. See in the above story, the person manifested a new life on the basis of his past karmas that was based on his awareness, knowledge and intentions. That karmic vibrations/information in his mind attracted the place, time and relations which are in-tune to his stored impressions/vibrations for the settlement of his unrealized dreams, desires or settlement of pending karmic account.

And he is reborn with the same degree of consciousness that he left in his past life. Let us understand this with example of your school (classes are like your degree of consciousness; class 1 is the lowest level of consciousness, class 2 is next to class 1 and class 3 is next to class 2 and so on). Like in school, you move from class 1 to 2 to 3 to 4 sequentially, likewise, in one life or in the past, present or future lives, your evolution is sequential, step by step. There cannot be any jump from 1st to 4th or 3rd to 9th and there cannot be any demotion either. You need to go through all phases of ups and downs in life, learning from them to successfully move up in life. If you are stuck at one place, you can't move up the ladder unless & until, you clear that hurdle in life. **Like in school, if you fail you remain in the same class unless you repeat, learn, understand and pass the exams.** If you need to grow, you need to cross that level through right karma in life.

Also, in life, once you have crossed any level, you can only move further up to new levels or you can remain stuck at the already achieved level but you will never fall back to the previous level/degree of consciousness. Like in school, if you reached class 4th, either you can go to class 5th or you can exit school in class 4th but you won't be demoted to class 3rd. Then, if you want to pass class 4, you need to re-join school, work hard and pass it in order to reach class 5. In the same way, for example, someone died in class 4, then he will take new birth at class 4 level only where he needs to work hard to reach class 5, then class 6 and so on. If he is lucky, he will understand self, life and universe leading to his growth at the speed of rocket powered by a catalyst called blessing.

Also be careful, **don't hurt anybody, and don't do bad karma which can attract curse in your life**, which can even throw you back down many levels in your life, a zero level from where you need to start your quest for evolution in life again. Thus, due to bad karma, you have to face many hardships again and you will keep on revolving up and down, round and round entangled in your bad karma and destiny derived from bad karma. This way, you won't be able to understand life, evolve spiritually and will never be able to find and live the purpose of life keeping you sad all the time.

Through good karma and blessings, you can achieve anything. And through bad Karma and curses, you will lose anything/everything. How does blessings and curses work? You must have seen some people get unexpected jump in life in terms of name, fame, money or a person gets huge jump in his status along with an increment in salary or a person escapes death and back to normal, healthy life again. How can it be possible? A good karma combined with blessings does the trick. For example, there are 2 people in the same organization, equally talented and hardworking but one gets the promotion and other was shown the exit door. Do you know the reason? The person who got the promotion was the one who was kind-hearted, has a caring, loving and helping attitude and thus, gets along with others very well and has a huge bank of blessings from others. The other person was rude, arrogant, creates problem for others and thus, is carrying the vibrations of curse that leads to his failure. This is a simple example of lifting your life through blessings. **I think blessings are nothing but what makes you lucky**. A hardworking person is like using stairs having a slow speed of growth and lucky person is blessed person who has the luxury of lift instead of stairs to enhance his speed of growth.

YOU) Once human, can we become an animal again?

ME) why you want to know this? Please live in the present and stop worrying about the future. Whatever will be, will be, God knows and let the mystery of the future be in an unknown zone/space. Let the super nature decide and your karma is just to accept and do your best. But still, when you have asked, I would try to answer from my observance, this is what I think:

Among all forms of life, human life is the highest in evolution. Once we are in human life, we will always take birth as humans. The chances of again becoming any animal are very minimal unless n until, an extreme bad karma attracts curse in our life. We get either blessings or curses from other humans, animals and plants, harming them in any way to attract curse and helping them in any way will attract blessings. Even if we can't help, at least we must not harm anybody to avoid curse in life which can manifest lethal tremors in life. Better choice with us is to get the blessings, by helping others which act as a catalyst in life. SO ALWAYS REMEMBER,

"Karma is the very essence of life, curse being a snake bite and blessing is the ladder/lift in the game of life."
        -Chetan Bansal

YOU) CAN WE ESCAPE THE KARMA?
ME) No way, nobody can escape karma, the truth is that the present moment is a result of past karma/actions and future shall be the result of your present karma. Karmic vibrations of your actions can't be removed or deleted from the universe, it is always present in the universe and is bound to attract equal and opposite reaction from other forms of life. So, we have to face the result in present moment which is inevitable.

YOU) CAN WE CHANGE THE PAST KARMA?
ME) No, the actions that are already done in the past can never be changed, as it has already happened in the past which is a gone moment, is history being time which will never come back in your life physically, though that past is present in the memory of your mind.

YOU) CAN I REDUCE THE IMPACT OF PAST KARMA?
ME) yes, to some extent, the impact of past karma can be dissolved/reduced. Even knowing and owning responsibility that today's results/problems are the outcome of your past deeds/karma can give immense strength, to bear the results and courage to act today in the most responsible way. Act now to change what you can change, reduce the impact with full focus on your present karma, to make and create your present and future destiny the way you want without being perturbed by your present situations, this is what is in your control and your focus area. A positive, responsible response from your side will definitely reduce the impact of past karma and the source of that positive response is your conscious presence in the present moment.

YOU) HOW OWNING RESPONSIBILTY ENHANCES MY KARMA?
ME) Owning responsibility of your past karma bring back your focus in the present moment and connects with your omnipotent reality which **1)** will give

you the intelligence for righteous perception **2)** intelligence/power/courage to take the best of decisions and actions with 100% focus.

All your life circumstances and your past, present and future are connected through karma and you can never escape the karma. You have to face the present inevitable moment which is the outcome of the past karma and the action/karma you do in present moment shall determine your future. You cannot change the past karma but can definitely change the present karma which is always under your control. Change/improve your karma to change your destiny and just focus on what you can change and leave every other thing to the God/almighty.

The purpose of your life is to understand your mistakes, learn and grow from them (growth in awareness, consciousness and spirituality) never to repeat them and keep moving forward in life. All the problems that come in your life teach you something or the other and even show you the right path of life. **For example, a person who drinks alcohol regularly** is facing severe health, relationship and financial issues today. His first understanding must be that his severe health condition is due to his own decision/choice/action of drinking too much alcohol in the past.

Now, what can be his responsible karma?
1) Stop drinking alcohol immediately.
2) Take expert advice and medication.
3) Pledge not to take alcohol in the present and future.
He has to go through immense pain in his body, the hospital bills and long course of strong medicines. All this is the result of past karma but now in present, he has chosen to get rid of his addiction. This present action of his will recover his health to normal where consistent, righteous actions will ensure his future destiny of good health. He may recover his health back to 100% normal or he may not, depending upon severity of his health conditions.

And when he recovers, he can always show the right path to others and may make helping others get over addiction his purpose of life. Many people after successfully overcoming a serious problem/challenge in life invariably make that purpose of life to help others in order to overcome the same problem. So, you can also say that your karma and destiny may also make you meet the purpose of your life. Once got, the purpose has the power to fulfil all voids in your life.

What is good karma, in case of the above alcoholic person?
Hard work with planning and right direction: Take expert advice and medication for de-addiction of alcohol.
Action for good of self and others: Saying goodbye to alcohol is not only good for his health but also for financial stability.
Action for higher purpose: Must start helping other alcoholics for de-addiction.
Action with focus: 100% focus and determination to leave alcohol.

Action with purity of intentions: Intention to help others for de-addiction.

Action of Gratitude: Gratitude to god and others who helped him overcome alcohol addiction.

Action of kindness: He must help other alcoholics to overcome addiction.

Action of unconditional love: For other alcoholics that they were on the wrong path like him and out of his love for humanity, he is here to help them.

WHAT IS BAD KARMA/ACTION? When we do something which is against humanity, against the rights of individuals; when we intentionally hurt someone or self, it is bad karma. When we don't respect other humans, other life forms, when we cheat and use unfair means to gain something, then it is bad karma. When, we don't fulfil our duties like to take care of self, parents, spouse, children, society and nature. When we delay good actions, don't act against the bad elements in society. When we blame or control or try to change others. When we are influenced negatively by others where we lose the ability to see the truth as it is without any bias; this is all bad karma which attracts curse in our life.

Good people, due to their unawareness may attract severe difficult situations which they are unable to find solutions in life. This causes frustration & depression in them and they might commit suicide. That decision is true suicide of life as they don't understand life; its laws and principles. If they know, they would never choose suicide. AN UNAWARE PERSON CHOOSES SUICIDE JUST TO ESCAPE THE PRESENT HARDSHIPS IN LIFE WHICH HE/SHE CAN NEVER ESCAPE THROUGH SUICIDE, LET'S SEE HOW. Even if they die, they have to take birth again and face the same situation which prompted them to commit suicide. That situation once created shall never stop haunting them unless and until they understand the situation, learn from it and solve it/resolve it to move into the next class/level in life. Like you fail in some class due to lack of knowledge because you did not study with focus or not studied at all. So, unless and until you study again, understand the subject and pass the exam you can't go in the next class. Even if you quit and change the school, you can't enter the next class in the new school, unless & until you pass the same old class in the new school, the class you failed in old school. The old school and new school can be compared to old life and new life. So, you can't escape the outcome of your karma by suicide of life. In your next life, the same situation will haunt you unless and until you learn, understand and fight to overcome your situation. So anyhow, you can't escape the hardships manifested due to your karma and the only solution is to fight back which you need to choose ultimately in your future life. Better choose to fight your difficult life situations now rather than delaying it by choosing suicide. Just choose to face your problems, fight them, do not give up and soon to your amaze, a universal help will make life easy for you.

YOU MUST BE WONDERING WHO KEEPS TRACK AND RECORD OF ALL THE PAST, PRESENT AND FUTURE OF YOUR LIFE CIRCUMSTANCES AND KARMIC ACCOUNT or how karmic vibrations are stored retrieved and give results?

See, you know how data is stored in computers and transmitted through internet. All the information is stored and transmitted in the form of frequencies vibrations. Same way, God is super intelligent and he does not need to store everybody's account separately or doesn't need to remember everybody's account. He has created one universal mind which is a store-house of all thoughts, emotions, actions; karma of all people including you. The records in this universal mind are decentralised, not in control of one or few persons but are a part of mind of all people, so karmic records are immutable and can't be deleted by anybody. One universal mind means that all of us have same mind and anybody if wants to can read/see/listen/perceive the thoughts, emotions, actions of any other person through WOW focus (*Dhyana*). Please remember, all your karma gets stored in your subconscious mind which is a part of one universal mind. You can't escape your own record, it was with you, is with you now, and shall always be with you in future and you can't hide your karmic vibrations from the universal mind. So, you can't avoid your karma. **Nobody else but only you can keep all records, direct your life according to your past and present karma.** When you don't tell anybody about your thoughts & actions, you only hide your karma from their conscious mind but you can never hide from the subconscious mind, a universal mind.

The only thing in your control is doing right karma which manifests right results in life. So better to focus on what you can do to control your life rather focusing on what you can't control. **Also, conscious way of life or spiritual way of life helps remove all the negative vibrations/impressions stored in your subconscious mind** which helps reduce the impact of your past karma and at the same time, enhances your present karma for right results in future.

THIS IS HOW LIFE FLOWS AND CAN BE CHANGED BASED ON KARMA: A person never dies but it is the death of a physical body and a soul carries the mind of a person with it at the time of death and chooses a new body, parents, time and place of birth according to the past impressions/vibrations (karma), which determines the next life story/destiny, people & situations coming to life.

When a person is born, comes out to the outer world from the mother's womb, the energy/karmic vibrations of the past life which the soul carries became the basic life energy/aura and is aligned to the energy of time & place of birth which ultimately determines his/her mindset, thought process, behaviour, inborn talents, likes, dislikes, needs & wants which ultimately determines his/her life path, situations and also, results in life. **The**

time & place of birth is chosen by vibrations of the past karma. The life energy field/aura is the basic mindset which almost remains same throughout his/her life with many major or minor changes, happening with change in time. Change in time changes the degree of position of the sun in relation to the planet earth which changes the degree of energy coming to the person's mind & body. The change in degree of energy changes the energy field of a person which ultimately changes his/her needs & wants, mindset, thought process. Hindu astrologers make a birth chart of a person based on time & place of birth where they are able to predict his/her mindset. They also predict future changes in the person's life situations due to changing times which are based on future planetary movements. **Does this means that everything is predetermined and there is no use of changing your actions/karma?**

Yes, you can change your life through your karma. This is very important for you to understand **the importance/power of your present karma** which can change your life positively, irrespective of negative times predictions based on planetary movements. **Positive/righteous karma dissolves the negative impact of negative times making your life timeless, a life not dependent upon planetary movements associated with changing times but a conscious choice of righteous karma. The people who are able to change their life positively or reduce the impact of negative times are the people who have understood and are practicing vertical alignment on a regular basis** and are able to maintain positive energy field. A positive energy field removes/dissolves negative impressions of past karma from subconscious leading to higher consciousness/awareness which leads to a truthful PDA and desired results in life. *So, your present is predetermined by your past karmas but you can change your future by changing your three core karma (PDA).*

YOU) I have seen many people who are born rich but their present actions are not good; they behave rudely with others, are wasting their hard earned money on unnecessary things, are wasting their time, are not taking care of their body but still they are earning huge money and are happy in life. **And I have seen many people who are born poor but working very hard** having good behaviour and attitude in life but still, they are unsuccessful in life. This means law of karma does not exist or if it exists, it is not universal. **ME)** Very good question! I would love to answer it, my *Dear REAL YOU*. First, always remember the law of karma exists and it is the universal truth, the problem is not the existence of law but the perception about the law.

Before directly answering your question, you must first understand this, **"The results of some karma are instant or some takes time." In mind, the manifestation is instant but in physical world due to concept of time and space, it requires constant, consistent action, planning and execution.** For example, **when you are in a coffee shop** and ask for coffee, it may come in 5 to 10 minutes but **when you are in your home and wants to have coffee in**

the coffee shop, you will first travel from your home to the coffee shop, say in about 20 minutes and there, you order and you receive your coffee in another 10 minutes. So, it took you 30 minutes in total to get coffee and in previous case just 10 minutes. See, this is the difference explained by the concept of time and space. **Same way, someone cheated somebody who was weak** mentally and physically. At that moment, he was not able to take his revenge because of his weakness. But he started working on his mental, physical and economic strength which took him say for example, 2 years. So, he will come back after 2 years and take his revenge. This is how the time duration of karma manifestation varies. So, some simple actions bear instant results and some complex actions involving too many people may take years or some difficult goals may also take decades or one or more life.

Simple action: Ask coffee and it is given to you instantly.

Difficult goal: You don't understand abcd of cricket and want to become a cricketer. You need to develop a skill which requires expert guidance, practice and hard work from your side but all needs a consistent, persistent action in real time which may take more than 2-3 years of time or even more.

Complex action: Somebody murdered somebody and the victim took revenge after rebirth.

I think the answer to your question lies in the above explanation. The rich man is rich and happy today because of his past good karma but his present bad karma will definitely manifest failure & unhappiness in his future depending upon the degree of his bad karma. And someone poor & unhappy today will definitely achieve success & happiness but again the results depend upon the degree of his righteous/truthful karma/actions. **I think we all have witnessed both types of stories in life; rags to riches and riches to rags.** I think we should not waste our precious time by analysing life of others but to give precious time & energy to our own life; how to improve and take it to the next level to make it a joyous and successful journey. So, **focus on your own growth & success and never waste your precious time by focusing on the life of others** as you never know about their journey; do not hate, envy, blame, judge, try to compare and control life of/with others. Doing so would only make your life miserable. Let us understand this:

1) Do not blame others: It is only your karma, karmic vibrations/impressions which chooses all your relations, life path, life situations or in other words, all your life situations and relations whether parents, family, spouse, children, friends, business or any other/all relations are attracted and manifested in your life through your own karma. So why would you complain about something which you have chosen. If your present life situations or relations are problematic, you need to change your karma to get the right result. Some people complain that they decided and acted under the guidance of someone else but I tell them that ultimately the final decision and action was their own, so they are to be blamed. Your perception was wrong and that is why you took wrong decisions and actions. The other person may have influenced you intentionally for his/her vested interest and took undue advantage of your innocence or he/she might be having lower consciousness/awareness. The life experiences, likes, dislikes, beliefs and perceptions of people are different and hence their opinions might not be in-tune with your life situations, so they, guiding you have 99% chances of wrong PDA and wrong results in your life. Whatever the case may be, you can't blame others and need to improve/enhance your consciousness/awareness for choosing right karma in life.

2) Do not try to change others, no expectations from others. Do not try to control others. Give them freedom of space, time and choice; it is their life, let them live on their soul path: But, what we do is opposite and we are not ready to understand that the present situations are a result of our own past karma. Even if people in our life are wrong, we have attracted them through our own vibrations of karma. So, to convert a miserable relation into a blissful relation, we must change our vibrations first. This will either change the other person positively or that person will move out from our life. Our job is to change karma positively and the rest will be taken care by the universe. Normally, we try to change the other person's perception, behaviour, beliefs and impose our opinions upon them which have been nothing but pure stupidity. Changing others is very difficult, better to change self which is easy and under your control.

Are you possessive of the other person, try to change/control them or let them live their life the way they want? Not giving freedom to others lead to suppression in them which leads to frustration. Unexpressed frustration leads to depression and if expressed, leads to anger. And many people find themselves confined in this loop of anger---frustration---anger---frustration. This leads to a series of action-reaction heated exchanges with them and ultimately, steels your own peace, happiness & prosperity. So, for your own happiness, your actions/karmas toward others have to be natural/spiritual.

Just give freedom of space & time to others as everyone loves their time & space. The best way to irritate somebody is to interfere with their personal space & time. The unconditional love is when we give freedom of space & time to the person we love. The best way to get the best out of people is by giving them the freedom of time & space; be it your employees, children, friends, spouse and more. You just have to give support & helping hand, everything rest will be managed by the freedom of space & time. **Freedom activates the nature of person which activates the best version of them.** So, if you are controlling and suppressing others, you are only making them negative which ultimately hurt your relations and biggest cause of failure in life.

3) Do not compare/judge your life and situations with others or do not judge others: We should not compare with others as everybody has their own karmas that have determined their life path/destiny. We do not know how much hard, smart and consistent work they have undergone to become what they are today. Everyone gets exactly what they deserve based upon their karma and universe is never biased. **Remember, the output results are directly proportional to your input efforts**. So, your focus should only be you and not in comparison with others, if something is good or bad in the life of others, it is due to their own karmic vibrations and if something is good or bad in your life, it is due to your own karmic vibrations. Judging and comparing your life with others will only activate feelings of hate or envy in you which will only divert your mind from productive work. Just appreciate the success of others, learn from them, and let them be a motivation for you. **So, the credit and debit of your own life situations belong to you only and to change or achieve something you need to work upon your own karma, shift your focus from others onto your own life.** Moreover comparing yourself with others is like disrespecting and devaluing yourself which never allows you to focus on to yourself or activate the best version of yourself; can you succeed like this?

GYAN YOG/**UNDERSTANDING DRIVEN OUT OF LAW OF KARMA:** The ultimate understanding of life is or ultimate *Gyan* of life comes from the Law of Karma and that is, **accept your past and present without any resistance, fully surrender to your present moment as it is inevitable** but you can change your future by choosing response to the present situation. Understand the present moment without any bias and give your 100% to your decisions and actions in present. **Whatever happened, happening and shall happen in future is bound to happen, is determined by karmic vibrations and for a cause.** Be strong, learn and understand life and keep on moving forward with a never give-up attitude in life. Keep on crossing all the hurdles and solving problems on your path of life. Not able to solve something beyond your control, leave it to the almighty, **have faith and belief in self/god** and let the time take care of all your worries. Just keep on doing good karma, find purpose and keep on growing in life, do something for others/ society, listen to your heart and align with your nature.

TILL NOW, YOU HAVE SEEN WHAT IS RIGHT OR WRONG THROUGH THE EYES OF THE LAW OF KARMA. You have also seen that destiny is in your karma and karma is in your hands; your conscious choice. The cause of all miseries in life is wrong perception which leads to wrong decision and wrong action in life. So, to activate righteous thoughts-----righteous perception, righteous decisions, righteous actions (3 core karmas of your life), you must walk on your soul path by raising your vibrations/consciousness/awareness. Let your soul path guide your karma (PDA) and not the influence of others.
Now let us understand how to activate righteous perception, righteous decisions, righteous actions and righteous results along with various techniques to enhance the degree of truthfulness in your real life as only

truth can take you towards the right path of life; a path to truly joyous and blissful journey.

7.1   ENHANCING   PERCEPTION   &   NATURAL INTELLIGENCE THROUGH WOW
RIGHTEOUS UNDERSTANDING, INTERPRETATION AND PERCEPTION

PERCEPTION: A simple understanding of perception is the way you think, see, understand and believe about something/anything in your life. **For example,** when a difficult situation comes in life, **one person becomes depressed,** gives up and makes his/her life miserable. **On the other hand, another person upon encountering a difficult situation may feel the pain**, go into depression and go in his/her shell, but that is all temporary. He/she bounce back even stronger because they believe life is a challenge and use difficult life situations as an opportunity to improve their life skills and grow in life. Their focus is on solutions, gives their 100% in actions and does not bother about results.

Everybody wants to be happy & successful but is it possible? Success is determined by perception and people experience varying degree of success only due to their varying degree of perception. Or even the same individual experiences a varying degree of success in life as his/her perception keeps on changing with changing times. **Perception is a base, based upon perception we take decisions and based on decisions, we take action** and based on actions we get results. So, if the first step goes wrong, the last output result is definitely going to be wrong. So we need to develop pure/truthful/unbiased perception to lead a truthful, happy, prosperous and successful life.

How to develop pure perception?
Walking on your **soul path through a spiritual attitude is the first step**, a big leap to a happy, successful and prosperous life. Walking on your soul path calms your disturbed emotions, raises your state of mind from unconscious to super-conscious state, converts disturbed mind to a peaceful mind and your vibrations are raised. Once your vibrations are raised, you get connected to your **spiritual space which activates your super intelligent nature.** Once your life starts to be guided by nature, your perception becomes pure, perfect, truthful and transparent without any bias. When you are fully focused in the present moment, your understanding comes from a natural, spiritual space making your perception pure and perfect which is the **first and most important step towards a truthful life**. A negative mind activity with too much irrational focus on past & future makes you unconscious leading to biased perception, away from the truth.

So, for pure and unbiased perception, it is very important to bring the mind back to the present moment, by making it free from emotional disturbances that were caused by negative, fearful and anxious thoughts. If you choose peace or not to be affected by negative thoughts irrespective of any situation, your emotional state remains steady which connects with your roots/source/**REAL YOU** leading to a pure perception. It also gives you **immense faith/belief in self/almighty** where nobody is able to influence you negatively and you do not follow/believe others blindly but you are able to see the truth as it is. Where you follow your intuition, listen to your inner voice and gut feelings.

A wrong perception is the only cause of all misery in your physical life. Perception is a base and source of all decisions and actions. The more is the perfection in perception, the more perfect will be results. But, a biased perception shall only give imperfect, wrong results. It is like a foundation of building; the more is the strength of the foundation, the more stable and perfect is the building. Even if you are putting immense effort in the building, its design, interior and exterior using the best of materials, still it will fall if it has weak roots. Same way, if a perception is cloudy, biased and under the influence of others, then you are bound to fail even if you put immense efforts in your actions. **Perception is like radar**, a compass which gives direction to you in the physical realms of life.

E.g. What if, diagnose of a doctor is wrong? He will keep on giving medicine based on the wrong diagnose but he won't be able to cure the patient. His observation about the disease was wrong as he/she was not focussed or his/her mind was elsewhere during diagnosis. He/she may not be disturbed emotionally but his waivered focus lead to wrong understanding/diagnose/perception. **Don't you think so, this happens in all professions or this happens with all people.** The one who are fully focussed/fully present in their job, are the ones with perfect understanding/perception which makes them successful and the unfocussed ones are the failures and cause of problems for self and others.

When your perception is right, you are able to see the situation as it is; the real cause of problem, the right decisions and actions for right results in life. For righteous/pure/truthful perception, you just need to master your focus and the best way to do that is WOW which you have already understood in the *PRESENT MOMENT LIVING/VERTICAL ALIGNMENT* section earlier in PART-B of this book.

FIRST OF ALL, WE ARE GOING TO UNDERSTAND IN DETAIL THAT HOW THIS AMAZING POWER OF FOCUS THAT GOD HAS GIVEN TO US can be used to activate higher faculties of our mind which automatically activates pure perception and removes all disempowering beliefs from mind & life leading to righteous decisions, actions and results in life.

Your mind & body are the tools given by the nature to experience life. It is through your mind & body that you perform 3 core karmas of life, PDA to fulfil all your needs, wants, desires and dream to live a happy life. People though having the same mind & body but varying degree of consciousness/awareness leads to varying degree of PDA and thus, varying results in life for the same situation, even with the same resources. So, you need to enhance your degree of consciousness and for that, you need to understand the **WORKING OF YOUR MIND** so as to activate its higher faculties to get your Karma (PDA) right, to get the desired results in your life. **THE ONLY KEY IS POWER OF FOCUS.**

FIVE MAJOR WORKING QUALITIES/PROCESS OF THE MIND

Conscious mind has got the power of thoughts & emotions through which it can achieve anything in life. The thoughts & emotions that you focus upon gets the energy and gives the direction to your actions and thus, life. So, focus is the key which chooses and controls your thoughts & emotions and thus, life. Everything that has happened, happening or happen in future in your life is always determined by your own thoughts & emotions, nothing else. If the results or current life situations are not to your liking, it clearly means that your thoughts & emotions are not under your control. And you always have the power to understand your wrong thought patterns and change them to change your life. **THE BEST WAY TO CHANGE YOUR THOUGHTS & EMOTIONS IS BY CHANGING THE FOCUS OF YOUR MIND.** Focus has the amazing power which can only be understood by your practice & experience of your conscious presence or present moment way of life.

These are the five major qualities/process of mind which makes it a valuable tool for us to understand, perceive, decide and act in life. The optimum functioning of these qualities is vital for right results to lead a happy & successful life.

THESE FIVE QUALITIES OF THE MIND ARE PROCESSED THROUGH THOUGHTS & EMOTIONS UNDER THE CONTROL OF FOCUS.

1) Belief & perceptions formation
2) Memorizing
3) Retrieval of information from the memory
4) Logical/intellectual qualities
5) Intuitive powers/creative ideas

So, let's understand it one by one

1) Understand the science of Belief formation

This we have already understood but still, it will bring more clarity to your mind. A conscious mind is like a RAM of computer. And a subconscious mind is like a Hard disk as it is store-house of all past incidences. **If the mind is occupied with numerous, varied thoughts on different life issues simultaneously, like constant thinking about the past, future and present or mind jumping from one issue to another and to another very fast; IT GETS JAMMED AND STOPS WORKING,** loses connection with the processor and is not able to process the information the way it needs to be processed, instead it corrupts the input data and gives the wrong output. So, the wrong output gets stored in the hard disk as a file of belief. Now in future, the mind uses those stored beliefs as filters to understand, interpret and perceive any/all situations related to a particular belief. And when the belief was untruthful, it will only create biased perception in the future. This is like a vicious cycle where one wrong belief will lead to another wrong belief and so on. **The files of biased beliefs are like corrupted files which have corrupted the original software of human mind leading to wrong karma (PDA)** and thus, wrong results. This way, one wrong belief will keep on haunting your life until and unless you detect it, edit it or delete it as per the truth which can only be possible through your focussed, conscious presence.

VARIOUS PARTS OF MIND, ITS WORKING AND MEDIUMS		
Input devices of mind	Ear, Eye, Tongue, Skin, Nose, 3rd eye	All the information from outside enter our mind through five senses and from the sixth sense(3rd eye) if it is activated
RAM of the mind	Conscious mind	The presence of thoughts ensures the working of conscious mind.
Hard disk of the mind	Subconscious mind	The subconscious is carrier of super natural intelligence or preinstalled software of our mind. This software can get corrupted by formation of wrong beliefs which leads to unnatural functioning of subconscious mind.
Information in our mind	Thoughts & emotions	All the information in our personal space moves in the form of thoughts & emotions and stored in the form of beliefs
Speed & accuracy of processing of information	Emotions, feelings	The more is the emotions and feelings attached to a particular thought the faster it is processed and stored in our memory.
Processor of our mind	Gap between mind powered by REAL YOU	The processor of our mind works at its best when the mind is fully focused on one issue/information at a time which connects the conscious mind with the **REAL YOU** leading to activation of higher faculties of mind.
Output devices of mind	Ear, Eye, Tongue, Skin, Nose, 3rd eye	All the information moves out from our personal space through speech, actions, gestures, body language and frequency vibrations of energy field in the form of thoughts & emotions which can be observed by the five senses of the other living being. This is how communication and interaction happen between various living beings.
Power source of mind	Cosmic energy	The higher the frequency vibrations of our energy field the faster, accurate, perfect is the functioning of all faculties of our mind.

Source: Meet the Real You **Copyright** Chetan Bansal

A conscious mind needs free space for free flow of input thoughts & emotions to activate higher powers/processors to get the final output in the form of right understanding/perception/decisions, like a car/vehicle needs a spacious road to activate higher gears for fast, hassle-free movement towards its destination. **So, if your mind is not focussed on one issue at a time or you are not able to give full focus on one thing, definitely your understanding, perception is going to be wrong leading to the formation of wrong beliefs or slow movement towards your goals or wrong direction of life.**

2) Memorizing
Same way, any information/thought that we either like or dislike becomes a part of our memory. Like or dislike activates emotion which actually focuses mind on that thought/information. **When the mind gets focussed on one information/thought, all other thoughts vanish from it.** The jam of

numerous, various thoughts has been cleared leading to a faster, clearer understanding and strong memory. **Imagine you have 10 cars and you have filled only one car with fuel and others are empty,** containing **no fuel.** So, this car containing fuel is the only car that has the power to move and reach its destination. Emotions, whether negative or positive fuels the particular thought/issue to become a part of memory.

To learn, understand and memorize something in a fast and accurate manner, we must invoke some feelings, emotions, interests, likes and dislikes by the following ways:

A) By correlating the subject with your own life experiences and real life examples---This makes learning interesting as people are always interested in themselves and stories of others.

B) By making the concept interactive through role play---This makes learning fun and interesting.

C) By making some diagrams, flow charts, pictures related to the subject/concept----This makes learning easy as mind understand, stores and retrieves data in the form of pictures.

Let's first understand this.

Close your eyes or you can do it without closing eyes. Speak or recall the name of your spouse or friend or anybody else you know in your mind, immediately the picture of that person comes in front of you reflected from the screen of your mind.

Or

Close your eyes, slowly spell "Success". To your amaze, you will find that as if you are reading from somewhere and that somewhere is your mind. Or spell any name, any word and observe, you will find yourself reading from somewhere and that somewhere is the screen or board of your mind. Amazing, isn't it! Your mind works like this; it stores and retrieves data in the form of pictures.

Well, we are not going into the details of the various ways of learning, understanding and memorizing as this book is not on memory but I have explained you the basic science for fast, accurate learning and permanent memory. You can always make your own creative ways of learning when you understand the science. And this is how the real understanding, learning and strong memorizing happen. If this step is taken care of accurately, then recalling is easy and accurate but still during recall, you need complete focus on the issue/subject/information that you are retrieving/recalling. **Strong memory helps you correlate various facts about your past with your present, hence, help you understand and perceive the present situations to take accurate decisions, right actions and desired results for future.**

3) Retrieval of information from memory

Information/data/thoughts are stored in our mind in the form of files. For every life issue, there are separate files. The information can be retrieved any time but again, the focus is required. **That focus again comes from**

emotions/feelings/interests/passion that you have for the **issue/information.** If the mind is jammed with numerous, various thoughts, it is not able to focus and thus, not able to retrieve the information at the right time or not able to connect with the required file in the hard disk/deep memory/subconscious. **We call this a loss of memory but actually the memory is already there but it is the loss of power to access the memory.**

Imagine your office having separate record rooms on different subjects like accounts, human resources, production, sales and you are trying to access the records of sales. You move towards the sales room but on the way, someone calls you from the accounts room and you move towards it. Again, someone calls you from the HR room and you move towards it. This way, you keep on moving between various rooms but you do not reach the room you wanted i.e. the sales room. Once you determine to focus on the sales room, you reach it ignoring all calls from all the other rooms. **And once you reach the sales room and start checking the records giving your precious time & focus, you get all the in-depth information related to the sales records. You must have experienced this many times, once you focus on something for a long duration your clarity about it enhances immensely. So, a perfect/specific retrieval of information from memory also comes from the focus of mind which ultimately enhances the quality of your PDA and results in life.**

4). Logical/intellectual qualities

Same way, to analyse, interpret, understand the data/information, we need focus on one thing as focusing on too many issues/information jams the RAM and once the RAM jams, the processor losses its power and intelligence. This will result in wrong understanding/interpretation/analysis as the logical operators of the mind become loaded with too many thoughts and they never knew which thought to work upon or which thought not to work upon or before processing the one thought completely, another thought came which hinders with the processing of previous thought.

Imagine you talking to your child and in between your chat, the second child came and started discussing about something else. Now, how can you talk to both of your children about different issues at the same time? So, you will ask the second one to shut and wait until your discussion with the first child ends. Otherwise, you will get confused and your understanding will go wrong which will lead to wrong decisions and actions.

This is how your logical and intellectual processors are being hijacked by too many thoughts on separate information/issues. The only solution is to focus on one subject/information at a time.

5) Intuitive powers/creative ideas

Again, when your mind is focussed on only one thing/issue at a time, it connects you with all the information about that thing that is available in your subconscious mind. **And also, your mind gets connected to all the higher/divine powers present in the universe which provides you all the** information in the form of intuition. **This connection happens through a 3rd eye, your 6th sense.** First, your desire to know about that thing/issue goes out from your mind to the universe through the 3rd eye and then the required information comes back to your conscious mind through that 3rd eye only. The information comes to your conscious presence in the form of thoughts only.

When you sit and think about something with a cool & calm mind, with full focus, with strong emotions and strong desires, your 3rd eye gets activated connecting your mind with the universal vibrations which has all the information about the universe. It is like Google which answers all your questions from its bank of information. But the powers of Google are limited as Google has limited information but the powers of the 3rd eye are unlimited as it has each and every bit of information about the whole universe. The more focussed you are, the faster and accurate are the results.

All the inventions, discoveries, creativity happens only through this 3rd eye which activates the intuitive powers. We can safely define intuition as the "right thought/idea at the right time." It may come from your own memory or the memory of the universal mind. From wherever it may come, it is the only solution for all your problems. **The power of 3rd eye is in everybody and needs to be activated through the connection with your omnipotent reality for which you need to practice conscious/focussed way of life** where you try to give your 100% focus on each & every thought and action of yours.

SO, CONTROLLING MIND IS ALL ABOUT FOCUS, YOUR ABILITY TO FOCUS ON ONE THING AT A TIME. When you focus, your higher faculties of the mind gets activated leading to perfection in your PDA, leading to perfection in work and thus, desired results. Everybody knows that focus gives perfection but the big question is how to get that 100% or near 100% focus or how to continually improve your focus for perfect results.

THREE THINGS, *RESPONSIBILITY/PURPOSE OR FEAR OR PASSION or all* help the person in activating the near perfect focus and thus, desired results in life.

LOVE & PASSION for something creates a strong desire in the person to live and achieve something. You must have observed that when someone loves something, he/she is ready to do anything about that thing. That is why it is always said choose your profession which you love because when you love something, your focus is automatic and so are the positive results. Or you must choose to love whatever you do or doing for activating the focus.

Even if you don't love something but you have a RESPONSIBILITY for that thing, it will automatically generate love and thus, focus for that thing. Life is all about giving in a responsible manner. The more responsible you are in all your action, the better is the focus and thus, perfect are results. The concern, responsible thoughts and actions are inbuilt in our nature but somehow due to overthinking, we have forgotten this virtue of ours. **Spiritually strong people are 100% inclined towards their**

responsibility/purpose of life and are thus, very sharp in focus. **They always prioritize purpose over something they like or dislike.** For example, if a person has two things to do but he has money for only one thing, obviously he is going to choose which is necessary or more important or for the benefit of the masses. Like, if a person has X amount of money which he can spend either on his dream vacation or for medical emergency of his parents, obviously he is going to choose to defer his dream vacation and pay for the medical needs of his parents. **See, responsibility/purpose always wins over love or passion or likes or even dislikes.**

The same way, **FEAR also activates your focus. For example, heavy fines/penalties are imposed by the Govt. for compliance of various laws.** This activates the focus of people out of fear of loss of money or fear of jail or other penalties. That is why you must have seen people have a habit of delaying tax returns but on the last day, their focus happens automatically and they prepare and file the returns. **Students focus in their exams days are automatic,** out of the fear of failure. **The focus of the driver of a vehicle is perfect** out of fear of accident. You can cite so many examples of fear activating your focus because fear is an amazing energy which is there to protect you. **So, the real fear is actually a positive emotion and helps us focus.** And the illusionary fear is a negative emotion which actually diverts our focus. We have already understood about real and imaginary fears in Sec 6.3 of this book only.

SO VARIOUS, NUMEROUS THOUGHTS CAUSE THE MIND TO JAM AND MAKING IT DEFECTIVE LEADING TO STORING OF WRONG INFORMATION OR DISEMPOWERING BELIEFS, LOSS OF POWER TO RECALL FROM MEMORY, LOSS OF INTUITIVE/CREATIVE POWERS, AND LOSS OF ABILITY TO UNDERSTAND & PERCEIVE THE TRUTH AS IT IS. Thus, it is very important to clear the jam for healthy functioning of the mind for a better life which we aspire for. The best way to optimize all the faculties of mind is by giving 100% of **FOCUS** in all your thoughts & actions. **And for the right focus, we need to create love or passion or real fear or all but above all, follow a responsible/purposeful way of life.** Or for that right focus, we just need to practice WOW in each & every moment of life which automatically activates right emotions of love, fear, passion, purpose and above all, responsible way of life leading to righteous PDA and thus, right results in life.

LET'S UNDERSTAND WOW FOCUS TECHNIQUE TO RELINQUISH DISEMPOWERING BELIEFS AND ACTIVATE PURE PERCEPTION IN LIFE

Normally people have a habit of judging the person/situation based on the past experiences of their life. Past experience has created a particular image of the person/situation in mind. Whether a guy is good or bad or intelligent or egoistic or cruel or any other image is already printed in our mind, which acts as a filter to judge that person in the present moment. This leads to prejudice where we already judge the person based on the past impressions without listening, seeing or analysing the truth as it is in the present moment.

See, nothing is permanent in this life. People and situations keep on changing with changing time, so how can a belief be permanent? A belief developed on the basis of a particular incident/situation may lose its base with change in the situation. So, once a situation changes, it being the base of belief; belief dies its natural death. For example, if someone was a beggar 10 years ago and now you find that person doing some very good business and earning good income, how would you react? "Oh! I can't believe my eyes, are you the same person whom I met 10 years back?" See same way, we judge and create a limiting belief that this is not possible, that is not possible. But Sir, this is life, it keeps on changing where possible becomes impossible or impossible becomes possible. So, we are limiting ourselves; our capabilities and dreams with bias, prejudice and disempowering beliefs which does not allow us to move forward or grow in life.

The only belief, sorry not belief but the truth is that......

"Whatever happened till now or happening today in your life was due to your decisions, judgment and actions done in the past and whatever that shall happen in your future life, it shall be based on your present actions."

And your actions were influenced by beliefs which were based on your experiences of people & situations in your life. And we may not have the clarity to understand/perceive those people & situations which will lead to the storage of wrong/biased information/beliefs in a subconscious/memory. So, maybe our beliefs were wrong at the first place which gave wrong perception and wrong results in life.

SO, LET'S PLEDGE TO HAVE NO BELIEFS IN LIFE FROM NOW ON. You won't judge anything based on beliefs but by giving your full focus through watching, observing and witnessing in order to understand the truth as it is. This will lead to fully conscious decisions and actions without the influence of any person, situation or belief. **Focus connects you with your source that guides all your actions, reactions, decisions, attitude, behaviour and perceptions leading to success in life.**

BIASED BELIEFS TO WRONG RESULTS IN LIFE

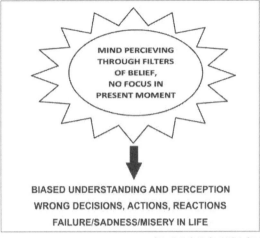

Source: Meet the Real You Copyright Chetan Bansal

MY BELIEF MANTRA: NO BELIEF, ONLY TRUTH, if you want to believe then, believe in self/almighty, believe in your capabilities, goals, dreams, desires and do not believe in what others say or think about you. GIVE YOUR CONSCIOUS FOCUS TO ARRIVE AT YOUR OWN JUDGMENTS/PERCEPTIONS/DECISIONS. Just live life with full acceptance, surrender and keep on doing your karma being consciously present in each and every moment of your life.

USING "WOW" TO KEEP AWAY FROM BIASED NEWS AND INFORMATION

As whatever you see, hear and speak, it draws your focus and whatever you focus upon expands in your life. That is why it is advisable not to listen, watch, read news on television, newspaper or any form of mass media which focus more on negative news and most likely influence you negatively. One rape news and mind perceives everybody to be a rapist or one case/news of theft and mind presumes everybody is a thief. This creates unnecessary fear among people and they start to doubt and distrust everybody leading to the spread of negative atmosphere.

See, this is how mind works which is attracted to the negativity out of fear as it wants to save us, protect us and send alert messages through thoughts, "be careful, this world is full of bad people." As **REAL YOU**, it is your duty is to make your mind understand the truth/facts as they are and save yourself from unnecessary fear & doubt. You should become fully aware of all news (do WOW), do statistical analysis of data to find the truth behind any news. Once we understand the complete picture about any news, it leads to perfect decisions, actions and removes unnecessary fear from the mind. **You should not follow or trust some news agency, politicians or any so-called authorities unless or until you WOW them perfectly.** By following someone blindly, you might become a victim of their vested interests.

Also, **media people should avoid giving instant/fast judgements on any news/incidents.** Their job is just to report the truth of any incident without any bias or opinion from their side. They must understand that people trust them and they have the responsibility to honour their trust. By highlighting some negative news just to raise their TRP, they are playing with emotions and lives of people. They should focus too much on positive news and too little on negative news to create a positive environment in the society. **It does not mean that media should not tell about some negative news**, they should make people aware of the threats or problems in the society but focusing on solutions and not to create unnecessary fear and doubt in the minds of people.

As majority of people do not watch, observe and witness with full focus about any/all the news and information coming on mass media, thus their perception is invariably biased which creates an environment of confusions leading to negative emotions; environment of fear, hate and anger where people might resort to unnecessary violence & protests in the society. So, whosoever is in any type of mass media, he/she must act with utter responsibility and must filter all the news/information through WOW focus before publishing, otherwise media which should be a source of peace, harmony and growth in the society will become a source of miserable society.

FOR WOW TO BE EFFECTIVE, FOR BETTER PERCEPTION, USE YOUR ALL FIVE SENSES---LISTEN, SEE, FEEL AND THEN PROCESS ALL THE INFORMATION TO UNDERSTAND IT. DO NOT HASTE INTO ANY DECISION/ACTION/REACTION BEFORE UNDERSTANDING IT.

Most of the times, we haste onto conclusions just by seeing or listening or feeling something without going into the details. Any decision based on one or two sources of information can be misleading as that is not complete information which is blurred away from the truth. Gather information from all your senses/medium of information; see, hear, feel, touch, taste or if not possible all, at least 3 senses should always be used before reaching to any conclusions.

Give a deep focus before reaching to any conclusions. Give some time and space to your mind, truth will pop up soon. Wait and watch, do not haste into decisions or actions. Let the super intelligent nature decide, let the awareness decide, let the time decide, let the space decide. Just observe patiently.

One interesting fact for you;
1). **Category A:** Approx. 30% of people in this world process information and **decide only on the basis of feelings**.
2). **Category-B:** Approx. 30% of people in this world process information and **decide only on the basis of what they hear**.
3). **Category-C:** Approx. 30% of the people in this world process information and **decide only on the basis of what they see.**
4). **Category-D: Approx. 10% of the people in this world decide only after gathering and processing all the information through all five senses or**

majority of them. The awareness level/conscious level of these people is highest in this world and they are the people who rule this world.

So, which category you are in from the above data? Whatever category you may be till now in your life, decide to immediately jump to category-D where you will use all your senses to process all data, to find clarity/clear perception before coming to any conclusions or decisions in your life.

PROCESSING, COORDINATING INFORMATION THROUGH ALL SENSES

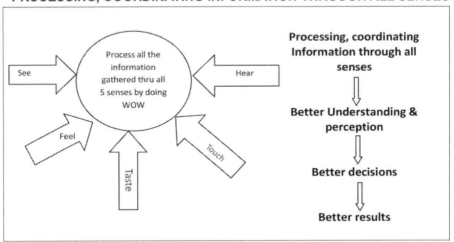

FIVE PATHS THROUGH WHICH INFORMATION ENTERS MIND

So, to arrive at the FINAL/TRUTHFUL DATA from RAW/INITIAL/FIR DATA, you must process and filter through maximum or all of your senses. Actually, WOW is a wonderful technique/process which not only activates all your senses but also your conscious presence to arrive at the truth. This is how you should be easily able to have clear perception by giving your full focus (WOW *Dhyana*) at any situation in hand.

So finally, always try to understand the truth of any information/situation and not to believe something just because others believe it or saying to you, be it anybody. Always believe in yourself and not others. It is not that you should not listen to others. You should but give your conscious focussed presence to whatever you listen, see, or feel to find the truth.

Find all beliefs that are letting you down in your life or not allowing you to grow in life, give your conscious thoughts on them. The best way to do that is to give your conscious presence to each & every moment/ situation in your life. This not only helps you to find the truth of the situation but at the same time, this dissolves the disempowering belief related to that particular situation.

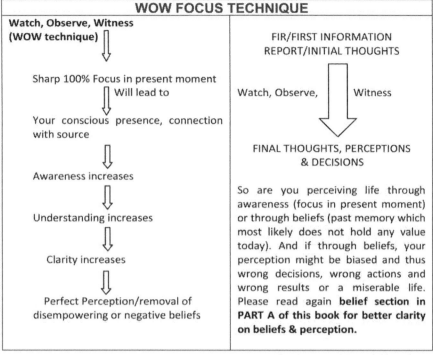

Source: Meet the Real You **Copyright** Chetan Bansal

For the things that are not in your control, **"always believe that whatever has happened, happening and shall happen in your life is for your good and having some divine purpose."** Start believing the above statement right now and forever and make it your habit to say it to yourself every day in the morning, "everything that is happening right now and everything that shall happen in the future shall only take you to the right path of your life." Actually when you believe, you are giving your **REAL YOU** a message that I trust you and will accept whatever you bring into my life, then, your **REAL YOU** takes control of your life guiding each & every action of your life.

7.2 DECISIONS & PPN SCAN
REAL LIFE DECISIONS; TOOLS & TECHNIQUES

"Any decision which gives pain or causes harm to self or others or all is a wrong decision. Decision which is good for you or others or all or beneficial to you and at the same time, does not harm others is definitely righteous decisions."
        -Chetan Bansal

Decisions taken under the influence of disturbed emotions are likely to be biased, away from the truth leading to wrong actions and thus, wrong results in life. On the other hand, decisions taken with a cool & calm mind upon connection with your nature are definitely going to be truthful leading to right actions and thus, right results in life. **The difference between successful and unsuccessful person** having same goal, same resources is just one and that is their DECISIONS. Unsuccessful one took under the influence of disturbed mind with a narrow perspective and the successful one took with a cool & calm mind, with a broader perspective after understanding each & everything in detail.

Your decisions are very important as your decisions give direction to your actions which gives results or determines your destiny. **So, you can control your destiny through your decisions.**

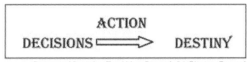

Source: Meet the Real You **Copyright** Chetan Bansal

You take decision in the present moment (present space) and result comes in the future (future space). There will always be a time lag between the decision and the result as result needs action in real time. The thought is instantly manifested in your mind but in physical world, it needs constant action which always consumes time.

Due to time lag, you can never be sure about what results your decisions/actions will manifest, so it becomes very important to continuously watch, observe and witness your actions, to check whether they are aligned with your decisions or not, are you going in the right direction at the right speed for that desired/right results, otherwise, a lot of your time will be wasted in hit & trials and correction of your actions. **WOW focus is the only secret to align your decisions, actions and results.** WOW brings back your conscious presence in the present moment, aligns you vertically leading to the activation of your super natural intelligence leading to perfection in your PDA. Life and its situations are just outcome of your PDA and your conscious presence is the key to righteous PDA and thus, righteous results in life.

Decisions are the most important part of your life and must be a choice of your inner voice and never be under the influence of others. One right decision or one wrong decision can totally change your life. But I always believe that it's your life, **you must take your own decisions** and even if your decision goes wrong, you will never regret it. But if somebody else decides for you, there will always be a feeling of regret/suppression in some corner of your mind, it does not matter whether you succeeded or failed. That suppression in decision making won't let you enjoy the success and even more terrible feeling if you fail. That is why always decide for yourself and for the same reason, let the others decide about their own life. **If you decide for**

others, they will keep blaming you and if others decide for you, you will keep blaming them. This way, there won't be any happiness but just a game of blame and complain will become a feature of your life.

You must have seen many successful people with very high salary/income leaving their job/business at peak of their career to start a new business/job from scratch in a totally different field, a field of their interest. **When it comes to happiness, it is more about living life on your own choice/freedom rather than money.** Their inner voice was pushing them somewhere else. Happiness comes from living on your soul path and not from success/failure determined by others. I ask you, will you leave your family if someone offers you a big mansion, huge wealth but slavery? No! My dear you, you will never because your inner voice/ your soul path will never let you take that decision.

But sometimes, situations do not allow you to make your own choices, may be because of some family/societal responsibilities. The people, who rise above their likes & dislikes, needs & wants for a higher purpose to help others, are the most powerful people in the world. They are truly real, I salute them. If you are the one who is doing something for a higher purpose to help family/society/others without caring about your own likes & dislikes, happily giving your 100% effort in that work, then I assure you that destiny shall make your life a blissful journey beyond all limitations and imaginations.

The above situations/decisions are rare in life and most of the times, you have a freedom/choice to decide for yourself and whatever you decide is always right, as it comes from inside you, *THE REAL YOU* which always gives an emotional high, strength and power. **While decisions based on the outside influence** of parents, teachers, friends and peers etc. are mostly not aligned with your source and thus, disempowers you. It does not mean that you should out-rightly reject their opinions and you don't have to be rude to them or disrespect them. You should listen and understand them, make them understand your thoughts/ideas, indulge in a healthy discussion and make a conscious choice. You can always convince others if you are focussed and determined. Only an unfocussed, unclear and a doubtful person can be influenced by others. But listening to others is very important as it helps you understand opinions/views of many people which ultimately enhances your awareness and helps you take intelligent decisions. Sometimes, many amazing thoughts/ideas come from others, if we have the patience, respect to listen to others. If you do not listen to others, you might miss the universal message which was meant for you through them. **So listen to all, respect all, have the intelligence to convince all but that can only be possible if you are convinced yourself. And you can only be convinced once you are on your soul path which helps you take your decisions consciously after listening and understanding everything in detail.** So, you should always be thankful to others for their support, help and guidance which help you to directly or indirectly arriving at the most wonderful/intelligent decision in your life.

So, don't look outside for decisions but surely for opinions and for your decisions, just look inside, listen to your inner voice, remain cool & calm, ask yourself what you want and I am sure the right answer will definitely knock on your mind. *IT'S YOUR JOURNEY, ONLY YOU, THE REAL YOU, YOUR SOURCE ENERGY KNOW EVERYTHING ABOUT YOU, SO ONLY IT CAN DECIDE FOR YOU AND NOBODY ELSE CAN EVER DECIDE FOR YOU, THEY CAN ONLY GUIDE YOU.* You can always take opinions from others, take help of your parents, teachers, experts in respective fields but you should always take your own decisions. **Taking decisions yourself helps in overall growth of mental, emotional well-being irrespective of the outcome of your decisions. It develops self-confidence, enhances ability to take on challenges and face uncertainties of life.**

If you dig deep, it is only you who decide even if you think you have taken decision under the guidance of others. The final decision is always yours, so you can't blame others when something goes wrong or you don't get the desired results. **Both credit and debit of the outcome of your decisions belongs to you only.** Whatever is the outcome of your decisions, you need to accept it without any resistance, analyse what went wrong, change what is required and restart your journey.

SOME MORE TIPS TO ARRIVE AT RIGHTEOUS DECISIONS:
- **Don't haste into your decisions** if not urgent. Always take decisions in a balanced state of mind, when mind is disturbed or at high emotions of anger or excitement, it clouds your intelligence leading to wrong decisions.
-**Take expert advice (Don't discuss it with every other person)**. You should not discuss your difficult times/life situations/problems with every other person as most people are unable to solve their own problems, so how can they solve yours. Most people do not understand self, so how can they understand you, more so when your life situations are different from them. Invariably they give wrong suggestions to you leading to wrong decisions by you. They may create fear in you making your energy field negative where your PDA can become biased causing wrong results in life. So, it would be much better to go to an expert professional for discussion and finding solution to your problems. But ultimate decision should always be yours.
-**Ask questions** to self, why do I want to do this/that? Can your decisions harm you or others in any way? Can your decisions be useful to you or others or all?
-**Analyse and visualize** the possible outcomes of your decisions.
-Once taken, **believe in** your decisions
-**Take 100% responsibility** of your decisions.
-**Think big**, set big targets, do not limit yourself and expand your boundaries or self-imposed limits. **Think for a higher purpose** where others will be benefitted from your work either directly or indirectly. The vibrations of people getting benefitted from your work will act as blessings for you which remove all hurdles on your path to success. For example, if somebody chooses to start writing books/taking seminars on life lessons, they will definitely get

the blessings of people who will get benefitted from their work. And you know blessings are nothing but vibrations to activate your luck.

YOU SHOULD KNOW WHAT TO DO/HOW TO DO IT (VISION) AND ABOVE ALL, WHY (REASON) TO DO WHAT YOU DECIDED TO DO.
In life, if you have a **clear vision and a reason,** nobody can stop your success. **The major cause of failure is your non-clarity on reason and vision.** The unclear reason and vision makes you puppet at the hands of others or you come under the influence of others or biasness clouds your mind leading to wrong results and failure.

For example, when you watch big movie stars or sports stars doing advertisements for some health clubs or health products, you invariably join those clubs/gyms or buy health products or both as you want to make your body like them. **You decided in haste under the influence of advertisements.** But soon, when you didn't get the results as promised/shown in the advertisement, you stop your subscription for those expensive health clubs or stop taking those expensive health products or both. **But it is too late as by then, you have wasted much of your hard earned money and time.** It is okay if you have a passion for body building, but if you just want to be a healthy person with a normal body, then it is not health clubs or health products but natural food and some simple physical activity that will solve the purpose.

So, if you had given your conscious presence and asked yourself that what type of body you wanted, will joining the gym is enough or you need to spend time and work very hard for very long hours in gym to get that six pack body, are those expensive healthy products really helpful or just an illusion to steal your hard earned money, how much money those stars are getting from these advertisements and from whose pocket that money would be paid to them? **If you have asked these questions before taking a decision, then you would have not wasted your money and time. *SO, YOU SHOULD KNOW WHAT TO GET (VISION), WHY TO GET (REASON), HOW TO GET (ACTION PLAN) FOR REAL SUCCESS.*** 95% of the success is determined here at this stage of perception, decisions and rest is your action in real time.

Now let's understand some decision-making techniques which will help you take righteous, efficient, accurate decisions in the most natural, scientific and fast manner, if practiced properly can enhance the degree of success & growth in any or all areas of your life.
D.1 HOW TO TRUST SOMEBODY (SKILL AND MINDSET)
D.2 RISE ABOVE FEAR AND GREED
D.3 INTUITIVE DECISIONS
D.4 DEFAULT/PREINSTALLED PSYCHOLOGICAL NEEDS MODEL (PPN)
D.5 DECISIONS FOR A HIGHER PURPOSE

D.1 HOW TO TRUST S0MEBODY (SKILL AND MINDSET)

Choosing a company for investment, business partner, employees like managers, technicians, machine operators, accountants, office staff drivers and maids etc., how to trust the product/service, suppliers, dealers; you are always in dilemma how to choose, how to trust somebody/anybody? How can I trust him/her? VERY BIG AND MOST IMPORTANT QUESTION, isn't it?

The answer lies in skill and mindset of a person both are important. **SKILL plus Mindset is equal to TRUST. The skill of a person is related to his job/profession; how proficient, knowledgeable, aware he is in his job/profession. And Mindset is about his behaviour, attitude, habits, beliefs, discipline, responsibility, moral values and integrity etc.**

Let's understand with a simple but very powerful example.

Suppose you have to choose a driver for your car. The prime responsibility of a driver is to drive the car, so he must be perfect in driving skills. To test his driving skills, you will take his test drive. **Judging the skills is very easy; you can quantify and instantly reach a conclusion.** Now, if he is bad at driving, you will straight away reject him without any second thoughts.

But what if he has good driving skills, will you recruit him immediately or some further inquiry or understanding about him is needed to fully trust him? The answer is yes. You need to understand his mindset/attitude/character which is difficult to judge and quantify accurately in less time but can be surely judged only through your conscious presence. **So, what if he is a good driver but has a bad character;** has bad behaviour, drinking habits, can you trust him? The answer is no. So, skill without good attitude/character/mindset or having good character/mindset but no skills, in both cases, you can't trust.

Another example (Cricket field): Say one is a good, hard-hitting skilful batsman but everybody knows he is weak mentally and has never performed under pressure situations. So, captain won't trust him and he will soon find his way out of the team.

Another example (Want to invest in some company): Suppose it is a product based company. So, the first thing I will analyse is **the character/mindset of the management of that company.**

1) Purity of intention of the Management.
2) Mental toughness, confidence, will, determination of the Management, Background of Directors.
   Then, the skills
3) The quality, usability, application, price acceptability, expected life span of that product in the market- Marketing skills.
4) Installed Machinery and technology- Technical skills.
5) Their Management skills.

Mindset/character/attitude/integrity should always win over skill. If the mindset of a person is negative more so if his/her integrity is in doubt, even then if he/she has good professional skills, you should not enter into any business relationship/partnership/job with that person. A person with high integrity, good character, positive attitude will soon develop a good skill but a person with good skills but bad character is highly unlikely to change his/her mindset towards positivity and any relationship with them is most likely to cause problem/misery in your life. **This way, you can easily decide to trust or distrust something or anything based on both skill and mindset (attitude, behaviour, habits, beliefs, integrity, and discipline etc.).**

D.2 RISE ABOVE FEAR AND GREED

In life, many or most of the people take decisions based on either fear or greed but do not go beyond that and think about what is right or wrong for them. See, that is why 80% of the world wealth is only with 5% of people. See, the talented/skilful people who work as employee in some company will take the company to newer heights. The boss of the company may be illiterate but still he is very courageous and exactly knows how to manage people, get work from them and earn huge profits. An employee is just happy with a monthly salary to meet with his/her monthly bills and **losing the job is his/her** *BIGGEST FEAR*. He/she does not want to go beyond this and does not want to calculate what amount of profits they are earning for their company which is growing bigger & bigger day by day just because of their efforts. **They are just getting peanuts in the form of salary.**

Can't they work for themselves instead of working for others, be it a small business or they can start consultancy or professional work in the same industry and can earn huge income way above of fixed salary. **Got it! If not read it again.** But, when an employee thinks of starting his/her own business and give resignation to his/her employer, the employer offers increment and the poor employee falls prey to the *GREED* of the increment. Not only that, they also **fear the unknown future** where they imagine facing hardships due to lack of money, due to not getting any business for themselves. This is just an illusionary fear having nothing to do with reality that does not allow them to leave the comfort of the job and monthly fixed salary.

Some company comes up with huge returns on investment schemes and people fall prey to the *GREED* **of mind** and start investing their hard earned money in such companies and even refer to other people citing their own example that they are getting the committed returns on time. The modus operandi of such companies is to collect money from people, pay back to the initial investors to gain trust and once their collection meets their target or when their liability becomes huge, they run away with investors' hard earned money. Can't we do some analysis before deciding and investing about the background of the company and of promoters? The source of income of the company, is it real or fake?, When other companies are giving very less return as compared to this company, what magic trick/strategy/technology this company has which others do not have? **The only magic trick they have is to trap people by spreading a net of greed.**

If you analyse your life, all decisions are taken either out of fear or greed. But you need to be consciously present, raise above all fears & greed to understand the situation as it is, without any bias to arrive at perfect decisions in your life. So, be wise and practice WOW to make wow decisions for wow results in life.

D.3 INTUITIVE DECISIONS—

Many a time or many people do not know what makes them happy or what is right or wrong for them. It clearly indicates that their nature has been clouded by disturbed emotions.

The only way to break the cloud is by living life with focus and practicing spiritual attitude to get that connection with your source. Once connected, all your decisions, actions, reactions, beliefs and perceptions becomes intuitive being guided by the divine, the God particle sitting inside you having the power to make your life joyous, purposeful and meaningful in alignment with your soul.

My decision to write this book was intuitive and the content of book is only based on intuitive ideas. Only the logical mind has been used for better presentation of the content. Intuitive decisions make the person happy irrespective of results; at least he will not have somebody to blame, he will not carry the guilt of being suppressed by others or suppressing his own needs, wants and desires. And to me, this is a big source of contentment, peace and happiness in life, although, I may not be successful every time.

Always remember that intuitive ideas always comes from the higher consciousness activated by your conscious presence but unfocussed/disturbed mind making you less conscious leading to wrong decisions/actions/results in life. Now the big question is, *HOW TO JUDGE THAT A MESSAGE/IDEA/THOUGHT/SUGGESTION IS FROM SPACE/REAL SELF/HIGHER SELF OR JUST A MIND ACTIVITY UNDER THE INFLUENCE OF NEGATIVE PEOPLE AND SITUATIONS?*

Messages from higher self (space)

1) The ideas/thoughts which are good for you or good for others or both.

2) The messages which are good for you and has nothing to do with others (not good or bad for others)

Thoughts/Ideas of mind activity

1). the thoughts/ideas that might be good for you but negatively impact others.

2). the thoughts/ideas which look good in short term but actually harmful in the long run.

3). the thoughts/ideas which are harmful to self and others.

When the percentage of good thoughts/ideas are dominant on your mind, it clearly indicates that your **REAL YOU** is active now or you are consciously focussed every now & then and the driving seat of your life has been taken over by your nature. This is when life shall start to flow inside you, through you and outside you.

D.4 SIX DEFAULT/PREINSTALLED PSYCHOLOGICAL NEEDS MODEL (PPN SCAN)--PPN SCAN IS A VERY STRONG ANALYSING, CHANGING AND DECIDING TOOL

Everybody's life has needs & wants. The fulfilment of needs & wants make you happy and non-fulfilment makes you sad. The more is the number of need fulfilment in life, the happier you become. The life of every person revolves around fulfilment of their needs & wants, nothing else. The knowledge, understanding of these needs is very important for you to analyse and decide about your life as a whole and various life areas/situations in particular. **No human on this planet earth can set himself/herself free from the fulfilment of these needs or escape these needs.** The needs of people may vary from each other depending upon the level of their consciousness/awareness or keep on varying with change in time but the need will always be there in life. **End of needs is the end of life. You can refer to NEEDS & WANTS section of PART-A of this book.**

Now the problem that most of us face is that we are not able to decide what is good for us or bad for us or in other words, what will make us happy or sad. Whether it is choosing a profession/career, relations, business partnerships, leaving a job and starting your own business or changing something/anything, **what is it that will give you real happiness? The solution here is six preinstalled psychological needs** of every human being.

      The happiness quotient (HQ) of a person is dependent upon the fulfilment of his/her default psychological needs & wants. For you to be happy at-least 4 out of 6 PPN needs shown in diagram below should be fulfilled in your life. Knowing and understanding PPN is a sure way to analyse your life and decide for positive changes in life. Let's see how?

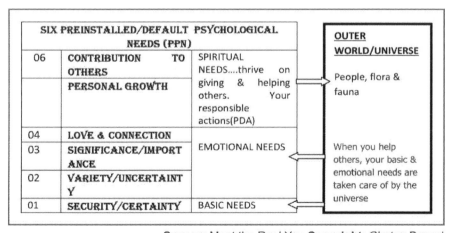

Source: Meet the Real You **Copyright:** Chetan Bansal

TRY IT YOURSELF AND DECIDE, the six default/preinstalled psychological needs of every Human which can help you understand your real needs & wants for a fulfilling and happy life.

Every human being on this planet earth has universal psychological needs & wants as mind is One Universal Mind. Every Human irrespective of caste, creed, colour, race, religion is born with six preinstalled psychological needs (PPN). Like mobile phone manufacturers install some default applications in the phone, in the same way your own manufacturer has preinstalled the above mentioned 6 needs/requirements in you which when fulfilled shall give you a fulfilling life, otherwise you feel some kind of lack or void in life. **The understanding of these default needs shall help you in understanding and deciding what is right or wrong for you** or what is good or bad for you or more precisely, what is fulfilling or void for you or what are your real needs & wants in life or what needs fulfilment, ultimately makes you happy & joyous and what makes you sad. Various decisions in your life can be taken by analysing these pre-installed needs pertaining to any particular situation/area of your life. For example, you can easily analyse your physical health, professional health, relationship strength with this PPN and can decide what kind of change is required for betterment. It helps you immensely in taking righteous, personal decisions.

You can easily analyse all major areas of your life, HWRC (physical health, material wealth, relationship, profession/job/career) with this PPN SCAN and can decide accordingly what changes are required in all or particular areas of your life. Balance in all areas of your life is very important for a fulfilling life. **A person who is too much focussed on his/her physical health** might not be able to focus on his/her relations, finances, career and will definitely become unhappy in life. **A person too much obsessed with earning money** will neglect his physical health, relations, personal growth, may not help others will also have a difficult/unhappy life. **A person who is too much focussed on relations** might neglect his/her physical health and career, will also have an unhappy life. **A person with too much focus on his job/career** might neglect his/her physical health, relations, helping others will also miss most colours of life making his life dull. **A person too much obsessed with helping others** might neglect his/her personal & family needs and thus, won't be happy in life. **So, what is the solution?** The solution is balance in HWRC as only balance in your vital areas of life will fulfil your PPN and gives you experience of all colours of life. Experiencing all colours give real happiness ensuring a joyous journey of life.

Now let's scan all vital areas of your life through a tool called PPN SCAN.
1). Physical health
A). Security/certainty---Having good, healthy physical body gives you a sense of security/certainty/confidence in life ensuring a healthy life free of diseases, on the other hand, an unhealthy person is always unsure/uncertain/fearful about his health and not able to enjoy life.

B). Variety/spice---Having good, physical health ensures that you can even satisfy your cravings of eating spicy food, sweats, junk food sometimes as a variety. An unhealthy person is not able to eat finger-licking spicy, sweat, junk food as that would further make them unhealthy. But always remember, not to make fast/junk food your routine habit as that would convert your healthy body to an unhealthy one. Having good, physical body also ensures healthy, pleasurable sex life which is not a privilege for an unhealthy body.

C). Significance/importance----Having good healthy physical body gives sense of pride, draws attention, appreciation and importance from others.

D). Love & connection---A healthy person always loves his/her body and shall always do whatever is needed to maintain a healthy body. He/she feels connected with his/her life thus, enjoy and always love his life.

E). Personal growth---Having a healthy physical body leads to personal growth, as only a healthy body will be able to take actions in all areas of life like earning wealth, growth in profession, growth in consciousness, etc.

F). Contribution/help to others---A healthy person is physically active, who is easily able to help others and you already know that helping and contributing for the well-being of others give the highest form of happiness in life.

See, a physically healthy person is able to meet all his 6 psychological needs and thus, enjoys a happy life. On the other hand, a PPN below 4 indicates an unhealthy body and thus, an unhappy life. So, an unhealthy person must enhance his health, to be able to raise the PPN satisfaction to 4 or above for happy and fulfilling life.

2). Material wealth

A). All wants a **certainty**, a comfort level in every area of their life. This is the first human need like we need security for food shelter and clothing etc. and that can only come from material wealth.

B). Variety/spice/luxury----Having material wealth ensures fulfilment of all your luxurious needs of good/quality/luxurious food, clothes, home, vehicle, and traveling etc.

C). Significance/importance---Having material wealth gives a sense of pride, also draws attention/importance from others.

D). Love & connection---Having good material wealth makes you feel connected, where you love your life as you have all the means to enjoy & celebrate your life.

E). Personal growth---Having material wealth give you extra time to work on your mind & body, to be able to pursue your hobbies, passion, purpose leading to personal growth in life.

F). Contribution to others---When you have enough money not only to fulfil your personal needs but also the needs of others, it gives a sense of joy beyond happiness.

Again, having enough material wealth ensures fulfilment of all your 6 PPN leading to happiness in life. And if you are not able to satisfy at-least 4

PPN, then you need to earn more money to raise the number of PPN satisfaction to 4 or above for fulfilling and happy life.

3). Relationship

A). Security--Does your relationship gives you a sense of security that it is a long term relationship and you can fully trust your partner that he/she will never leave you, betray you and that you both shall always be together, no matter what. That you feel you are made for each other, even in difficult times you feel secure and trust your partner. If answer to this is yes, your foundation of relationship is strong.

B). Variety/spice--Is there some uncertainty/variety in your relationship like you also fight sometimes, you are not always hooked to the other person but also give personal space & time to the other person? You have different opinions, many times and you accept & respect that difference. If yes, it is very good as your 2nd need is also fulfilled. But remember, never allow fights & disputes to become frequent, it is just for variety and let it remain a variety otherwise it will prove poisonous for you.

C). Importance--Do you get respect and importance from your partner? Does he/she make you feel special? If yes very good, your 3rd need is also fulfilled.

D). Love & connection--Do you feel loved by him or her? Do you feel a connection between each other where you are able to understand and **respect each other feelings?** Yes, great! 4th need is also fulfilled.

E). Personal growth--Is the relationship helping in your personal growth? Do you feel happy all the time or most of the time. Your relationship has given you so much confidence that you always feel on top of the world and it's helping you achieve success in other areas of life like career, finance etc. Great, your relationship is very good.

F). Contribution to others/society--Do you help each other or contribute to each other's success? Your relationship has helped you become a very kind person and you always help others, the needy ones and society as a whole. Yes, oh! Wonderful, you are soul mates then.

Women's prime need is emotional fulfilment in a relationship. If men can listen and understand her feelings, then she will always love him and stand by him. **On the other hand, men's primary need is of significance/importance.** If a woman can make her man feel important and give respect, then he will do anything for her. This is just a matter of difference of prime importance (priority differs) between men and women, otherwise we all, irrespective of the sexes, requires fulfilment of all PPN.

So if in relationship, all your 6 PPN are satisfied, then you are in a wonderful and happy relationship. Any PPN satisfaction below 4 is alarming and a sign of a problematic relationship, for that you need to bring about a positive change in your relationship to enhance the number of PPN satisfaction to 4 or above.

4). Career/Job/Profession

A). Security/certainty---Are you getting enough financial returns, you feel that your job/business is secure and can feed your all financial needs for long term, then you are in the right profession/job/career.

B). All need **some variety** in their work life. For example, for variety's sake you need a break from your job like weekend holidays and long term holidays once or twice a year. At the same time, your job should not be monotonous; doing same things daily, over and over again can be very boring and may take away your focus from work which negatively impacts your productivity. For example, if you have a job of sitting in front of a computer, then you should also be given some outdoor work and obviously not always but sometimes, maybe once in a week to make it more satisfying for you emotionally.

C). Significance is the importance that you get from your colleagues, juniors, seniors and industry that you are in and even the respect/importance from your family & friends about your job. If you are getting so, then you are in the right job.

D). Love and connection is the next emotional need in the hierarchy. If you feel love and connected to your profession, passionate about it, then your focus is automatically laser sharp on it and thus, success & growth in your profession is inevitable.

E). Growth is the next emotional need. If you are growing as a person, both mentally & spiritually, if you are growing financially, in social status due to your profession, then that profession is fulfilling for you.

F). Contribution- Everybody loves to help others or contribute for the success of others. If you have achieved enormous financial growth, you would love to give charity, love to contribute for the growth of society. Look we are born like that, once our personal needs are fulfilled, we all by nature always help/contribute for the benefit of needy people in the society. Giving is your nature and gives you the highest form of happiness i.e. joy beyond happiness.

Again, if your profession is such that it is satisfying all 6 PPN, then you are in a wonderful profession. Having PPN satisfaction below 4 means you in an unhappy profession and you need to bring some change in the same profession or change the profession itself to increase the number of PPN satisfaction to 4 or above.

PPN SCAN IS A VERY STRONG ANALYSING, CHANGING AND DECIDING TOOL

Let's find out how to use PPN scan for making a logical, reasonable, natural, truthful and righteous decisions in life. It is the universal truth that at least 4 psychological needs must be fulfilled to declare that job, relation to be a real source of happiness for you.

Suppose you are in a particular job in a certain company or you are doing your own business of any type. So, how will you decide that it is the right job or right business for you or do you need to change your job or business? So, if your job/profession/business is not fulfilling at least 4 PPN, then you need to do something to somehow get 4 needs fulfilled from the same business/job/profession or change your profession/business to find the one that fulfils at least 4 PPN.

Now suppose for example, you are in bad relationship or bad business partnership and you did PPN SCAN. You found that only 2 psychological needs are satisfied, it is not that you need to change the relationship right away. You need to do some introspection of your own attitude and behaviour, whether you are fulfilling all your responsibilities, whether the other is fulfilling his/her responsibilities and if not, what are his/her intentions? **This scan helps you find out the current status of your relationship so that you can improve on it.** Changing a relationship is not a solution in most of the cases if both are willing to come forward and work on a relationship. **You can sit together, analyse together and start working on your relationship so that you can satisfy 2 more psychological needs.** Now, your 4 needs are satisfied. You will yourself feel the difference. Then you can go further to satisfy 2 more needs to make it 6, a huge success for both of you. **See how easy it is. Just do it, I know you will find success, in fact success was waiting for the both of you for very long and now, success is delighted to meet you both,** Isn't it? Are you laughing? Good! At least I have succeeded in making you laugh aloud.

REMEMBER, ONE SECRET TO HEAL YOUR LIFE, ANY AREA OF YOUR LIFE I.E. JUST FOCUS ON YOUR PERSONAL GROWTH AND HELP OTHERS, THESE 2 THINGS WILL AUTOMATICALLY FULFILL ALL YOUR 6 PPN. A SPIRITUAL ATTITUDE AND FOCUS IN LIFE IS A SURE WAY TO ALL SUCCESSES, BALANCE AND HAPPINESS IN LIFE.

This way, you can easily decide whether you are in the right profession/Business, relation or not and if not, you need to change something, you need to work on it or find new option and that new option can also go through this PPN SCAN for taking a right decision for yourself. PPN SCAN will help find your real needs & wants where you will come to know what you want from your life or from any area of your life. This realization of what you really want in your life will give you the right direction, reason, path and vision to take the best decisions in your life.

But sometimes, situations are beyond your control and you know that change is required but still you are unable to change, like you have a disturbed marriage and things are not changing positively but you have children also. Or you are not able to pursue your hobby/passion as you don't have enough time and money for that. In that case, just one thing, keep on trying to improve/change your life with acceptance of the present situation with faith/belief in self/god and a never give up attitude where you decide for **HIGHER PURPOSES beyond personal needs & wants.**

D.5 DECISIONS FOR A HIGHER PURPOSE
Decisions for higher purpose fulfil your spiritual need of giving and helping others which is the highest need in hierarchy. This single need which thrives on giving and helping others without any vested interest has the power to change your life where all your basic and emotional needs are ultimately

taken care of by the universe. **Rising above your own personal needs to fulfil your responsibilities is what we call decisions for a higher purpose.** Only a spiritually strong person can do that.

You want to change a business partnership or job but you are weak financially, you can still carry on the old business partnership/job until & unless you make yourself financially stronger or find some way out of this old job/business partnership. This is a case of higher purpose as you have a family who is dependent upon you financially.

Many people leave their comfortable/normal life to become social reformers or join armed forces where their only focus is to help and support other people/society/country/world without worrying about the fulfilment of their personal needs; these are surely decisions for higher purposes.

MANY PEOPLE CHOSE TO CARRY ON WITH THE DISTURBED RELATIONSHIP. Even if they are not getting their personal needs fulfilled in a relationship, but still they chose to be in that relationship for the well-being of their children and spouse. See, **99.9% of the times the problems in relationships are due to disturbed emotions which leads to miscommunication and ultimately misunderstandings.** So, you both need emotional healing and that may take time. And emotional healing comes with giving, when you help others without expectations. This heals both of you and ultimately, automatically you both will start fulfilling the needs of each other. You should keep on helping even if the other person looks stubborn and does not want to change; it's a sure sign of deep pain and misunderstanding within him/her. You tried a lot and it's not working. What to do?

If you think it is impossible now, still you should give it a try and do not haste into such decisions of prime importance in your life. See here, the future of your children; the source of immense happiness to you is involved. Would you like your children to live an unhappy life? If your spouse wants to break the relationship, then you do not have a choice but if your spouse wants to carry on the relationship, you should continue and give it another try. At least try, try and only try; give some space & time to the relationship before thinking of breaking it. I have seen many people who keep on changing their relationship but never find happiness or never experience ideal relationship or they keep facing same problems in all their relations.

So, the problem is with everybody else and I am perfectly fine, I am just unlucky as I am attracting all fools in my life but I am still hopeful, determined and will definitely find a perfect person for me. This is a typical thought process of a person who is never satisfied in his/her relations, keep on blaming or finding faults in others but never try to introspect, the problem can be with their attitude as they might be suffering from ego and bias in life. So, changing the relationship is not working and I think it will never work for them. Then what to do?

What works is finding and connecting with your original nature. Once you connect to your nature, your behaviour changes positively which not only positively impacts the other but also their nature gets activated. Then, a communication between the two happens from the level of heart and not at the level of disturbed emotions. Even if after changing yourself positively, the other person does not change himself/herself positively, you still need to remain positive. Because once you are on the soul path, everything, all the required changes in life will happen automatically. So just surrender, relax, pray and let the nature decide the destiny of your relationship. And once the nature takes over your life, all problems be it any, are transformed into solutions.

This is surely a decision for higher purpose where you think and act for the benefit of your family and ultimately, things gets back to normal. This is how nature works but the ultimate choice and decision is always yours as you know your situations better than anybody else. First learn to drive the car, changing the car won't make you a driver, you need to understand the mechanism and systems of driving the car, you need to practice, you need to have patience, you need to have faith & belief in self/almighty. **So, go for a higher purpose, use your higher powers of your nature/soul and live a happy life.**

7.3 ACTIONS & 3G TO 4G MODEL

ACTION: Action simply means any movement in your mind (thoughts movement) or in your body (physical movement) which causes change either in some non-living things or living organism or both. But somehow, action shall definitely cause a change in something. The change may be what you desired or it may be an undesired change. So, action causes change. And you must have observed that life is never constant, it keeps on undergoing change and every change is a result of action and every change initiates some reaction from us. **So, change is inevitable, where there is life, there is change**. If we want to stop change, we need to stop action and as soon as we stop action, life will stop.

See, even the universe is moving constantly; planet earth is moving about it axis and revolving around the sun, other planets are also revolving. Earth moving about its axis brings about changes in the light, it causes day and night. And earth revolution around the sun leads to different seasons. Birds are flying, animals are on the move, water is moving/flowing constantly (waves of sea), air is blowing constantly, and sun rays are coming towards the earth and other planets constantly. So, everything in this universe is in the movement or in constant action and every movement/action of universe has some purpose. Air is giving oxygen and sun is giving heat energy; both important to sustain life. So mother-nature is alive only due to movement/action and we, the creatures of mother-nature are also alive only due to constant action/movement of our vital organs. **It simply means life means movement/action.** Imagine what will happen if the movement of all planets stops, energy coming to the earth stops; will life end?

The actions/movements of the universe follow some laws of nature and are beyond your control. Same way, working of your mind & body is beyond your control or very difficult for you to control. Check it yourself, can you wilfully stop your thoughts, your breathing or stop the functioning/movement of your vital organs or can you stop yourself from eating food or drinking water and if yes, then for how long? These actions are important for life to sustain and nature being super intelligent has not given this control to you.

But we can choose our breathing patterns, we can choose the amount and quality of water, food that we intake or we can choose which thoughts to focus upon. Different people have different perceptions and attitude towards life, healthy or unhealthy body because of the quality of energy or the quality of five elements in their personal space are different leading to different mindset or different blue prints or different DNA. Having different DNA means different life patterns. **So, your choice of input shall determine the quality of your physical/mental health and ultimately, the quality of external life.**

Some **external actions are voluntary** like, "to travel a distance you might choose to walk or drive a car or use train or an airplane". Or **action might be compulsive, involuntary and automatic** means it has been forced upon us by some undesirable situation like if someone physically attack us, an instant natural reaction comes to protect us. You never wanted to hurt someone physically but your nature wanted to protect your life, so it initiated a physical or emotional reaction or both in you against the attacker.

Action is the essence of life and no action means miserable or disturbed life. See, we have been given a physical body & mind to take action only. Your body has needs & wants of food, pleasure, love, personal growth and of helping others. And your mind has been designed to think and direct body to take a planned action so that you get the desired result in the perfect way, within an optimum span of time.

So, we cannot stop action as action is life but what we can do is we can choose our action. Yes, the power to choose our actions lies with us. The results in our life will depend upon the action we choose. And that choice makes a difference in two individuals. **Every action has an equal and opposite reaction or a particular action yields a particular result** and if the result is not to our liking or not as desired, it means **either we were not aware of the results** that our actions will yield, otherwise, we would have not taken those actions or **we do not have the right skill** to take the perfect action or **our**

action was unfocussed. For example, having **physically unhealthy** body means my food habits, my water intake or my breathing pattern is not right or I am living in some unhygienic conditions. Having bad **financial health means I** am not working the right way to earn money or I do not know how to earn money. So, whatever the case may be, we need to change our actions exactly the way it needs to be done to get the results exactly the way we want. **If we are not getting what we want in life, we need to change the input action to get the desired output. If we keep doing what we have been doing till now, we shall only get the same results what we have been experiencing/manifesting till now. "So change the input to get the changed output."**

SO, ACTION MEANS MOVEMENT WHICH BRINGS ABOUT A CHANGE OF SOME KIND AND TO PREDICT THE OUTCOME OF THE INPUT ACTION WITH PRECISON IS KNOWLEDGE/INTELLIGENCE AND THAT KNOWLEDGE COMES FROM RIGHTEOUS PERCEPTION WHICH COMES FROM THE FOCUS OF MIND WHICH COMES FROM PATIENCE WHICH COMES FROM WATCHING, OBSERVING AND WITNESSING (WOW)

Our purpose here is to understand the righteous action which we can choose/control/change to make our life happy, meaningful, and successful.

WRONG ACTION TO RIGHTEOUS ACTIONS
Righteous action = Right intention + Right emotion+ right action in real time
Righteous action = Benefit of all or self without giving pain/harm to self/others.
Are your actions harming you or others or all, what is right or wrong action? Let us understand with an example. For example, you felt the **urge (emotion)** to drink coffee and you decided to drink it but you will only be able to drink it once you or someone else make it for you. A thought, decision alone was not enough. So, a combination of **thought + emotion + action** gives result.

But, what if someone moving on a street felt the urge to drink coffee and do not have the money? He stole money from the pocket of passer-by and then got caught by cops. So, he had the **urge (emotion)**, thought to drink coffee but his action was to harm or give pain to someone. **What he manifested is prison instead of coffee.** So, the right intention and action both are a must for right result, **right action leads to right results and wrong action leads to wrong results**.

NON-ACTION AND DELAY IN ACTION (PROCASTINATION) TO TIMELY ACTION
An idle mind is a devil's mind. If you are sitting idle, invariably you will attract negative thoughts as mind feeds upon negativity, it loves negativity and the only way to calm your negative mind is to give it some work/some activity. So, do not sit idle, start doing some work, make your mind work hard as that will make your mind more creative, productive and positive; once that happens, it forgets all negativity.

Your time is limited. With each passing minute, hour, day, month, year and so on your life time is being reduced. If you have a habit of thinking and you think that thinking will lead to manifestation, then you are wrong; nothing will happen. Check it yourself, if something has manifested in your life which you dreamt and never took action on it. **Only actions give results. No action, no result.** It is okay that thoughts lead to emotions, decisions and actions. But result comes only after action. Thought is the source but for results in real life, we need action in real time. Due to the concept of time and space in real life, action/movement is required to reach your destination/goal but in the spiritual world or world of vibrational energies, a thought is manifested the moment it is conceived in your mind. But to make it happen in your physical life, an action is required and to make it happen fast, a planned action is required, and to make it happen accurately, a skill is required. But without actions, there shall be no manifestations.

Delaying your action only delays your manifestations and what is the use of delay when ultimately you know that real action is required for real results. By delaying your action, you may or may not lose the opportunity forever, but you have definitely lost the precious time that you have wasted which will never comeback. Do whatever you want to, don't delay and keep on doing karma as it is the only source of happiness in life.

An idle body is like a dead body, an unfocussed mind is like a hell. Have you observed still water when becomes dirty, becomes useless and you can't drink it or even can't use that water for washing. And that dirty water to be used needs some treatment. **Same is with your mind & body. An idle person mind & body becomes sick and needs treatment of ACTION.** Start taking actions for the benefit of self/others with the focus & pure intention and it cures all sickness of mind & body. **Giving your 100% in your each & every action is the only secret to success.**

Better to take action and fail rather than sit idle. Because when you have chosen a non-action, you have chosen and ensured your failure but if you choose to take action, you have given yourself a chance to succeed and in case of failure, you get the wisdom/experience/learning for the right action next time.

Taking action transmutes all negative emotions to positive ones. All your fears, doubts, anger are vanished and transmuted to love, faith and confidence. But sitting idle and worrying only creates fear, anger, anxiety, hate, envy and jealousy in you. *SO FOR A HAPPY, MEANINGFUL AND RESULT-ORIENTED LIFE, JUST KEEP ON DOING KARMA WITH RIGHT PERCEPTION, RIGHT DECISION, PURE INTENTION, 100% FOCUS IN ACTIONS.*

LAW OF KARMA (KARM YOG)
The only way to live life is to keep on doing your work, giving your 100% focus with full responsibility, purity of intentions, without any fear or greed and not giving any undue favour or bias towards anybody without being worried about the result. And your actions should not harm or bring about

pain to anyone, including you. If you are doing this, you are true karma yogi, you are the REAL YOU. True karma yogi always chooses righteous karma without any attachment to the results.

RESPONSIBLE ACTION FOR THE BENEFIT OF ALL, PEOPLE WHO ARE RESPONSIBLE GETS THE POWER AUTOMATICALLY.

Everybody wants power but nobody wants to take responsibility. Power and responsibility are two sides of the same coin. Power comes with responsibility or when you get power you have to be responsible, otherwise soon, you are going to lose that power. Same way, to get right results, you need to take right, responsible actions. And responsible actions are when you take care of all the people concerned, giving them equal opportunity without any bias or favour to few or some.

For example, if you are the head of your family, you need to take care of needs & wants of every family member of yours on equal basis without any undue favour or bias towards anybody. And for that, you may need to rise above your own needs & wants and you may need to work consistently, persistently & relentlessly for the benefit of all. This creates an atmosphere of love and harmony in family where everybody respects you, takes care of you, loves you, blesses you and always wants you to be their family head/leader.

Don't you think that this is the case with any head/leader of any organization, society, state and country? The leaders who are responsible get the power automatically. You must have seen a person rising from nowhere to top within no time in any private or govt. organization or some political leader. The emergence of a true leader from nowhere to top is only possible when the person has incredible persona and that incredible persona comes from relentless work for the benefit of all and society as a whole, without any vested interest or bias or favour to anybody.

SO IF YOU TAKE CARE OF YOUR RESPONSIBILITIES, POWER SHALL COME AUTOMATICALLY, THIS IS THE LAW OF NATURE. It applies everywhere in life be it managing family, any institution, any business, any group, any society, any state, any country or any govt. body. **Responsibility and power coexist, they cannot be separated.** An irresponsible leader is always a cause of disharmony and misery. All the successful organizations have true responsible leaders and unsuccessful ones have irresponsible leaders.

Same is the case with you, the boss/master of your mind & body. If you are not getting right results or desired results in your life, it clearly indicates that you are not taking responsible action. **If your mind & body is unhealthy,** it means eating, sleeping and drinking habits are not good or you are irresponsible in your actions. **If you don't have good relations with people,** it means you are not responsible in your behaviour towards others. **If you are not rich,** it means you are not taking responsible actions in managing your money in the right way or you are not working responsibly in your work/job/career/profession. Life is good, happy and successful but only for those who are responsible. **People who have a habit of passing their responsibility to others or are habitual in blaming others are the ones who pass their luck to others, become unlucky and thus, lead a miserable life**. They are the people who never understand this secret of life i.e., **"To be happy and successful, people need to realize, accept and practice responsibility."** And if everybody in the family, society, state, country, the whole world realize, understand, accept and work with responsibility, the day is not far off when this whole world will witness love, harmony, creativity, prosperity and happiness for all; such is the power of responsible action.

"I request you to be selfish as far as responsibility is concerned, meaning for your own happiness and success, practice responsibility in your every action and every deed. The best expression of selfishness should be responsibility."
        -Chetan Bansal

Do you know the secret to become a powerful, successful leader? The leader always takes responsible actions for the benefit of his/her followers/subordinates. He/she always takes care of their needs & wants, help them realize their potential, gives them appropriate opportunities to grow, give them freedom to work their own way. He understands that only a happy person can give good performance, can give 100% in his/her actions and if you have won the heart of people, they will definitely give their best efforts in every work as all their actions will always be out of love and full of energy. There will be harmonious relations in the organization leading to effective communication, cooperation and coordination at the highest level resulting in success at individual and organization level. **On the other hand, the leaders who suppress their subordinates;** do not give them the freedom to work, equal opportunities, or create an atmosphere of fear among them, either unknowingly or knowingly, distances themselves from their subordinates. This causes disharmony in relations which leads to miscommunication, lack of trust, lack of cooperation and coordination resulting in failure of organization and thus, leader.

DUTIES AND RESPONSIBILITIES ARE THE SEEDS WHICH GIVES RISE TO THE FLOWERS OF RIGHTS.

Everybody wants rights but what if their expression of rights is hindering the rights of others? Can those rights are sustainable or really rights? No! A big No! Every right comes with a duty/responsibility to not disrupt the right of the other. If I am not responsible in my actions, or my actions are hindering rights of the other person, how can my rights are RIGHT, in fact they are WRONG.

Let us understand with some examples. **See, I have a right to freedom of expression/speech** but at the same time, it is my duty not to use any language which is against the dignity of others. If my words reflect disrespect for others, then I should not have the right to freedom of speech.

If I have a right of freedom to worship any religion, it does not, by any means give me the right to force others to follow my religion. In that case, the right of freedom to worship religion by the other person is being disrupted by me. So, how can it be my right if that is not the right of the other person? Rights and freedom comes only with duties and responsibilities to protect the right of others.

I have a right to live but that right only comes with a duty not to cause any harm to the life of other. If I am causing harm to the life of other, then the other person has a right to take an action against me.

There is no right, no equality and no freedom possible without responsibility and duty to safeguard the rights of others. So, it is much better to focus on duties and responsibilities rather than rights. Rights and duties co-exist and they cannot be separated. **Duties are the cause and Rights are the effect**. And the law of karma says, **"Focus on the cause and not on the effect"** and if we take care of the cause, there is nothing to worry about the effect. But if we neglect a cause, then we have no right to expect a perfect effect.

YOU) what are my action areas or where should I focus or what is in my control or what is not in my control?
ME) I have explained many times earlier in this book only, but still I will explain. Your action area is you; your personal growth.
CHANGE WHAT YOU CAN and you can change only yourself; bring about a positive change in you. Focus on your inner happiness and personal growth. **Shift your focus onto yourself** as it is only you who is under your control. Other people & situations are not under your control. Most of us keep on trying to control the outer people & situations which we are unable to or can control only for a short period, it is temporary. The urge to control and blame others leads to anger, frustration & depression and ultimately, leads to misery in life. See, everybody has their own life means everybody has a different level of consciousness leading to varying degrees of self-realization, perceptions, beliefs and hence, varying success & failures in life. They have their own life path, only they understand themselves better and will only do what they think is right for them. So, to get the best out of them or to make them the best version of themselves you need to give them freedom. If we can't control ourselves, how can we control the life of others, if we cannot understand self how can we understand the other and if we cannot understand anything, how can we change that thing?

As you want to change and control your outside situations & people, it clearly indicates that people & situations in your life are not to your likings today, but wait, who is responsible? Only you are responsible for it and nobody else. Your past karma has manifested your present problematic life situations. So, your life situation has become problematic. What to do?

See, everybody faces problems in life, life itself means problems which helps in your personal growth. So, problems are the stepping stones for your growth. To overcome problems, you need to make many changes which even maintain the charm of life and without change life will become monotonous, boring and dull. If big problems are coming your way, it's a sure sign that the universe wants a big growth in your life, which may require big changes in your life and we should welcome them with open arms. So, keep on doing your karma, do not fear change, accept change, take it as challenge, change is life, change is necessary for us to learn & grow in life.

And to face challenges and problems, you need to understand the life science, universal laws, laws of your mind & body to bring about the positive changes in your life. And these are **your action areas which are under your control, your life purpose and you need to work upon them. And by reading this book, you are already doing that.** This is a sure way to growth in awareness/consciousness/wisdom/intelligence which ultimately brings about the balance and success in all areas of life i.e., HWRC and this is what I, you and everybody want.

Keep on learning and growing in life, there is no limit to knowledge, it is as infinite as the sky. Always keep an open mind; life stops, becomes dull and loses its charm if you stop learning in life. And the best way to learn and grow in life is through books, watch videos, listen to audios, attend seminars, attend workshops and do whatever you can to enhance your knowledge. **"The greatest asset a man has is his knowledge which nobody can steel."** So, life is all about self-realization, personal growth and we must shift our focus to that.

Once we realize, understand self & life, it activates the best version of you; *THE REAL YOU.* It is then, it becomes very easy for us to understand others and handle them in the most responsible way as we connect and communicate with them from a higher level of consciousness/awareness. Not only that people feel loved in your gracious presence and are even transformed positively. That is why it is also said, **"Be the change you want to see in others". If you want to change others or your life situations or all, first bring about a positive change in you.**

Many of us also keep worrying about things which are beyond our control like issues of our body shape, height, skin colour, etc. See, we cannot change them as these have already been manifested and are determined by the laws of nature which we cannot change. Some worry about future, about death and are just wasting their precious time. Your gracious presence is now; the real action place & space. Just shift your focus to **"giving your best in all areas of your life now through WOW, to make your life WOW".**

YOU) But Sir, you told earlier to accept everything that is happening in your life. To me, acceptance means no action.
ME) *MANY THINK ACCEPTANCE MEANS JUST ACCEPT AND DO NOT TAKE ANY ACTION BUT THE REAL MEANING OF ACCEPTANCE IS **TO ACCEPT, PERCEIVE, DECIDE AND ACT.*** Accept the situation means not to create any internal resistance or emotional disturbance inside you so that you are able to See the situation as it is, without any bias to understand it the way it is, to understand what action needs to be taken, then deciding the final action plan and finally take the real

action in real time, to change what you can change by putting your best foot forward or by giving 100% in your actions and leave to god or pray to him what you cannot change.

HABITS: Energy determines consciousness which determines thoughts that decides action and repeated actions on a regular basis become habits.
Your habits determine the quality of your life. Good habits mean good actions which gives good results in life and bad habits yields bad results. Your life is an accumulation of small actions. Small actions when taken repeatedly bring about a big change in your life over a period of time. So, it is very important to analyse your habits, to change them, to bring about a positive/desired change in your life. Let us now understand a **3G to 4G model** technique to analyse and bring about change in your habits to ultimately change your life positively.

TECHNIQUE TO CHANGE HABITS: 3G TO 4G MODEL
FEELING (COMFORT) VERSUS FACT (REALITY)

3G TO 4G MODEL TECHNIQUE TO RELENQUISH BAD HABITS AND ADOPT GOOD HABITS

ACTION/DECISION/ HABITS	FEELS GOOD OR BAD	GOOD FOR YOU (GY)	GOOD FOR OTHERS (GO)	GOOD FOR FUTURE (GF)	RIGHT OR WRONG DECISION/ HABIT
EXCESS USE OF TV, VIDEO GAMES, SMART PHONES	YES OR NO	NO	NO	NO	WRONG
SMOKING	YES OR NO	NO	NO	NO	WRONG
DRINKING ALCOHOL	YES OR NO	NO	NO	NO	WRONG
PROCASTINATION	YES OR NO	NO	NO	NO	WRONG
LATE WAKE UP FROM SLEEP	YES OR NO	NO	NO	NO	WRONG
UNDUE ANGER	YES OR NO	NO	NO	NO	WRONG
TIME WASTING	YES OR NO	NO	NO	NO	WRONG
EXCESS USE OF SOCIAL MEDIA	YES OR NO	NO	NO	NO	WRONG
JUNK FOOD	YES OR NO	NO	NO	NO	WRONG
HEALTHY DIET	YES OR NO	YES	YES	YES	RIGHT
PHYSICAL EXERCISE	YES OR NO	YES	YES	YES	RIGHT
GOOD BEHAVIOUR, RESPECT FOR OTHERS	YES OR NO	YES	YES	YES	RIGHT
SPENDING QUALITY TIME WITH YOUR FAMILY	YES OR NO	YES	YES	YES	RIGHT
SMART WORK, HARD WORK, FOCUSED WORK	YES OR NO	YES	YES	YES	RIGHT

Source: Meet the Real You Copyright Chetan Bansal

This model will help you both in deciding which habit is right or wrong and why & how to speed up (3G to 4G) adaption of good habits and deleting bad

habits from life permanently. You choose your actions on the **BASIS OF FEELINGS**. *Feeling good about something does not guarantee it to be good in reality.* In fact, actions and habits based on feelings might be bad in reality and cause an irreversible damage in the long run which you must realize now. It's high time for the sake of you, your family, beloved ones and for the sake of God, start analysing your habits now to change the bad ones and adapt the good ones. **It is not difficult to break bad habits and adopt the right habits;** it just takes a second/moment to decide now and a mere 21 to 40 days of repetition to make this new adoption a permanent habit.

Now, we will analyse one right habit and one wrong Habit to get a deep insight into the 3G to 4G model. This is a very simple model to analyse your habits and find out which habits are wrong and pushing you away from your life. Which habits are right that will help in your overall growth, in all areas of your life viz. HWRC.

Take 1 RIGHT HABIT --- Physical exercise, Healthy diet---Now for example, there is some Mr Raj and he is overweight. He is **lazy, eats a lot of junk food (Wrong habits)** and at the same time, he wants to be slim and healthy. So, his habits at present makes him feel good (as he enjoys the taste of junk food) but actually, it is not good for his physical health, even in the long run, his obesity is going to create more health issues like heart problem, diabetes, joint problems etc., moreover, his working capacity will decrease which may weaken him financially and because of his health problems, his family, his dependent family members will also suffer. So for him, the analysis is **"Feels good to him to be lazy and eat junk food"**

But ---Actually not good for him
   ---Actually not good for others (his family members)
   ---Actually not good for his future
SO WHAT HE NEEDS TO DO, somehow he needs to become aware and realize the outcomes of his habits which are pushing him away from life. He should **somehow start feeling bad (Visualize his future outcome due to bad habit)** and **somehow start feeling good (visualize the desired results of right habits). This will help him shifting to the right habits of eating healthy food, doing some physical exercise, etc.** Even if he feels comfortable to be lazy and eating junk food, he must start some form of physical exercise like walking and eat healthy food.

       THIS IS A TRANSITION PHASE. Here, strong determination, strong will and right expert advice is needed to cross this barrier of transition phase. Slowly and gradually, increase the activity of physical exercise and adding more healthy food into the diet will bring about a desired change. It takes just 21-40 days of repetition to adapt to good habits. He needs to be strong for just 40 days and moreover, he will witness some positive results over a period of 15-20 days which will inspire him further to strengthen his RIGHT habits.

THEN, HE WILL START FEELING GOOD ABOUT DOING PHYSICAL EXERCISE AND HEALTHY DIET AS HE HAS WITNESSED POSITIVE RESULTS. **Means all four G's (4G) are active now in his awareness—1G, FEELS GOOD; 2G, GOOD FOR YOU; 3G, GOOD FOR OTHERS AND 4G, GOOD FOR FUTURE.**

Previously, when Mr Raj was thinking, dreaming of adopting the good habit of regular physical exercise but he was not able to because doing exercise did not give good feelings (comfort) to him. His goal of becoming healthy has only **three G's (3G)--1G, GOOD FOR HIM; 2G, GOOD FOR OTHERS; 3G, GOOD FOR FUTURE but there is no 4ᵗʰ G, means he FEELS BAD/UNCOMFORTABLE TO DO. Now, he has converted 3G to 4G**. Means he has happily adopted good habits, now he feels good about his good habits, habits which are right for him, habits which will give him good life from darkness to light.

So, your ultimate goal should be to analyse habits, remove bad habits and adopt good/right habits; after adoption, convert a good habit from 3G to 4G. Only then my dear friends, you will enjoy the real fun and thrill of 4G speed of growth in your personal life.

EXTERNAL WOW MEDITATION TECHNIQUE FOR SKILL DEVELOPMENT

For developing or enhancing the quality of your action, you just need to be fully focussed in your actions, nothing else. And for that laser sharp focus, you just need to watch, observe and witness your actions to develop that laser sharp skill. WOW connects with your source which activates your super natural intelligence which guide/help you become skilful in your actions leading to completion of your work in optimum time and with ultimate precision/perfection. With a regular practice of WOW, your perfection about everything will keep on increasing to make you a skilful master. The more is the WOW, the more is the focus and faster is the speed of learning and mastery. Let's understand it with some examples.

Example 1: Try to remember, when you learned cycling for the first time, you were always told to watch/observe/witness in front of you or in the direction of the movement of your cycle. Have you ever noticed why? Because when you WOW, focus becomes automatic, then your legs will paddle automatically and your hands automatically keep the handle of cycle in the direction of your focus and in case of any obstruction, your hands automatically press the brakes or changes direction. And you are always told to keep your body normal, relaxed without any resistance or fear because when there is no internal resistance your super natural intelligence works for you perfectly; it activates the perfect action in you. And doing WOW reduces internal resistance, enhances your energy, it activates your natural intelligence.

The same way, when you play some sports like cricket, table tennis, football, you are always told to keep your eye on the ball. The more you watch/observe/witness the ball, the sharper is the focus and better are the responses/reflexes of your body. Who is making your body play perfectly, obviously **THE REAL YOU** inside activated by your focus through "WOW".

7.4 RESULTS

There is nothing right or wrong about results, they are simply an output of the input. The output is directly proportional to your input efforts. The undesired or unexpected result looks wrong to you and desired or expected result looks right to you. Right and wrong are your own perception but from the perspective of your efforts, every result is just a reflection of your efforts, nothing else. **The universal law of results** "the result is directly proportional to your input efforts".

OUTPUT RESULT α INPUT EFFORT

The law is the same for everybody, if two people in the same exam got different result; it simply means that their efforts were different. *SO, YOUR FOCUS AREA SHOULD BE YOUR INPUT EFFORT AND NOT THE RESULT.* **Everyone gets what he/she deserves based upon his/her karma (PDA), so in life, focus upon PDA and not the results.**

So, why care about results and have concern about input efforts which are the resultant of your thoughts, perceptions, decisions, actions, reactions, habits, attitude, behaviour, and skills. If results are not as per the desire, then we need to analyse our mistakes, work upon them, correct them and change the input to get the desired output. This way, we learn and grow in life. Nobody is perfect, everyone makes mistakes and fails but the smarter ones improve, they come back, bounce back, rise above their emotions, change their actions and they never sit back to repent life and its situations. They enjoy the challenges, problems and the whole journey irrespective of ups and downs in life; the best way to live, learn, succeed and grow in life.

If you have an open mind if you are learning, constantly improving, growing and enjoying in life. If you accept success and failure alike, if you think you are nothing, you know nothing and there is so much to learn from every situation, person and each & every moment of life. **If you think hard work/karma matters and not the results, then my dear friend you are alive, otherwise, you are accumulating burdens and miseries in life.**

"Results do not matter, what matters is righteous, responsible intentions, perception, decisions, actions, reactions, habits, attitude, behaviour, skills and I am constantly, continually working and improving on that. Only this is the secret to successful & happy life."
-Chetan Bansal

LIFE IS ALL ABOUT A RESPONSE TO THE SITUATION and the situations may not be in your control but surely response to a situation is always under your control; **make it your conscious choice**. And for the right response, you need to control your mind (thoughts and emotions) which can only be possible through a spiritual FABP (Food, water, attitude, DLS breathing, Physical body language, posture and voice). And being lucky is nothing but having the ability to respond to situations in the most responsible manner. The response to your situations changes the outcome of the situation and thus, your destiny. Your response is nothing but your 3 core karmas PDA which are dependent upon your mindset/DNA stored in your subconscious mind.

So if your mindset/DNA/blueprint of your life is negative/wrong, you can change it positively by consciously choosing a spiritual attitude of acceptance, PML, faith/belief in self/god, gratitude, happiness, kindness, love, forgiveness, celebration to deep cleanse all negativity and fulfil your personal space with all positivity, making it highly energetic and vibrant. This activates your super natural intelligence leading to righteous/truthful PDA making you valuable/strong/powerful/lucky; a person who automatically attracts & manifests good health, wealth, relations, job/career/profession leading to happy, vibrant and joyous journey.

Even understanding and choosing a right karma activates a spiritual attitude in you. **So, it works both ways, either make a spiritual attitude your way of life or choose right karma or choose both,** all aligns you vertically leading to deep cleaning of your personal space, leading to enhancement of your energy field/aura activating right/responsible PDA in you, making you lucky. **Remember just one thing about karma,** the right/responsible karma is when your PDA is for the benefit of self or others or society or universe as a whole but without causing any pain/misery to self or others or all. This way, you attract good opportunities and become lucky. Any karma which causes pain to self or others or all is a bad/wrong karma which attracts miseries in life making you unlucky. **So, life is all about choices** and always choose spiritual FABP, right karma which can even dissolve/dilute your bad past karmas. The power to choose is always with you and for the right choices just practice conscious presence through WOW focus/meditation/dhyana now and forever in your life.

A tree with strong roots always become strong, healthy, powerful, valuable that produces juicy, healthy, delicious fruits in all areas of your life viz. HWRC, also serves others and gets the respect, appreciation and love from them leading to increase in the overall happiness quotient in life. **All is**

easier said than done but everything becomes easy once you believe and take action. **Start practicing the spiritual attitude from now on and keep on practicing/analysing/improving as nothing comes without practice. And best way to practice and experience is through experimenting in your real life situations. The beauty of spiritual attitude is such that** even if you practice one attitude out of all above, the rest would automatically be embedded in your mind, body and soul. **So always remember, the magical formula to meet the *REAL YOU*, to become the *REAL YOU* and that is a real diamond already inside you and many of us were searching for it outside**. The more you are focussed persistently and consistently with this diamond inside you, the brighter and colourful becomes the physical realms of your life.

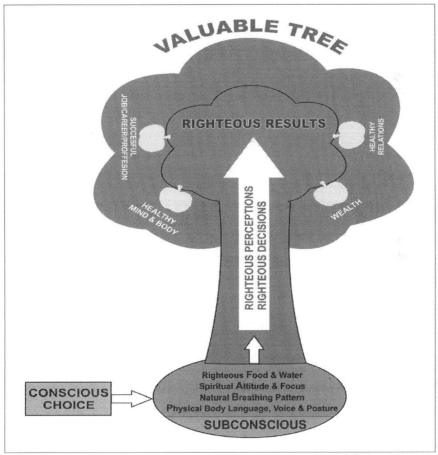

Source: Meet the Real You Copyright: Chetan Bansal

Till now, you have worked on your mindset (attitude) but to maintain positive energy field/aura, you also need to work on your physical body. Working on one, either mind or body will not yield you the right results. You might be working on your mind and neglecting your physical body leading to an unhealthy body and an unhealthy body can never maintain/sustain a healthy mind. Or you are working on your physical body only but not following the right attitude of life, soon your body will also become unhealthy due to disturbance in emotions. Mind & body are inter-related, co-exist and the slightest of negativity in one is going to negatively impact the other. So, for complete transformation, for permanent connection with your omnipotent eternal reality you need to maintain high energy field which can only be possible by simultaneously working on both mind & body.

Simply putting together, you need to control and balance the five elements of your life to enhance the quality/degree of your energy vibrations and thus, your life to put your life back on its natural path by understanding and bringing about positive changes in **FABP** (Food & water, Attitude, Breathing, Physical body language, postures & voice); powerful changing agents of your life.

ELEMENTS OF LIFE	SOURCE OF ELEMENTS	
Air	Breathing pattern, Attitude & focus	THIS IS THE MOST BASIC SCIENTIFIC AND ONLY WAY TO CONTROL/CHANGE YOUR LIFE POSITIVELY
Water	Water, Attitude & focus	
Fire	Food, Attitude & focus	
Earth	Food, Attitude & focus	
Space	Energies, Emotions, Thoughts dependent upon your attitude & focus	MUST BE FOREMOST KARMA OF YOUR LIFE

Source: Meet the Real You Copyright: Chetan Bansal

In PART-B, you have just worked on **A** out of **FABP and FBP are pending, to be brought into your conscious presence. Let's move to PART-C of this book, *RAISING ENERGY & CONSCIOUSNESS THROUGH PHYSIOLOGY.***

MEET THE REAL YOU

A Recipe to Find Meaning and Purpose of Life; Master Emotions and Focus; Raise Prana Energy; Awaken Conscious; Enhance Love, Joy, Success, Growth and Happiness in Life

PARTC: RAISING ENERGY & CONSCIOUSNESS THROUGH PHYSIOLOGY

ONE CHAPTER
8.0 FUELLING YOUR PHYSICAL VEHICLE

Enhancing your Physical Quotient (PQ), Emotional Quotient (EQ), Intelligence Quotient (IQ) and Spiritual Quotient (SQ)

8.0 FUELLING YOUR PHYSICAL VEHICLE

8.1 FOOD & WATER

8.2 PHYSICAL EXERCISE

8.3 REST & RELAXATION

8.4 SLEEP

8.5 DLS BREATHING PATTERN

8.6 MEDITATION TECHNIQUES

8.7 DISEASE: CAUSE & CURE

8.8 PPLV

8.9 GIVE TREAT TO YOUR SENSES

8.10 CLEANING INTERNAL & EXTERNAL SPACE

Your body is a Physical house in which you live but as it moves also, we can call it a moving house or more appropriately a PHYSICAL VEHICLE. It is also an interface to interact with the physical world, meaning you experience your life through it, so you can easily call it a *PHYSICAL VEHICLE THROUGH WHICH YOU EXPERIENCE LIFE*. If this is perfect and healthy, you will be able to experience/enjoy your life to the fullest. No matter what valuable cars/vehicles, bungalows, immense wealth, and all material things you possess, you won't be able to enjoy life if your body is unhealthy. So, it is your prime duty/responsibility of life to maintain a healthy body. That is why it is a common saying, "*YOUR HEALTH IS YOUR REAL WEALTH*".

Till now, you have seen that living a life on a spiritual path with a spiritual attitude converts your unconscious or weak mind to a super conscious mind. **The mind which is Software of your Existence** is the source of your physical life and it being cool, calm and still makes it energetic/conscious which is the only secret to righteous PDA and thus, happy & successful life. **Not only spiritual attitude, but also a healthy physical body (Hardware of your life)** is the key to a cool, calm, still and thus, energetic/conscious mind.

As your mind and body are connected, a change in one affects the other. A healthy mind has a positive impact on the body and an unhealthy mind has a negative impact. Same way, an unhealthy body has negative impact on the mind and a healthy body has a positive impact on the mind. **So, along with maintaining a healthy mind, we need to maintain a healthy physical body** as well. Working on either mind or body alone won't work, what works is a simultaneous working on both mind & body for optimum attainment of energy/consciousness/awareness. Even if you find difficult to work on your mind initially, the best way to control your mind is to work on your physical body, as working on the body is easy as compared to working on the mind, particularly when your mind is disturbed or is not under your control.

The physical body of a human is supreme to all creations in this world as far as the degree of consciousness is concerned. Human body having the biggest brain and the vertical spine is the most sophisticated, most intelligent, most evolved hardware/instrument/machine; being the supreme form of life on this planet earth created by nature so far. A human physical body ensures optimum movement of energy/consciousness within the body, allowing the mind to work at its full potential or work at the highest degree of consciousness among all creatures. This gives humans the privilege to process and understand all the information about self and universe in a much better way than all other beings present on the earth. **So, 1) Vertical backbone, 2) Largest brain** among all creatures result in larger awareness/consciousness in humans which helps them to read, process, understand and use all the information, energy, awareness, and consciousness to create something/anything for the betterment of self/others/society or planet as a whole. Thus, maintaining a healthy brain and spine is a must to keep enjoying the highest degree of consciousness for a creative, purposeful, happy, joyous and successful journey.

The physical body of all humans is the same but still they have varying degree of consciousness, what is the reason? People have varying degree of physical health which leads to varying degree of consciousness that results in varying degree of success/failures/happiness/sadness in life. To enhance your consciousness, you need to enhance the degree of your physical health, for that you need to bring about positive changes in your physical body. And for that, you first must understand your physical body.

For a healthy life, you need an optimum release of hormones (biochemical) which requires a healthy endocrine system, chakra system and other vital organs to be at their natural best. And the best way to do that is to maintain the original nature of all your body cells or if your body cells have become defective, you need to repair them, but how?

All your body cells, tissues, organs and thus, the complete body is made up of 5 elements, fire, earth, water, air and space. And to maintain a healthy body is nothing but to maintain a balance of all those five elements in each and every cell of your body. **The following are important inputs/sources of energy to your body** which are variable, under your control and is required by your body on a regular basis to maintain the balance of five elements in your body; **FABP. *1) Food & Water 2) Attitude 3) Physical exercise 4) Right Breathing Pattern 5) Healthy Sleep, Relaxation/Rest 6) Physical body postures, language and voice.*** The right quantity & quality of these input sources determines the quality or balance/unbalance of five elements in each and every cell of your body and thus, determines the health/energy field/consciousness of your body & mind.

The major source of 5 elements is the food that comes from flora & fauna, water that we drink and the air that we breathe in. But the modernization of the world with machines, factories and many high-tech products has resulted in deforestation, indiscriminate killing of flora and fauna, air pollution, soil pollution, water pollution, disruption of natural water bodies etc. and has caused an imbalance in the nature; the source of our food, water and air has thus, become unnatural or defective. **The food, water and air coming from the polluted environment, unnatural chemically-processed food from factories,** wrong breathing pattern, negative thinking, excessive/low/wrong physical exercise, unhealthy sleep patterns, unrest, wrong physical postures and unnatural body language has disrupted the elementary balance of your cells leading to the disturbance in energy, biochemistry and thus, the physics of your body that has made the present human life miserable and may make life of generations to come a misery. The sooner you realize it, the better it is for everybody, the whole humanity.

The right change/choice in above inputs/sources of energy will ensure a positive/natural change in your energy, bio-chemistry and thus, the physics of your body.

"Life is all about quality physics and quality physics comes from quality bio-chemicals, and the quality bio-chemicals comes from your conscious connection with your eternal reality"
-Chetan Bansal

Always remember the solution to all your problems in all areas of your life, be it health or wealth or relationships or job/career/profession or all is simple. You just need to understand the basic fundamentals of life and work upon them. Here, we shall be discussing basic science of your physical body to consciously replace the wrong inputs with the right inputs for making each & every cell of your body completely natural, healthy and vibrant again. Let's begin with Food & water.

8.1 FOOD & WATER

Food and water, both are the most important sources of energy for all human being and all living organisms. No human can survive without food or water or both for long, say not more than 15 days, have you ever given a thought on it? Why it is so that such a huge body made up of million, billion and trillions of cells, collapse in the absence of food and water? The simple reason is that all cells are in a constant state of degeneration which can only be regenerated by regular intake of food and water. All your body cells are being constantly replaced by new cells on a daily/regular basis; it's a routine/natural process of your body. All food and water gets converted into your cell/tissues/organs and ultimately becomes your body. An intake of unhealthy/unnatural food means unhealthy/unnatural cells and thus, unhealthy/unnatural mind & body. The unhealthy food & water intake practices had made your body unhealthy/unnatural but the big question now is how to make them healthy again? The answer is simple, by understanding & choosing the right food & water intake practices from now on in your life. This will enhance life energy in you that will remove/clean all the toxins from each & every cell of your body, making it healthy, vibrant, energetic and full of life.

HUMAN DIGESTIVE SYSTEM
For treating your body with the five elements, God has given you an elementary canal. The elementary canal runs from mouth till your anus, helping in the process of eating, digestion, and absorption of digested food into the blood stream and finally, removal of unabsorbed food/waste from your body through anus. Normally, it is called alimentary canal but I call it elementary for a simple reason that it is associated with 5 elements of life.

Mouth: Your mouth is the entry point of food, where you break & chew your food **with your teeth. The taste bud on your tongue** helps in identifying the food like sweet, sour, salty etc., and helps in the release of enzymes that enhances the digestion of food. **The saliva** in your mouth contains many enzymes, which not only speeds up the digestion but also kills many bacteria and viruses. **Your mouth, teeth, tongue and saliva** are sensitive to both the right and wrong food. They immediately sense, reject and filter out all the unnatural food and on the other hand, if the food is natural & tasty, they instantly accept, filter in and start chewing the food. Any foreign body like hair, stone etc. if found in your food gives a bad feeling and you immediately detect & remove it from your mouth.

Stomach: Food from mouth goes to the stomach through food pipe. The real or more vigorous digestion or breaking of food into the energy happens in your stomach.

Small intestine: The digested or broken food enters the small intestine from the stomach where the food is absorbed by the surface wall of the intestine and transmitted ultimately to our blood stream. This means that the food we ate becomes a part of our blood which through circulatory system, reaches and energizes each & every cell/tissue/organ of body. Thus, our body cells are made up of the food that we ate and that is why it is said that a man becomes what he eats.

Large intestine: The unabsorbed food from the small intestine further moves down to the large intestine which stores and removes the unabsorbed food waste through anus from time to time.

LET'S UNDERSTAND DO'S AND DONT'S ABOUT EATING AND DRINKING WITH ALL THE NATURAL SCIENCE BEHIND IT

We already know that our body is made up of five elements. **Our body contains approx. 70% water, 10% earth, 8% air, 6% fire and the rest is space/ether.** You need to maintain a right balance of all the above 5 elements in your body through intake of food & water. The first and foremost need of all cells of your body is food & water, so you need to analyse and understand the types of food that you eat and the percentage of water content in it. Earth element percentage is very less 10% of your total body requirement, so the quantity of solid food that you take should be very less as compared to the water element. To evaluate it further, let us divide the food into various categories so that you can understand the righteous food and water practice.

TABLE DEPICTING THE VARIOUS CATEGORIES OF FOOD (ABCD FOOD CATEGORY)

Category	General Examples of food	Approx. Digestion time in stomach	Rank based on water content	Rank based upon degree of natural energy	Rank based upon balance in nutrients	Rank based on earth/fire content
A	Raw foods in its natural form are fastest in digestion like fresh seasonal fruits & juices	2 hour	1st	1st	1st	4th
B	Seasonal salads , uncooked /boiled vegetables	3 hour	2nd	2nd	1st	3rd
C	The cooked vegetables, grains & pulses (wheat, rice etc.)...and like	5 hour	3rd	3rd	2nd	2nd
D	The fried food, junk food, packaged food, Non-vegetarian food	9-10 hour	4th	4th	3rd	1st

Source: Meet the Real You **Copyright** Chetan Bansal

So, category A & B is the best natural food having maximum water content, natural energy, balanced nutrients, lowest earth & fire element, is obviously fastest in digestion and thus, results in a healthy physical body. **Category D is** the most unnatural food for human body and thus, results in various diseases. **Category C** comes in between, is also very important for your body but in lesser quantity, as compared to category A & B. This table will help you immensely in making various decisions related to your food & diet.

1. What to eat or what is healthy/natural food for me? Your body is 70% water, so you need to take food which has maximum water content. Foods like fruits, salads, sprouts have almost 70% water content are the rich sources of vitamins, minerals, protein, fats, carbs and fibre; fulfils natural needs of your body. And when the natural need of your body is fulfilled, it also reduces the hunger of your body, which in turn reduces the urge to eat cooked, fatty, and junk food. Also, the food that has high fibre/water content takes less time to digest or is digested very fast by your body and at the same time, helps in the fast removal of waste from your intestines.

Food that is cooked or fried, has a very little or no water, high in earth & fire elements and at the same time, also low in nutrients. This does not mean that you should not eat cooked food, you should but a large percentage has to be of fresh fruits and vegetables.

In present times most people are eating junk and packed food which is processed, refined, chemically treated contains artificial flavours and all with very low nutrient value leading to an imbalance of 5 elements in your body. Your food has become artificial which corrupts your body cells leading to unnatural/unhealthy/disease-prone bodies. Moreover, white sugar, junk food, undigested food get stuck and forms a thick layer on the wall of your intestines which; A) does not allow the absorption of nutrients in your bloodstream B) give a perfect environment for various types of disease-causing microbes bacteria, virus, and worms, etc. to flourish.

Do you know when the majority of your food is junk, you keep on eating in large quantities but still, you feel hungry, why? The simple reason is when you eat junk food which has a very little or zero water content and nutrients, your body is not getting fulfilled with its natural requirement (water & nutrients) and your body will keep asking for more food in anticipation to the natural food that never arrives and thus, makes you overeat every time. This in turn makes your body obese a store house of excess fat & toxins and your cells become unhealthy leading to many physical ailments.

The food that you eat also needs some spice or fire element but in a very small percentage, that is why your food has very less spices and pickles. Adding pickles & spices to your food not only makes the food tasty, but also helps in fast digestion by activating various enzymes in the mouth and stomach.

The above table also suggests you to eat maximum category A & B (fruits & vegetables in raw form) food. Ideally, category A & B should be around 70% of your meal, category C (cooked vegetables, grains) should be around 30% but ideally you should avoid category D (artificial/chemically treated food, and animal products) foods. We will discuss about the right permutations and combinations of all the food categories in **point no. 8 of this FOOD AND WATER section, where I will share some formulas so that you can customize your diet, to be able to enjoy all categories of food and at the same time, maintain a good, healthy body.**

2. Vegetarian food versus Non-vegetarian food.

So, what you think or what I think or someone else thinks does not matter, what matters is the reality of what happens to your mind and body when you eat vegetarian and when you eat non-vegetarian food.

Vegetarian food has all five elements in almost same ratio as in humans. All plants are grown on soil (earth) and get its energy from air, water, and sun (fire). The quality of soil and sufficient watering, proper air, proper sunlight and sufficient space to grow are all needed for a plant to become a tree and ultimately, produce fruits and vegetables. Now, these fresh fruits and vegetables have everything that your body requires as food. The fresher the fruits and vegetables are, the better it is as the vegetables if stored over a period of time or on cooking lose both water content and nutrition. That is why it is always better to eat fresh vegetables and that too in its primary form (uncooked).

The plants and trees are a very simple form of life or the primary form of life on earth (they have simple non-moving cells & body but are emotionless), animals being second in evolution (have a complex body cells & voluntary moving physical body, having a small size brain and mind with emotions), and Man being the top most (in terms of evolution has a vertical physical body and a big size brain with highly evolved mind and emotions). As what he eats becomes a part of his cells/tissues/organs and thus, the body of the man becomes what he eats. If you eat a simple form of life (plant-based diet), then your body & mind retains its natural form getting all the five elements in a balanced form.

On the other hand, if you eat animals, the emotions of those animals gets absorbed in your body and slowly, if you eat too much of non-vegetarian food, soon you will find a change of pattern in your feelings and emotions. Unknowingly, you have imbibed the emotions of the animals you ate in your mind & body. The more evolved is the animal or more close the animal to the humans in evolution that you ate; the more complex will be the body, mind, and emotions of the animal and thus, more harmful it is for your mind. The aggressive you might become in your behaviour and you do not know from where this aggression has become a part of your body. If you want to eat any non-vegetarian food, you should eat animals which are very primitive in the evolution stage, small-size sea animals like fish, prawns etc. for a simple reason that they have very less or almost zero emotions.

Try this out, watch the behaviour of 3 to 4 vegetarian and non-vegetarian people around you. To your amaze, you will find people who are vegetarian are peace-loving and non-vegetarian people are more aggressive. It may vary from person to person but the general tendency remains the same.

Moreover, non-vegetarian food has very less water content, takes very long to digest at least 9-10 hours and will always lead to digestion problems that ultimately will lead to obesity, heart diseases, high B.P., and high blood sugar, etc. as non-vegetarian food has more solid and fat content. In fact, the digestive system of a carnivore and herbivore are different and human digestive system is almost similar to that of herbivores, undermining the fact that the human digestive system is more effective in digesting vegetarian food.

Also, there is a myth that non-vegetarian food gives more power & strength to your body. Yes, it's a myth. If this were to be true, then why an elephant, which is purely vegetarian, is so much strong and powerful? As we already know that our body is made up of five elements and water being maximum (70%), so your food also requires 70% of the water content. People who know the right intake of water and right breathing techniques can live without solid food for months, feeding only on water and air. Think of *sadhus* in India who used to live without solid food for days/months in jungles facing harsh weather conditions.

Moreover, if we have enough vegetarian food for every human being on the planet earth, then why should we be killing animals to satisfy our taste buds? In case of shortage of vegetarian food, non-vegetarian food can be eaten but I don't understand why if there is enough vegetarian food on the planet. **Unknowingly, we are causing various problems by killing and eating too many animals which are as follows:-**
A) We are snatching food from other animals and directly or indirectly, are hindering natural food chains, disrupting the prey-predator cycles and thus, creating some imbalances in nature which will somehow, directly or indirectly, harm us in the long run. Let the nature take care of its food cycle, where one animal is killed & eaten by another.
B) By eating animals, we are absorbing their feelings/emotions/negative energies in our body which is negatively impacting our behaviour.
C) As your body is 70% water, so it also needs more water intake but non vegetarian food has a very little or zero water content and a high fat content that slows down the digestion process or make the digestion difficult.
D) Non-vegetarian food is difficult to chew on, grind by your teeth, and difficult to digest by your stomach, it takes a very long to digest and the longer presence of non-vegetarian food results in the birth of various microbes; bacteria, viruses, and worms in your body leading to various diseases. Also, the undigested, unabsorbed non-vegetarian food makes a thick layer on the walls of the intestine thereby closing the mouth of pores going to the blood stream causes the non-absorption of nutrients in the blood stream leading to the deficiency of nutrients and various diseases.

3. What is the right quantity of food? How to determine the right quantity of food that you eat? It is very easy as your own body signals you when you have eaten enough. **As soon as you feel your stomach is filled, there occurs confusion if to eat that little extra, it is the exact time you should stop eating.** Your brain signals the exact quantity that you ate, only after 20 minutes of complete eating. If you felt say 25% emptiness in your stomach and immediately stopped eating, then after 20 minutes, you will feel not empty but filled. But if you felt 25% emptiness and continued eating, you will find your stomach to be very heavy after 20 minutes as you have eaten extra. **So, the only thumb rule is to eat a little less than you feel** as only after 20 minutes, your brain will signal the exact quantity of food in your stomach.

Also, your stomach should never be completely filled and 20-25% of space in the stomach should be empty. If there is no empty space, the process of digestion stops/jams. Everything requires some open space for the movement/actions to happen properly, like when you grind & mix some food in the mixture machine, you never fill the mixture jar completely. Same way, your stomach requires some open spaces for the digestion process to happen effectively, a stomach 100% filled with food won't be able to activate the process of digestion or the process of digestion slows down or becomes defective and causes various diseases related to digestion. Imagine a restaurant without open spaces, how will waiters move and serve you with the food? The same way open space in your stomach gives the space to the vital energy/god power inside you to act swiftly/efficiently.

The habit of eating too much in one go leads to the feeling of extreme overload, heaviness in the stomach which also stretches the muscles of the abdomen area making it bulge-out or D-shaped over a period of time. So, never make over-eating your habit if you want your belly to look slim. **But sometimes, people overeat, so is there any remedy?** Yes there is:

A) The best would be to do some slow walking, say for 2 kilometres, to help activate the process of digestion.

B) Also, what you can do is drink some hot water mixed with a lemon, sip by sip after about 1 hour of eating and never gulps it.

C) You can skip your next meal to balance out the extra food eaten in the previous meal.

D) Or you can do fasting for the whole day which will help in complete digestion of undigested food in your body and also, the removal of waste/toxins from your body.

4. What is the right sequence of eating different categories of food or 3-4 course meal?

Suppose you have to eat more than one category food in a single meal and this happens normally in parties where you have 3 course or 4 course meals. The right sequence of eating different categories will let your digestive system work properly and effectively or the sequence should be such that if it harms your digestive system, the harm must be barely minimum, temporary and easily recoverable by your body itself. But remember, if you make it a routine to eat 3-4 course meal, then even the right sequence won't be able to help much. So, you should avoid taking 3-4 course meal on a routine/daily basis but you can take it as a variety, ideally not more than once or twice a week.

The thumb rule is to eat first the food that is faster to digest, the slowest one in the last and the medium one in between. We must eat the raw food first and the cooked food afterwards when eating different kinds of foods in the same meal or the food that digests faster must be eaten first as compared to the food that are slow to digest.

The reason is very simple, if we first eat the food that takes more time to digest and then, the second food that is faster to digest; this is what will happen in your stomach. The fast digesting food eaten the second time will rot due to delay in its digestion caused by the slow digestion of slowly digesting food eaten first. Then, that rotten food releases harmful chemicals which will lead to the problem of acidity, gas and other digestive problems. On the other hand, if we had eaten the fast digesting food first, then it would have easily been digested in its due time as there are no hurdles in its path. **Eating cooked or fried food first and fruits afterwards is like creating hurdles/blocks for a high speed car (fruits & raw vegetable) whose nature is to run fast and it's forced slowdown by slow moving vehicles (fried/cooked food) in front of it will only make its engine to behave unexpectedly/unnaturally leading to release of harmful chemical/gases that will pollute the environment.** Same way, eating cooked food first and raw food afterwards will disrupt the normal functioning of body leading to acidity, indigestion and resulting in various diseases.

For example, when you go to some party, where there is 2/3/4 course meal. How you decide what to eat first, then second and so on; it's very simple. Say the food has fruits, salads, soups, fried snacks, cooked vegetables, chapatti, rice, ice cream, hot sweets. What should be your sequence? **Refer to the above chart of ABCD food category.**

1st is Fruit, 2nd Soups, 3rd Salads before or with cooked vegetables, rice, chapatti and then, 4th is Ice creams/hot sweets.

I would avoid fried snacks or I would eat them with cooked vegetables (in conjugation with category C). What people normally do is they eat fruits after eating the main course i.e. after cooked vegetables, rice, chapattis which is an eating blunder not to be committed at least now, when you know the scientific natural logic that works for perfect digestion.

5. What is the right way to chew the food? Normally, people chew very less leading to large size particles of food going into their stomach. The large size food particles are difficult to digest and thus, reduce the quality of digestion and at the same time, increases the time of digestion. **Chewing is directly in your control but the digestion in stomach is not your voluntary activity**, it is done by the vital life energy sitting inside you. **Your vital energy does one job at a time; it either does digestion or removes the waste from your body.** The lesser the time required in digestion, the more time it will spend on the removal of waste/toxins from your body. And by chewing more, you indirectly reduce the digestion work of your vital energy thereby giving more time for it to clean your system. **Think of your teeth as a knife and your stomach as a mixer-grinder, the smaller the size of the food cut by that knife (teeth), the faster is the breakdown by that mixer-grinder (stomach).**

The more you chew your food, the more it is broken into small particles and more of it is mixed with your saliva making it watery that has tremendous advantages.

A) **Chewing more starts instant digestion right in your mouth,** giving you the instant energy where even a tasteless food gives you a feeling of sugary taste in your mouth. The sugary taste is nothing but conversion of food into glucose/energy which we call digestion. So, chewing longer activates digestion in your mouth only.

B) **Getting instant energy balances/reduces your hunger** or makes you feel filled, overcomes compulsive excessive eating thereby helping in overcome the problem of obesity and many diseases associated with obesity like high blood pressure, heart diseases, cholesterol, etc.

C) **The watery food mixed properly with your saliva** also helps with fast digestion in your stomach/small intestine and fast removal of waste from the large intestine.

The thumb rule of chewing effectively: Chew until the solid food in your mouth becomes watery or dissolves fully in your saliva. Or if you love numbers, chewing 25 to 32 times shall make your food watery.

6. Temperature of the food and water that you eat. Just observe your body temperature, **it is around 37 degree Celsius** and it is an ideal temperature decided by the nature for your body where all the vital functions of your body happens in an effortless/perfect/natural way. And the best way to disrupt the normal functioning of your body is by changing the internal body temperature by feeding food or liquid or both having temperature way above or way below your normal body temperature.

Low temperature reduces the vital energy making the functioning of your vital organs inefficient. Do you know people living in extreme cold climatic conditions suffer from depression which is nothing but the decrease in the energy level of body? So, extreme cold is not suitable or ideal for human life to flourish. On the other hand, **extreme hot is very high energy which increases the fire element** in the body that burns the human body cells disrupting the normal functioning of the body. **Still, it is the outside temperature from which we can protect by** wearing clothes, controlling the temperature of the buildings through heaters and air coolers and it takes time to affect our body temperature but the food that directly enters our elementary canal instantly affects the temperature of body.

So ideally, the temperature of the food & liquids that we eat should be around 37 degree Celsius. The maximum temperature deviation allowed is around +/- 20% from the normal body temperature. The closer the temperature of food to your normal body temperature, the better would be the functioning of all your body organs.

Sometimes, you are served a very hot or very cold food. In that case, you can wait for hot food to get cooled down first or allow cold food to become hot at the room temperature and eat it afterwards.

Chewing food properly and keeping food in the mouth for long time also changes/matches the temperature of the food to become one with the body temperature, thus, ensuring the right temperature of food entering your stomach thereby enhancing the digestion and normal functioning of your vital organs. The right way to eat an ice-cream is to keep it for a long duration in your mouth, doing so, will reduce the temperature of the ice-cream making it suitable for the stomach.

Drinking too much cold water also hinders the speed of your digestion and doing so on a regular basis severely disrupts your digestive system. **Drinking too much hot water can burn and damage your body cells** leading to defective food pipe, stomach, and intestine hindering the release of various enzymes required for proper digestion and functioning of the body. Thus, water must be taken at the room temperature or temperature near to body temperature.

It is your responsibility to maintain the nature of your body temperature if you want your body to function normally and if you want a disease free healthy body.

7. Feelings and mental state of person making food

The person who makes/prepares the food, his/her feelings and mental state directly impacts the quality/energy of the food. The vibrations of feelings and emotions of a cook becomes a part of the food being cooked. So, if the person cooking the food is positive, happy and loves to cook with joy, then those positive feelings/energy becomes a part of that food which would obviously naturally be full of energy and at the same time, will taste very good. This food when eaten enhances the vital/life energy in the person thereby enhancing digestion and healing of the body. That is why when we eat at religious places or in large social gatherings where everybody is in celebration mode, vibrant and energetic; the food is also very tasty and energetic.

On the other hand, the food cooked by a depressive, unhappy, sad person will result in only tasteless food devoid of energy. That is why we should avoid eating food at places where people are grief-stricken due to some tragedy, like death, etc.

So if you want yourself, your children, parents, spouse and the whole family to be healthy and happy, you must ensure a happy state of mind of the cook. That is why the women in the house must always be in a happy state of mind as they are the ones who cooks or serves food most of the times.

In houses where the food is prepared by servants on a regular basis, you must ensure that they have a happy state of mind. Also, women in the house should always contribute in making the food, if not in full preparation, at least add some spices to food and/or serve the food etc. The reason is simple because women by nature are more caring & loving and their positive vibrations will make the food more energetic and healthy.

8. What is right number/frequency/combination of meals?

There is no thumb rule to this. You should decide as per the requirement of your body. Listen to it, feel its hunger and feel its fullness. Normally, people can eat 3 meals in a day but the quantity and number of meals the person eats should reduce with age or with reducing physical activity of your body as all this slows down your digestion.

You have to check how many meals you are eating at present times, are you overweight, too thin or healthy in your physique? Accordingly, you should decide and **make your own permutations & combinations** of different categories of food, quantity to eat and frequency of eating. You can easily decide based on your present physical health condition and by referring the above *ABCD FOOD CATEGORY CHART.*

Whatever numbers of meal you are eating or decide to eat, make sure to follow these rules.
A). You should **never overeat** and should always keep your **stomach at least 20% empty** in a way that you never feel hungry or overloaded in your stomach anytime/all time.

B). Whatever food category you decide to eat, check its digestion time and eat another meal only one hour after the completion of the digestion time of the previous meal. Say for example, you ate Fruits (category A) in your breakfast at around 10 a.m. Fruits take around 2 hours to digest in your stomach, add one hour extra for the rest to your digestive system. So, you can eat your 2nd meal after 3 hours i.e. 10 a.m. + 3 hours = 1 p.m. Now, you ate category C food cooked vegetables, rice etc. in the 2nd meal (Lunch) which takes around 5 hours to digest, add one hour extra. So, you can eat your 3rd meal after 6 hours i.e. 1p.m. + 6 hours = 7p.m. This way, you can take a maximum of 3 meals in a day. Now, you again ate category C food at 7p.m. which will take another 5 hours for digestion. So, your digestion will come to a halt at 7p.m. plus 6 hours= 1a.m. It does not mean that you should eat another meal at 1a.m. Give another 6 to 8 hours for digestion, absorption of nutrients in the small intestine and for the removal of waste/toxin from your large intestine. And if you are overweight, give another 2 hours i.e. total of 10 hours after 1a.m. for your body to remove stubborn fats/toxins accumulated in your body over the years. So finally, the next morning you have to eat at around 9 a.m. if you are healthy and 11a.m if you want to lose weight.

C). The same way if you want to eat more than 3 number of meals in a day, you should eat more of category A and B foods in your meal as their digestion time is very less.

D). If till now you were eating only category C and D foods, then I fear you might be overweight and or you may have many diseases like high cholesterol, high BP and diabetic, etc. It is high time to add/insert category A and B food in your diet otherwise your health is going to deteriorate further very fast.

E). It is highly advisable to eat one quarter plate of fresh salads (category B) just before eating category C or D food. Or you can also eat category B and category C/D together like take one piece of salad, then one bite of category C, then one piece of salad and then category C, and so on. This has immense benefits that will make your food watery leading to fast digestion or reduction in digestion time of category C and D foods. For example, if you mix category B and C in 1:1 ratio, the digestion time of category B is 3 hours and category C is 5 hours, so 3+5= 8hours divided by 2 = 4 hours. This way, you reduced the digestion time from 5 hours to 4 hours. And to reduce the time of digestion further, you need to increase the percentage of category B to category C.

F). The dinner has to be light means it should have fast digesting food like category A/B or mix of category A/B/C and that too in lower quantities, as we do not require energy after dinner for a simple reason, that the amount of both physical and mental activity is very less, almost nil at night as it is our sleeping time, a time to give rest to your mind & body. Sleep is a natural process to heal and repair your body and when we eat heavy or slow digesting food in dinner, the focus & time of body shifts to digest the heavy food instead of healing/repair of body during the sleep. This leads to the accumulation of waste/undigested food/fats in your body leading to various lifestyle diseases and at the same time, weaken the immune system also. That is why eat light, give a gap of at-least 2-3 hours between dinner and sleep, do some slow walking to digest the food before going to bed. **The crux is not to sleep with undigested food in your stomach so that the natural process of healing/digestion in intestines, removal of waste from your body keep on going perfectly for your body to remain balanced and healthy.**

G). Morning time is the time for cleaning of your elementary canal, so you should never hinder with this process of cleaning, doing so will lead to accumulation of wastes on the walls of intestine, will reduce your metabolic rate and will surely invite various diseases. At-least you should give a gap of 12 hours between yesterday's dinner and today's breakfast. **And if you are overweight, or unhealthy,** then the gap/fasting time should be between 14-16 hours as during this time, your body will clean and remove all the extra fats and toxins built-up in your body over the years. **Your vital energy has two roles when it comes to digestive system; 1) digestion and 2) removal of waste/toxins and the first priority is always digestion.** So, if you eat in this period, your internal power will leave cleaning work and will get busy in digestion. This way, your body will never be able to free itself from the waste/toxins and it will keep on accumulating in your body, making you obese and the host of various diseases.

H). To remove toxins on a daily basis, your **morning breakfast after 12-16 hours should not be heavy carbohydrates** but a light food of fresh fruits & juices (category A) which are also very powerful cleaning agents and enhances the cleaning of your elementary canal.

I). **Also, drinking water with food is a big no.** You should not drink water within 40 minutes before the meal and within 60 minutes after the meal. Drinking water with the food will kill the fire inside the stomach necessary to digest/decompose the food. **So, what to do if you feel thirsty while eating food**? Again, adding salads with your food, eating less spicy food will take care of your thirst and you won't feel the urge to drink water. If you still feel thirsty, you can take lemon water or fresh juice along with your food.

J). At the end of the meal, **you can eat Jaggery (gur)** which is very sweet in taste, also quiches your thirst, magically enhances your digestion and helps in swift removal of waste from your elementary canal.

RECOMMENDATIONS ON YOUR DIET

TIME	DURATION BETWEEN MEALS	CATEGORY OF FOOD	BENEFITS/REASON
Morning starter 8 a.m.	12 hour after dinner	1 glass of Fresh fruit juice or coconut water or any other fresh vegetable juice	They give instant energy, nutrients without any load on your digestive system and also helps cleanse waste from your body.
Morning Meal 10 a.m.	2 hour after starter	Minimum One quarter plate Fresh seasonal fruits	Very strong cleaning agent, very fast digestion, instant natural nutrients & energy
Lunch 1 p.m.	3 hours after morning meal	1st one quarter plate of fresh salad 2nd Category C your normal food as per your hunger	Mixing of category B with C ensures reduction in digestion time, balance in nutrients and eating category C makes you feel filled.
Evening snacks 6 p.m.	5 hours after lunch	1 or 2 fruits (optional)	This is optional only if you feel hungry. In between meals always take category A foods
Dinner 8 p.m.	2 hours after evening snacks	Vegetable soup (optional), then one quarter full fresh salad and then category C your normal food as per your hunger	Mixing of category B with C ensures reduction in digestion time which gives more cleaning time to your body thus will ensure complete removal of waste from your body, balance in nutrients and makes you feel filled.
Just start following the above recommended diet or make your own diet plan as per the above knowledge and rules.			

WATER

Water is energy, energy is life and no water means no energy & no life. So, life can't exist without water. Our planet is 70% water and our body being no exception. As per scientific studies, water is only available on earth and is the only planet where life exists. We need water on a continuous basis, to replenish our cells which are continually using water energy for their normal activities. Low water content in your body makes your body cells defective and unhealthy leading to various health problems.

Water being in liquid form gets absorbed in the body immediately and thus, gives us instant energy. The quantity, timing, frequency and way of drinking water determine the overall physical and mental well-being of your body & mind.

<u>**Practice the following righteous water drinking habits for a healthy physical body & mind.**</u>
1). Always drink water sip by sip and you should never gulp the water. Drinking water sip by sip has many advantages: **a)** it ensures a slow movement of water which helps dilute all the waste stuck on the walls of elementary canal leading to its easy removal. **b)** It helps in complete mixing of saliva with the water. Saliva contains various enzymes which not only enhances the speed of digestion in the stomach but also kills various microbes in our elementary canal.

On the other hand, **gulping water** does not allow movement of saliva from the mouth to the stomach & intestine which slows the digestion and hinders the removal of waste stuck on the walls of elementary canal.

2). Drink hot water having a temperature little higher than the body temperature, say around 40 degree Celsius helps in the cleaning and removal of toxins from your whole body, helps maintain healthy cells/tissues/organs and also kills various microbes like bacteria and virus in your body.

Drinking refrigerated water on regular basis having temperature way below your body temperature; **1)** harms your cells/tissues/organs **2)** cold water instead of removing waste on the walls of elementary canal thickens and hardens it **3)** cold water is not able to break/digest the food, thus slows down the digestion **4)** it also leads to various ailments like cold, cough and various infections of throat, lungs and nose.

3). Drink hot water mixed with lemon after 1 hour of meal to increase the speed of digestion and cleansing of your intestines.

4). Do not drink water with meal. Drink it before 40 minutes and/or after 60 minutes of meal. The stomach needs fire element for fast digestion of food and drinking water extinguishes that fire which slows down/hinders the digestion process.

5). Quantity of water should be decided by the feeling of your body and not by any advice coming from somebody else. Just follow one rule, keep yourself hydrated at all times. You should never feel extreme thirst. The below is the recommended schedule to drink water which will keep you hydrated properly.
A). Drink 2-3 glasses of water immediately on waking up from your sleep. Drinking water in the morning helps in complete elimination of undigested food/waste. It also refreshes all the cells of body with instant energy, the best treat that your body deserves on waking from sleep.

B). Drink 1 glass of hot water before sleep helps in dilution of digested food in your intestines, helps the cleaning process during the sleep and also keep your body hydrated.

C). Drink 1 glass of hot water after 1 hour of every meal. This helps you keep hydrated and helps in removal of toxins from the body.

D). Eating category A and B food in sufficient quantity also keeps you well hydrated and you won't feel the need to drink water on a regular basis which is quiet normal and healthy.

6). Eating too much spicy food, fried food, junk food will force you to drink water with the food which is the biggest cause of indigestion and defective digestive system. So, avoid these types of food or you can eat these foods as a variety, say once or twice a week or you should take 1 full plate of fruits/salads along with these types of food.

The above change is very easy to adopt as I am just asking you to eat whatever you are eating, just change the sequence and add a little bit fruits & salads before or with every meal. Right/natural food habits, right intake of water is a sure way to balance the five elements in your body leading to a healthy mind & body. Within no time or very less time, say 10-15 days, a considerable positive change will be visible in your body; **you will start feeling light**/easy in your stomach, you will move towards your **ideal weight**, witness **higher energy** levels, **feel good** factor will rise, and your blood tests will witness positive changes in your **blood sugar, cholesterol and biochemical levels** which will motivate you further to practice a healthy/natural way of life making it a lifelong habit in you. **Any knowledge is incomplete without experience and continuous practice is the only way to experience the right knowledge.**

The energy vibrations of natural food and right intake of water will remove all the toxins from your body leading to rise in your energy field (Aura). **Right/natural food & water habits-----removal of toxins (-ve energies)-----increase in energy-----natural/healthy cells-----healthy body & mind------connection with real you-----rise in consciousness----Success/growth/happiness for you.**

The quantity, quality, frequency, timing and the way we chew food & drink water determines the overall physical, mental and spiritual well-being.
-Chetan Bansal

8.2 PHYSICAL EXERCISE

A physically fit person is always full of energy, happy, looks very attractive, has a good positive mind and is always the centre of attraction among the masses. **Doing physical exercise helps in improving your digestive system,** endocrine systems, circulatory system, excretory system, strengthens the muscles, bones & joints and all types of body functions thereby making each & every cell of body healthy, happy and vibrant. **Less physical activity or no physical activity or sedentary lifestyle** makes all your body systems and functions defective leading to various kind of diseases which can even become life threatening over a period of time. An unhealthy person is not able to enjoy his/her life and they miss many experiences of life. Along with a healthy diet, a right physical exercise is must for a healthy life. **When it comes to health, it is almost 80% of diet and 20% of physical exercise**. It does not mean that you should ignore physical exercise, it is mandatory for a healthy life.

Physical activity does not mean you have to hit a gym on a regular basis or you need to join some aerobics classes. Physical exercise just means any type of physical activity which could be as simple as walking, running, jogging, and stair stepping, etc. The simple rule is to use your legs and arms for the movement on a regular basis. **Normal movement of a body like walking for half an hour, using stairs instead of lift is enough to maintain a healthy physical body and there is no need to do extreme forms of exercises in gyms etc.** The basic fundament is to consume the food that you have eaten so that it does not get stored in the form of extra fat in your body. The amount of intake of food on a daily basis must be consumed on a daily basis, to ensure no toxins become a part of your body. Accumulation of waste/toxins is the basic cause of almost all diseases in your life. **Doing physical exercise on a regular basis deep cleanses your body of all the toxins thereby maintaining energy, vibrancy and health of your body cells.**

I am not saying no to the gym or aerobic classes or any other classes for physical exercise; I am just making you realize that you can be healthy even without them. **All depends upon your physical health goal and your choices of physical activities.** If you want big muscles, you can join the gym, if you love aerobics go and join the classes, if you don't like doing physical exercise alone go and join some classes, if you love walking then walk, if you love yoga then do it. Just remember to do some form of physical exercise on a daily basis which could be walking, running, yoga, aerobics, weight training, playing cricket, football, badminton, table tennis and volley ball etc. or whatever you like. There are so many forms of physical exercise available, the choice is always yours but doing half an hour of physical exercise on a daily basis is must for all.

But what if you don't have the time for all the above? Well! In that case, your dream of a healthy body will remain a dream only. Dear, somehow you need to find a way to do some form of physical activity. Use stairs instead of lift and try to walk to public transports, offices or whenever you get a chance. Avoid personal vehicles, instead, use public transports, if you don't have the time to go out, you can do exercise at your home. You cannot escape physical exercise, no job/career/profession is more important than your physical health. Better to change any job/career/profession which is adversely affecting your mind & body.

I would recommend 30 minutes of brisk walking or 30 minutes of aerobics on a daily basis and in addition 30 minutes of yoga. At least 1 hour of physical exercise is a must-do 4-5 times every week. You can make your own recipe of physical exercise. **The best would be to consult some doctor, professionals in the field for advice on the best type of exercise as per your body requirements, as per your physical health goals, as per your own liking etc. and it** may vary from person to person.

Yoga is also very important in today's world where people have long sitting jobs, they drive for long hours which deforms the posture of their body and thus, creates many blockages which hinders the free flow of energy in the body leading to many physical, mental and emotional disturbances. The best solution for correction in your posture is yoga which aligns you vertically. **Yoga means union of mind, body and soul which aligns your physical geometry to become one with the universal cosmic energy**. *Yog asana* makes your physical geometry normal & natural and once geometry is natural, all cells, tissues, organs and mind draws the optimum amounts of energy from the cosmos making their functioning natural & perfect. All *yoga asanas* mainly work on the core of your body; your vertebrae. All the nerves, energy chakras, the vital organs and your endocrine system, all are connected with your spine & brain constitutes your core which yoga strengthens. So, you should try yoga for at-least 40 days under the guidance of some expert to be able to experience the benefits of yoga in your life; in your emotional, mental, physical and spiritual wellbeing.

Remember one thing, never overdo any physical exercise, it may harm your body. **The problem is that many people overdo it on the first day** and their body responds painfully or gets injured. So, that painful memory of exercise does not allow them to try or practice physical exercise next time. **For this reason, you need to enhance your physical fitness level step by step.** The key to developing a successful habit of exercise is to increase your time and intensity of exercise on a regular daily/weekly basis. You should stretch yourself little by little everyday so as to feel a little pain while increasing your physical intensity. A little pain means a little gain every day or each time you work out. **So the quantity and intensity of physical exercise must be a little hard above your comfort zone and increase the quantum & intensity of exercise in a phased manner step by step.** Remember, to have a little pain and stress every day, only then your growth will happen. If you stop stressing yourself beyond the point of fearing pain, then your growth will stop and you may miss your target/goal. By following this technique, you will find to your surprise that your perfection and skill in exercise which you practiced will increase immensely in just a few days, say 15-20 days.

For example: If you are comfortable with 5 minutes of walking. Just walk for 5 minutes on the first day, then on the 2nd day, go for 6 minutes, 3rd day, go for 7 minutes, 4th to 10th day 10 minutes, 10th to 20th day 15 minutes and so on till you reach the maximum target time for your walk. **Say for example, your target is to walk for 30 minutes every day**, so you should keep on increasing your time till you are comfortable walking 30 minutes every day. **Once you achieve your time goal of walking, then start increasing your speed of walk so as to cover more distance day by day in those 30 minutes.**

Physical exercise gives energy, the more you do it, the more active you become. That is why immediately, after any physical exercise, you don't feel hungry as the physical exercise has already generated the energy by breaking down the fats and carbohydrates in your body. So, doing physical exercise also reduces your hunger leading to a more healthy body.

Regular physical exercise and rest is a sure way to balance the five elements in your body leading to a healthy mind & body. Within no time or very less time, say 10-15 days, a considerable positive change will be visible in your body; **you will start feeling light/easy** in your stomach, you will move towards your **ideal weight**, witness **higher energy** levels, **feel good** factor will rise, and your blood tests will witness positive changes in **blood sugar, cholesterol and biochemical levels** which will motivate you further to practice a healthy/natural way of life making it a lifelong habit in you. Any knowledge is incomplete without experience and continuous practice is the only way to experience right knowledge.

The energy vibrations generated by regular physical exercise and proper rest will remove all toxins from your body leading to rise in your energy field (Aura). **Regular physical exercise & rest-----removal of toxins (-ve energies)----increase in energy-----natural/healthy cells-----healthy body & mind------connection with real you-----increase in consciousness----- Success/growth/happiness for you.**

8.3 REST & RELAXATION

You must take rest at regular intervals to ensure recharging of lost energy from your personal space. There are 3 core/basic rests: **1) Physical rest 2) Mental & emotional rest 3) Rest to the digestive system and other vital organs of your body. After a long duration of work, the sharpness/efficiency of your mind & body reduces due to the reduction in energy.** Rest is nothing but a way to enhance the vital energy/life energy/energy field or aura, **it is like sharpening the axe** so that you are able to work in a fast and efficient manner.

Body & mind needs rest of 5-10 minutes after continuous physical or mental work of 45-60 minutes. That is why in sports, there is a rest after every 45 minutes, in all types of games, for example, hockey, football, badminton, lawn tennis, in cricket there are drink intervals after every 1 hour etc. In schools, colleges and other educational institutes, there is break of around 3-5 minutes in between 45-60 minutes period of study. This you all must have experienced in your educational/sports life.

Also, we all love to have holidays on weekends, once or twice a year to relax, enjoy, celebrate through travel, watching movies, going to live shows, playing sports and games etc. **The means, the enjoyment may be different for different people but we all need holidays or rest or break from our routine patterns of work. Why it is so?** Remember the SIX DEFAULT PSYCHOLOGICAL NEEDS where *VARIETY* is also one of the natural basic psychological needs of your life and *REST* also comes under the *VARIETY* need of your life.

Excess of rest makes you lazy. You must have seen people who keeps on resting every now and then, never looks active and their face looks sleepy all the time, their body language is down. What does that mean? It means the person who rests for longer durations is less energetic and lazy, whereas the person who is active, he/she is active all day long and his facial expressions & body language says it all. Rest is an important need of your body which must be exercised as a **VARIETY** only, as your body is designed to work more with small intervals of rest, excess of rest will corrupt your mind & body leading to decrease in aura/energy field. From this, we can safely presume that **"Our body needs longer duration of work (Approx. 1 hour) and less duration of rest (5-10 minutes) but at frequent short intervals (approx. every 1 hour) to be more active and energetic."**

So, it is very important to give rest to your mind & body at regular intervals on hourly, daily, weekly, monthly, yearly basis like you plan regular preventive maintenance & service of your vehicle for it to run efficiently and to avoid unexpected failures. Same way, if you want your mind & body to be effective at their natural best, then you must give your mind & body the following rests more so when the rest is absolutely free. Free! Just joking!

1) **Rest to your taste buds, digestive system, and other vital organs** of your body by **FASTING**.
2) **Rest your vocal cords** by remaining silent for at least 1 hour a day or full one day once a week or once fortnightly or once a month as per your choice.
3) **Rest to your mind & body** through a **sound sleep, meditation, short meditation, sleep meditation, breathing exercises** and above all, practicing of spiritual attitude each & every moment of your life are the best way to rest, relax and rejuvenate yourself.

The surrender and acceptance of people & situations as they are without any resistance that we understood in SPIRITUAL ATTITUDE part of this book is the best form of rest to your mind & body. It is like giving rest to your overthinking mind under the influence of difficult life situations and surrendering to the almighty is like giving rest/holiday to the thoughts & emotions invoked by your fearful/anxious/unconscious mind.

Once you surrender your physical body & mind to the almighty through various forms of rests/fasting on a regular basis, your nature, the supreme power, "***THE REAL YOU***" inside takes over the steering of your life.

1) Which guides, directs and transforms your unconscious mind to become super-conscious setting you on automatic/natural path of life.

2) Which heals/repairs/rejuvenate your physical body inside out completely, removing all toxins from your body and curing almost all diseases.

This leads to overall physical, mental and spiritual well-being. **The only thumb rule to rest is that you must rest but duration, frequency and the techniques of rest all depends upon your choice, nothing else.**

We will understand sleep, breathing exercises and various meditation techniques in next sections of PART C of this book only. Here we will only understand REST TO YOUR DIGESTIVE SYSTEM & OTHER VITAL ORGANS. But how can we give rest to our vital organs as their function is not in our control? Yes, we know that functioning of all vital organs is beyond our control. But due to unhealthy eating, disturbed sleeping, unhealthy drinking habits, and sedentary lifestyle, we have disrupted the functioning of these vital organs. If we can give rest to our digestive system for a day or two once in a month, we can indirectly give rest to all the vital organs of body. Let's see how?

Your vital energy has two functions of 1) digestion & absorption of nutrients 2) removal of waste/toxins from your body. But it can perform one function at a time and its first priority is digestion. So, we eating frequently on a daily basis engage and consume the maximum time of that energy in digestion and it does not get the appropriate time to remove waste/toxins from vital organs of body. Non-removal of toxins puts an extra burden on the vital organs which reduces the life of cells, tissues, organs and overall body. The presence of toxins is also the major cause of almost all diseases in the human body.

Doing fasting or not eating at all for a day or two shifts the focus & action of the vital force to deep cleanse your body at a cellular level. Fasting gives rest to your digestive system and your vital force gets the extra time to remove toxins from your body.

Initially, you may find it difficult to practice fasting. The best would be to prepare your mind & body in a phased manner like:

1) First try to practice 14-16 hours fasting every day popularly known as intermittent fasting. Actually, it is being practiced since ages by Hindu, Jain and other communities in India. Eat your morning breakfast only

after 14-16 hours after your last night dinner. Practice it for 7-10 days. Once mastered, try to make it your regular habit.

2) Then you can try one full day fasting with fresh seasonal fruit juices.

3) Then after seven days try one day fasting with water.

4) Then after seven days try dry fasting where you don't drink and eat at all.

Fasting for a period of 24-72 hours gives rest to your digestive system, deep cleanses and removes toxins at cellular level, helps in the rejuvenation of body, enhances vital energy; overall develops physical, emotional and spiritual strength boosting your life. **It is like auto cleaning and servicing of your complete presence at a cellular level.** Doing fasting once in a month or after every 2 weeks or once a week for a period of 24-72 hours is the best way to deep cleanse your body. Choice is always yours.

Warning! Doing more than 72 hours of fasting may harm your body. **Better to do fasting under medical supervision,** particularly if you are suffering from any disease. There are also longer versions of fasting but again that requires expert guidance and supervision. So, be careful and take note of the warning.

8.4 DLS BREATHING PATTERN

Breath is the most important gift given by god, it is nothing but life. It binds your mind & body together. The only cause of misery in life is your unaware, unconscious & unnatural short, shallow and fast (SSF) breathing pattern and the only way back to a healthy, happy, joyful, peaceful & harmonious life is your conscious choice of natural deep long slow (DLS) breathing pattern.
-Chetan Bansal

Breathing plays a very important role in your physical life. If breathing is stopped even for a minute or maximum for two, your physical body will die. As your body cells need continuous supply of oxygen and continuous exhalation of carbon dioxide from your body, breathing can easily be termed as the **life line of your body**. Oxygen must reach each & every cell of the body in the right proportion and carbon dioxide must be exhaled completely from each & every cell of the body, to maintain healthy cells and thus, a healthy body & mind. **Your normal breathing pattern should have equal time or equal speed of inhalation and exhalation.** In other words, the quantity of carbon dioxide exhaled from your body must be equal to the quantity of oxygen inhaled. If you exhale less, excess carbon dioxide will be left in your body which will damage your cells. If you exhale more and inhale less, then also there can be shortage of oxygen in your body which can also damage your body cells.

Your natural breathing pattern is very simple (deep, long, and slow—DLS breathing) but it has been disturbed by uncontrolled/disturbed emotions driven by unconscious mind focusing too much on negative memories, unpleasant situations and illusionary future worries. **DLS breathing is a natural way of breathing leading to optimum levels of oxygen** in each and every cell, tissue, and organ of the body making them healthy, energetic and vibrant. It also relaxes your mind and helps to come out of a negative/disturbed state of mind.

And what is the proof that DLS is natural pattern of breathing? Well, **observe the in and out movement of navel/tummy of any person during his/her sleep,** to your amaze **1)** easily visible movement of navel/tummy proves he/she is breathing up to the navel, a deep and long breathing **2)** the slow in and out movement of navel proves slow speed of breathing. And a person gets maximum amount of energy during sleep. This means DLS breathing pattern gives immense energy.

A negative emotion of anger, fear, greed, hatred, jealousy, etc. invariably activates a wrong pattern of breathing (shallow, short and fast— SSF breathing) leading to shortage of oxygen and accumulation of carbon dioxide in the body further leading to unhealthy cells/tissues/organs making them prone to diseases. **Emotional disturbances & physical exertion make your breathing pattern shallow, short and fast (SSF); the process is subtle, involuntary, and automatic which happens without you being aware of it.** You must have noticed your breath becoming SSF during any physical pain, exertion or any/all unpleasant situations. But within a span of 2-3 minutes, your breath becomes normal (DLS) which calms your mind & body by giving you much needed oxygen or energy.

But what if a little of physical exertion is making your breath SSF or a small unpleasant situation is causing an emotional disturbance in you or you easily get irritated with small things & issues; it clearly means you have become weak, both physically & mentally and it will surely be reflected in your breathing pattern and to your amaze, you will find it to be SSF. **Check right now to verify it.**

If emotional disturbances become a pattern of your life, then SSF breathing also becomes a pattern of your life leading to low levels of oxygen in your body, accumulation of carbon dioxide in your body which ultimately leads to an unhealthy physical body. That is why people with long history of emotional disturbances also acquire many physical ailments, particularly unexplained pains in some or any parts of their body. Not only that, with a disturbed mind and SSF breathing pattern, **you also lose your natural intelligence to deal with unpleasant/difficult situations,** meaning your PDA invariably goes wrong leading to wrong results in life.

But the good news is that you can anytime consciously understand, learn, practice and master some breathing techniques to consciously change your breathing pattern from SSF to DLS. The DLS breathing pattern gives you a tremendous amount of physical, emotional, mental & spiritual strength by balancing the right amount of oxygen in your body. All in all, DLS breathing is the simplest and the most basic way to connect with your omnipotent eternal reality, **"THE REAL YOU"** to set your life on automatic/natural path of your life, to make your life energetic, vibrant, happy, joyous and harmonious again.

Whatever may be the status of your physical and mental health, it is very important to check your normal breathing pattern by checking your breathing rate.

Exercise: Check yourself and analyse your breathing pattern.

1) Notice the breath of people around you. To your surprise you will find:

a) That people who are mostly calmer, joyous, happy, healthy are having a DLS breathing pattern.

b) That people who mostly seem disturbed, unhappy, unhealthy are having a SSF breathing pattern.

c) That even in a temporary state of anger, the breathing pattern of humans becomes SSF.

2). Measure and observe your own breath rate. Stand straight with a relaxed mind & body. Press your navel/belly button with your right hand so that you can sense that in and out movement of your navel due to breathing. Set the stopwatch to 1 minute. As soon as you start the stopwatch, start counting the in and out movement of your right hand placed with a little pressure on your navel. **One in and one out makes one breath**. Now, count the number of breaths in one minute.

People with 17-18 breaths in one minute are the ones with an average control over their mind focus and emotions. **People with breath rate of 12-14** are the people with tremendously focussed mind and steady emotions. **People with breath rate above 20** are the ones with the most disturbed emotions and wandering with an unfocussed mind.

The emotional/mental/spiritual strength is inversely proportional to your breath rate. The more is the breath rate, the lesser is the strength or vice-versa. Less breath rate also means healthier body cells which mean a long life. **If your breath rate is above 15 or below 15, in either of the cases,** you should practice the below mentioned techniques to maintain a healthy breath rate at around 12-14, so that you remain healthy at all levels of your existence physical, mental, emotional and spiritual. Here are the two very important, basic, simple and most effective techniques which will help you change your breathing pattern to DLS with rate/count of 12-14 if practiced on a regular basis. **1) Deep breather technique, 2) Internal and external "wow" meditation/dhyana/focus technique which you will get to know in sec 8.6.**

The energy vibrations generated by **DLS breathing pattern** will remove all toxins from your body leading to rise in your energy field (Aura). **DLS breathing pattern-----removal of toxins (-ve energies)----increase in energy-----natural/healthy cells-----healthy mind & body------connection with real you-----increase in consciousness-----Success/growth/happiness for you.**

8.5 SLEEP

"It is not the lack of money but the lack of sleep or disturbed sleep or no sleep that makes a person poor". A person with poor sleep or no sleep is the poorest person on the planet earth.

Sleep is the natural process of recharging of cosmic energy in your body. See, a **restful mind** draws the optimum cosmic energy and a man is **restful in his sleep.** It is involuntary, subtle and an automatic way of recharging your body. After working for the whole day, you lose your vital energy and naturally, you are inclined towards sleep. When you wake up in the morning after sleep, you feel fresh and energetic but only if you had a sound sleep.

A disturbed mind or a disturbed sleep hinders the absorption of cosmic energy in your body. That is why people with disturbed sleep or disturbed state of mind becomes irritable, restless and are unhappy because they are lacking life energy. Nobody can be at ease without life energy. If the life energy in a person increases, happiness increases. Think of someone after an angry emotional outburst or after excessive physical work, he/she loses his/her vital energy, are not able to control his/her sleep and falls asleep automatically. You know the reason why, he/she wants to get back the lost life energy/vital energy/cosmic energy.

When your energy level is low, your body becomes lethargic and your mind becomes negative or disturbed; you experience negative emotions like anger, fear, hatred, jealousy, anxiety, etc. **But when you have optimum energy levels, your mind & body becomes healthy and active, where you** experience positive emotions like calmness, confidence, love, kindness, happiness, feelings of gratitude, etc. You can easily understand the negative effects of disturbed sleep or sleepless nights on your mind & body; some people suffer from **insomnia**, some have a **problem getting up from sleep** in the morning and even after 8 hours of sleep, they feel drowsy and lethargic. The simple reason is that they have unwanted thoughts, their mind is not at rest and it keeps on thinking negatively. And negative thoughts repel the inflow of cosmic energy in your body making you restless, tired and unhappy.

Your body consumes energy in doing activities like talking, walking, thinking, digestion, reading, writing etc.; the energy is consumed by your mind & body for doing routine activities. So, it is very important to recharge your body with energy on a daily basis without which your mind & body will come to standstill. Without the recharge of your cells, the rate of regeneration of cells will become slower than the rate of degeneration which will lead to faulty, unhealthy cells making your body prone to disease. A normal person would die if deprived of sleep for 3 to 4 continuous days. It is during sleep that you get cosmic energy which helps in energizing, repairing, and healing of your mind & body. That is why a person with deprived sleep or disturbed sleep feels very low, lethargic, restless, and irritated and people who suffer from disturbed sleep for longer periods of time, their mind & body becomes defective leading to various diseases.

Like you recharge your cell phones with electrical energy, the same way you recharge your body through sleep (by absorbing cosmic energy). Sleep helps you absorb the cosmic energy which is very vital for the normal functioning and survival of your body. Through normal, healthy, and sound sleep, your mind & body gets the treat of life energy leading to happy, prosperous and joyous journey.

The recommended normal sleeping hours for people for various age groups is as under:-

S.NO	AGE GROUP	NORMAL SLEEPING HOURS
1	CHILDREN 2-5 YEARS	
2	CHILDREN 6 TO 12 YEARS	
3	TEENAGERS 13 TO 19 YEARS	
4	ADULTS 19 TO 60 YEARS	
5	OLD 60 TO 120 YEARS	

Source: Meet the Real You Copyright: Chetan Bansal

Yes, you don't need the above normal sleep hour table according to age group or any criteria, but just let your body decide the time of your sleep. There are people who sleep not more than 4 hours a day and still feel healthy & energetic. If you feel restful in your mind all day long, you won't feel the urge to sleep more. **There are individual differences and the best way to judge your sleep quality or how to know your sleep is normal & healthy is this;** if you feel energetic & happy on waking up in the morning, then this is a clear indication that your sleep is normal, sound and healthy and it does not matter whether you slept for 2 or 4 or 8 hours. And if you feel lethargic, lazy and does not want to get out of bed even after sleeping for long hours (more than 8 hours), then this is a clear indication that your sleep is disturbed and unhealthy.

There may be various reasons for an unhealthy, disturbed sleep. People who are under mental stress due to any kind of problems in life like physical health issues, problems in relationships, financial problems, stress due to any type of failure tend to worry a lot and are constantly feeling sad which does not allow their mind to rest. When the mind is not at rest, means it is constantly thinking, worrying and fearing which depletes the vital energy from mind & body. **A constantly worrying mind is not at rest and is not able to sleep properly or his/her mind also keeps on thinking during sleep which hinders the natural process of absorption of cosmic energy.** Thus, it doubly and negatively impacts you; **1)** by depleting the vital energy **2)** not allowing the cosmic energy to enter your body. You can again refer to **3.6 section (fig 1) in PART-A of this book to understand how negative thoughts or too much thoughts repulse the cosmic energy.**

Mental stress leads to disturbed sleep and if this becomes your pattern over a period of long time, it leads to a mental disease called Depression. Depression is the decrease in levels of energy below optimum levels of energy. Depression or decrease in the energy is the cause of almost all physical & mental diseases which causes havoc in the life of a person involved. **Many people suffer from various kinds of sleep disorders like; 1)** Disturbed sleep due to mental stress, 2) Insomnia where the person is not able to sleep at all.

1). MANY PEOPLE SLEEP FOR LONG HOURS (say 9-10 hours) and still feel lethargic, low on energy all the day. They are not able to get up early in the morning and on getting up, they feel headache and laziness etc. The reason is that they are sleeping for long hours but not getting a sound sleep. Their sleep is disturbed due to uncontrolled mind activity. They are constantly worrying and regretting their life and are not able to bring their mind to rest or in present moment.

2). MANY PEOPLE FIND IT VERY DIFFICULT TO SLEEP AND JUST SLEEP FOR 2-3 HOURS OR ARE NOT ABLE TO SLEEP AT ALL. In medical terms, we call it **Insomnia.** A person who is not able to sleep is the poorest person on the planet, no matter how rich he/she may be. They can never be happy in their life. Their life becomes a constant struggle for peace, happiness which no money can buy. They also feel lethargic and low on energy. These are small words to define their plight; in fact, their physical & mental state is horrible and terrible. They try many medicines/drugs/tranquilizers.

Drugs or sleeping pills or alcohol, is this real solution: People with disturbed mind are not able to sleep well or at all because their endocrine glands are not able to release the 'feel good' hormones in the blood stream and people need to take many medicines/drugs/tranquilizers. These medicines are chemical alternatives to your natural feel good hormones (biochemical) but never activate or correct your defective endocrine glands. These medicines only give relief/peace to your mind temporarily. Your body becomes addicted to these medicines, tranquilizers or drugs for the feel good factor and sleep. With regular dependence on these drugs, the body develops resistance towards them requiring higher doses to remain effective. This harms your body & mind immensely, particularly in the long run.

Unless and until you found a way to control your thoughts and steady your emotions, no medicine in the world without any side effects can give you sound sleep on a regular basis. **The only solution is within you;** all the medicines are within you, so why search for medicines outside when you have everything inside? **The omnipotent eternal energy** is the source of your life, maintains your life and the super intelligence which has all the solutions to your plight.

We have already understood and about to understand many ways and techniques to calm your disturbed mind; the spiritual attitude, right food, right water intake, right rest, right sleep, right breathing pattern, WOW meditation, right body postures, right focus of mind, all increases the source energy in you. Once you treat your mind & body with its source energy, no negativity, no physical and mental diseases can stay in your life including disturbed sleep. **You absorb cosmic energy when your mind is at rest** and resting mind means it does not have disturbing thoughts or very less thoughts or mind is focussed in the present moment or it is vertically aligned. This activates your energy chakras & your endocrine glands which releases the optimum amount of biochemical in your blood stream; **the real natural medicines for a peaceful, happy and joyous journey.**

Meditation/*Dhyana*/focus is a sure way to absorb the optimum amount of life energy. Whereas, sleep is an involuntary and automatic process of absorption of cosmic energy but meditation is a voluntary process of absorption of cosmic energy. Sleep is natural but for meditation, we need to learn and master through practice.

The best, simple, basic and the most effective way to make your breathing pattern DLS, to make your sleep sound, to steady your emotions, to overall healthy mind & body is a practice of meditation through focus on breathing or on your chakras or core of your body. So, if you know how to breathe, you can easily meditate and you reading this book confirms that you are breathing but may be your breathing pattern is disturbed or it is SSF or disturbance in your emotions have distorted your breathing pattern and you are not aware about it. **Don't worry! Now, you can not only control your breathing pattern but thoughts, emotions, sleep, mind and thus, your life with the following breathing/internal focus techniques:-**

A) Deep breather
B) WOW Internal and External meditation/dhyana/focus technique
C) Short Meditation
D) Sleep Meditation

8.6 MEDITATION TECHNIQUES

A). DEEP BREATHER TECHNIQUE

In this technique, we consciously practice deep breathing, a natural breathing pattern proved by observing the breathing pattern of humans during sleep already discussed in section **DLS *BREATHING PATTERN.***

DEEP BREATHER	IN THE RATIO OF 1:1
Inhale time	= 1x number of count
Breath hold time	= 0x zero count
Breath exhale time	= 1x number of count

BOTH INHALE AND EXHALE TIME ARE SAME--deep, long and slow, hence deeper penetration of oxygen in each & every cell and complete removal of carbon dioxide from each & every cell, makes every cell energetic, vibrant, and calmer.

DURATION: 10-15 MINUTES OR 150-200 COUNTS OF BREATH

FREQUENCY: ATLEAST 2 TIMES IN A DAY

IMPORTANT NOTES
1) Can be done any time of the day but ideally before meal or after 1 hour of meal
2) Preferably before sleep and on waking up from sleep as this is natural Alfa state of mind.
3) Can be done anywhere but not while driving any vehicle or working on some machine.
4) You should not be doing anything else. Full focus must be on technique.

PROCESS
Move 1: Just sit on chair with back support and hands resting on thighs with palms downward **or 2ⁿᵈ option** lie down straight with face & body upwards on any comfortable surface while resting hands with palms downwards on navel. Relax and loosen up your body. Close your eyes. Just ensure straight backbone during the whole process.
Move 2: Take 2-3 deep breaths while counting 1 to 7 breathe in, halt for a count, while counting 1 to 7 breathe out, and repeat 2-3 times
Move 3: Main Technique (if you are doing while sitting)-Breathe in while counting 1 to 5, then breathe out while counting 1 to 5. Depending on your capacity, you can also increase the count to say 1 to 7 (but not more than 7) or if you don't like counting just watch your breath right from nostril to navel and from navel back to nostril--One in and out of breath completes 1 breathe and now repeat the same process for 150-200 breaths.
OR
Move 3: Main technique (If you are doing while lying down)-Take your full focus on to your navel. Just watch in and out movement of your hands resting on navel. Very simple, equally effective and recommended for beginners--One in and out movement of navel is equal to 1 breathe---Repeat the same process for 150-200 breaths.

CLOSING: After completing the desired no of breathing cycles--- say it in your mind that **"I am now coming out of this meditative state by counting 1 to 10"**. Then, count 1 to 10 slowly approximately at the speed of 1 count per second. Then slowly open your eyes.

KEY: Keep on doing this technique with your full focus on your breathe if doing while sitting and full focus on navel if doing while lying down, does not matter if your focus goes elsewhere or some thoughts come, bring your focus back to your breathe consciously and keep on doing the technique even if the focus does not come back on your breathe.

MAKING IT A HABIT: Practicing and performing anything for continuous 21 days to 40 days becomes your habit and if done continuously for 11 months it become part of your subconscious and if continued for 3 years, it will permanently become part of your DNA.

BENEFITS: Deep breather is also a WOW internal meditation, read benefits of WOW internal meditation.

B) WOW INTERNAL AND EXTERNAL MEDITATION/*DHYANA*/FOCUS TECHNIQUE
Meditation is just *Dhyana* (Focus) and **watching, observing and witnessing (WOW)** is a process of *Dhyana*. The more you WOW, the sharper becomes the *Dhyana* and calmer & intelligent becomes your mind. **There are two types of meditation-**
Internal meditation- Watching, observing and witnessing your internal thoughts, emotions, body parts, feelings, and breathing etc. is internal meditation. WOW increases awareness, energy and consciousness of your mind & body.
External Meditation- Watching, observing and witnessing the job/work/people/situations in your life is external meditation.

Both types of meditations when done on a regular and consistent basis, **activates your 7 chakras/minds and endocrine glands that leads** to increase in your awareness, energy and consciousness which ultimately enhances the quality of your PDA, increases the quality of your work, reduces the time of completion of work, removes stress from mind, increases the emotional strength, enhances physical well-being, enhances the quality of your sleep, reduces the quantity of your sleep, cures many chronic diseases, and removes unwanted people & situations from your life, Attracts righteous people & situation in your life; all in all, increases your luck, sets you on your natural path of life leading to success and growth in all areas of your life viz. HWRC thereby, **enhancing your overall happiness quotient.**

We have already learned about the WOW focus/*Dhyana*/meditation earlier in PART-B of this book only. Now let's understand and practice internal meditation technique.

INTERNAL MEDITATION TECHNIQUE
There are two types of internal meditation.

M1. BASIC MEDITATION----TO RAISE YOUR VIBRATIONS: This meditation de-clutters your mind of all negative emotions leading to increase in your energy field/aura and synchronization of your mind, body and souls with the source energy. This is a wonderfully, amazing technique for a vertical alignment to bring back the focus of your wandering mind in the present moment.

M2. MEDITATION FOR A SPECIFIC PURPOSE: This is the second phase of meditation for the fulfilment of specific purpose like for achievement of your goals/targets. It may be your health, financial or relationship goals or for healing a specific disease. This technique is done only in continuation to a basic meditation technique or you can say this technique can't be performed directly. If you do it without the 1st step, it won't harm you but it may not be effective or will have less effect. The first step of this technique is BASIC MEDITATION and MEDITATION FOR A SPECIFIC PURPOSE IS 2nd step without any break between 1st and 2nd step. This technique is like installing new software in your subconscious mind (deep memory) for a specific goal or for overall success & growth in all areas of your life or for solving some problems or healing some diseases or healing some relations etc.

M1. INTERNAL MEDITATION---BASIC MEDITATION TECHNIQUE

The purpose of all meditation practices is to shift the focus of your mind from the past & future to the present space, a space of creator/divine/nature. **It's a process to calm your mind.** To calm your disturbed mind, to get connected to the source energy, to expand your energy field/aura, to expand your consciousness, to remove all negativity from your mind is the basic purpose of meditation.

Let's understand the basic breathing technique for achieving a restful/meditative state of mind and is the base of all advanced meditative technique. It is a very powerful technique to grab energy from cosmos/universal space just like sleep. Even half an hour of meditation will give you the energy equivalent to approx. 4 hours of sleep which may vary from person to person depending upon their level of practice. **Now, what is meditation and how to do it**? Most of us are alien to the word meditation as we think it is meant for saints only. It is for everybody, easy and must be practiced from a very young age till death. It has an immense benefit; you just need to practice it in order to experience it.

Air or breath is a connecting link between mind & body. Breathing binds your mind & body together. Once breath leaves your body; mind and body gets separated; the absence of mind is just a dead body, nothing else. So, breath is nothing but life; it 100% leaves the body means the death of the body and less or short breath/oxygen in live body causes disturbances in physical cells & mind. **The percentage of oxygen is inversely proportional to the disturbance in mind,** i.e. the more is the oxygen in the body, lesser is the disturbance of mind or vice-versa.

Therefore, right breathing pattern leads to a peaceful/conscious/normal/natural mind. **Right breathing patterns and** focusing on your breath leads to the optimum levels of oxygen in the body; steadies the emotions, super charges the whole body (brain, vertebrae, nerves, endocrine gland, energy chakras) with energy and brings your focus back to the present moment leading to the vertical alignment and activation of your 3rd eye. Right breathing pattern is the way to the divine light and that is why breathing techniques are the best way to do internal meditation/*dhyana*/focus.

As in your physical body, all the chakras, endocrine glands, and major body organs are present on the centre line/core of your body; right from the bottom of the vertebrae to the top centre of your head, you must focus on the centre line or core of your body. And this is the centre line which is also place of breathing, so focusing on your breath will automatically shift the focus of your mind to the centre line/core/vertebrae of your body and thus, chakras/mind. This way, breathing is an effortless, easy way to focus on the core of your body which is the lifeline to your healthy body & mind. You can also focus on individual chakras directly without the focus on your breath but that will be difficult for a beginner and I recommend you to use focusing on breath, the best way for internal meditation.

MEDITATIVE STATE OF MIND

Meditation is a process to steady your emotions or to remove negative emotions so as to achieve a restful state of mind, the only state which draws/absorbs energy from the cosmos. Meditation is a state from many to one thought or zero thoughts. It is an Alpha state of mind where both your conscious and subconscious are actively connected and are on the same wavelength synchronized. Only a mind devoid of all noises (too much negative thoughts) can connect with the subconscious mind.

THE LOGIC OF ABSORPTION OF COSMIC ENERGY THROUGH A PROCESS CALLED MEDITATION.

You can refer to 3.6 section (fig. 1) of PART-A of this book to understand how negative thoughts or too much thoughts repulse the cosmic energy. Also, you can refer to the vertical alignment or present moment living in section 6.2 of PART-B of this book only. Disturbed mind means negative emotions having low frequency vibrations and cosmic energy is characterised by high frequency vibrations; low and high frequency vibrations repel each other. So, cosmic energy is not attracted or absorbed by a disturbed mind. A peaceful mind means positive emotions having high frequency vibrations which attracts and absorbs the high frequency vibrations of cosmic energy. The more peaceful is your mind, the more energy you draw from universe.

HOW TO ACHIEVE MEDITATIVE STATE OF MIND; A SIMPLE BREATHING TECHNIQUE

MOVE 1: You can either sit on a chair with a back support, resting your palms on your thighs or you can lie down straight on any comfortable surface with your face upwards and palms resting on your navel/stomach **or** you can sit in *Padma asana* **or** *sukh asana*, choice is all yours.

Note: Please ensure a straight backbone and never forget to give your back a support so that you can comfortably maintain a straight backbone during the process of meditation. Straight backbone helps in the free and speedy flow of energy which is the most important part for effective meditation.

MOVE 2: Close your ears with cotton or sit in a place where there is no external sound or sit in a natural place with soothing sounds of water, animals, birds etc. Don't eat anything during the process to give rest to your digestive system. In fact, practice the process of meditation after two hours of eating or best would be on an empty stomach.

Close your eyes, relax and loosen up your body, consciously stop all the body movements, try to maintain stillness of your body but at the same time, your body should be fully relaxed without any stiffness.

Note: The idea to shut the working of your senses in order to cut your connection with the outer world so that you can focus on to yourself. Connection with the outer world will invoke unnecessary thoughts & emotions which will hinder the process of meditation.

MOVE 3: This is the main technique where you will use your breath to bring back the focus of your mind in the present movement. For ease of understanding, learning and practicing, it has been divided into 3 Steps.

Step 1: After shutting your senses, take 3-4 deep breaths and then **consciously start breathing up to your navel**. Take your full focus on to your breath; simply observe, watch and witness the movement of breath right from the nostrils to the navel and back from the navel to the nostrils. One in and out of breath constitutes one breath, do it for 40 counts. This way, focus of mind will shift from many thoughts to counting of your breath and **your mind cannot focus on two or more things at a time.**

Step 2: Then, take your focus of breath right from the nostril up to your chest and back to the nostrils. Repeat 40 cycles of breath i.e. 41 to 80.

Step 3: Then, take your focus of breath right from the nostril to top of your nose or in between your eye brows or your 3rd eye and back to your nostril. Repeat 40 cycles of breath i.e. 81 to 120.

STEPS TO INTERNAL MEDITATION

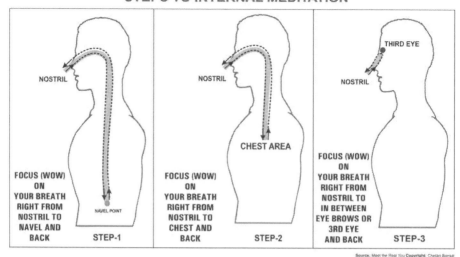

Source: Meet the Real You Copyright: Chetan Bansal

Once you complete 120 breaths in these 3 steps, stop counting but still maintain your focus on your breath, slowly you will witness your breath becoming narrow. Now your breath movement is only at the nostril and ultimately, you will feel no breath as if you are not breathing. At this stage, your focus will move to one point and that is in between your eyebrows; the point of third eye or pituitary gland.

Or instead of above 3 steps you can just watch, observe and witness your breath giving your full focus without any counting and slowly, you will feel your breath movement gradually getting very narrow. First, it was up to your navel (stomach) from the nostril. Then, you will witness its movement up to base of your chest, then upper part of your chest, then up to your throat, then the movement of your breath will become very narrow just confined within your nose, then only to nostrils and ultimately, you will feel no breath as your focus comes on one point, i.e., 3rd eye.

So, your focus has reached your 3rd eye. You feeling zero breath does not mean that you are not breathing, just that your focus has shifted from breath to 3rd eye and your breathing is obviously happening. At this stage, the number of thoughts within you would be very less or some would even experience zero thoughts or there would be no disturbing thoughts. All depends upon the degree of your focus. Whatever you may experience, you must consciously focus on this point in between your eyebrows or if you have not reached this point just keep on focusing on your breath. The longer you stay in this state the better would be the results. **But you don't have to worry about the results you just need to focus on your breath.**

The direct benefits of this technique are two which will result in many other benefits given at the end of technique.

1) Once the negative thoughts go or your focus is on breath or on third eye, you will achieve a peaceful, restful mind where you will draw

immense **cosmic energy** as there are no hindrances due to low frequency vibrations associated with negative thoughts and emotions.

2) **The 3rd eye is a connecting link between you and the universe,** it is centre of your perception, focusing on this point for longer periods laser sharpens your perception, removes all negative beliefs and it makes you see things as they are without any bias.

CLOSING: After staying long enough in the meditative state, you can come out of it but by following a simple process. Never open your eyes instantly, first say in your mind that **"I am now coming out of this meditative state by counting 1 to 10"**. Then, count 1 to 10 slowly, approximately at the speed of one count per second. Then slowly open your eyes.

WHAT YOU WILL EXPERIENCE PHYSICALLY & EMOTIONALLY? Once you achieve the meditative state where you start to absorb energy from the cosmos; **1)** you will feel some energy movements in your body as if some magnetic movements or goose bumps near your naval or entire body **2)** your body will become warm **3)** you will feel peace/calmness/serenity in your mind **4)** you won't feel the presence of your body as if your body is under the influence of anaesthesia **5)** you will feel yourself everywhere as if there is nothing else but only your consciousness **6)** many creative thoughts/ideas may come to your mind regarding any aspect of your life like relationships, career, profession, wealth which you should note on some paper or any digital medium, who knows what million dollar idea it may turn out to be **7)** you might also witness rotating rings of light having mix of yellow, bluish and black colour just like colour of fire flame. In between those rings, you might also witness some images, pictures or videos. But how can you see something with closed eyes, this is just an indication that you have deeply connected with your subconscious/deep memory and you might be witnessing some images present in your deep memory and this could be a process of deleting/washing all your bad negative memories/beliefs. Whatever you may witness or experience, don't think about it, just keep your focus on your breath or your 3rd eye point and enjoy the flow.

Once you are deeply connected, you forget everything like the place where you are doing meditation, the duration of sitting, all your thoughts/worries etc. During the meditation process, time runs very fast without you being aware of it as you might think that you have been sitting for say 15 minutes. But actually, if you note the starting and closing time of your meditation, don't get surprised if it is like say 50 minutes. This indicates that you focus and connection was very good having your mind completely in the present moment; a timeless journey. **Verify it yourself** when you are fully focussed in some/any activity and during sound sleep you always experience timelessness.

PROBLEMS DURING MEDITATION: People complain that when they try meditation, they are not able to stop their thoughts and they give up on meditation. One thing is sure, thoughts will come and you can't stop them as stopping thoughts means stopping your mind. **Meditation may not stop your thoughts but surely raises the degree of your thoughts by raising your consciousness.** So, it is normal to have thoughts during meditation. Do not worry or bother about it. The thoughts may be negative/bad/disturbing or good but the key is that you should not bother about thoughts, let them come and don't resist your thoughts. The more you resist your thoughts, the more will follow. You might also feel some itching somewhere in your skin at the beginning of the technique, you just need to ignore it or do itch once, but the second time, you need to ignore it and keep your focus on the breath.

These are just the games of egoistic mind which does not want to lose its identity and wants to divert focus from meditation. Do not bother, just keep on doing the process without any resistance, irrespective of any physical/mental distraction and accept every thought coming to your mind, best would be to consciously shift your focus to your breath again. **The more you sit and focus on your breath, irrespective of any thought, the better becomes your focus and meditation becomes a child play for you.** So, practice it again & again and with every passing day, increase your time of meditation. **This is the only key to mastery, nothing else.**

DURATION OF TECHNIQUE: This is a basic technique and very useful. The advance state of this technique is only when we increase the time of our *Dhyana*/focus/meditation, you can increase its time to say 30, 40, 60, 90, 120 minutes or more. It all depends upon your interest. The best said about its ideal time is the minutes = age. For example, if someone age is 40 years, then he/she should do it for at least 40 minutes and people with age of 25 years should do for 25 minutes and so on.

FREQUENCY: Start doing today the above for at least 20 minutes any time during the day but preferably on waking up or just before sleep to experience the benefits of meditation. And keep on increasing the duration with every passing day.

SUMMARY OF PROCESS: Close your eyes, relax your body, relax your mind, take a 3-4 deep breaths, start focusing on your breath, watch your breath, and just observe your breath. Witness your breath, amazing breath, and keep on observing your breath. If a thought comes, do not resist but consciously take your focus back on to your breath, experience the magic of observance, being aware of everything, anything inside you through nothing but your beautiful breath.
BENEFITS: The benefits of above techniques are amazingly and wonderfully positive on your body, emotions, mind and intellect.

1) Meditation makes your normal breathing pattern DLS. It also detoxifies all your body cells.
2) You will feel energetic all day long, your urge to overeat will reduce and your sleep time will also reduce.
3) Your body postures will improve immensely leading to vertical alignment and activation of energy chakras.
4) Your nervous system, circulatory system, excretory system, endocrine glands, immune system, digestive system and all body systems will start to function normally.
5) Biochemistry of your blood will become normal & natural leading to increase in feel good factor and happiness quotient.
6) Focus of your mind will become laser sharp where you are able to give your full focus in every work you do.
7) Your communication skills will improve immensely.
8) Positive emotions of gratitude, happiness, kindness, faith, celebration, love, forgiveness, acceptance, surrender will become your way of life.
9) Negative emotions of hate, procrastination, undue anger, jealousy, envy, all negative beliefs, negative memories, disempowering soft-wares which were causing failures and miseries in your life will disappear from your life; it is like cleaning your personal space of all negativity.

FOCUSING ON YOUR BREATH OVER A PERIOD OF 20 MINUTES SUPERCHARGES your brain, vertebrae, nerves, chakras, endocrine glands. And once all chakras are balanced/energized, it activates right thoughts, right emotions leading to right perception/decisions/actions in your life. It also balances your nervous system, your endocrine system, digestive systems, circulatory systems, excretory systems, and in fact, all your body systems start to work in a most natural way leading to a healthy body & mind. In fact, meditation if done on a routine basis can immensely enhance your energy field/aura which can ultimately enhance your physical, mental and spiritual well-being. All in all, meditation gives back the steering of your life to your nature, **THE REAL YOU** which sets your life on automatic path leading to success and growth in all areas of your life viz. HWRC.

THE KEY TO SUCCESS OF ALL MEDITATIVE TECHNIQUES is not to focus on results and/or not to focus on distractions but to focus on the technique, do it on regular basis. Initially, for a period of 40 days, do it thrice a day to activate your energy field. Once activated; you can always reduce the frequency to twice or once a day but a regular practice is must to continue and to maintain the energy field and thus, enjoy the benefits. **The first 40 days of regular practice with discipline is the key to the development of your meditation skill and then it will be like a child's play for you.** With growing experience of your meditation, your love for meditation enhances where it automatically becomes your habit like you bath and brush your teeth on daily basis. Once experienced, it can give you pleasure beyond your imagination and to experience you must practice and only practice.

C). SHORT MEDITATION
Sometimes, we may not have enough time to go about the full breathing and meditation technique. Suppose you are in office or traveling or doing something where you have very less time to relax and rest. Well, in that case, even 3-5 minutes of meditation can give you tremendous amount of much needed relaxation and energy. The technique is very simple as you have already learnt.

Technique: Close your eyes, relax your body, relax your mind, take a 3-4 deep breaths, and start focusing on your breath. Watch your breath, just observe your breath, witness your breath, amazing breath, and keep on observing your breath. If a thought comes, do not resist but consciously take your focus back on to your breath, experience the magic of observance, being getting aware of everything, anything inside you through nothing but your beautiful breath.
Do it just for 3-5 minutes and experience the magic.

D). SLEEP MEDITATION
After lying down on your bed you can practice this sleep meditation for a healthy, sound sleep.
Step1: Start with a short meditation technique explained above for 2-3 minutes.
Step2 Affirmations: Then consciously start speaking in your mind, "Oh my dear God, thanks for solving all my problems, fulfilling all my needs and making my life a happy, prosperous and joyous journey; I love you for that".
REPEAT THIS ATLEAST 7 TIMES.
Step3 Affirmations & visualisations: Now I am going into a deep sleep. Oh! God thanks for giving me a healthy, sound, deep sleep. Say this for 5-6 times and then **just visualize this,** "Imagine a digital clock lying on your bedside, imagine you getting up, grabbing the clock and then setting morning wakeup alarm say at 5.30 a.m. and then keep the clock back on bedside. Now imagine yourself going in to deep sound sleep and then imagine your-self waking up at 5.30 am feeling very happy & energetic and thanking the God for the same."
Step4: Just keep your eyes closed and keep your focus on your breath, soon sleep will take over
Notes:
1) The above technique is a mental sleeping technique where you set up your mind clock to the wake up time of your choice.
2) It is a virtual clock of imagination in your mind and not a real clock.

3) Everything about the technique you need to do while lying down with closed eyes.
4) Wake up time you have to decide by yourself, above 5.30 a.m. is just an example.
5) In the above technique, you can use subconscious mind, *the Real You*, God, Divine or any power you believe in. Me using God here is just my choice.

E). AFFIRMATIONS FOR POSITIVE MINDSET OR INFLUENCING THE MIND POSITIVELY OR MEDITATION FOR MAKING YOUR LIFE A HAPPY, PROSPEROUS AND JOYOUS JOURNEY.

Speak affirmations in your mind quietly 3 times a day and particularly just before sleep and immediately on getting up in the morning. Doing **affirmations for positive mindset and happy life** on a daily basis brings about a positive change in your subconscious mind leading to positive changes in life. Doing affirmations after internal breath meditation or short meditation enhances the speed of results. Or you can do affirmations directly also, choice is always yours.

My mind, body and soul are always synchronised & harmonised, having permanent connection with the divine.

All my actions, reactions, decisions, attitude, behaviour, beliefs, habits are guided by divine and are constantly giving me immense happiness, health, wealth, peace, prosperity, harmony, strength and power in life.

All my thoughts & feelings are positive, optimistic, strong and permanent. I am the master of my thoughts. All my thoughts and feelings are constantly giving me immense happiness, health, wealth, peace, prosperity, harmony, strength and power in life.

My emotions are steady and under my control. All my emotions are constantly giving me immense happiness, health, wealth, peace, prosperity, harmony, strength and power in life.

My mind is very active, cool & calm, each & every moment/second of my life. It is under my control and is constantly giving me immense happiness, health, wealth, peace, prosperity, harmony, strength and power in life.

My focus is on my personal growth, on solutions, on prosperity and on happiness of all. Instead of all problems/distractions, I keep on moving forward, improving myself, learning new skills and achieving newer & newer heights with a never give up attitude in life.

I love, help, understand, respect and forgive myself and others in my life.
My body language, my communication skills and sense of humour is always perfect.

I am rich, was rich and shall always remain rich forever in my life; this life and all lives.

My mind & body are perfect, were perfect and shall always be perfect, forever in this life and all lives.

I am happy, was happy and shall remain happy forever in this life and all lives.

I am thankful to all the people & situations in my life for they has always taken care of my financial, emotional needs, intellectual and spiritual needs.

With every breath I take, I am becoming younger, more beautiful, healthier, wealthier, intelligent and happier in life.

Oh god! Thank you for everything you have given to me in life. Life is a wonderful journey and it's amazing when you hold on to my hand. Oh god! Just keep on holding my hand forever in this life and all lives. Thank you from the bottom of my heart, thank you from the bottom of my heart. Thank you, thank you and thank you!

8.7 DISEASE: CAUSE & CURE

WHAT IS DISEASE? Any abnormality in physical structure and malfunction of any, one, many or all cells/tissues/organs or particular part of the body or body as a whole is what we call disease. **Disease is never natural or automatic but the only thing natural and automatic is your healthy mind & body. What does it mean?** It means that the nature of your body is to remain healthy & happy and it never wants any disease. Disease is an unnatural phenomena caused by unnatural/unhealthy way of living induced by an unaware human mind.

What are foreign bodies or disease-causing microbes? Any micro-organism or any chemical or many drug or any unnatural food etc. or all having physical structure not friendly to your body cells is called a foreign body. **All the microbes like viruses, bacteria, fungi etc. are foreign bodies having the potential to harm your body causes various infections & diseases.**

Pro-biota or disease-fighting or helping bacteria in your body: The pro-biota is the family of friendly bacteria living in your body. These bacteria live in your nose, mouth and maximum in your gut (stomach & intestine) but these bacteria lives only in a healthy body. **The pro-biota** in your body helps in 2 ways: **1) in the complete & easy digestion of food and 2) help in killing harmful viruses and other disease causing bacteria.** The moment the number of positive/healthy bacteria in your gut reduces immensely or become zero; your immune, digestive and all body systems becomes weak. **Remember just one thing that taking high percentage of raw vegetables and fresh fruits in** your daily diet not only increases the number of pro-biota in your gut but also makes your immune, digestive and all your body systems perfect & healthy.

Working of immune system: It is an involuntary, automatic defence system to protect against any foreign body or microbe or both and it is also healing system of your body to heal and recover from various ailments & diseases. Your body is super intelligent and it knows exactly how to deal with any kind of threat and maintain a healthy disease free body.

Your super intelligent body recognizes cells which are compatible with it, accept & absorb it. Your immune system will do everything/anything to remove any foreign particle or microbe from your body and heal any injury. **To understand its action, let's divide it in two parts A and B.**

A) PHYSICAL CUTS & INJURIES

Whenever some cut/injury happens on your skin, your immune system heals it automatically, although, sometimes some oral medicines and or application of local ointments and/or liquids are required to prevent the infection from various microbes. But one thing is sure that healing happens automatically. Sometime pustules appear on the site of cut/injury which is nothing but white blood cells (WBC) which absorbs and prisons all the microbes in it. These are all natural defence mechanism of your body to protect against infections.

--**Whenever some bone fracture occurs, your immune system re-joins the bone**, the plaster done by doctors is just a support to your bone so that it does not get displaced from its original place, so that once it joins automatically, it remains in its original shape & position.

The swelling, pain, inflation, fever etc. associated with any injury are just the natural responsible actions of your immune system to cure and heal the injury which takes its due course of time.

B) INFECTIONS INSIDE BODY

Many disease-causing viruses & bacteria are easily killed and removed from your body by your healthy immune system.

--Whenever some foreign particles or harmful microbes enter your nose, **you sneeze.**

--Whenever some foreign particles or harmful microbes enter your throat or lungs or both, **you cough.**

--Whenever some foreign particles or harmful microbes enter your stomach/gut, **you vomit or remove it through loose motions.**

--Whenever some foreign particles or harmful microbe is able to escape all above actions and enters your blood stream, it may cause infections in one or many organs leading to pain, swelling, inflation, fever etc. **So, all above actions of your immune system are natural response/reactions to defend against any infection/disease caused by any microbe.** The above are also symptoms of the presence of some kind of microbe in your body and not disease in itself. The fever (rise in temperature of your body) is not a disease but an immune response to kill the infection-causing microbe (which cannot live in high temperature) in your body. The fever & other symptoms subsiding early means your immune system is healthy and has successfully removed the foreign body/microbe from your body.

The beauty of your immune system is such that it can successfully fight and kill almost all types of microbes. The severe symptoms of high fever, severe pain and, or constant vomiting and, or constant diarrhoea or all may happen only on first interaction with the microbe and the next time, the same microbe is not able to cause any symptoms or only cause mild symptoms and is easily killed by your immune system. **How is it so?** On first interaction with any microbe your immune system, naturally & automatically, it **develops antibodies against that microbe/antigen.** Next time, when the same microbe attacks your body your immune system already having antibody against it developed during the first encounter, easily fights and kills that microbe. **It simply means that your body has become resistant to that microbe/foreign body which cannot cause any infection next time. This is what we call self/auto-immunization against the microbe.** This is how super natural intelligence of your body work making it capable enough to fight any attack by any foreign body.

Understanding the chronology of infections from new born to adulthood: You must have seen children getting frequent infections in childhood which keep on reducing with the age and ultimately, becomes almost zero. During childhood, they interacted with many microbes/bacteria/viruses for the first time which caused various infections but they also developed antibodies against them leading to very low symptoms or no symptoms next time. And almost after 7+ ages, every person looks healthy or you can say has developed resistance against almost all microbes. *Letting the child play in open spaces, on mud or with mud, in green fields/parks is the sure way to interact and develop friendship with many microbes; the more they are given the chance to interact with the microbe, the stronger becomes their immune power through a process called auto-immunization.*

But sometimes, during the first interaction with the microbe, the intensity and duration of symptoms increases and may become life threatening, **particularly in new-born babies.** So, as a preventive measure against almost all deadly microbes, all new born babies are given vaccinations. **Now what are vaccinations? A vaccination is a small dose/load** of natural microbe injected in the body of a human either through oral drops or injections. Some vaccines, but not all may cause mild fever, pain, swelling etc. as an automatic response of your immune system to kill that microbe but in the process it leads to the development of antibodies, making your body immune to that microbe.

But if an adult is not able to fight any microbe, it clearly means that he is having a **poor immune system and is already suffering from many chronic diseases. So the presence of the disease makes the immune system**

weak. A person free of diseases always has a healthy immune system. Till now, we have read about infections from microbes, immune system and foreign bodies etc. and you must be wondering there are so many diseases other than microbial infections but why I have not talked about them? Yes, **you are right,** there is lot of other diseases which might be more lethal than infections from microbes but studying the immune system first was the most basic and fundamental way to understand almost all the diseases; their causes & cures.

CAUSE OF A DISEASE: The presence of disease is due to the imbalance of five elements in the body which leads to some deficiency or accumulation of toxins in the body. This cause of imbalance in your five elements is due to, **1) your uncontrolled, unfocussed negative thoughts which changes your cell structure negatively OR 2) your defective digestive system induced by your unaware, unhealthy eating habits OR both.**

1). UNFOCUSSED, UNCONTROLLED NEGATIVE THOUGHTS: A weaker mind or mind with an emotional disturbance loses its inability to deal with difficult life situations leading to negative emotions of illusionary fear, anxiety, stress etc. Disturbance in emotions causes internal resistance, makes you sad leading to depletion of vital energy. The low vital energy leads to weakening of cells/tissues/organs which ultimately makes your immune system and all systems of your body defective leading to almost all diseases. Almost all diseases start at a subtle level which becomes physical & visible over a period of time.

2). DEFECTIVE DIGESTIVE SYSTEM DUE TO UNAWARE UNHEALTHY EATING HABITS. When you eat too much of cooked food, animal protein, fast food, chemically-processed food with very less or nil quantity of fresh fruits & raw vegetables, this is what happens in your body:-
a). Nutritional imbalance: The above food are not complete food in itself has very less or nil nutrients or leads to nutritional imbalance leading to unhealthy, weak and disease prone cells and body.
b). Unhealthy digestion: The above food has very less water content, is very slow to digest and does not fulfil the nutritional need of your body and in anticipation of its natural/balanced/nutritional food, your body keeps on asking for more & more food and you keep on eating more & more and you overeat. All above factors leads to slow/defective digestion and accumulation of toxins/fats over a period of time making you obese.
c). Presence of disease causing bacteria and very less or nil positive bacteria: The above food is not natural food to positive bacteria which dies in the absence of its natural food. And once the positive bacteria dies, negative/disease causing bacteria automatically rises in your gut. The absence of positive bacteria weakens or slows down digestion and increases the disease causing bacteria & viruses in your body which otherwise, would have

easily been killed by positive bacteria. **So, your digestive system and immune system become weak and defective in the absence of their very loyal and powerful warriors (pro-biota).**

All this leads to the accumulation of toxins, absence of positive biota in your gut and overall body which leads to weaker digestive system, nutritional imbalance in cells making your body a perfect host for many diseases like obesity, high blood sugar, high blood pressure, high cholesterol etc. **The above may sound simple life style disease but are actually root cause of all other diseases and if not cured or allowed to remain in your body will keep on weakening your cells/tissues/organs and ultimately, cause organ failures like** cardiac failure, kidney failure, brain strokes, etc., disease like cancer and severe microbial infections due to weaker organs and body systems, particularly the immune system. The list is endless. Medical professionals had given many names to diseases based on the symptoms and the organs they affect. **Our focus here is not to know all the names but just to understand the root cause of all diseases** so that we can work on root to cure or prevent almost all diseases. All these can lead to untimely/unnatural death of a person.

How lifestyle diseases weaken your immune system? See, when there are internal health issues your vital force energy is consumed in repairing and normalizing your body organs and it does not have enough time & energy to deal with the external threat. **For example, a country with many internal problems** spends all its time and energy in resolving internal issues, its defence system becomes weak making it prone to attack by other countries. Then, even the friendly looking, militarily weaker smaller countries may try to seize the opportunity which might attack and cause severe damage to the country. **Same way, millions, billions and trillions of bacteria, viruses and other microbes** are a part of your body being always present in and outside your body that are living peacefully without causing any harm to you. But once you suffer from many lifestyle diseases that make your body organs defective and immune system weak. A weak immune system becomes incapable of handling infections caused by otherwise friendly bacteria or viruses present in your body.

All the diseases are all result of imbalance in 5 elements caused by **unhealthy digestive system and unhealthy mind.** An unhealthy digestive system is a result of unhealthy/unnatural eating and unhealthy mind is a result of constant negative thinking. **As the health of your digestive system and mind is in your control only you are to be blamed or your unawareness about your mind & body is to be blamed.** If you have survived even after such bad eating & negative thinking habits over a period of long time, you are immensely powerful and you being alive today proves that. But you might be carrying many diseases, taking many medicines on regular basis which might be making life difficult for you. But you can reverse any or most diseases, let's see how?

We just need to remember one thing i.e. the cause of all diseases is just one and that is the imbalance of all the five elements in your body. Excess or low of one or more elements causes either accumulation of toxins or deficiency in body. If you can maintain the balance of the five elements in your body, no disease can even think of entering your body. Or if you are suffering from any diseases it means that your body is carrying many toxins. Whatever the case may be, the only solution is to balance your five elements by following natural way of life; **righteous intake of food, water, physical exercise, spiritual attitude (right thought process), right rest to mind & body, right practice of breathing exercise.** This all will balance the five elements making your cells, tissues and organs natural & healthy again, removing all toxins and fulfilling all deficiencies ultimately leading to healthy disease free mind & body.

The focus here is particularly on digestive system, to cure/free yourself from almost all types of diseases. Now, we have two ways to cure almost all types of diseases: **1) Cure through natural food & positive thinking 2) Cure through modern science & medicine.** Both have their own importance depending upon the severity of the diseases. **Cure through natural food is the best way to reverse, prevent and maintain a healthy disease free body for lifelong but in case of severe medical conditions, life threating emergencies etc., there is a role for modern science & medicine. So here, we will understand both.**

1). CURE THROUGH NATURAL FOOD & POSITIVE THINKING
A simple, natural, cost effective and the best solution to live a healthy, disease-free life. Now from the above, you must have understood that you need to balance the five elements by maintaining a healthy digestive system and by steadying your emotions. This will surely enhance the vital force/life energy, thereby strengthening your immune system which can easily reverse & prevent diseases and maintain a healthy mind & body.

A) Prevention/Cure through positive thinking/mind energy or spiritual healing for any/all physical & mental diseases: Your mind creates, controls and can also destroy your each & every cell, tissue, organ of your physical body. Your mind commands and control each & every moment of your body. See, when you want to walk, talk, run, lie down, sleep etc. a thought/information is passed from your brain to your body through nerves. So, you are controlling every body movement of yours by directing and controlling your cells/tissues/organs. **You must be wondering that you never told your body to become unhealthy but how has it manifested diseases? 1)** Wrong knowledge/unaware thoughts about eating leads to unhealthy eating and **2)** the inability to handle difficult life situations leads to **disturbance in emotions which** cause serious depletion of vital energy which develops energy blocks leading to unhealthy cells, tissues, organs and body. Thus, to maintain a healthy body and cure/heal/rejuvenate the damaged/disease-ridden cells, you need to steady your emotions and at the same time, practice conscious positive affirmations to prevent/cure all diseases. This is the basic concept of spiritual healing.

SPIRITUAL HEALING AFFRIMATION TECHNIQUE "Close your eyes, relax your body, relax your mind, take a 3-4 deep breaths, start focusing on your breath, watch your breath, just observe your breath, witness your breath, amazing breath and keep on observing your breath. If a thought comes, consciously take your focus back on to your breath, experience the magic of observance, being aware of everything, anything inside you/within you through your beautiful breath." **Do it for 3-5 minutes and then start speaking in your mind, "I am thankful to God for a perfectly healthy body & mind. All my cells/tissues/organs/body were, are and shall always be perfectly healthy, happy & fine, forever in this life and all my future lives. With every breath I take, I am becoming more & more young, beautiful, healthy, happy, vibrant and full of life energy."**

DURATION: Do repeat the affirmation for at least 9 times, the more you repeat the better it is.

FREQUENCY: At least 3 times a day after waking up, before lunch, and before sleep.

RESULT OF THE AFFIRMATION:

a) Will lead to increase in the vital force/life energy and a positive affirmation/thought will give positive energy to your cells helping them heal faster.

b) Will give you the intelligence to make best/perfect decisions/actions for your health.

c) Your positive vibrations will attract all information, knowledge & peoples in the form of doctors, books, seminar etc. that are perfect for the cure of your diseases.

B). Cure through natural food: Now, if you minutely observe, we need to do "something" which will **a) balance the nutritional** requirement of body so that each and every cell of body remains healthy, **b) make digestive system healthy** so that no toxins gets accumulated in the body, **c) increase the percentage of healthy/positive bacteria** in your gut which not only helps in digestion but also kills many disease causing bacteria & viruses. And that "**something**" is nothing but the right/natural food & water habits that we learnt in section 6.1 of this book. **Plant based diet with fresh fruits & raw vegetables as your major diet being 50-70% of your whole day diet will lead to:-**

i) Nutritional balance: Raw vegetables & fresh fruits being wholesome i.e., it takes care of nutritional balance having all the vitamins, minerals, carbs, proteins etc., all that your body requires. **Eating all regional & seasonal fruits & raw vegetables ensures complete balanced nutrition.** If we limit the food intake to one or two or three variety of food your body might miss some vitamins, minerals, carbs, proteins etc. and maximum variety ensures wholesomeness. Your job is to just treat your body with all varieties of seasonal & regional fresh fruits & raw vegetables, instead of worrying and calculating what vitamins, minerals, carbs, proteins it has and in what percentage. **Your body being super intelligent draws & absorbs everything exactly in the percentage that it needed by it in the balanced form during digestion.** Your body needs variety, provide it and let it decide what it wants to absorb and what it wants to reject & throw out of the body. This ensures nutritional balance leading to a healthy, strong and disease-free cells and body.

ii) Healthy digestion: The above food has maximum water content, thus, very fast in digestion leading to the complete removal of waste & toxins from your body on a daily/regular basis. So, your body weight automatically becomes ideal.

iii) The presence of positive bacteria and very less or nil negative bacteria: The fresh fruits and raw vegetables are the natural fibrous food which leads to the growth and maintenance of positive biota in your gut. **They help in fast & effective digestion;** eat the fibre in raw food, separate the nutrients from food to be absorbed by your blood stream and helps in fast removal of food waste from your gut. **This biota also helps in killing many disease-causing bacteria and viruses,** helping your immune system immensely in fighting infections. So, pro-biota is boon to your digestive system, immune system and thus, overall health of your body.

Instead of cooking the raw food in manmade kitchen, let it be cooked in the internal/natural kitchen of your body; let your teeth perform the function of the knife, grinder, mixer & juicer, let it get mixed with the natural water (saliva) in your mouth, like you mix water when you cook food and let the cooking be done by the fire inside your stomach.

     For a diet chart, create your own combination of food, sequence of food, frequency of food, quantity of food, temperature of food, water intake rules, you can refer to FOOD & WATER SECTION 8.1. The above system will lead to almost complete reversal of almost all lifestyle diseases like high BP, obesity, high cholesterol, high blood sugar etc. and in almost 1 to 3 months with freedom from regular medicines and will also bring back the energy, vigour & vitality of all your body cells/tissues/organs. Your all body systems like digestive, immune, circulatory, excretory, endocrine etc. will become normal & healthy again. And the positive results will become visible in just 4-5 days. **The time taken to cure any or all diseases will depend upon the severity of the diseases, the degree of damage already done in the particular organ or organs or the complete body and your disciplined actions.**

     If the degree of diseases present in your body is very severe, you need to eat 90% of your daily diet as natural diet and if it is medium 70% and if low 50%. But your daily percentage of natural raw food has to be minimum 50% irrespective of you being healthy or unhealthy so as to

maintain healthy body lifelong. So, natural lifestyle is sure way to live a healthy life and prevent almost all types of diseases.

But then what is the role of modern medicine? The role of modern medicine is immense when it comes to helping you deal with many life threatening diseases, organ threatening diseases and/or in case of accidental emergencies etc. Let's see how?

ROLE OF MODERN MEDICINE/SCIENCE TO CURE DISEASES

Many people think that they have learned a natural way of life and they can reverse all diseases, they can but only if they are ready to change their bad habits and are ready to take expert advice of doctors.

A doctor is a doctor, an expert in the field of medicine, understands body, its functions, role of nutrition and role of medicines perfectly, they have spent almost 8 to 10 years in learning the science of human body and are practicing doctors with enhanced knowledge coming from experience. So, it is always advisable to take advice of expert doctors if your disease is severe or you are on regular medicine of any kind may be it is of high BP, high blood sugar, high cholesterol etc. The doctor could be an allopath or naturopath, the choice is yours with only one condition that a doctor must have a valid medical degree and practicing license. Tell them that you now want to practice a natural diet, discuss & share your diet plan with them and they will make changes in your medicines accordingly. It is not that the above food practice will cause any harm to your body but if you are on medication, then the medicine needs to be reduced/altered once you move from unnatural/unhealthy to natural/healthy diet, not doing so will harm your body.

All doctors always want their patients to be healthy and happy. Normally, people ignore the advice of doctors; the precautions, food habits, physical exercise and other changes in lifestyle they prescribe to live a disease free healthy life. A poor doctor is left with no choice but to give you medicines on a regular basis which he never wanted to, as many times, he warned and cautioned you about the side effects of these medicines. These medicines can never cure your diseases but gives temporary relief from symptoms or delay the dire/severe consequences which are inevitable in the absence of your conscious shift in your life style from unhealthy to healthy.

All lifestyle diseases, if left uncontrolled, not cured or reversed may lead to severe infections, severe organ damage, development of huge lump of cancerous cells (tumours), majorly blocked arteries & veins etc. and accidents/injury are all medical emergencies which needs to be treated with the help of modern diagnostic tools, life support systems, modern surgeries and modern medicines like antipyretic (in case of high fever/temperature), antibiotic (in case of high bacterial infections), anti-inflammatory (in case of severe inflammation), analgesic (in case of unbearable pains) etc. I mean your first aim should be to save your life which need timely precise laser sharp action and once you are safe with the help of modern medicine & surgery, you can start your normal natural way of living, so that you remain healthy & happy thereafter and forever with less or no burden on doctors & society.

The advancement in the medical science is a boon to the society where they have developed various amazing diagnostic and corrective tools/machines having instant successful results for the patients in emergency. Being preacher of natural lifestyle does not mean that we should not respect/value the tremendous amount of hard work, smart work where so many number of doctors, scientist, assisting staff have spent endless number of sleepless nights to bring back life & smile on the faces of endless number of patients suffering from endless number of diseases. We all salute, respect and appreciate them. And above all, use their valuable treatment to get instant relief from all the chronic, severe life and/or organ threatening diseases.

PRECAUTIONS & SIDE EFFECTS OF MODERN MEDICINES

Let's take the example of Antibiotics. Antibiotics are also foreign bodies and you know that your body throws out everything/anything which is alien to it. Your doctor knows it and gives a specific dose according to the weight and age of a person. These are all medical calculations for enforced absorption of antibiotics in your blood. If taken less dose or empty stomach, your intelligent body removes it through vomiting or loose motions or normal motions without getting absorbed in your blood, so infection won't be cured. When on an empty stomach, your vital energy is very high & vigilant and does not allow the entry of any foreign body into the blood stream but if you take the same antibiotic after eating food, your vital energy gets busy in digesting the heavy rush of food and might miss to act on the antibiotic and it gets digested & absorbed in your blood stream. When someone body does not accept the antibiotics even after taking food, doctors administer the antibiotic directly into the blood stream through injection. **This confirms that antibiotics are foreign bodies and needs to be taken with extreme care & precautions.**

Antibiotics, as name suggests is an anti-life but it is used to kill infection-causing bacteria in your body and its potency is very low which has a very little and temporary negative effect on your body. **Antibiotics though given to kill the infection causing bacteria but it also kills the positive healthy bacteria in your body. Almost all antibiotics are of broad spectrum which kills almost all kinds of micro-bacterium without any differentiation between good and bad bacteria.** That is why taking antibiotics over a period of long durations causes more harm to your body 1) by killing the pro-biota in your body which leads to unhealthy digestive system and weaker immune system 2) By making your own body cells/tissues/organs weak.

Bacteria develop resistance to antibiotics: The way your body develop resistance towards any foreign body, the same way the disease-causing bacteria in your body also develop resistance towards the antibiotics. So, to treat the same bacteria, we need to change the salt of the antibiotic. Again, after sometime, the bacteria develop resistance towards the changed antibiotic and you need to change the salt of antibiotic again. This way, almost all antibiotics become ineffective in the long run.

Maintaining your pro-biota is the ultimate solution to the problem of pro-biota being killed by antibiotics. So, antibiotics must be taken under medical supervision only, in severe infections and obviously not for long durations. **In case of severe infections along with taking antibiotics, you should increase natural fresh fruits and vegetable in your diet so as to maintain the presence and growth of positive bacteria in your body.** Probiotic drinks these days prepared in factories serve this purpose only but again, better to eat fresh fruits & raw vegetables, the best natural source of probiotics for your body which also provides nutritional balance.

Body also develops resistance against many other medicines & drugs if taken on a regular basis like for pain, sleep, anxiety, stress, alcohol etc. After some time, your body will start resisting these medicines and you may need to increase the dose/quantity of medicine to get the same effect. This is how people become addicted to most of the medicines and drugs. These medicines do not cure the disease but gives only temporary relief from the symptoms of the diseases. **The real solution is to increase the vital force of your body to reverse/cure all diseases and medicine with the side effects to be used under medical supervision for a temporary basis only.**

So, what is the ultimate solution to cure almost all the diseases? Cure through nature or modern medicines or both? The only solution is to adopt the natural way of life where you practice righteous food, righteous water, righteous breathing, and righteous thought process to balance all the five elements of your life. And also to use the tremendous amount of beneficial applications developed by the medical science and never forget to take the expert advice. The right responsible attitude of yours can cure, reverse and prevent almost all types of diseases; just your conscious presence is required in your PDA regarding the prevention and cure of any or all types of diseases.

8.8 PPLV

PHYSICAL BODY POSTURES, LANGUAGE AND VOICE (PPLV) FOR VERTICAL ALIGNMENT

The mind & body are connected: You must have seen the body language of a depressed or a sad person; their head & shoulders are down, shallow, short, fast (SSF) breathing pattern, they are not able to speak properly and they walk slowly. **On the other hand, a confident happy person** will always have smiling face, deep, long, slow (DLS) breathing pattern, head and shoulders up, they walk fast and they speak fluently, confidently.

What does that mean? **It means that the overall physiology; language, postures, voice, breathing pattern of people with positive and negative mindset is different.**

Mind & body of a person are connected through emotions. A positive, energetic, physical body will definitely bring about positivity in the mind of a person. Same way, the positive thoughts in your mind makes your body language energetic. Or a negative change in either mind or body will definitely have a negative impact on each other. This is the universal truth about your mind & body. So the mind, either happy or sad, it reflects on your body and vice-versa and if you consciously change your PPL, it will definitely change your mind.

And your PPL is under your control or you can consciously choose a positive body language, right physical postures and voice to raise the vibrations of your mind. Wow! If you are feeling sad, depressed, then you can bring about a change in your PPL to raise your mood, feel good factor and thus, mind instantly.

Changing your PPL positively smoothens and speeds up the flow of energy in your personal space and when energy rises in body, mind also gets the treat. Your body is an instrument/machine which runs on the fuel called energy. For the perfect functioning of each & every cell, tissue, organ, in fact, your whole body needs energy in each & every cell/part/corner/section of your body. The movement and flow of energy in your personal space depends upon the posture of your vertebrae, limbs, etc.

The centre lining of your physical body is where all the energy chakras, endocrine glands, nerves lies and all vital organs are situated either to the right or left of the centre lining. The optimum energy in the centre lining/core of your body ensures energy to each & every cell of your body. **Straight vertebrae lead to optimum flow of energy without any hindrances. Bends in vertebrae leads to hindrances and blocks the flow of energy.**

Don't believe me unless you try these simple tips to improve your PPL to enhance your energy, consciousness and wellbeing:-

Whenever you feel sad, low on energy, depressed consciously bring about a change in your PPL and best would be to adopt the following PPL in your habits:-

1) **Consciously practice smiling face all the time** even if you are not feeling happy inside.
2) **Consciously start breathing DLS** which ensures optimum amount of oxygen reaching each & every cell of your body.
3) **Consciously raise your head and shoulders, straighten your backbone:** Straight vertebrae/back all the time whether you are standing, walking, running, sleeping, sitting or doing anything.
4) **Keep a little focus in between your eyebrows each & every moment** of your life. This ensures your conscious presence and thus high vibrations in your personal space.
5) **Always walk fast** and straight.
6) **Voice: Consciously start speaking clearly**, loudly without any hitch. (Next Sec 8.8.1)

The moment you do that, you will start feeling the confidence, happiness and flow of positive thoughts within you. Keep on practicing these unless and until it becomes your permanent habit. This will always keep you high on energy and vertically aligned ensuring connection with your nature/spiritual space/source of life.

8.8.1 RAISING YOUR VIBRATIONS THROUGH VOICE FOR VERTICAL ALIGNMENT

Your voice plays an important role in influencing your mind and mind of others. **A mentally disturbed person has a low depressive voice or unclear words or aggressive voice or uses abusive language or abusive tone which cause disturbance in the mind of others also** and creates further negativity in his/her own mind. All in all, this causes depletion of energy. This leads to disconnection with your own spiritual space and spiritual space of the other person leading to miscommunication which leads to wrong understanding & perception and thus, leading to problematic relationships.

So, **if you are at the receiving end (means other is throwing tantrums at you),** then you must understand that the other person is mentally disturbed and needs your support, blessings and your positive response. Or if you cannot manage them, you should know how to ignore them and protect your mind from attracting the negativity of that person. **FTIPP** already learnt in PART-B of this book is the way to deal with all people & situations.

And **if your voice, tone is negative** means **you are giver,** then there is something bothering you inside, some negativity has become a part of your mind. You should first give a deep thought on what's bothering you, what is the root cause of that problem and remove that root cause. **For example,** if your frustration is due to your bad health, then you should take expert advice, medication if needed and change in your food habits to improve your health.

But the instant and most natural way to raise your vibrations is to make a conscious shift in your voice; choose your words, tone that are sweet, clear, loud, and strong. This shall convert your negative mindset to positive one leading to increase in your vibrations.

You must have seen a sports person consciously using some techniques of voice and body language to uplift a self-spirit if it is an individual sport or uplift self-spirit/spirit of other team members to uplift the performance instantly during the game. **Like high fives, high tens, jumping in air, punching the air, motivating self and other with good positive words.** This all activates the spiritual space of person and hence, enhances performance.

A mentally cool/calm/happy person has strong/clear/sweet voice, uses good language which also causes calmness in the mind of others. This leads to the connection with your own spiritual space and spiritual space of the other person leading to effective communication which in turn leads to perfect understanding, perception and thus, wonderful relations. And thus, enhances the overall happiness quotient of all.

THIS IS HOW A STRONG, POSITIVE VOICE AND BODYLANGUAGE INSTANTLY CONVERTS YOUR NEGATIVE MINDSET INTO A POSITIVE ONE AND BRING BACK THE MIND INTO THE PRESENT MOMENT.

8.9 GIVE TREAT TO YOUR SENSES

OF NATURAL ENERGY

It is through your five senses that all information enters and influences your mind. If the information is useful/truthful/beneficial, it impacts your mind positively, otherwise negatively causing emotional disturbance that disconnects you from your omnipotent eternal reality. The food that you eat, water that you drink, air you breathe, the smell of food, air and atmosphere around you, the interaction with people around you, the thoughts coming to your mind are all energy and the more it is close to the nature, the more energetic it will be. More energy means positive energy field and thus, ensures connection and vertical alignment.

1) **Cleanliness:** Maintain good cleanliness everywhere both inside you and outside you. Clean your mind of all negativity, regular cleaning of your mind, physical body, clothes that you wear, Home, office, car, public place, environment or any place or space that you are in. **More on it in NEXT SECTION 8.10**

2) **See, listen and read good:** Anything that makes you feel good, you must do that like listening to good music, watch good movies, knowledge enhancing shows, comedy shows, motivational shows, read good books, etc. Anything which makes you happy, anything which enhances your knowledge and thus, personal growth. Avoid any information which is depressing, which is not based on truth, which spreads hate/anger, anything that is against humanity. Even if you cannot avoid do not let that negative information influence you in any way.

3) **Eat Good:** Eat a food as natural as possible i.e. plant-based diet. You can also eat fast food, spicy food, sweets but in very less quantity and not on regular basis but as variety only.

4) **Smell Good:** Plant more plants & trees in and outside your house/office/everywhere to treat yourself with fresh air and fragrance of flowers. Use natural perfumes made from herbs and avoid artificial perfumes made from chemicals which may give good fragrance but may also turnout to be harmful to your mind/body/energy field in long run.

8.10 CLEANING INTERNAL & EXTERNAL SPACE

Once, all the negativity leaves your personal space the omnipotent eternal light present inside you rises and shines brightly permanently. This whole book is an antivirus which will clean all negativity from your personal space leading to real connection with your eternal omnipotent reality, "**THE REAL YOU**" which will take your life on the natural path of a purposeful, prosperous, joyous and successful journey.

In Hindus, it is a common belief, **"Where there is cleanliness, there is God or in spiritual terms, you can say there is energy and you know where there is energy, there is prosperity & happiness."** It is very important to clean and maintain that cleanliness in your **inner and outer space**. Your **inner space being your thoughts, emotions and physical body** and **outer space being the place/space where you live like home, office, work place or any other place you visit and spend time. And obviously, all places & spaces consists of the people you interact with, air you breath in, water you drink, flora & fauna that gives food to you, soil which gives space to you, and the complete universal environment & atmosphere.**

Imagine not bathing, even for a single day or not washing your hands for full day, how do you feel? Obviously you feel bad, low and at the same time, it's unhygienic which may lead to development of disease in your body. But what about cleaning of the negative thoughts & emotions which are draining all vital energy from your mind & body? What about the negative impact of company of bad people on your mind and, thus life? What about the effect of polluted environment; soil, water and air? What about the effect of imbalance in nature due to undue/unnatural/irrational killing of flora & fauna? What about effect of the destruction of various natural structures like mountains, forests, disruption of natural water bodies, etc.?

So, cleaning & maintaining each and every space is very important right from your personal space to all the universal spaces in your proximity because directly or indirectly everything inside you and outside you, it influences your mind & body and thus, life. If the environment, people and places in your life are good & positive you also become positive and thus, live a good life. The negative environment, negative people and places disrupt your mind and thus, caused havoc in your life.

As modern life is full of challenges and many things are not in your control, so everyone in life, irrespective of age, colour, caste, creed, sexes, socio-economic status etc. faces difficult times, negative people & situations which need a right response from your side. The only solution to fight any negativity is to maintain your own positive attitude by maintaining constant connection with your omnipotent eternal reality. And that connection is only possible by cleaning both your inner and outer space on daily/regular basis.

So you need to clean all negativity to maintain positivity in your life. These are the spaces that need regular positive action from your side to maintain cleanliness and thus positive life energy.

CLEANING BOTH INTERNAL AND EXTERNAL SPACES

S. NO	SPACE/PLACE CLEANING	INNER/OUTER	WHOSE KARMA/RESPONSIBILITY
1)	MENTAL HOUSE CLEANING	Inner space	Only You (Individual Karma)
2)	PHYSICAL BODY CLEANING	Interface of inner and outer space	Only You (Individual karma)
3)	HOME CLEANING	Outer space	You and all in the family (Family karma)
4)	CAR/VEHICLE CLEANING	Outer space	You or someone deployed by you(Individual karma)
5)	OFFICE/WORKPLACE/PUBLIC PLACE CLEANING	Outer space	You and all in the office/workplace (Joint karma)
6)	PEOPLE IN YOUR LIFE/SOCIETIES	Outer space	You and all in the society(Joint societal Karma)
7)	UNIVERSAL ENVIRONMENT CLEANING	Outer space	You and all in the society (Joint societal Karma)

Source: Meet the Real You **Copyright** Chetan Bansal

Start your day with mental house cleaning, then physical body cleaning, then either yourself or through someone take care of the cleanliness of all outer spaces.

1). Mental house cleaning: A spiritual attitude is a way to all positivity in life. But still, due to many challenging situations or hectic lifestyles stress sometimes become inevitable leading to disturbances in mind. To clean the all stress and negativity from your mind **along with the spiritual attitude,** you need to practice many techniques on a daily/regular basis.

    A) Meditation and Deep breathing techniques; already discussed

    B) Affirmations for positive mindset; already discussed

These techniques are like a **whistle of a pressure cooker** which removes all pressure, stress from your mind leading to optimum presence of life energy and thus, a healthy/conscious mind & body. **A mental house cleaning is the first and foremost cleaning that you must focus upon because it being the base/source to your automatic perfect actions for cleaning of all other spaces.**

2). Physical body cleaning like washing hands, bathing, sun bath, taking fresh air, eating healthy food, physical exercise, right water drinking habits on daily basis to maintain healthy disease free body and thus healthy life.

3). Home, car, office and other spaces cleaning: A good clean spaces smells good, free of disease causing microbes, insects & mosquitos, is a visual treat to your eyes which directly/indirectly give good feelings and raises your happiness quotient in life. This is what you can do.

A). Regular cleaning of buildings & spaces, putting garbage in designated containers or places with regular decomposition, reuse and recycle of all wastes.

B). Sort out everything: A place for everything and everything in place. Make a specific place for everything in your house and keep things only at specifically defined places. This not only make your wardrobes, sections, rooms, cabins and complete building look neat & clean but will also saves your time & energy on searching & retrieving all necessary stored stuff which, otherwise always seems lost in the absence of cleaning and sorting.

C). Remove all old stuff from your home/office which is no longer of any use to you like old cloths, old furniture, old crockery, old machinery etc. You can either sell these items or give to some needy people a sure way to earn blessings. This way, you will also create space for new useful items to enter in your valuable spaces.

4). Clean, service & preventive maintenance all your car/vehicles on daily, monthly, yearly basis and as & when required.

5). Clean, service & preventive maintains all the office places/public places, spaces, tools, machines, furniture on daily, monthly, yearly basis and as & when required.

6). People in your life/societies: Stay away from negative people & situations as everything and anything which you interact with on regular basis influences your mind and thus, life. This is the universal law of mind. **We all are copy cats and subconsciously, absorb the language, habits, behaviour, attitude, beliefs of the people we surround with.** Good & positive people have a positive influence on your mindset and negative people influences your mindset negatively.

A simple example to make you understand on how a human mind learns or grabs the information subconsciously from the people he/she is surrounded with. A person never needs to learn his/her mother tongue but a foreign language needs to be learnt and practiced over a long period of time, why is it so? Why is he proficient in his mother language even when nobody taught him and after taking so many lectures/classes of foreign language, he still struggles with it? The answer is simple, your subconscious mind absorbs, learns and becomes a master of whatever it encounters or exposed to on a regular basis. That is why repeated training helps a person become a master in anything. The best way to learn a foreign language is to surround your-self with the natives of that foreign language and best way to do that is to go and live in that country for at least 5-6 months. This is the best way to fast and accurate learning.

So, whatever types and company of people you are surrounded with, you subconsciously absorb their mind patterns that became your mind patterns which influences your perception, beliefs, decisions, actions,

reactions and determines the path/direction of your own life. So, it is your prime responsibility to choose people in your life wisely, otherwise it may have very negative impact on your mind and thus, life.

If we do not find company of good people, better to be alone rather than to be in bad company. A lonely person is with his inner world of thoughts, emotions and ideas. So when alone, spend your time to understand and change your inner world positively. Learn to enjoy your own company and if you can master that, no people or situation outside shall be able to disturb you in any way or by any means.

What if you are not able to remove negative people/situation from your life? You have to make yourself so much emotionally, mentally & spiritually powerful that you are not influenced by anybody or any negativity be it any. Well! In that case, it is your conscious presence which would even influence others positively.

Same way, you need to clean/remove all bad elements from your society/country/world. If you do not raise your voice and take appropriate action against any or all bad elements in your society, it will become dirty and will definitely cause havoc in everyone life including you either directly or indirectly. **Spiritual attitude, WOW focus, FTIPP** is the best way to deal with people & situation in your life be it your family, office and society.

7). Universal environment/spaces: It is your **prime responsibility to take care of the universal environment/spaces;** air, water, soil, all flora & fauna, water bodies, mountains, forests etc. And the best way to do that is not to interfere with their natural functioning, not to cause any pollution, no to disrupt the natural habitats of flora & fauna and not to disrupt the natural food cycles of prey predator relationships. If you try to disrupt the nature it will balance itself through natural calamities, diseases etc. which will ultimately bring pain & misery in your life.

Nature has created everything/anything with a purpose; everything/anything in this universe has a role, all help each other exist by fulfilling the needs of one another. Everything co-exists, you can't exist alone, and biodiversity is a must for you to survive. It is for your own good for the good of every life to prosper on planet. So, we just need to respect each and every creation of nature and nature will take care of you. By killing other creations of nature, by polluting the environment we are inviting problems for ourselves which will definitely show up in due time and has already started showing up. The intelligence of human mind is limited and can never compete with the nature; the creator. We must accept & respect all the creations of nature as it is. Nature runs on its laws, rules and regulations without any bias towards any of its creation and works on the law of karma. So, what you sow shall definitely come back to you. Now the choice is yours, whether you want to pollute/disrupt the nature or want to respect the nature.

A strong, positive mind may get negative thoughts but is unperturbed by them which forces the negative thoughts to run away. **A clean physical**

body inside out may be attacked by bacteria, fungus, or virus but in the absence of dirt/toxins, they run away. **A clean house/office/public place** is visited by rats, mosquito, insect etc. but in the absence of dirt, cluttered spaces, they run away. **Negative people & situations** with or without vested interests may try to influence you, but when you are not disturbed or unperturbed by them, they run away. **When the people & governance of any society is positive**, it promotes human values of equality, freedom and has strict laws against crimes then no bad elements can remain in that society, either all run away or are transformed positively.

Practice regular cleaning of your inner and outer space, make it your habit and you shall definitely experience a positive impact & happiness in your life. A neat & clean place/space is highly energetic, full of God's energy. Cleaning your inner and outer space ensures your conscious presence and connection with your omnipotent eternal reality; *THE REAL YOU*, the super intelligence of nature which no problem, challenge or negativity can withstand, be it any.

Spiritual attitude, the right/natural food habits, right intake of water along with regular physical exercise & rest, right breathing, meditation, healthy sleep, right physical body postures, language and right usage of voice etc. is a sure way to balance the five elements of your body and thus, a healthy body & mind. Within no time or very less time, say 10-15 days, a considerable positive change will be visible in your body; you will start feeling light/easy in your stomach, you will move towards your ideal weight, witness higher energy levels, increase in feel good factor, and your blood tests will witness positive changes in your blood sugar, cholesterol and other biochemical levels, your communication skills will improve, a visible improvement in your ability to deal with people & situations, money and time leading to overall improvement in your relations, job/career/profession which will motivate you further to practice healthy/natural/spiritual way of life, making it a lifelong habit in you. Any knowledge is incomplete without experience and continuous practice is the only way to experience right knowledge.

When it comes to bringing about positive changes in the society, many think of changing the others first or think that changing themselves won't bring about any change in others, so what is the use of changing my-self? That is the big problem, if everyone thinks like this, nobody will change. Okay, I understand the first ones need to be patient, may face many hardships, they need to be consistent in their positive responsible actions against all popular disempowering beliefs. It may take time but society can, will and shall change. But why worry about the change in others, it is your life if you want to live a joyous journey, then you must change and you reading this book this far prove that you want to change and millions, billions reading this book also proves that everyone wants to change; just your conscious presence is required.

So let's take a pledge.

"IT IS MY LIFE, I AM GRATEFUL TO THE NATURE FOR GIVING ME LIFE, MAINTAINING MY LIFE, FULFILLING MY NEEDS AND I RESPECT & LOVE THE NATURE FOR THAT. I SHALL CHANGE MYSELF POSITIVELY AND I SHALL ALIGN MYSELF WITH MY NATURE. IT DOES NOT MATTER TO ME IF OTHERS DON'T WANT TO CHANGE, AS THAT IS THEIR CHOICE. MY CHOICE IS LIFE, MY CHOICE IS JOYOUS JOURNEY, MY CHOICE IS PURPOSEFUL JOURNEY AND MY CHOICE IS MY NATURE; A UNIVERSAL CONSCIOUSNESS, MY SOURCE/MY ROOTS/MY POWER, MY REAL ME."

The beauty of your eternal reality is such that it is always present within you, around you, above you, below you, to your left, to your right and everywhere/anywhere you can think of and once all the negativity starts leaving your personal space, it will automatically rise in you leading to an overall growth in your physical, mental, emotional and spiritual well-being, setting you on an automatic path of your life. So, never think it is too late to change; the moment you get the knowledge, the moment you start changing yourself is *NOW* perfectly destined for you, the best present the life has offered you, "***MEET THE REAL YOU***" waiting for your conscious presence to take conscious repetitive actions to transform your life positively forever...

9.0 A NEW BEGINNING

END OF BOOK BUT A NEW BEGNINNING FOR YOU, MY DEAR *REAL YOU*

It is time to practice whatever you have learned in this book. Keep on practicing, perfection comes only with practice. Read this book once, twice, thrice and even more number of times or refer it at any point of time in life. With practice it has all the power to transform your DNA positively towards success, growth, happiness and joy in life. It is a psychological fact that any change if practiced for 21 days continuously becomes your habit, for 40 continues days becomes part of your subconscious and for 3 continues years it becomes part of your DNA. So what are you waiting for my dear "Real You", destiny has already knocked your door. Destiny has given you the opportunity, take action now.

The foremost learning from this book is that **the destiny is in your hands**, nobody else but only you who creates and writes your own destiny. Everything that has happened, is happening, will happen is determined by your own thoughts (perception & decisions) and actions. Nobody else, only you are responsible for your own life. If you are not happy in life it is your responsibility to make yourself happy, nobody else will do it for you. And for making yourself happy you need to work on yourself; mind, body, energies, emotions, karma (PDA) for success in all areas of your life HWRC.

You learned everything about life; universal laws, source of life, mind, thoughts, emotions, beliefs, needs & wants, relations, how life became problematic, and the ultimate solution to all your problems is only one i.e. strengthening the connection with source simply by working on your FABP. Positive change in your FABP is the only secret to all the success, growth, happiness and joy in life. FABP is the input, under your control and determines the quality/degree of your energy & consciousness of your mind & body which determines your perceptions, beliefs, decisions, actions, habits, behaviour and thus results in life.

Your birth, death, functioning of vital organs, relations and situations in your life are not in your control. The only thing that you can control is your energy & consciousness. Your first, foremost and only focus must be to maintain your conscious connection with source, the creator of your mind & body and thus life. It knows everything about your life; past, future, hidden talents, purposes having solution to all your problems. Connecting with it enhances energy & consciousness, develops immense emotional & spiritual strength, laser sharp focus, memory, logic, intellect, intuitive powers, truthful perceptions, righteous decisions and actions in each & every moment and situation of your life. So once you enhance the degree of your connection, your life comes on an automatic/natural path of life where everything that is needed to your comes towards you in an effortless way rather than you chasing.

Due to your enhanced truthful PDA all unnecessary, undue, irrelevant problems will end in life. It's not so that now you will never experience problems, but you will find solutions in very easy, fast and effortless way or the problems that looked bigger to you earlier will now look small or problems will not bother you with the same intensity anymore. You may not avoid bad times but can surely shorten the span, reduce the intensity and reverse the bad times. It all depends upon the degree of mastery of your life skills dependent upon your degree of practice in real life situations.

With regular practice of spiritual FABP, your degree of mastery over life shall keep on increasing which will ultimately lead to success in the outer world making you lucky. This is what you should keep on practicing in life to master your life or to take charge of the steering of your life.

1) **Keep on maintaining a healthy, energetic, conscious mind & body** by practicing righteous FABP (Righteous food & water, Spiritual attitude & focus, DLS breathing, righteous physical body language, postures & voice) to balance 5 elements to maintain strong connection.

2) As **life is all about response to the situation** and for right response you must practice your conscious presence where you are fully focussed/present in each & every thought and action of yours. Keep on practicing WOW focus technique to master your conscious presence.

3) **Accept all your situations without any internal resistance** and maintain cool & calm of your mind. Internal resistance reduces your vital energy, creates emotional disturbances, disconnects with source leading to decrease in natural intelligence and thus biased PDA and miseries in life.

4) Use **WOW focus** to perceive the truth as it is, remove all disempowering beliefs and take conscious decisions & actions for right results in life.

5) Use **PPN scan** model to analyse and decide for any or all situations in life.

6) Use **3G to 4G model** to choose positive actions/habits in life.

7) Be **flexible in your thoughts & actions** and always decide & act for the benefit of self or others or all but without paining anyone.

8) Be **grateful for everything in life**, even your difficult life situations as these are nothing but blessings in disguise. It has come to teach you something, enhance your life skills and take you to the next level of success & growth in life.

9) **No problem is bigger or stronger than you**, you are extension of supreme nature which is source of life and has solution to every problem in life. You just need to have faith, determination, focus, patience and courage to live a happy & successful life.

10) The **best way to deal with people** is to listen to them first, understanding the situation/issue and then responding with a cool & calm mind. Practice conscious presence and FTIPP.

11) The **unknown zone of future may pose problems**, do not get perturbed or disturbed or worry about them, live moment by moment fully focused and consciously present, the super intelligent power inside will take care of anything/everything.

12) Every **problem comes with an opportunity** and being fully present/focused help tap that.

13) Life is a mix of ups and downs. **Failure is not to fall in life but not to stand up after the fall.** The real success is in maintaining inner peace, happiness, love & joy in life and keep on doing karma without expectations in life.

14) As this is life, we all face challenges and it is **absolutely normal to become sad, disturbed, uneasy or anxious in life** but we should never give permanent space to any negativity and must bounce back in life.

15) **Spend your time wisely;** give your time and energy on regular basis for continual growth of your mind, body, wealth, relations, and career/job/profession, hobbies and celebration in life.

16) Give **permanent space to your intentions, dreams, desires and goals** in your mind. Do not let any negativity/hurdles/distractions hamper your dreams be it external distractions in the form of people/situations or internal distractions of your mind. Don't stop and keep on taking positive actions with a never give up attitude in life.

17) Always remember to **help & support others** in whatever possible way without any expectations in return. Helping others is a source of immense happiness, peace, love, joy and blessings in life.

18) And lastly **love yourself and life** unconditionally.

Results will definitely come but the speed may vary depending upon your determination, speed & accuracy of your actions. But keep moving with righteous spiritual attitude & focus in life.

Having knowledge is one thing but applying knowledge is another thing; it is the next level of your evolution. Although knowledge and understanding is the base for taking right action but without action your knowledge is incomplete. It is through actions you get results, experience life which enhances your knowledge and life skills. So, real knowledge comes from experience of actions. But for right actions we need right knowledge, understanding and planning. Actions not backed by right knowledge lead to waste of time, energy, money and cause of failures & frustrations in life. So action without understanding & planning is very risky & dangerous and not taking any action even after having knowledge will never get results. **So both knowledge and action complete each other and your life journey is also incomplete without balance of both.**

Now my dear real you, I have shared with you my knowledge and understanding about life and now it's your conscious choice. But what will you choose, **it's already inside you waiting for you to be enhanced and**

expanded by you. The darkness in life is due to darkness in mind which can only be removed by light of awareness, knowledge and consciousness. Even a small candle can lit the whole dark room and my job was to just touch that eternal light within you which was just sleeping or not activated fully to its potential. Choice is yours, the very reading of this book has activated it in you and just holding on to it will expand it further. No matter what happens never let your light of consciousness sleep again in your life. Once it is expanded and enhanced to its full potential you will become your own guru/master/guide and you won't need anybody else to guide you, in-fact you will become guide and help to others.

It's your life, decide and start taking actions right now with your conscious presence without influence of anybody outside. Nobody else can decide for you or responsible for you but only you. Take charge of your life now, and start living the way you want. Living life your way is just a matter of your conscious choice and source of immense happiness, love, joy and success in life.

Nothing matters! Except living life your way
And to live life your way, MEET THE REAL YOU, the eternal secret to find
Meaning, Purpose, Everlasting Peace, Love, Joy, Success, Growth and
Happiness in Life
-Chetan Bansal

I shall keep writing books, blogs, articles etc. on different subjects for the purpose of helping people. This is my purpose, what is your purpose? Find and live yours.

Send your feedback/suggestions at bansalchetan911@gmail.com; this will help me improve my writings, books, blogs and contents on continual basis. You can also ask any question on the above mail and I will definitely answer you back either directly or through an article on my website **meettherealyou.org**

Your quest for knowledge should not end here as knowledge is never complete or absolute. Keep on enhancing your knowledge through books, audios, videos, seminars or by any means. Keep on learning and trying new things in life.

In this book you learned how and why to connect with your omnipotent eternal reality "**THE REAL YOU**". You have raised your vibrations, entered a divine space, a higher consciousness which will lead to automatic manifestation of your real source driven dreams, desires, and purposes in life. Still to make you understand the practical step by step process or impeccable actions in real time for actualisation of your dreams, desires and purposes in life, I am launching my 2nd book on 9th Dec 2020; "SRCAA". Just need your love and blessings, really grateful to you.

I wish all the success and growth in all areas of your life. My best wishes are always with you.

-SD-
Chetan Bansal
A Keen observer, thinker & learner of life...
Bansalchetan911@gmail.com
www.meettherealyou.org

Your valuable **review and rating** at **amazon** shall help other readers make a right decision to buy this book. Your kind action shall be highly appreciated.

MEET THE REAL YOU
REAL PURPOSE & FOCUS

THE PURPOSE AND FOCUS OF THIS BOOK IS TO
Enhance the degree of consciousness/Awareness

Which will enhance your aura; energy field
Which will connect to your true identity beyond mind & body
Which will put your life on your soul path an automatic path of life

Will remove all negativity/toxins/disturbances (Fear, anxiety, undue anger,
stress etc.) from your Mind & Body
Will make your Mind & body at its natural best
Your intuition, creativity, luck, confidence will get activated

Activation of ability to Manage Thoughts, Emotions, Mind
Activation of laser sharp Focus & stillness
Activation of crystal clear unbiased truthful righteous Understanding &
Perception/Decisions/Actions/Behaviour
Activation of ability to manage People & situations in a most efficient way

Will ultimately  lead to

A PURPOSEFUL LIFE FULL OF LOVE, HAPPINESS, JOY, CELEBRATION, AND
SUCCESS & GROWTH IN all areas of life viz. Health, Wealth, Relations,
Career/Job/Profession (HWRC)

Printed in Great Britain
by Amazon